THE ULTIMATE

Barbie® Doll Book

Marcie Melillo

Published by

**krause
publications**

700 E. State Street • Iola, WI 54990-0001

Please call or write for our free catalog of publications. Our toll-free number to place an order or to obtain a free catalog is (800) 258-0929. Please use our regular business telephone (715) 445-2214 for editorial comment and further information.

Library of Congress Catalog Number: 96-76686
ISBN: 0-87341-397-0
Printed in the United States of America

Contents

Dedication

This book is dedicated to the memory of my father, Peter Melillo, and my mother, Margaret Porto Melillo.

Acknowledgments

Many people were instrumental in the creation of this book. The unselfish group listed below inconvenienced themselves in a number of unthinkable ways. Some people packed up and shipped their precious dolls or permitted me to invade their homes to photograph them. Some people made gifts of dolls, and some insisted I rip open their doll boxes to properly record all facts. Some people offered advice, support, and clerical assistance. Everyone wanted information to be shared. Their generous contributions enrich the book beyond measure.

Pamela S. Anderson
Michael Antony
Joe Blitman
Sandra Brake
Carrie Breckenridge
Sally Coulter
Cyndy Donaghue
Patience Eiker
JoAnne Faulkner
Alice Hasenbank
Greg Hill
Sandi Holder
Donna Horgan
Liz Horn
Lisa Larkin

Gina Lumpkins
Sharon McLaughlin
Emma Melillo
Lynne Ohrt
Beth Owens
Helene Giel Rapport
Arlene Rehor
Kimberly Rehor
Vicky Scherck
Bill Simpson
David Trinidad
Julie Vanderploeg
Andrea VanOutryne
Priscilla Wardlow

My sister, Emma Melillo, provided enormous assistance in setting up the initial database in a careful, concise manner. Her support and enthusiasm were unwavering.

Joe Blitman, with a million ongoing projects, not only took the time to loan a truckload of dolls, but kept searching for missing items and put me in touch with others who could help.

Gina Lumpkins unselfishly loaned dolls, provided information, and relentlessly combed doll shows, unearthing many hard-to-find pieces in the process.

Beth Owens not only sent many of her favorite Midges, but insisted I open sealed doll boxes. And with great tolerance, permitted me to talk out loud at her.

Sandi Holder and Lynne Ohrt exhibited great faith and nerves of steel when they packed up large boxes of valuable dolls and shipped them to be photographed and examined for this book.

Bill Simpson, a professional photographer with a degree in engineering, created a portable photography studio, which made the daunting task of taking almost two thousand transparencies feasible. He generously shared his art and taught me the basics.

Thanks to the people at Krause Publications: Roger Case, who initially approached me about this project; Patricia Klug, who made all the correct decisions; Deborah Faupel, who worked so hard to ensure everything turned out right; Melissa Warden, who accurately read my mind; and all those unseen who conscientiously handled the book.

And finally, Greg Hill, my husband, who not only designed four separate databases and software to integrate them for this project, but was forced to live in a chaotic, vinyl-littered house for five months. All for a hobby he has no interest in and can't fathom why I do. Thankfully, he has great reserves of patience and humor.

How to Use This Book

I am astounded by people who want to "know" the universe when it's hard enough to find your way around Chinatown. – Woody Allen

What is here?

Over 1,070 U.S. issue dolls produced by Mattel, Inc. from 1959 through 1995 are pictured. Most dolls have a close-up and a long shot—approximately two thousand photographs. But this is not just a picture book. Concise blocks of information next to the photographs contain name, model number, hair color and style, clothing, body type and markings, head mold and markings, accessories, booklets, and pertinent notes. Abbreviations are kept to a minimum, but for those used, check the Terms and Abbreviations key. Also, a Pictorial Key illustrates some of the frequently cited arms, shoes, accessories, and doll stands. Finally, an alphabetical Price Guide and Index lists the dolls, price in and out of box, average retail price, and page number with extensive cross-referencing.

What isn't here?

No foreign dolls are pictured unless available for sale in the U.S. and ordered directly from Mattel by a primary retailer. Every doll in this book could be purchased by the general public. Not included are special event Barbie dolls, which are usually very small productions of regular issue dolls with a different hair color, or one-of-a-kind items created for charitable auctions. Also excluded are regular issue dolls repackaged in gift sets or repeatedly reissued with minor box changes. These dolls are already pictured once, and for completeness, relevant detail is included in the "Notes" section of the corresponding regular issue doll. Finally, not reported are dolls produced by Mattel, Inc. with no direct stated association to a Barbie or friend.

How to use this book.

Organized by type of doll rather than year, Ken, Barbie, and Skipper have their own chapters. This permits speedy identification of an unknown doll. Rather than paging through the entire book, perusal of a specific area or two is sufficient. The exceptions are special collector and series dolls. These are unlikely to be found without boxes, as most are purchased by adult collectors, and they are grouped alphabetically by series in their own chapters. The entire group may be viewed in a quick scan.

To identify a doll, first determine whether the doll is female or male, adult or child. Basic height measurements are noted on a schedule with that name. Look in the appropriate chapter and then study the body, face, hair color, and hairstyle. Many of these dolls use the same head mold, but are painted in a particular way or possess a unique hairstyle.

Next, check markings. On some dolls a country may be indicated on the bottom of the foot. These markings are considered subsidiary and are not normally used for identification. Relevant body markings are usually on the back torso; head markings are on the inside rim/neck hole or on the back of the neck. The year on the back of the doll is a date of patent/copyright registration, not manufacture. So, although providing substantial information, it is not the date of issue. Also, the date on the box is sometimes, but not always, the patent date. Please note: To conserve space and add consistency, the start of a new line is noted by a slash (/). Also, the markings are noted in uppercase and lowercase letters although they may appear on the doll in all caps. Look for a match of the words and numbers, not capitalization. Also, a particular Barbie doll may be manufactured in several countries. Included is a small schedule of "Countries Manufacturing Dolls by Decade." Use that if everything matches but the country. Clothing is easily removed and replaced, and is not a reliable method to use for identification. Once the doll is identified, the photographs and written information will detail the correct outfit and accessories to accompany it.

Booklets and accessories are noted, but Mattel used items until depleted, so a previous year's booklet may be found, accessories may be substituted, or neither may be included, even within the same series of dolls. The packaging of these items at the factory is clearly not a precise science.

Among dealers and collectors, dates are used inconsistently. Some people use issue date; some use box date. In this book, box date is used because it is readily confirmed by all. In the past, Mattel wholesale catalogs were used to determine when dolls were on the market. A former regional buyer for a major retail chain during the 1970s told me use of these catalogs would render inexact dates at best. He said that although a doll is included in a Mattel wholesale catalog, it may not be available. Catalogs are printed before final decisions are made regarding the production of certain dolls, availability of items, and many other variables. Box date is tangible. For identification purposes, that date is usually the year prior to actual release, so a box dated 1994 probably holds a 1995 doll. A few issue dates are included for dolls with confusing box dates or acknowledged production spanning more than a few years.

Keep in mind that the spelling of a name may vary, or names may switch between different characters. Stacey is an adult female friend of Barbie's, Stacie is also a teenage friend of Jazzie's, and yet another Stacie is Barbie's little sister. Use of "and" or 'N or 'n fluctuates, locations of apostrophes dance about, names of series change in midstream. Whether it is Doctor or Dr., Allan or Alan, Living or Livin'—all add to the confusion and are part of the collecting experience.

A parting word.

There is nothing in this field as consistent as its inconsistencies. But this is no reason to abandon an effort to record solid general information about the dolls. This book represents what was in each particular doll box I examined. Countries vary, arm molds are interchanged, facial screening differs, skin tones are divergent, booklets are not mandatory, slight alterations in fabrics and other accessories occur, and different styles of shoes may be found. And as fascinating as it might be to note any and all variables, it is also an impossible task. There is no guarantee every modification for each doll could ever be found, so something would always be missing. This is in large part what holds our long-term interest in the hobby—the never-ending discoveries and surprises. So, view this book as a basic accounting of the dolls and their detail. Not a map of the universe, but something to get you around Chinatown.

Terms and Abbreviations

Terms

bent = permanent bend at elbow
b/l = bend leg
cello = cellophane
dipped = same mold used for all ethnic variations
MIB = Mint in box
NRFB = Not removed from box
ptr = palm to rear
pts = palm to side
reg = regular
s/l = straight leg
s/s= swim suit
titian = red color hair
tnt = twist and turn

Booklet Abbreviations

B&K = Barbie and Ken
BF&F = Barbie Fashion & Fun
BFG = Barbie for Girls
BIC = Barbie International Collectors
BK&M = Barbie, Ken, and Midge
BWBSN = Barbie's World, Bright, Swinging, Now
BWOB = Beautiful World of Barbie
BWOF = Barbie World of Fashions
COA = Certificate of Authenticity
EFBM = Exclusive Fashions by Mattel
F&PABM = Fashions and Play Accessories by Mattel
IIB = I'm Into Barbie
JES = Junior Edition Styles
LB = Living Barbie
LB&S = Living Barbie and Skipper
LWOB = Lively World of Barbie
MFB = My First Barbie
PB = Product Brochure
WOBF = World of Barbie Fashions
WOF = World of Fashion

Arms

Top row, left to right:
Bent arm
Mexico arms (a style) Note: Each arm has a different hand position.
Busy hands

Bottom row, left to right:
Regular arm – arm for vintage Barbie® doll and friends
Francie® doll arm – same arm as Skipper® except longer
Skipper® doll arm – same arm as Francie® except shorter
Two different Barbie® doll ptr arms

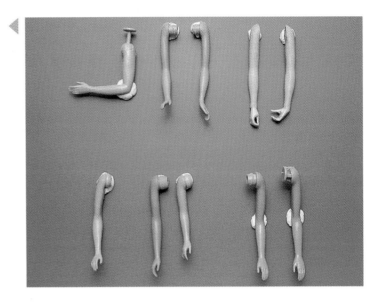

Ballerina style arms
Definition: Besides the usual up and down movement, arms move away from sides.
Ballerina arms are palms to rear (ptr) and the Shani® arms are palms to side (pts).
Note: Ballerina split finger arms (not pictured) are also pts.

Ballerina body in back
Shani® body in front

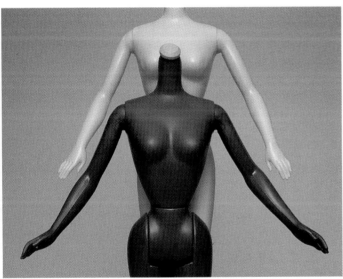

Living arms
Definition: Arms with joint at elbow and wrist.

Living Barbie® in back
Living Skipper® in front

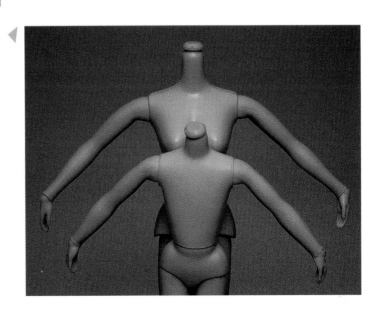

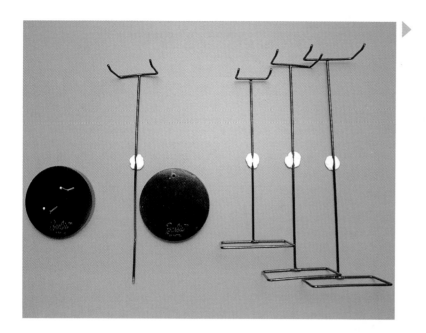

Doll Stands I
Left to right:
#1 Barbie® doll display stand
#2 or #3 Barbie® doll display stand – hole position in #2 stand varies; first stands marked TM, then ® Skipper®, Barbie®, and Ken® doll black wire display stands, later issued in gold color

Doll Stands II
Left to right:
Colored two-piece display stand
Clear "X" display stand
Two-piece clear display stand

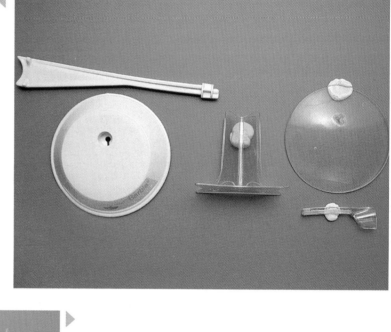

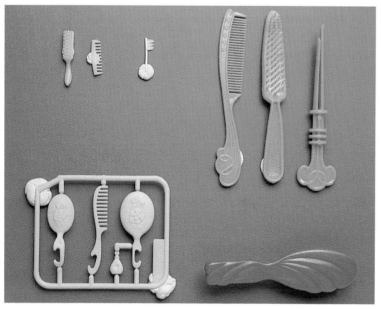

Hair Care
Top row, left to right:
Small brush and comb
Francie® doll eyelash brush
Pointed comb, brush and quick curl curler

Bottom row, left to right:
Brush, comb, and mirror with hand grip
Oval brush

Shoe I

Top row, left to right:
Mules
Flats
Male cork sandals
Ricky® doll sandal
Tutti® doll bow flats
Francie® doll soft high heel

Bottom row, left to right:
Jazzie®/gymnast flat
Francie® doll soft buckle flat
T-straps
Soft pointed flat
Ankle strap ballet
Female tennis shoe
Ankle straps
Square toe low heel
Pilgrim shoes

Shoe II

Top row, left to right:
Narrow pumps
Brazil pumps
Wide pumps
Wide bow pumps

Bottom row, left to right:
Male doll tennis
Male doll dance oxford
Male doll loafer
Male doll lace-up oxford
Male doll cowboy boot
Female doll cowboy boot

Countries Manufacturing Dolls by Decade

1959 and 1960s
Hong Kong
Japan
Mexico
Taiwan
United States

1970s
Hong Kong
Japan
Korea
Philippines
Taiwan
United States

1980s
China
Hong Kong
Japan (just porcelain)
Malaysia
Mexico
Philippines
Taiwan

1990s
China
Indonesia
Malaysia
Mexico (just My Size)

Doll Heights

Barbie and female friends	11-1/2 inches
Supersize and Pretty Dreams Barbie	18 inches
My Size Barbie	3 feet
Francie and Casey	10-7/8 inches
Skipper, Skooter, Ricky, etc.	9 inches
Modern Skipper	9-1/2 inches
Kelly and Teacher kids	4-1/4 inches
Stacie, Todd, Janet, Whitney, etc.	7-3/4 inches
Ken and male friends	11-3/4–12 inches
Tiny babies for Dr. Barbie, Babysitter etc.	2-5/8 inches

Model #: 850 **Name:** Barbie Ponytail #1 **Box Date:** 1959 **Hair Color:** blonde brunette **Hairstyle:** below shoulder-length ponytail, hard curl on end, curly bangs **Face:** no eye color, blonde or brown brows, red lips & blush **Clothing:** black & white striped 1-piece strapless swimsuit, gold hoop earrings, white sunglasses with blue lenses, black mules with holes in ball of feet **Extras:** 2 metal prong black plastic disk stand with Barbie ™ logo **Booklet:** Barbie Fashion - pictures rare first 3 outfits **Head:** Barbie **Arms:** reg **Body:** small neck knob, tan solid vinyl s/l, painted nails, copper tubes inserted in holes in feet to fit on display stand prongs **Body Markings:** Barbie T.M./ Pats.Pend./ ©MCMLVIII/ by/ Mattel/ Inc. **Notes:** body fades to ivory color, smells like crayon, variety of styles in eye paint, but always pointed brows & no iris color, box has ™ markings

Model #: 850 **Name:** Barbie Ponytail #2 **Box Date:** 1959 **Hair Color:** blonde brunette **Hairstyle:** below shoulder ponytail, hard curl on end, curly bangs **Face:** no eye color, blonde or brown brows, red lips & blush **Clothing:** black & white striped 1-piece strapless swimsuit, gold hoop earrings, white sunglasses with blue lenses, black mules **Extras:** black wire pedestal with black disk base & Barbie ™ logo, variations in distance of hole for wire from edge of disk **Booklet:** Barbie Fashion with Commuter Set outfit **Head:** Barbie **Arms:** reg **Body:** small neck knob, tan solid vinyl s/l, painted nails **Body Markings:** Barbie T.M./ Pats.Pend./ ©MCMLVIII/ by/ Mattel/ Inc. **Notes:** body fades to ivory color, smells like crayon, box has ™ markings

Model #: 850 **Name:** Barbie Ponytail #3 **Issue Date:** 1960 **Box Date:** 1959 **Hair Color:** blonde brunette **Hairstyle:** below shoulder ponytail, hard curl on end, curly bangs, factory braid variation **Face:** blue eyes, blonde or brown brows, red lips & blush **Clothing:** black & white striped 1-piece strapless swimsuit, gold hoop or pearl stud earrings, white sunglasses with blue lenses, black mules **Extras:** black wire pedestal with black disk base, Barbie ™ markings, later in year ® symbol **Booklet:** Barbie Fashion **Head:** Barbie **Arms:** reg **Body:** small neck knob, tan solid or partially solid vinyl s/l, painted nails **Body Markings:** Barbie T.M./ Pats.Pend./ ©MCMLVIII/ by/ Mattel/ Inc. **Notes:** eyeliner color blue or brown, only time brown color used, but blue is rarer, body fades to ivory color, smells like crayon, box has ™ or ® markings, gift sets: Mix' N' Match, Trousseau, & Party Set

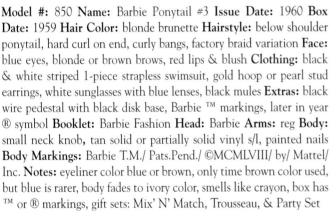

Model #: 850 **Name:** Barbie Ponytail #4 **Issue date:** 1960 **Box Date:** 1959 **Hair Color:** blonde brunette **Hairstyle:** shoulder-length or below ponytail, hard curl on end, curly bangs, factory braid variation **Face:** blue eyes, blonde or brown brows, red lips **Clothing:** black & white 1-piece striped strapless swimsuit, gold hoop or pearl stud earrings, white sunglasses with blue lenses, black mules **Extras:** black wire pedestal with black disk base, ® markings or black wire stand **Booklet:** Barbie Fashion **Head:** Barbie **Arms:** reg **Body:** small neck knob, tan partially solid s/l, painted nails **Body Markings:** Barbie T.M./ Pats.Pend./ ©MCMLVIII/ by/ Mattel/ Inc. **Notes:** 1st year to retain tan tone in body, gift sets: Mix' N' Match, Trousseau, Party Set, Barbie & Ken Gift Set

Model #: 850 Name: Barbie Ponytail #5 Issue date: 1961 Box Date: 1959 Hair Color: blonde brunette titian Hairstyle: ponytail, hard curl on end, curly bangs Face: blue eyes, blonde, brown or reddish brows, red lips Clothing: black & white striped 1-piece strapless swimsuit, pearl stud earrings, optional white sunglasses with blue lenses, black mules, wrist tag Extras: black wire stand Booklet: B&K 1961 Head: Barbie Arms: reg Body: small neck knob, tan s/l, painted nails Body Markings: Barbie®/ Pats.Pend/ ©MCMLVIII/ by/ Mattel/ Inc. Notes: some dolls have greasy face, first hollow body doll, gift sets: Mix' N' Match, Barbie & Ken Gift Set

Model #: 850 Name: Bubblecut Barbie Issue Date: 1961 Box Date: 1959 Hair Color: titian, shades of blonde & brunette Hairstyle: small bouffant Face: blue eyes, blonde, brown or reddish brows, red lips Clothing: black & white striped 1-piece strapless swimsuit, pearl stud earrings, optional white sunglasses with blue lenses, black mules, wrist tag Extras: black wire stand Booklet: B&K 1961 Head: Barbie Arms: reg Body: small neck knob, tan s/l, painted nails Body Markings: Barbie®/ Pats.Pend/ ©MCMLVIII/ by/ Mattel/ Inc. Notes: some dolls have greasy face, particularly rare hair colors are white ginger & sable brown

Model #: 850 Name: Barbie Ponytail #6 & 7 Issue Date: 1962-66 Box Date: 1962 Hair Color: shades of blonde, titian & brunette Hairstyle: ponytail, hard curl on end, curly bangs Face: blue eyes, blonde, brown or reddish brows, coral lips Clothing: 1-piece red stretch swimsuit, pearl stud earrings, red mules, wrist tag Extras: black or gold wire stand Booklet: B&K 1962 or BK&M white 1962 Head: Barbie Arms: reg Body: large neck knob, tan s/l, painted nails Body Markings: Midge T.M./ © 1962/ Barbie®/ © 1958/ by/ Mattel, Inc./ in 1964 add word "Patented" Notes: face paint varies both lip color and brow to match hair color, many shades of lip paint used, variation: painted legs

Model #: 850 Name: Bubblecut Barbie Issue Date: 1962-67 Box Date: 1962 Hair Color: titian, shades of blonde & brunette Hairstyle: bouffant Face: blue eyes, blonde, brown or reddish brows, coral lips Clothing: 1-piece red stretch swimsuit, pearl stud earrings, red mules, wrist tag Extras: gold wire stand Booklet: B&K 1962 or BK&M white Head: Barbie Arms: reg Body: large neck knob, tan s/l, painted nails Body Markings: Midge T.M./ © 1962/ Barbie®/ © 1958/ by/ Mattel, Inc./ in 1964 add word "Patented" Notes: new box illustrations, many hair colors, lip & brow paints, & sizes of bubble-cut style hair, variation: painted legs, gift sets: Sparkling Pink, Round the Clock, Wedding Party, Mix 'N Match version 2, Barbie & Ken, On Parade

Model #: 850 **Name:** Bubblecut Barbie Sidepart **Box Date:** 1962 **Hair Color:** titian, shades of blonde & brunette **Hairstyle:** bouffant combed to one side **Face:** blue eyes, blonde, brown or reddish brows, coral lips **Clothing:** 1-piece red stretch swimsuit, pearl stud earrings, red mules, wrist tag **Extras:** gold wire stand **Booklet:** BK&M white 1962 **Head:** Barbie **Arms:** reg **Body:** large neck knob, tan s/l, painted nails **Body Markings:** Midge T.M./ © 1962/ Barbie®/ © 1958/ by/ Mattel, Inc./ in 1964 add word "Patented" **Notes:** various shades of paint used for lips & brows, some dolls found in b/l boxes on b/l bodies, hair has cross-hatch rooting pattern, may have American Girl head markings

Model #: 870 **Name:** Fashion Queen **Box Date:** 1962 **Hair Color:** painted medium or dark brown **Hairstyle:** molded head with removable blue band **Face:** blue eyes, brown brows, coral or pink lips **Clothing:** gold & white striped 1-piece strapless swimsuit with matching turban, white plastic 3 head wig stand, red flip wig, blonde bubble wig, brunette pageboy wig, pearl stud earrings, white mules, wrist tag **Extras:** black wire stand **Booklet:** BK&M white 1962 **Head:** Fashion Queen **Arms:** reg **Body:** large neck knob, tan s/l, painted nails **Body Markings:** Midge T.M./ © 1962/ Barbie®/ © 1958/ by/ Mattel, Inc./ in 1964 add word "Patented" **Notes:** wig colors may alternate between styles, gift sets: Fashion Queen Barbie & Her Friends, Fashion Queen Barbie & Ken Trousseau Set

Model #: 871 **Name:** Fashion Queen Wig Wardrobe **Box Date:** 1963 **Hair Color:** painted brown or dark brown **Hairstyle:** molded head with removable blue band **Face:** blue eyes, brown brows, pink or coral lips **Extras:** pearl stud earrings, 3 wigs: red flip, brunette pageboy & blonde bubble with white plastic wig stand **Head:** Fashion Queen **Notes:** wig colors may alternate between styles, gift sets: both Color 'N Curl

Model #: 850 **Name:** Barbie Swirl Ponytail **Issue date:** 1964 **Box Date:** 1962 **Hair Color:** titian/red, light blonde, ash & lemon blonde, brunette **Hairstyle:** ponytail, swirl of hair across forehead pulled back into ponytail, end tied with yellow ribbon secured with bobby pin, no curl at bottom, cello on head **Face:** blue eyes, blonde brows, coral lips **Clothing:** 1-piece red stretch swimsuit, white pearl stud earrings, red mules, wrist tag **Extras:** gold wire stand **Booklet:** EFBM Book 1 1963 **Head:** Barbie **Arms:** reg **Body:** large neck knob, tan s/l, painted nails **Body Markings:** Midge T.M./ © 1962/ Barbie®/ © 1958/ by/ Mattel, Inc./ in 1964 add word "Patented" **Notes:** numerous lip & brow colors appear with each hair color, red replaced titian hair color on box, some dolls found in b/l boxes on b/l bodies gift sets: Little Theatre Gift Set & On Parade

Model #: 1060 **Name:** Miss Barbie **Issue Date:** 1964 **Box Date:** 1963 **Hair Color:** painted brown with orange band **Face:** blue "sleep" eyes, light brown brows, coral lips **Clothing:** 1-piece pink swimsuit with gold paint dots or glitter, pink yarn cap with gold glitter, light pink mules, wrist tag, white plastic 3 head wig stand, blonde pageboy, red bubble, brunette flip wigs **Extras:** gold wire display stand, go together lawn swing, 3-piece palm planter, Barbie Home magazine, clock radio, purple princess phone, tray, 2 glasses **Booklet:** EFBM Book 1 1963 & instructions **Head:** Miss Barbie **Arms:** reg **Body:** small neck knob, tan b/l, painted nails **Body Markings:** indented © 1958/ Mattel, Inc./ U.S. Patented/ U.S. Pat. Pend **Notes:** only doll with eyes to open and close, hard plastic head develops 'melt' marks from soft vinyl wig cap if left on for extended period

Model #: 1070 **Name:** American Girl **Issue Date:** 1965 **Box Date:** 1964 **Hair Color:** brunette, titian/red, blondes: light, ash or yellow **Hairstyle:** parted in middle chin-length bob with bangs, cello on head **Face:** blue eyes, brown brows, yellow lips **Clothing:** 1-piece swimsuit with multicolor striped top & solid turquoise bottom, turquoise mules, wrist tag **Extras:** gold wire stand **Booklet:** EFBMB Book 1, 1964 **Head:** Barbie **Head Markings:** inside rim Copyr. © 1958 Mattel Inc **Arms:** reg **Body:** tan b/l, painted nails **Body Markings:** indented © 1958/ Mattel, Inc./ U.S. Patented/ U.S. Pat. Pend **Notes:** available with a variety of lip & brow colors

Model #: 1070 **Name:** American Girl Side-Part **Issue Date** 1965-66 **Box Date:** 1964 **Hair Color:** shades of blonde, brunette & titian/red **Hairstyle:** left side part, hair flipped up or under at base of neck or below shoulder with rubberband holding hair in place & turquoise ribbon headband **Face:** blue eyes, brown brows, orange lips & blush **Clothing:** 1-piece swimsuit with multi-striped top & solid turquoise bottom, turquoise mules, wrist tag **Extras:** gold wire stand **Booklet:** WOBF 1965 **Head:** Barbie **Head Markings:** inside rim Copyr. © 1958 Mattel Inc **Arms:** reg **Body:** tan b/l, painted nails **Body Markings:** indented & later raised letters: © 1958/ Mattel, Inc./ U.S. Patented/ U.S. Pat. Pend./ Made in/ Japan **Notes:** available with a variety of lip & brow colors, including high color or Color Magic face

Model #: 1070 **Name:** American Girl **Issue Date:** 1966 **Box Date:** 1964 **Hair Color:** shades of brunette, blonde & titian/red **Hairstyle:** parted in middle, chin or shoulder length with bangs - softer texture than 1965, cello on head **Face:** blue eyes, brown brows, raspberry lips & blush **Clothing:** 1-piece swimsuit with multicolor striped top & solid turquoise bottom, turquoise mules & wrist tag **Extras:** gold wire stand **Head:** Barbie **Head Markings:** inside rim Copyr. © 1958 Mattel Inc **Arms:** reg **Body:** tan b/l, painted nails **Body Markings:** indented & later raised letters: © 1958/ Mattel, Inc./ U.S. Patented/ U.S. Pat. Pend./ Made in/ Japan **Notes:** available with a variety of lip & brow colors including high color or Color Magic face

Model #: 1162 **Name:** Barbie trade-in twist & turn **Box Date:** 1966 **Hair Color:** titian/red, shades of blonde & brunette **Hairstyle:** sides pulled to top of head tied with orange bow, rest mid-back uneven length, bangs, cello on head **Face:** blue eyes, rooted lashes, brown brows, deep pink lips & blush **Clothing:** orange vinyl bikini with white net cover-up with orange stitching at neck, arm & leg hole openings, wrist tag **Extras:** clear X stand **Booklet:** WOBF 1966 **Head:** tnt **Head Markings:** inside rim © 1966 Mattel Inc & country **Arms:** reg **Body:** pink tnt, painted nails **Body Markings:** © 1966/ Mattel, Inc/ U.S. Patented/ U.S. Pat. Pend/ Made in/ Japan or © 1966/ Mattel Inc./ U.S. Patented/ Other Pats Pend/ Made in/ Japan **Notes:** different shades of brow paint used to correspond with hair color, face & arms may pale, packaged in clear bag within box

Model #: 1160 **Name:** Barbie twist & turn **Box Date:** 1966 **Hair Color:** titian/red, shades of blonde & brunette see notes **Hairstyle:** sides pulled to top of head & tied with orange bow, rest mid-back to waist length, uneven ends, bangs, cello on head **Face:** blue eyes, rooted lashes, light brown brows, deep pink lips & blush **Clothing:** 2-piece orange vinyl bikini, white net 1-piece cover-up with orange stitching at neck, arm & leg hole openings, wrist tag **Extras:** clear X stand **Booklet:** WOBF 1966 **Head:** tnt **Head Markings:** inside rim © 1966 Mattel Inc & country **Arms:** reg **Body:** pink tnt, painted nails **Body Markings:** © 1966/ Mattel, Inc./ U.S. Patented/ U.S. Pat. Pend/ Made in/ Japan **Notes:** brow paint corresponds with different hair colors, face & arms may pale, odd hair color names: blondes: Sun Kissed (light), Summer Sand (gray), brunettes: Go Go Co Co (medium), Chocolate Bon Bon (dark brown) Sears exclusive gift set: Beautiful Blues

Model #: 1150 **Name:** Color Magic **Issue Date:** 1966 **Box Date:** 1958 **Hair Color:** golden blonde/scarlet flame or midnight/ruby red **Hairstyle:** side part, below shoulders, uneven ends, 1 side held with turquoise bobby pin, pulled back with multicolor diamond print headband, cello on head **Face:** blue eyes, blonde brows, raspberry lips & blush or pale peach lips & blush **Clothing:** 1-piece multicolor diamond print swimsuit with turquoise tie belt, 4 hair ribbons, 3 colored bobby pins, light blue tulle tie, color changer A & B, sponge applicator & wrist tag **Booklet:** WOBF 1966 & instructions **Head:** Barbie **Head Markings:** inside rim Copyr. © 1958 Mattel Inc **Arms:** reg **Body:** tan b/l, painted nails **Body Markings:** indented letters: © 1958/ Mattel, Inc/ U.S. Patented/ U.S. Pat.Pend./ raised letters: Made in/ Japan **Notes:** plastic box converts into closet, color change solution alters hair color & swimsuit colors, which stop changing with time, midnight hair may turn to ruby color while still in box & won't turn back, gift set: Color Magic Doll & Costume Set

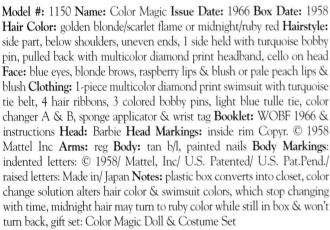

Model #: 4042 **Name:** Hair Fair Barbie **Box Date:** 1966 **Hair Color:** brunette blonde **Hairstyle:** chin length, side part **Face:** blue side glance eyes, rooted lashes, light brown brows, deep pink lips & blush, 1 dangle triangle brass earring in left ear **Extras:** Brunette hairpieces: crownette=braid on brass headband with blue roses & green leaves on either end, fashion fall=long hair on blue elastic headband, braided switch=long braid with blue satin ribbon intertwined with hair & oval brass barrette at top, blonde flip wig, brass oval barrette, triangle dangle earring (same as on head), plastic navy disk with pink dangle earrings, 6 bobby pins, made in Japan **Head:** tnt **Head Markings:** inside rim © 1966 Mattel Inc & country **Notes:** sold as head with hairpieces, blonde head had blonde hairpieces with brunette wig

Model #: 1190 **Name:** Standard Barbie **Box Date:** 1966 **Hair Color:** titian/red, shades of blonde & brunette **Hairstyle:** sides pulled up & tied with pink ribbon, mid-back to waist length, uneven ends, bangs, cello on head **Face:** blue eyes, light brown brows, deep pink lips & blush **Clothing:** 2-piece swimsuit, solid pink scoop neck top & matching bottoms with white plastic flower with green leaves, wrist tag **Extras:** clear X stand **Booklet:** BWOF 1966/67 **Head:** tnt **Head Markings:** inside rim © 1966 Mattel Inc & country **Arms:** reg **Body:** pink s/l, painted nails **Body Markings:** Midge T.M./ © 1962/ Barbie®/ © 1958/ by/ Mattel, Inc./ Patented **Notes:** gift sets: Travel in Style & Twinkle Town Set

Model #: 1160 **Name:** Barbie twist & turn **Issue Date:** 1967 **Hair Color:** titian/red, shades of blonde & brunette see notes **Hairstyle:** sides pulled to top of head & tied with pink bow, rest mid-back to waist length, uneven ends, bangs, cello on head **Face:** blue eyes, rooted lashes, light brown brows, deep pink lips & blush **Clothing:** 2-piece swimsuit, top sleeveless shell of pink, red, light & dark green checks with thin light green belt with gold buckle, pink vinyl shorts, wrist tag **Extras:** clear X stand **Booklet:** WOFB 1967 **Head:** tnt **Head Markings:** inside rim © 1966 Mattel Inc & country **Arms:** reg **Body:** pink tnt, painted nails **Body Markings:** © 1966/ Mattel, Inc./ U.S. Patented/ U.S. Pat. Pend/ Made in/ Japan **Notes:** shades of brow paint used to correspond with different hair colors, face and arms may pale, weird hair color names, blondes: Sun Kissed (light), Summer Sand (gray), brunettes: Go Go Co Co (medium), Chocolate Bon Bon

Model #: 1150 **Name:** Color Magic **Issue Date:** 1967 **Box Date:** 1958 **Hair Color:** golden blonde/scarlet flame or midnight/ruby red **Hairstyle:** side part, below shoulders, uneven ends, 1 side held with turquoise bobby pin, pulled back with multicolor diamond headband, cello on head **Face:** blue eyes, light brown brows, raspberry lips & blush or pale peach lips & blush **Clothing:** 1-piece multicolor diamond print swimsuit with turquoise tie at waist, matching headband, 4 colored ribbons & 3 colored bobby pins, blue tulle hair tie, A & B color changer, sponge applicator, wrist tag **Extras:** gold wire stand **Booklet:** WOBF 1966 & instructions **Head:** Barbie **Head Markings:** inside rim Copyr. © 1958 Mattel Inc **Arms:** reg **Body:** tan b/l, painted nails **Body Markings:** © 1958/ Mattel, Inc./ U.S. Patented/ U. S. Pat.Pend./ Made in/ Japan **Notes:** color change solution alters color of hair & swimsuit, with time color stops changing, midnight color dolls have darker brows & often turn ruby by themselves in the box & won't turn back, gift set: Color Magic Doll & Costume Set, doll & outfit

Model #: 8348 **Name:** Talking Barbie Spanish **Box Date:** 1967 **Hair Color:** brunette **Hairstyle:** side mid-back-length ponytail tied with 3 pink bows, curled sideburns, bangs **Face:** blue eyes, rooted lashes, brown brows, deep pink lips & blush **Clothing:** hip-length pink swimsuit top with pink & yellow yarn trim at hem & pink vinyl shorts with wrist tag **Extras:** clear X stand **Booklet:** WOBF 1967 **Head:** tnt **Head Markings:** inside rim © 1966 Mattel Inc & country **Arms:** reg **Body:** pink talking **Body Markings:** ©1967/ Mattel, Inc./ U.S. & Foreign/ Pats.Pend./ Mexico **Notes:** speaks when string pulled, usually mute, limbs fall off, same doll & model # also available in cardboard box

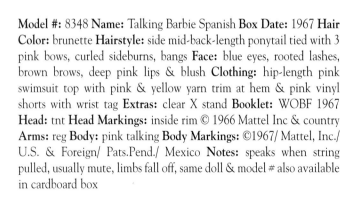

Model #: 1115 Name: Talking Barbie Box Date: 1967 Hair Color: blonde, titian/red, shades of brown Hairstyle: side mid-back-length ponytail tied with 3 pink ribbons, curled side burns, bangs Face: blue eyes, rooted lashes, light brown brows, deep pink lips & blush Clothing: hip-length pink swimsuit top with yellow & pink yarn trim at hem, pink vinyl shorts, wrist tag Extras: clear X stand Booklet: WOBF 1967 Head: tnt Head Markings: inside rim © 1966 Mattel Inc & country Arms: Mexico Body: pink talking Body Markings: ©1967/ Mattel, Inc./ U.S. & Foreign/ Pats.Pend./ Mexico Notes: speaks when string pulled, usually mute, limbs fall off, same doll & model # also available in cardboard box, JCPenney gift sets: Pink Premiere & Silver 'N' Satin, Sears gift set: Dinner Dazzle Set, Go Formal 2-doll set with Ken

Model #: 1160 Name: Barbie twist & turn flip hair Box Date: 1968 Hair Color: blonde brunette brown-red Hairstyle: shoulder-length flip, part on side, pin curl on forehead, cello on head Face: blue eyes, rooted lashes, brown brows, deep pink/red lips, blush Clothing: 1-piece multicolor diamond pattern swimsuit of yellow, red, pink, light green with wrist tag Extras: clear X stand Booklet: WOBF 1968 Head: tnt Head Markings: inside rim © 1966 Mattel Inc & country Arms: reg Body: pink tnt, painted nails Body Markings: © 1966/ Mattel, Inc./ U.S. Patented/ U.S. Pat. Pend/ Made in/ Japan Notes: different shades of brow paint used to correspond with hair color, face & arms may pale

Model #: 4043 Name: Hair Fair Barbie Box Date: 1968 Hair Color: blonde brunette Hairstyle: chin length, side part Face: blue eyes, rooted lashes, light brown brows, deep pink lips & blush, 1 gold triangle dangle earring in left ear Extras: Blonde hairpieces: wiglet=curly bun with pink bow & elastic strap, curly swirls=ringlets held at top with blue barrette, switch=lock of long hair held with pink ribbon bow, brunette flip wig, small white comb & brush, 2 white flowers, brass triangle dangle earring, 6 bobby pins, made in Japan Head: tnt Head Markings: inside rim © 1966 Mattel Inc & country Notes: brunette head has brunette hairpieces and blonde wig, #4043 was revamped & issued in 1974 with center glance eyes

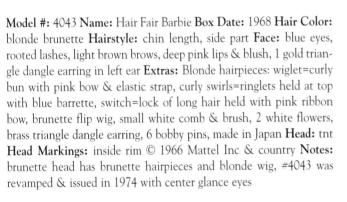

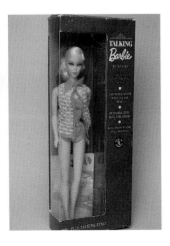

Model #: 1115 Name: Talking Barbie Box Date: 1968 Hair Color: blonde brunette red Hairstyle: side part with pin curl on forehead & at each ear, hair drawn back to nape of neck in softly curled bun Face: blue eyes, rooted lashes, blonde brows, orange lips & blush Clothing: coral bikini with white elastic band belt & metal accent, silver & white net cover-up with coral collar & trim, wrist tag Extras: clear X stand Booklet: LB 1969 or LB&S 1970 Head: tnt Head Markings: inside rim © 1966 Mattel Inc & country Arms: Mexico Body: pink talking Body Markings: ©1967/ Mattel, Inc./ U.S. & Foreign/ Pats.Pend./ Mexico Notes: speaks when string pulled, usually mute, limbs fall off, same doll & model # also available in light purple box, Sears exclusive gift set: Perfectly Plaid

Model #: 1160 **Name:** Barbie twist & turn flip hair **Box Date:** 1969 **Hair Color:** blonde brunette brown-red **Hairstyle:** shoulder-length flip, part on side with pin curl on forehead, cello on head **Face:** blue eyes, brown brows, rooted lashes, deep pink lips & blush **Clothing:** 1-piece pink & white nylon swimsuit & wrist tag **Extras:** clear X stand **Booklet:** LB&S 1970 **Head:** tnt **Head Markings:** inside rim © 1966 Mattel Inc & country **Arms:** reg **Body:** pink tnt, painted nails **Body Markings:** © 1966/ Mattel, Inc./ U.S. Patented/ U.S. Pat. Pend/ Made in/ Japan **Notes:** different shades of brow paint used to correspond with hair color, face & arms may pale

Model #: 1160 **Name:** Barbie twist & turn flip hair **Box Date:** 1969 **Hair Color:** blonde brunette brown-red **Hairstyle:** shoulder-length flip, part on side, pin curl on forehead, cello on head **Face:** blue centered eyes, rooted lashes, brown brows, pink lips & blush **Clothing:** 1-piece swimsuit with multicolor hot pink, purple, green, orange pattern with solid pink high collar straps, wrist tag **Extras:** clear X stand **Booklet:** LB&S 1970 **Head:** tnt **Head Markings:** inside rim © 1966 Mattel Inc & country **Arms:** reg **Body:** pink tnt, painted nails **Body Markings:** © 1966/ Mattel, Inc./ U.S. Patented/ U.S. Pat. Pend/ Made in/ Japan **Notes:** different shades of brow paint used to correspond with hair color, face and arms may pale

Model #: 1116 **Name:** Dramatic New Living Barbie **Box Date:** 1969 **Hair Color:** blonde brunette red **Hairstyle:** shoulder length, center part with bangs, cello on head **Face:** blue eyes, rooted lashes, shades of brown brows, orange red lips & blush **Clothing:** gold & silver metallic v-neck swimsuit with elastic at waist & orange net hooded cover-up with gold trim around edge & foil wrist tag **Extras:** clear X stand **Booklet:** LB 1969 **Head:** tnt **Head Markings:** inside rim © 1966 Mattel Inc & country **Arms:** living **Body:** pink living **Body Markings:** © 1968 Mattel, Inc./ U.S. & For Patd/ Other Pats.Pend./ Taiwan **Notes:** Sears gift set: Action Accents

Model #: 1190 **Name:** Standard Barbie **Box Date:** 1969 **Hair Color:** red, shades of blonde & brunette **Hairstyle:** sides pulled to top of head tied with pink bow mid-back to waist length, uneven ends, bangs, cello on head **Face:** blue eyes, light brown brows, deep pink lips & blush **Clothing:** 1-piece swimsuit of alternating strips of hot pink & green in a v-neck with pink plastic flower & metal bead center, wrist tag **Booklet:** LB&S 1970 **Head:** tnt **Head Markings:** inside rim © 1966 Mattel Inc & country **Arms:** reg **Body:** pink s/l, painted nails **Body Markings:** Midge T.M./ © 1962/ Barbie®/ © 1958/ by/ Mattel, Inc./ Patented

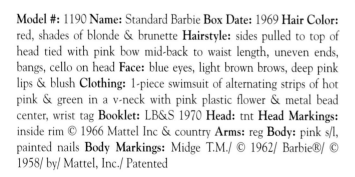

Model #: 1115 **Name:** Talking Barbie Stacey head **Box Date:** 1969 **Hair Color:** blonde brunette titian **Hairstyle:** side part, pulled back to nape of neck with large curls. pin curl on forehead & cheeks **Face:** blue eyes, rooted lashes, blonde brows, coral lips & blush **Clothing:** coral 2-piece bikini with white & silver net cover-up, coral collar & trim, wrist tag **Extras:** clear X stand **Head:** Stacey **Head Markings:** inside rim © 1965 Mattel Inc & country **Arms:** Mexico **Body:** pink talking **Body Markings:** ©1967/ Mattel, Inc./ U.S. & Foreign/ Pats.Pend./ Mexico or Hong Kong **Notes:** speaks when string pulled, usually mute, limbs fall off, also made in a Spanish talking version

Model #: 1115 **Name:** Talking Barbie **Box Date:** 1969 **Hair Color:** blonde, red, shades of brown **Hairstyle:** side part, side ponytail at nape of neck with loose curls, pin curl on forehead & over each ear **Face:** center blue eyes, brownish brows, peach lips & blush **Clothing:** white vinyl bikini, gold net knee-length sleeveless cover-up with lamé collar, wrist tag **Extras:** clear X stand **Booklet:** LB&S 1970 **Head:** tnt **Head Markings:** inside rim © 1966 Mattel Inc & country **Arms:** Mexico **Body:** pink talking **Body Markings:** ©1967/ Mattel, Inc./ U.S. & Foreign/ Pats.Pend./ Mexico **Notes:** speaks when string pulled, usually mute, limbs fall off, Sears exclusive gift sets: Perfectly Plaid & Golden Groove

Model #: 1144 **Name:** Barbie with Growin' Pretty Hair **Box Date:** 1970 **Hair Color:** blonde **Hairstyle:** parted on side, flipped up on either side at eye level & ringlets at chin level, bun on top of head & long retractable ponytail, cello on head **Face:** blue eyes, rooted lashes, brown brows, pink lips & blush **Clothing:** pink satin sleeveless dress with pointed hem detail, gold sewn on waistband, sewn in panties, wrist tag **Extras:** small white comb & brush, 2 hot pink flowers, 8 bobby pins, hairpieces: tiny looped braids on hot pink oval barrette & 4 long ringlet curls tied with pink bow **Booklet:** LB&S 1970 & instructions **Head:** tnt **Head Markings:** inside rim © 1966 Mattel Inc & country **Arms:** Mexico **Body:** pink b/l grow hair **Body Markings:** © 1967 Mattel, Inc./ U.S. Patented/ Other Patents Pending/ Patented in Canada 1967/ Taiwan

Model #: 4044 **Name:** Hair Fair Barbie **Box Date:** 1970 **Hair Color:** blonde brunette **Hairstyle:** chin length, side part **Face:** blue center eyes, rooted lashes, brown brows, bright pink lips & blush **Extras:** brunette hairpieces: wiglet=small hairpiece with blue bow on top and double flip curls on each side with elastic strap, curly swirls=ringlets held together with blue bow, switch=lock of long hair held with blue bow, includes blonde wig, small white comb & brush, 2 small white flowers, 8 bobby pins. made in Japan. **Head:** tnt **Head Markings:** inside rim © 1966 Mattel Inc & country **Notes:** blonde head comes with blonde hairpieces and brunette wig

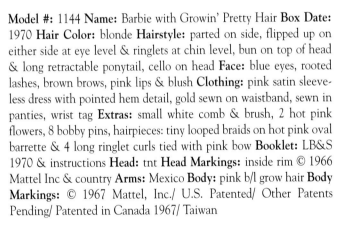

Model #: 1155 **Name:** Live Action Barbie **Box Date:** 1970 **Hair Color:** blonde **Hairstyle:** middle part, below shoulder length, ends curled under with light brown headband across forehead **Face:** blue eyes, rooted lashes, brown brows, peach lips & blush **Clothing:** multi-color long sleeve top of pink, fuchsia & orange with brown faux suede wide waistband accented with long fringe, fringe on wrists, matching multicolor pants, tan Skipper flats, wrist tag **Extras:** clear touch 'n go stand **Booklet:** LB&S 1970 & instructions **Head:** tnt **Head Markings:** inside rim © 1966 Mattel Inc & country **Arms:** living **Body:** pink live action **Body Markings:** © 1968 Mattel, Inc./ U.S. & Foreign Patented/ Patented in Canada 1967/ Other Patents pending/ Taiwan **Notes:** also available in Live Action on Stage # 1152

Model #: 1116 **Name:** Living Barbie **Box Date:** 1970 **Hair Color:** blonde brunette red **Hairstyle:** middle part, shoulder length with bangs, cello on head **Face:** blue centered eyes, rooted lashes, deep pink lips & blush **Clothing:** off-the-shoulder body suit with white background & pink & red bubble print, matching long wrap skirt, wrist tag **Extras:** clear X stand **Booklet:** LB&S 1970 **Head:** tnt **Head Markings:** inside rim © 1966 Mattel Inc & country **Arms:** living **Body:** pink living **Body Markings:** © 1968 Mattel, Inc./ U.S. & For Patd/ Other Pats.Pend./ Taiwan

Model #: 1067 **Name:** Sun Set Malibu Barbie **Issue Date:** 1971-77 **Box Date:** 1970 **Hair Color:** blonde **Hairstyle:** side part, waist length, cello on head **Face:** aqua eyes, brown brows, peach lips & blush **Clothing:** aqua 1-piece high neck swimsuit with round lavender sunglasses, yellow towel & wrist tag **Head:** Stacey **Head Markings:** inside rim © 1965 Mattel Inc & country **Arms:** reg **Body:** dark tan tnt **Body Markings:** © 1966/ Mattel, Inc./ U.S. Patented/ U.S. Pat. Pend/ Made in/ Japan **Notes:** through 1970s same doll & model # manufactured in Japan, Korea & Taiwan, with regular or Mexico arms, Stacey or superstar face, aqua, red square neck or red gathered swimsuit, different forms of packaging see white Sun Set Malibu Ken 1974, for pink box see Malibu Barbie 1975

Model #: 1174 **Name:** Barbie Hair Happenin's **Box Date:** 1971 **Hair Color:** red **Hairstyle:** side part chin-length hair, cello on head **Face:** blue eyes, rooted lashes, light brown brows, pink lips & blush **Clothing:** white short sleeve scoop neck blouse with elastic at edges, black felt belt with gold bead, pink skirt with ruffle at hem, wrist tag, black t-straps **Extras:** clear X stand, red hairpieces: mini curls=topknot of large curls, mini swirls=elastic band modified pageboy, fashion fall=long straight section of red hair on hot pink band **Extras:** small white brush & comb, mini bobby pins, small flowers, rubberband **Head:** tnt **Head Markings:** inside rim © 1966 Mattel Inc & country **Arms:** regular **Body:** light tan tnt **Body Markings:** © 1966/ Mattel, Inc./ U.S. Patented/ U.S. Pat. Pend/ Made in/ Japan **Notes:** initially thought to be a Sears exclusive, but sold by many retailers

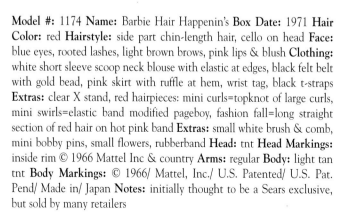  

Model #: 3311 Name: Busy Barbie Box Date: 1971 Hair Color: blonde Hairstyle: shoulder length, part on side, 1 side pulled back with brass oval barrette Face: blue eyes, brown brows, pink lips & blush Clothing: blue denim halter top with attached white panties, long multicolor skirt with self fabric ruffle of red, white, blue, green, pink print, white square toe low heel shoes, wrist tag Extras: clear X stand, brown princess telephone, TV, travel case, record player, record, tray, 2 glasses, stickers Booklet: LWOB 1971 & instructions Head: tnt Head Markings: inside rim © 1966 Mattel Inc & country Arms: busy Body: pink tnt Body Markings: © 1966/ Mattel, Inc./ U.S. & Foreign/ Patented/ Other Pats/ Pending/ Made in/ U.S.A. or Hong Kong Notes: arms fall off

Model #: 1195 Name: Busy Talking Barbie Box Date: 1971 Hair Color: blonde Hairstyle: shaggy chin length with bangs Face: blue eyes, rooted lashes, brown brows, peach lips & blush Clothing: red long sleeve turtleneck blouse sewn to turquoise satin short cuffed overalls with light green belt & gold buckle, matching red wide head-band, green lace-up knee-high boots, wrist tag Extras: clear X stand, brown princess telephone, TV, travel case, record player, record, tray, 2 glasses, stickers Booklet: LB&S 1970 & instructions Head: tnt Head Markings: inside rim © 1966 Mattel Inc & country Arms: busy Body: pink talking Body Markings: © 1967/ Mattel, Inc./ U.S. & Foreign/ Pats.Pend./ Hong Kong Notes: pull string doll talks, usually mute, arms fall off

Model #: 1182 Name: Walk Lively Barbie Box Date: 1971 Hair Color: blonde Hairstyle: middle part below shoulder length, ends curled under Face: blue eyes, rooted lashes, brown brows, pink lips & blush Clothing: 2-piece sleeveless red pantsuit with 2 thin brown gold buckle belts, yellow vinyl shoulder bag, red pilgrims, wrist tag Extras: light brown round walking stand Booklet: LWOB 1971 & instructions Head: tnt Head Markings: inside rim © 1966 Mattel Inc & country Arms: Mexico Body: pink walking Body Markings: © 1967 Mattel, Inc./ U.S. Pat.pend/ Taiwan

Model #: 1144 Name: Barbie with Growin' Pretty Hair Box Date: 1972 Hair Color: blonde Hairstyle: front pulled back into bun with retractable ponytail, sides bobbed, cello on head Face: blue eyes, rooted lashes, brown brows, pink lips & blush Clothing: sleeveless scoop neck empire gown, blue faux suede bodice with white lace-up front & eyelet trim, multicolor red, white, blue & yellow pattern skirt with self ruffle at hem, sewn in white panties, blue square toe low heel shoes, wrist tag Extras: bobby pins, hairpieces: long thin braided strip each end with blue ribbon bow & 4 long ringlet curls with blue ribbon bow at top Head: tnt Head Markings: inside rim © 1966 Mattel Inc & country Arms: Mexico Body: pink b/l grow hair Body Markings: © 1967 Mattel, Inc./ U.S. Patented/ Other Patents Pending/ Patented in Canada 1967/ Taiwan

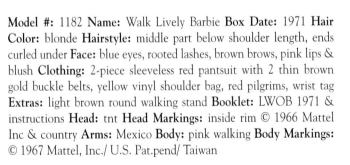

Model #: 4220 Name: Quick Curl Barbie Box Date: 1972 Hair Color: blonde Hairstyle: middle part, double row flip with sides fastened with tiny seed beads, cello on head Face: blue eyes, brown brows, pink lips & blush Clothing: pink & white gingham long dress with sheer sleeves, white satin collar, black ribbon accents at neck and cuffs, 3 white barrettes, 4 ribbons, 2 rubber bands, wrist tag, white square toe low heels Extras: white X stand & hot pink pointed comb, brush, curler Booklet: BWOB 1973 Head: tnt Head Markings: inside rim © 1966 Mattel Inc & country Arms: Mexico Body: pink tnt Body Markings: © 1966/ Mattel, Inc./ U.S. & Foreign/ Patented/ Other pats/ Pending/ Made in/ Taiwan

Model #: 7807 Name: Newport Barbie Box Date: 1973 Hair Color: blonde Hairstyle: waist length, side part, cello on head Face: blue eyes, brown brows, peach lips Clothing: white cotton pants with red buckled self belt, sleeveless sailor style top with red buttons, orange, red & white striped bikini, pink round sunglasses & wrist tag Extras: white sailboard, 2-piece mast, red or pink sail & sheet of stickers Head: Stacey Head Markings: inside rim © 1965 Mattel Inc & country Arms: Mexico Body: tan tnt Body Markings: © 1966/ Mattel, Inc./ U.S. & Foreign/ Patented/ Other pats/ Pending/ Made in/ Taiwan Notes: also available in box

Model #: 7806 Name: Sun Valley Barbie Box Date: 1973 Hair Color: blonde Hairstyle: waist length, side part, cello on head Face: blue eyes, brown brows, peach lips & blush Clothing: 1-piece yellow & orange turtleneck long sleeve ski suit with orange belt & yellow buckle, yellow parka with white fake fur collar, orange poles & goggles, yellow skis, orange ski boots & wrist tag Head: Stacey Head Markings: inside rim © 1965 Mattel Inc & country Arms: Mexico Body: tan tnt Body Markings: © 1966/ Mattel, Inc./ U.S. & Foreign/ Patented/ Other pats/ Pending/ Made in/ Taiwan Notes: also available in box

Model #: 7796 Name: Sweet 16 Box Date: 1973 Hair Color: blonde Hairstyle: below shoulder length with hair framed around face in front, cello on head Face: blue eyes, blonde brows, pale pink lips & blush Clothing: long pink dotted swiss dress with sheer ruffles at armholes & white bow at waist, pink Barbie makeup case with 2 shades of blush, white square toe low heel shoes, optional wrist tag Extras: yellow small oval brush & comb with handgrip, 4 yellow barrettes, makeup applicator, fragrance stickers for barrettes Head: tnt Head Markings: inside rim © 1966 Mattel Inc & country Arms: Mexico Body: pink tnt Body Markings: © 1966/ Mattel, Inc./ U.S. & Foreign/ Patented/ Other pats/ Pending/ Made in/ Taiwan Notes: also available with extra outfit

Model #: 7270 Name: Free Moving Barbie Box Date: 1974 Hair Color: blonde Hairstyle: side part, 1 side tied with red ribbon rest below shoulder-length flip, cello on head Face: blue eyes, blonde brows, pale pink lips & blush Clothing: white 1-piece playsuit with red insert at waist, red long skirt with white & black flowers, golf club, tennis racket, ball, white tennis shoes Head: tnt Head Markings: inside rim © 1966 Mattel Inc & country Arms: ptr Body: pink free moving Body Markings: © 1967/ Mattel, Inc./ Taiwan/ U.S.Pat.Pend. Notes: pull down lever on back of doll permits free movement

Model #: 7233 Name: Gold Medal Olympic Barbie Box Date: 1974 Hair Color: blonde Hairstyle: mid-back length, side part, cello on head Face: blue eyes, brown brows, peach lips Clothing: red, white & blue sleeveless bodysuit & gold medal pendant Booklet: coupon Head: Stacey Head Markings: inside rim © 1965 Mattel Inc & country Arms: reg Body: tan tnt Body Markings: © 1966/ Mattel, Inc./ U.S. & Foreign/ Patented/ Other pats/ Pending/ Made in/ Taiwan Notes: gift sets: Sears exclusives Winter Sports set & Olympic Wardrobe

Model #: 7262 Name: Gold Medal Olympic Barbie Skater Box Date: 1974 Hair Color: blonde Hairstyle: waist length, parted on side, cello on head Face: blue eyes, brown brows, peach lips Clothing: red, white & blue long sleeve turtleneck bodysuit with white pleated short skating skirt, pair of white skates & gold medal pendant Extras: 2-piece blue & white skating stand Head: Stacey Head Markings: inside rim © 1965 Mattel Inc & country Arms: Mexico Body: tan tnt Body Markings: © 1966/ Mattel, Inc./ U.S. & Foreign/ Patented/ Other pats/ Pending/ Made in/ Taiwan

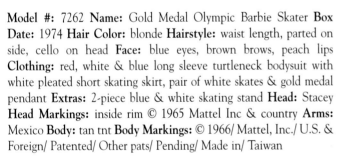

Model #: 7264 Name: Gold Medal Olympic Barbie Skier Box Date: 1974 Hair Color: blonde Hairstyle: waist length, parted on side, cello on head Face: blue eyes, brown brows, light red lips & blush Clothing: 1-piece red, white & blue long sleeve turtleneck ski suit, blue vinyl belt, navy #9 on yellow entry vest, red goggles, blue poles, yellow skis, gold medal, red hat, white ski boots Head: Stacey Head Markings: inside rim © 1965 Mattel Inc & country Arms: Mexico Body: tan tnt Body Markings: © 1966/ Mattel, Inc./ U.S. & Foreign/ Patented/ Other pats/ Pending/ Made in/ Taiwan

Model #: 9093 **Name:** Ballerina Barbie **Box Date:** 1975 **Hair Color:** blonde **Hairstyle:** parted in middle, part of sides pulled to back of head, rest in shoulder-length ponytail, gold crown **Face:** blue eyes, brown brows, pink lips & blush **Clothing:** white tutu with gold trim tulle, 3 red plastic roses with green leaves, white ankle strap ballet slippers **Extras:** 2-piece white stand **Booklet:** instructions **Head:** tnt **Head Markings:** inside rim © 1966 Mattel Inc & country **Arms:** ballerina **Body:** pink tnt **Body Markings:** © Mattel, Inc.1966/ U.S. Patent Pending/ Taiwan **Notes:** hairstyle may vary, also gift set: On Tour with extra outfit

Model #: 9217 **Name:** Deluxe Quick Curl Barbie **Box Date:** 1975 **Hair Color:** blonde **Hairstyle:** middle part, shoulder-length flip, cello on head **Face:** purple & aqua eyes, blonde brows, peach lips & blush **Clothing:** turquoise long sleeveless dress, sweetheart neckline ruffle at hem, white fringed shawl, blonde fall with turquoise ribbon tie, 2 white barrettes, 2 ribbons, rubber band, white choker, turquoise pilgrims **Extras:** white pointed brush, comb & curler **Head:** tnt **Head Markings:** inside rim © 1966 Mattel Inc & country **Arms:** ptr **Body:** pink tnt **Body Markings:** © 1966/ Mattel, Inc./ U.S. & Foreign/ Patented/ Other pats/ Pending/ Made in/ Taiwan **Notes:** also packaged with free beauty kit

Model #: 7470 **Name:** Hawaiian Barbie **Box Date:** 1975 **Hair Color:** black **Hairstyle:** below shoulder length, parted in middle, side pulled into band in back, ends curled under **Face:** brown eyes, brown brows, light red lips & blush **Clothing:** multicolor bikini with long wrap skirt of fuchsia, orange, green & green headband with flowers, white sailboard & mast & red sail & orange ukulele **Head:** Steffie **Head Markings:** inside rim © 1971 Mattel Inc & country **Arms:** Mexico/ptr/Francie **Body:** dark tan tnt **Body Markings:** © 1966/ Mattel, Inc./ U.S. Patented/ U.S. Pat.Pend./ Made in/ Korea **Notes:** doll released in 75, 77 & 1982 with fabric, arms, accessory & country changes(Philippines last country)

Model #: 1067 **Name:** Malibu Barbie **Box Date:** 1975 **Hair Color:** blonde **Hairstyle:** mid-back length, side part, cello on head **Face:** blue eyes, brown brows, pale pink lips **Clothing:** red/orange nylon 1-piece swimsuit **Head:** Stacey or superstar **Head Markings:** inside rim © 1965 Mattel Inc & country or inside or outside rim © Mattel Inc 1976 =/- country **Arms:** Mexico/ptr **Body:** tan tnt **Body Markings:** © 1966/ Mattel, Inc./ U.S. Patented/ U.S. Pat.Pend./ Made in/ Korea **Notes:** pictured is 2nd version with superstar face issued in 1977, doll also available with usual Malibu Stacey head mold, red square neck swimsuit, gift sets: Fashion Combo, Plus 3 & Super Fashion Fireworks

Model #: 9599 **Name:** Beautiful Bride **Box Date:** 1976 **Hair Color:** blonde **Hairstyle:** shoulder-length flip, part on side **Face:** blue eyes, rooted lashes, pale peach lips, light brown brows **Clothing:** scoop neck white gown with leg of mutton sleeves, veil with white crescent shaped head piece, pearl necklace, plastic pale blue flowers on green stem bouquet tied with blue ribbon & white pilgrims **Head:** tnt **Head Markings:** inside rim © 1966 Mattel Inc & country **Arms:** ptr **Body:** pink tnt **Body Markings:** © 1966/ Mattel, Inc./ U.S. Patented/ U.S. Pat.Pend./ Made in/ Korea

Model #: 9828 **Name:** Supersize Barbie **Box Date:** 1976 **Hair Color:** blonde **Hairstyle:** side part, mid-back length, cello on head **Face:** aqua eyes, blonde brows, peach lips & blush **Clothing:** silver & white satin sweetheart neck halter bodysuit with matching long skirt & pants, rhinestone stud earrings, choker, ring, extra ring, earrings and necklace out of white plastic & silver paint, white ankle straps **Extras:** 3-piece stand, child's bracelet, barrette & necklace **Booklet:** instructions **Head:** supersize **Head Markings:** Taiwan/© 1976 Mattel, Inc. **Arms:** bent **Body:** tan tnt supersize **Body Markings:** © Mattel, Inc. 1976/ U.S.A. **Notes:** 18 inch body

Model #: 9720 **Name:** Superstar Barbie **Box Date:** 1976 **Hair Color:** blonde **Hairstyle:** side part waist length, ends turned under **Face:** turquoise eyes, blonde brows, pink lips & blush **Clothing:** hot pink satin halter gown with silver & pink lace ruffled boa, rhinestone stud earrings, pendant, ring, pink ankle straps **Extras:** 2-piece pink star stand **Head:** superstar **Head Markings:** inside or outside rim © Mattel Inc 1976 +/- country **Arms:** bent **Body:** tan tnt **Body Markings:** © Mattel Inc 1966/ Taiwan **Notes:** gift sets: Barbie & Ken, In the Spotlight, Fashion Change Abouts & variations of outfit &/or free gift variations

Model #: 2210 **Name:** Fashion Photo Barbie **Box Date:** 1977 **Hair Color:** blonde with golden streaks **Hairstyle:** middle part, sides pulled to back of head, rest waist length **Face:** blue eyes, dark blonde brows, pink lips & blush **Clothing:** gold spaghetti strap body suit with fuchsia, orange & yellow chiffon long skirt, orange pants, orange rhinestone earrings, pendant & ring, orange ankle straps **Extras:** 2-piece pink modeling stand & cable, pose changes by turning lens on black camera, preprinted photos **Booklet:** instructions **Head:** superstar **Head Markings:** inside or outside rim © Mattel Inc 1976 +/- country **Arms:** bent **Body:** pink tnt **Body Markings:** © Mattel Inc 1966/ Taiwan **Notes:** special leg joint allows greater flexibility at hip

Model #: 9975 Name: Supersize Barbie Bridal Box Date: 1977 Hair Color: blonde Hairstyle: side part, waist length, cello on head Face: blue eyes, blonde brows, peach lips & blush Clothing: white lace long sleeve scoop neck wedding gown with ruffle at hem, matching veil, rhinestone earrings, pendant, ring, yellow & green plastic flower bouquet, white ankle straps Extras: 3-piece star shape stand Head: supersize Head Markings: Taiwan/© 1976 Mattel, Inc. Arms: bent Body: tan tnt supersize Body Markings: © Mattel, Inc. 1976/ U.S.A. Notes: 18 inch body

Model #: 9907 Name: Beautiful Bride Issue Date: 1978 Box Date: 1976 Hair Color: blonde Hairstyle: below shoulders, part on side Face: blue eyes, brown brows, pink lips Clothing: off-white lace gown with leg of mutton sleeves, veil with ribbon headband, bouquet of pink plastic flowers on green stems tied with off-white satin bow, rhinestone stud earrings, ring & clear plastic choker, off-white ankle straps Extras: white star shaped stand Head: superstar Head Markings: inside or outside rim © Mattel Inc 1976 +/- country Arms: bent elbow Body: pink tnt Body Markings: © Mattel Inc 1966/ Taiwan

Model #: 2597 Name: Kissing Barbie Box Date: 1978 Hair Color: blonde Hairstyle: sides pulled to back of head rest mid-back length Face: turquoise eyes, brown brows, mauve lips Clothing: square neck long sleeve pink floral gown, pink & purple plastic flower & green leaf bouquet, pink ankle straps Extras: 2-piece clear stand, pink liquid lipstick & sheet of cardboard punch outs Booklet: BWOF 1979 & instructions Head: Kissing Head Markings: © Mattel, Inc/ 1978 Taiwan Arms: bent Body: tan tnt Body Markings: © Mattel Inc 1966/ Taiwan Notes: press back panel for pucker & smack noise, also gift set with extra outfit

Model #: 2598 Name: Pretty Changes Box Date: 1978 Hair Color: blonde Hairstyle: short bouffant tied with yellow & white lace halo Face: blue eyes, blonde brows, pink lips & blush Clothing: spaghetti strap yellow satin jumpsuit, yellow & white sheer overskirt, yellow fabric rose tie at throat, pink necklace, barrette, white net & yellow wide brim hat, yellow & white matching bolero jacket, yellow ankle straps Extras: 2-piece white star stand, white pointed brush, light brown fall & 2-tone blonde fall Booklet: BWOF 1979 & instructions Head: superstar Head Markings: inside or outside rim © Mattel Inc 1976 +/- country Arms: bent Body: pink tnt Body Markings: © Mattel Inc.1966/ Philippines Notes: also sold as lamp

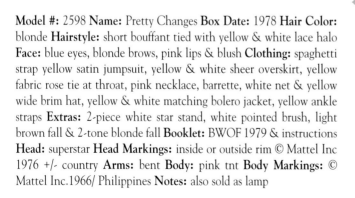  

Model #: 1067 **Name:** Sun Lovin' Malibu Barbie **Box Date:** 1978 **Hair Color:** blonde **Hairstyle:** middle part, waist length **Face:** turquoise eyes, black brows, peach lips & blush **Clothing:** turquoise bikini with 'B' initial on hip, turquoise vinyl tote bag, purple mirror sunglasses **Booklet:** BWOF 1980 **Head:** superstar **Head Markings:** inside or outside rim © Mattel Inc 1976 +/- country **Arms:** ptr **Body:** dark tan tnt, painted tan lines **Body Markings:** © Mattel Inc 1966/ Taiwan **Notes:** head of some dolls made in Philippines, some in Taiwan

Model #: 2844 **Name:** Supersize Super Hair Barbie **Box Date:** 1978 **Hair Color:** blonde **Hairstyle:** middle part, ends curled up at nape of neck, cello on head **Face:** blue eyes, brown brows, hot pink lips & blush **Clothing:** white knee-length spaghetti strap dress with pink ribbon trim & lace overskirt, pink hoop earrings, pendant, ring, white ankle straps **Extras:** pink nail polish/blush & 2-piece clear stand **Head:** supersize **Head Markings:** Taiwan/© 1976 Mattel, Inc. **Arms:** bent **Body:** tan tnt supersize **Body Markings:** © Mattel, Inc. 1976/ U.S.A. **Notes:** 18 inch body, pull string in back of neck releases long section of hair in top of head

Model #: 1290 **Name:** Beauty Secrets Barbie **Box Date:** 1979 **Hair Color:** blonde **Hairstyle:** thigh length, part in middle with ponytail and bangs **Face:** blue eyes, brown brows, pink lips & blush **Clothing:** hot pink teddy with lace trim, short jacket, long slim skirt with slit in back, hot pink mules or ankle straps **Extras:** 2-piece clear stand, pink brush, comb & mirror with handgrip, pink perfume bottle, large mirror, powder puff, wash cloth, purple toothbrush, hair dryer, compact, carryall **Booklet:** BWOF 1979 & instructions **Head:** superstar **Head Markings:** inside or outside rim © Mattel Inc 1976 +/- country **Arms:** Living Barbie **Body:** tan tnt **Body Markings:** © Mattel Inc 1979,/ Taiwan 1966 **Notes:** also gift set with 3-way mirror, press panel on back & arms move

Model #: 1703 **Name:** Malibu Barbie The Beach Party **Box Date:** 1979 **Hair Color:** blonde **Hairstyle:** mid-back length, side part, cello on head **Face:** turquoise eyes, brown brows, dark peach lips & blush **Clothing:** fuchsia 1-piece swimsuit with purple trim, green snorkel, mask, flippers, small yellow comb, burlap tote bag with blue trim, orange & yellow table with green umbrella, yellow beach chair, orange surfboard, orange grill & stickers **Extras:** white vinyl beach party carrying case **Booklet:** Instructions **Head:** superstar **Head Markings:** inside or outside rim © Mattel Inc 1976 +/- country **Arms:** ptr **Body:** dark tan tnt **Body Markings:** © Mattel Inc 1966/ Taiwan

Model #: 1874 **Name:** Golden Dreams Barbie **Box Date:** 1980 **Hair Color:** 2 shades of blonde **Hairstyle:** mid-back length, curly, parted in middle or large & puffed-up in front **Face:** blue eyes, blonde brows, pink lips & blush **Clothing:** metallic gold halter jumpsuit with white sheer & metallic gold stripe overskirt, long handless gloves, rhinestone earrings, pendant, ring, sheer tie-on wrap, 2 combs, 2 barrettes, 2 rubber bands, clear ankle straps **Extras:** white with gold accent brush, comb, curler & clear hair arranger **Booklet:** BWOF 1979 & instructions **Head:** superstar **Head Markings:** inside or outside rim © Mattel Inc 1976 +/- country **Arms:** bent **Body:** tan tnt **Body Markings:** © Mattel Inc.1966/ Philippines **Notes:** department store special with white faux fur coat

Model #: 1922 **Name:** Happy Birthday Barbie **Box Date:** 1980 **Hair Color:** blonde **Hairstyle:** side pulled back, curly bangs, rest mid-back length, ends curled under **Face:** turquoise eyes, blonde brows, pink lips & blush **Clothing:** rainbow color halter dress with lace trimmed bodice & flower appliqué skirt, clear ring, pink ribbon, gift box, white platform ankle straps **Extras:** clear child's ring, birthstone sticker sheet, pink Barbie head charm birthday gift **Booklet:** BWOF 1979 & party ideas **Head:** superstar **Head Markings:** inside or outside rim © Mattel Inc 1976 +/- country **Arms:** bent **Body:** tan tnt **Body Markings:** © Mattel Inc.1966/ Philippines

Model #: 1880 **Name:** Roller Skating Barbie **Box Date:** 1980 **Hair Color:** blonde **Hairstyle:** side part, sides pulled to back of head rest mid-back length, ends curled under **Face:** light blue eyes, blonde brows, pink lips & blush **Clothing:** 1-piece red & black bodysuit with long sleeves, purple short jacket, red knee socks, rhinestone stud earrings & ring, white roller skates with red wheels **Head:** superstar **Head Markings:** inside or outside rim © Mattel Inc 1976 +/- country **Arms:** bent **Body:** tan tnt **Body Markings:** © Mattel Inc 1966/ Taiwan

Model #: 1757 **Name:** Western Barbie **Box Date:** 1980 **Hair Color:** 2 tones of blonde **Hairstyle:** curly bangs, rest pulled back to shoulder-length ponytail, cello on head or parted on side & pulled into mid-back side ponytail **Face:** aqua eyes (1 winks), blonde brows, pink lips & blush **Clothing:** 1-piece western style jumpsuit white with silver lamé & black ribbon trim at bodice, collar, cuffs, belt, white plastic cowboy hat & boots **Extras:** turquoise brush, comb, mirror with handgrip, turquoise Barbie stamper, sheet of cardboard punch outs **Booklet:** BWOF 1980 & instructions **Head:** winking **Head Markings:** Mattel Inc./ 1976-1980 Taiwan **Arms:** bent **Body:** pink tnt **Body Markings:** © Mattel Inc 1966/ Taiwan **Notes:** press panel on back to activate winking

Model #: 5315 **Name:** Fashion Jeans Barbie **Box Date:** 1981 **Hair Color:** blonde **Hairstyle:** middle part, waist-length ponytail pulled back at nape of neck **Face:** blue eyes, dark blonde brows, pink lips & blush **Clothing:** pink short sleeve fuzzy top, blue jeans with pink piping & belt, rhinestone earrings & ring, pink cowboy boots **Extras:** pink pointed comb & brush **Booklet:** BWOF 1981 **Head:** superstar **Head Markings:** inside or outside rim © Mattel Inc 1976 +/- country **Arms:** bent **Body:** pink tnt **Body Markings:** © Mattel Inc.1966/ Philippines

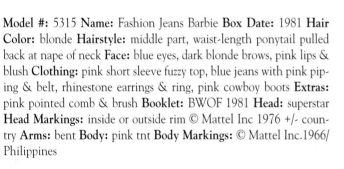

Model #: 3856 **Name:** Magic Curl Barbie **Box Date:** 1981 **Hair Color:** blonde **Hairstyle:** pulled back into mass of small curls held with yellow ribbon **Face:** blue eyes, blonde brows, peach lips & blush **Clothing:** long yellow dress accented with yellow lace & wide yellow ribbon belt, square neck & large puffed sleeves, wraparound towel, yellow mules **Extras:** white pointed brush & comb, purple brush & comb with handgrip, mirror, 2 barrettes, 2 hair ornaments, applicator bottle, magic mist packet, hand towel, vanity tray **Booklet:** BWOF 1981 & instructions **Head:** superstar **Head Markings:** inside or outside rim © Mattel Inc 1976 +/- country **Arms:** bent **Body:** tan tnt **Body Markings:** © Mattel Inc 1966/ Taiwan

Model #: 3551 **Name:** Pink n' Pretty Barbie **Box Date:** 1981 **Hair Color:** blonde **Hairstyle:** shoulder-length ponytail at top of head, ends curled under **Face:** blue eyes, light brown brows, pale pink lips & blush **Clothing:** pink sleeveless top with silver dots, floor-length slim nylon pink skirt, matching pants, chiffon skirt of varying lengths from floor to knee with pale faux fur hem, matching stole, headband, clear rhinestone dangle earrings, pendant, ring, pale pink mules **Extras:** small lavender brush, comb & mirror with handgrip **Head:** superstar **Head Markings:** inside or outside rim © Mattel Inc 1976 +/- country **Arms:** bent **Body:** tan tnt **Body Markings:** © Mattel Inc.1966/ Philippines **Notes:** also modeling gift set

Model #: 1067 **Name:** Sunsational Malibu Barbie **Box Date:** 1981 **Hair Color:** blonde **Hairstyle:** side part mid-back length **Face:** turquoise eyes, brown brows, peach lips & blush **Clothing:** fuchsia 1-piece halter-style swimsuit with flower appliqué, pink towel, purple mirror sunglasses **Booklet:** BWOF 1981 **Head:** superstar **Head Markings:** inside or outside rim © Mattel Inc 1976 +/- country **Arms:** ptr **Body:** tan tnt **Body Markings:** © Mattel Inc.1966/ Philippines

Model #: 5640 **Name:** Angel Face Barbie **Box Date:** 1982 **Hair Color:** blonde with dark brown streaks **Hairstyle:** mid-back length parted on side pulled into ponytail at nape of neck **Face:** turquoise eyes, brown brows, pink lips & blush **Clothing:** white lace long sleeve blouse, pink ribbon trim with cameo at neck, black belt & long pink taffeta skirt, 2 plastic hot pink hair ornaments & headband, rhinestone ring, hot pink mules **Extras:** pointed white comb & brush, pink applicator, comb & brush with handgrip, pink compact with makeup **Booklet:** instructions **Head:** superstar **Head Markings:** inside or outside rim © Mattel Inc 1976 +/- country **Arms:** bent **Body:** pink tnt **Body Markings:** © Mattel Inc.1966/ Philippines

Model #: 5868 **Name:** Dream Date Barbie **Box Date:** 1982 **Hair Color:** blonde **Hairstyle:** waist length, side part, pulled back at nape of neck, ends curled under **Face:** lavender eyes, blonde brows, pink lips **Clothing:** fuchsia sequin top with rose satin long slim skirt slit up side & matching sleeve detail both edged in purple satin, purple satin belt with fabric rose, rhinestone stud earrings & ring, rose mules **Extras:** lavender comb, brush & mirror with handgrip, perfume bottle **Booklet:** instructions **Head:** superstar **Head Markings:** inside or outside rim © Mattel Inc 1976 +/- country **Arms:** bent **Body:** tan tnt **Body Markings:** © Mattel Inc 1966/ Taiwan

Model #: 1757 **Name:** Horse Lovin' Barbie **Box Date:** 1982 **Hair Color:** blonde **Hairstyle:** mid-back-length ponytail **Face:** blue eyes, light brown brows, pale pink lips & blush **Clothing:** red vinyl pants, fake shearling vest, red & white blouse, rhinestone stud earrings & ring, light tan cowboy hat, saddle bag & boots **Extras:** pointed white comb & brush, cardboard punch outs, brown Barbie signature stamp **Booklet:** instructions **Head:** superstar **Head Markings:** inside or outside rim © Mattel Inc 1976 +/- country **Arms:** bent **Body:** pink tnt **Body Markings:** © Mattel Inc.1966/ Philippines

Model #: 5579 **Name:** Twirley Curls Barbie **Box Date:** 1982 **Hair Color:** blonde **Hairstyle:** middle part, mid-thigh-length side ponytail banded at nape of neck **Face:** blue eyes, blonde brows, pink lips & blush **Clothing:** hot pink halter-style bodysuit with matching long slim skirt with fabric ruffle & silver wide belt, rhinestone ring, hot pink mules **Extras:** pink pointed comb & brush, 4 white barrettes, 2 pink ribbons, purple chair with suction cups, pink twirley curler **Booklet:** instructions **Head:** superstar **Head Markings:** inside or outside rim © Mattel Inc 1976 +/- country **Arms:** bent **Body:** tan tnt **Body Markings:** © Mattel Inc 1966/ Taiwan **Notes:** also gift set with 3-way mirror, press plate on back and arms move

Model #: 4598 **Name:** Crystal Barbie **Box Date:** 1983 **Hair Color:** blonde **Hairstyle:** pulled back into 3 intertwined ponytails **Face:** lavender eyes, blonde brows, deep pink lips & blush **Clothing:** white spaghetti strap opalescent gown with ruffle hem & matching boa, fuchsia & purple waistband, rhinestone drop earrings, pendant & ring, narrow clear silver glitter pumps **Extras:** white pointed comb & brush, crystal pendant for child **Booklet:** BWOF 1983 & instructions **Head:** superstar **Head Markings:** inside or outside rim © Mattel Inc 1976 +/- country **Arms:** bent **Body:** tan tnt **Body Markings:** © Mattel Inc.1966/ Philippines

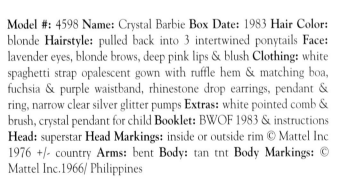

Model #: 7025 **Name:** Great Shapes Barbie **Box Date:** 1983 **Hair Color:** blonde **Hairstyle:** side part, mid-back-length side ponytail, ends turned under **Face:** turquoise eyes, blonde brows, pink lips & blush **Clothing:** turquoise 1-piece sleeveless full-length bodysuit, multi-striped leggings, pink sash, turquoise headband, pink workout bag & booklet, pink ankle strap ballet shoes **Booklet:** BWOF 1983 **Head:** superstar **Head Markings:** inside or outside rim © Mattel Inc 1976 +/- country **Arms:** ptr **Body:** tan tnt **Body Markings:** © Mattel Inc.1966/ Philippines **Notes:** next issue came with doll size walkman

Model #: 1922 Name: Happy Birthday Barbie Box Date: 1983 Hair Color: blonde Hairstyle: side part, rest curly mid-back length Face: turquoise eyes, blonde brows, pink lips & blush Clothing: hot pink polka dot long sleeve high collar mid-calf dress with white belt, rhinestone ring, lilac ribbon, gift box, pink mules Extras: child size ring & pink Barbie head charm birthday gift, birthstone sticker sheet Booklet: BWOF 1984 & party ideas Head: superstar Head Markings: inside or outside rim © Mattel Inc 1976 +/- country Arms: bent Body: tan tnt Body Markings: © Mattel Inc.1966/ Philippines Notes: also available in gift set with paper products

Model #: 7072 Name: Lovin' You Barbie Box Date: 1983 Hair Color: blonde Hairstyle: mid-back-length ponytail on top of head, ends curled under Face: blue eyes, light brown brows, red lips & blush Clothing: red flocked heart shaped bodice top with sheer white puffed sleeves with small red flocked heart detail, matching skirt, white panties with red edging, red rhinestone stud earrings & ring, white mules Extras: red pointed brush & comb, white Barbie stamper, sheet of stickers, heart shaped note paper in box Booklet: BWOF 1983 & instructions Head: superstar Head Markings: inside or outside rim © Mattel Inc 1976 +/- country Arms: bent Body: tan tnt Body Markings: © Mattel Inc 1966/ Taiwan Notes: also gift set with purse for child

Model #: 1067 Name: Sun Gold Malibu Barbie Box Date: 1983 Hair Color: blonde Hairstyle: side part, sides pulled back, rest mid-back length, ends curled under Face: light blue eyes, brown brows, light red lips & blush Clothing: gold checked halter-style 1-piece swimsuit, gold tote bag converts to blue mat, turquoise mirror sunglasses, extra glasses in pink & purple Booklet: BWOF 1984 Head: superstar Head Markings: inside or outside rim © Mattel Inc 1976 +/- country Arms: ptr Body: dark tan tnt Body Markings: © Mattel, Inc. 1966/ Hong Kong

Model #: 7929 Name: Day-to-Night Barbie Box Date: 1984 Hair Color: blonde Hairstyle: side part with front sections pulled to back of head, rest waist length, ends curled under Face: blue eyes, blonde brows, pink lips & blush Clothing: spaghetti strap metallic hot pink bodysuit, pink chiffon scarf, pink jacket with white lapels & buttons, matching reversible skirt, white hat with pink & white hatband, white briefcase, rhinestone stud earrings & ring, white plastic clutch purse with pink strap, hot pink mules, narrow white & pink pumps Extras: pink pointed comb & brush, sheet of cardboard punch outs Booklet: BWOF 1984 & instructions Head: superstar Head Markings: inside or outside rim © Mattel Inc 1976 +/- country Arms: bent Body: tan tnt Body Markings: © Mattel Inc 1966/ Taiwan

Model #: 9180 Name: Dream Time Barbie Box Date: 1984 Hair Color: blonde Hairstyle: side part, sides pulled to back of head, rest mid-back length, ends curled under Face: blue lavender eyes, blonde brows, hot pink lips & blush Clothing: long lilac spaghetti strap nightgown with white lace at neck & matching peignoir of pink, white, lavender with front tie, rhinestone ring, pink teddy bear, lilac mules Extras: lilac pointed comb & brush Booklet: BWOF 1986 Head: superstar Head Markings: inside or outside rim © Mattel Inc 1976 +/- country Arms: bent Body: tan tnt Body Markings: © Mattel Inc 1966/ Taiwan Notes: 1988 version w/pink gown made for Toys R Us

Model #: 7926 Name: Peaches n' Cream Barbie Box Date: 1984 Hair Color: blonde Hairstyle: side part with sides pulled to back, waist length, ends curled under Face: blue eyes, blonde brows, orange lips & blush Clothing: gown with spaghetti strap iridescent sweetheart bodice & full pink & orange chiffon skirt with ruffle hem, matching boa, orange chiffon belt, rhinestone stud earrings, pendant & ring, narrow peach pumps Extras: white pointed comb & brush, 2 orange barrettes, 2 hair combs, orange costume spinner & sheet of cardboard punch outs Booklet: BWOF 1984 & instructions Head: superstar Head Markings: inside or outside rim © Mattel Inc 1976 +/- country Arms: bent Body: tan tnt Body Markings: © Mattel Inc.1966/ Philippines

Model #: 2449 Name: Astronaut Barbie Box Date: 1985 Hair Color: blonde Hairstyle: side part, mid-back length pulled to nape of neck, ends curled under Face: blue eyes, blonde brows, deep pink lips & blush Clothing: metallic fuchsia & silver long sleeve turtleneck bodysuit with Barbie appliqué, matching pants with silver belt, matching pleated mini skirt, silver tights, wide fuchsia belt, silver purse, computer, clear helmet, silver backpack, flagpole, fuchsia over-the-knee boots Extras: pink pointed brush, sheet of stickers & sheet of cardboard punch outs Booklet: BWOF 1986 & instructions Head: superstar Head Markings: inside or outside rim © Mattel Inc 1976 +/- country Arms: bent Body: tan tnt Body Markings: © Mattel Inc 1966/ Malaysia

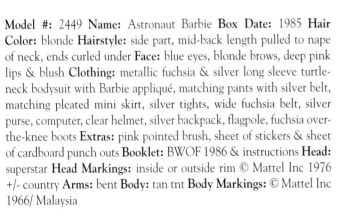

Model #: 2248 Name: Dream Glow Barbie Box Date: 1985 Hair Color: blonde Hairstyle: thigh length, middle part, sides pulled to back of head Face: lavender eyes, brown brows, hot pink lips & blush Clothing: halter-style gown, hot pink bodice trimmed in silver lace, full skirt of sheer pink fabric with white dayglo stars & silver lace, matching stole, rhinestone earrings, pendant, ring, pink plastic parasol, narrow pink pumps Extras: white pointed brush Booklet: BWOF 1985 & instructions Head: superstar Head Markings: inside or outside rim © Mattel Inc 1976 +/- country Arms: bent Body: tan tnt Body Markings: © Mattel Inc 1966/ Taiwan Notes: stars in outfit glow in dark

Model #: 1922 **Name:** Gift Giving Barbie **Box Date:** 1985 **Hair Color:** blonde **Hairstyle:** side part, pulled back into shoulder-length ponytail, ends turned under with lavender satin bow at side of head **Face:** turquoise eyes, brown brows, pink lips & blush **Clothing:** sleeveless knee-length dress with lilac top, lilac, pink, hot pink skirt, iridescent petal trim at neckline, matching belt, rhinestone stud earrings & ring, gift box, hot pink no strap ballet slippers, narrow dusty blue pumps **Extras:** pink pointed brush, lilac brush, comb & mirror with handgrip, pink pendant heart & ribbon for child, sheet of stickers & cardboard punch outs **Booklet:** BWOF 1986 & instructions **Head:** superstar **Head Markings:** inside or outside rim © Mattel Inc 1976 +/- country **Arms:** bent **Body:** tan tnt **Body Markings:** © Mattel Inc 1966/ Malaysia

Model #: 2126 **Name:** Magic Moves Barbie **Box Date:** 1985 **Hair Color:** blonde **Hairstyle:** side part, banded in 2 long ponytails **Face:** blue eyes, blonde brows, pink lips & blush **Clothing:** aqua halter gown with slim skirt, metallic top with silver collar & belt, matching cape with faux fur trim, rhinestone earrings & ring, narrow aqua pumps **Extras:** lavender pointed brush, fake hair dryer, small oval brush & comb, 2 sheets of cardboard punch outs **Booklet:** BWOF 1984 & instructions **Head:** superstar **Head Markings:** inside or outside rim © Mattel Inc 1976 +/- country **Arms:** bent **Body:** tan tnt **Body Markings:** © Mattel Inc 1966/ Taiwan **Notes:** box liner may be hot pink or metallic

Model #: 1140 **Name:** Rocker Barbie **Box Date:** 1985 **Hair Color:** blonde **Hairstyle:** middle part, very curly, large pigtails, purple nylon headband tied in hair **Face:** blue eyes, blonde brows, radical blue and purple eyeshadow, pale pink lips **Clothing:** silver scoop neck tank top, white vinyl mini skirt, pink 3/4 sleeve blazer with silver glitter dots, purple glitter belt, pink & silver striped footless tights, dangle earrings & ring, purple snake bracelet, pink faux fur headband, pink Rockers T-shirt, white vinyl fake boot tops with silver & white cuffs, narrow white pumps **Extras:** hot pink pointed brush, white microphone, Rockers theme Dressin' Up cassette, 2 sheets of cardboard punch outs, 1 iron-on Rockers transfer **Booklet:** BWOF 1985 & instructions **Head:** superstar **Head Markings:** inside or outside rim © Mattel Inc 1976 +/- country **Arms:** bent **Body:** tan tnt **Body Markings:** © Mattel Inc.1966/ Philippines **Notes:** many different clothing combinations found

Model #: 1017 **Name:** Tropical Barbie **Box Date:** 1985 **Hair Color:** 2 tones of blonde **Hairstyle:** middle part, banded at nape of neck with yellow fabric flower, twisted mid-thigh-length ponytail **Face:** blue eyes, brown brows, deep pink lips & blush **Clothing:** 1-piece off-the-shoulder navy, light blue, yellow, fuchsia swimsuit **Extras:** yellow pointed brush **Booklet:** BWOF 1986 **Head:** superstar **Head Markings:** inside or outside rim © Mattel Inc 1976 +/- country **Arms:** ptr **Body:** dark tan tnt **Body Markings:** © Mattel, Inc. 1966/ Hong Kong **Notes:** gift set: Deluxe Tropical with surfboard & fashion

Model #: 3421 Name: Feelin' Groovy Barbie Box Date: 1986 Hair Color: black Hairstyle: hair pulled into mid-back-length ponytail with bangs, cello on head Face: lavender eyes, brown brows, red lips & blush Clothing: gold spaghetti strap fuchsia mini dress, matching long slim skirt, iridescent & black pattern knee-length coat with black faux fur trim at cuffs and hem, long fuchsia handless gloves, hot pink drop earrings, black sunglasses, pink shoulder purse, hair dryer, hanger, cosmetic bag with luggage tag, black beaded necklace, clear fuchsia glitter mules Extras: black pointed brush Booklet: Billy Boy 1986 & instructions Head: Steffie Head Markings: inside rim © 1971 Mattel Inc & country Arms: ptr Body: tan tnt Body Markings: © Mattel Inc 1966/ China

Model #: 1738 Name: Funtime Barbie Box Date: 1986 Hair Color: blonde Hairstyle: waist length, 1/2 of front section in ponytail at side, other 1/2 pulled back, ends curled under Face: blue eyes, blonde brows, deep pink lips & blush Clothing: pink metallic crop top with short sleeves, glitter disk in center of bodice with clock hands, matching pink shorts, pink disk earrings & watch, blue, lavender & coral knee socks, pink tennis shoes, pink metallic headband, pink wrap sunglasses Extras: pink oval brush & child's digital watch with pink band Booklet: BWOF 1987 & instructions Head: superstar Head Markings: inside or outside rim © Mattel Inc 1976 +/- country Arms: bent or ptr Body: tan tnt Body Markings: © Mattel Inc.1966/ Philippines Notes: Philippine dolls developing white blotches on legs, dolls also available with bent arm variation & may also be dressed in #3718 purple or #3717 blue

Model #: 1737 Name: Jewel Secrets Barbie Box Date: 1986 Hair Color: blonde Hairstyle: side part, front section pulled to side, remainder sectioned into 3 with bands on ends, thigh length Face: light blue-lavender eyes, blonde brows, pink lips & blush Clothing: silver halter mini dress with full skirt, pink satin & silver glitter stripe bag for child which doubles as full skirt for doll, blue accent ruffle mini skirt, silver & pink jeweled choker, rhinestone stud earrings & ring, narrow clear silver glitter pumps Extras: pink oval brush & "The Night of Jewel Secrets" book Booklet: BWOF 1986 & instructions Head: superstar Head Markings: inside or outside rim © Mattel Inc 1976 +/- country Arms: bent Body: tan tnt Body Markings: © Mattel Inc 1966/ Malaysia

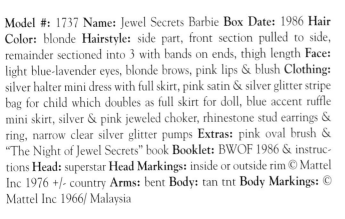

Model #: 3055 Name: Rocker Barbie 2nd issue Box Date: 1986 Hair Color: blonde Hairstyle: sides pulled up to top of head with rubber band, waist-length hair with curly bangs Face: blue eyes, light brown brows, radical aqua & purple eyeshadow, deep pink lips & blush Clothing: long sleeve pink satin top with high collar decorated with silver stars & Rockers logo, pink cuff with long fringe, pink & silver star print mini skirt, metallic silver pants, silver star earrings & ring, deep pink hair ornament, clear with silver glitter narrow pumps Extras: deep pink oval brush, sheet of cardboard punch outs, silver microphone Booklet: BWOF 1987 & instructions Head: superstar Head Markings: inside or outside rim © Mattel Inc 1976 +/- country Arms: bent Body: tan tnt Body Markings: © Mattel Inc.1966/ Philippines Notes: many variations available

Model #: 3101 **Name:** Super Hair Barbie **Box Date:** 1986 **Hair Color:** 2 tone blonde **Hairstyle:** partial topknot held with white curler in front, rest waist length with ends curled under **Face:** blue eyes, blonde brows, pink lips & blush **Clothing:** 1-piece long sleeve high collar jumpsuit with gold & silver trim on bodice, wide silver belt, rhinestone stud earrings & ring, narrow white pumps **Extras:** purple oval brush & matching mirror, fake hair dryer, hair ornament, 4 barrettes, small comb & brush, assorted ribbons **Booklet:** BWOF 1986 & instructions **Head:** superstar **Head Markings:** inside or outside rim © Mattel Inc 1976 +/- country **Arms:** bent **Body:** tan tnt **Body Markings:** © Mattel Inc.1966/ Philippines

Model #: 4439 **Name:** California Barbie **Box Date:** 1987 **Hair Color:** blonde **Hairstyle:** front pulled into curly topknot, sides pulled back, rest mid-back length with ends curled under **Face:** blue eyes, blonde brows, hot pink lips & blush **Clothing:** blue & white bikini, yellow & white dot sleeveless shirt with multicolor pattern, blue & white dot & pink pattern mini skirt, fake pink camera, visor, Frisbee, black beach bag, green palm tree earrings, blue knee-high socks, yellow high-top tennis shoes **Extras:** hot pink oval brush, sheet of stickers & cardboard punch outs, comic book, blue Beach Boys record **Booklet:** BWOF 1987 & instructions **Head:** superstar **Head Markings:** inside or outside rim © Mattel Inc 1976 +/- country **Arms:** ptr **Body:** tan tnt **Body Markings:** © Mattel Inc.1966/ Philippines **Notes:** may develop pale splotches on legs

Model #: 4439 **Name:** California Dream Barbie **Box Date:** 1987 **Hair Color:** blonde **Hairstyle:** front pulled into curly topknot, sides pulled back, rest mid-back length with ends curled under **Face:** blue eyes, blonde brows, hot pink lips & blush **Clothing:** blue & white bikini, yellow & white dot sleeveless shirt with multicolor pattern, blue & white dot & pink pattern mini skirt, fake pink camera, visor, Frisbee, black beach bag, green palm tree earrings, blue knee-high socks, yellow high-top tennis shoes **Extras:** hot pink oval brush, sheet of stickers & cardboard punch outs, comic book, blue Beach Boys record **Booklet:** BWOF 1987 & instructions **Head:** superstar **Head Markings:** inside or outside rim © Mattel Inc 1976 +/- country **Arms:** ptr **Body:** tan tnt **Body Markings:** © Mattel Inc 1966/ Malaysia **Notes:** may develop pale splotches on legs

Model #: 3850 **Name:** Doctor Barbie **Box Date:** 1987 **Hair Color:** blonde **Hairstyle:** side part, sides twisted & pulled back rest waist length **Face:** lilac-blue eyes, brown brows, deep pink lips & blush **Clothing:** pink spaghetti strap knee-length dress, white lab coat, white shimmering top with boa, beeper, stethoscope, 2 bottles, blood pressure cord, x-ray frame, cast, clipboard, notepads, reflex hammer, watch, adhesive strip box, ear checker, medical bag, 3 fuchsia roses on green stems, strap, rhinestone stud earrings & ring, wide pink pumps **Extras:** pink oval brush & sheet of cardboard punch outs **Booklet:** BWOF 1987 & instructions **Head:** superstar **Head Markings:** inside or outside rim © Mattel Inc 1976 +/- country **Arms:** bent **Body:** tan tnt **Body Markings:** © Mattel Inc 1966/ Malaysia

Model #: 4061 Name: Island Fun Barbie Box Date: 1987 Hair Color: 2 shades of blonde Hairstyle: middle part, mid-thigh-length ponytail banded at nape of neck, split in 3 Face: blue eyes, brown brows, pink lips & blush Clothing: 1-piece white swimsuit, hot pink Hawaiian print wrap skirt, hot pink & yellow lei Extras: hot pink seahorse comb Booklet: BWOF 1987 & instructions Head: superstar Head Markings: inside or outside rim © Mattel Inc 1976 +/- country Arms: ptr Body: dark tan tnt Body Markings: © Mattel Inc 1966/ China Notes: legs may develop light splotches

Model #: 4551 Name: Perfume Pretty Barbie Box Date: 1987 Hair Color: blonde Hairstyle: sides & front pulled up with pink ribbon, rest mid-thigh length with bangs Face: blue eyes, blonde brows, pink lips & blush Clothing: pink stretch halter gown with multi-layer tulle flared skirt at mid calf, pink bow detail on bodice, pink tulle bolero jacket, pink bow stud earrings & ring, clear & silver dot bow necklace, wide pink pearl bow pumps Extras: pink pearl oval brush, 1/2 circle comb, Barbie fragrance perfume & sheet of cardboard punch outs Booklet: Perfume Pretty Barbie Tips & instructions Head: superstar Head Markings: inside or outside rim © Mattel Inc 1976 +/- country Arms: bent Body: tan tnt Body Markings: © Mattel Inc 1966/ Malaysia

Model #: 4931 Name: Sensations Barbie Box Date: 1987 Hair Color: blonde Hairstyle: mid-back-length ponytail with bangs Face: blue eyes, blonde brows, deep pink lips & blush Clothing: silver halter dress, full hot pink satin skirt, sewn in panties & hot pink tulle slip, hot pink satin & white vinyl long sleeve jacket, hot pink drop earrings & ring, black microphone, pink & black glasses, silver string with pink grip to hold eyeglasses, white lace anklets, black & white saddle shoes Extras: hot pink oval brush, Sensations cassette & 2 sheets of cardboard punch outs Booklet: BWOF 1988 Head: superstar Head Markings: inside or outside rim © Mattel Inc 1976 +/- country Arms: bent Body: tan tnt Body Markings: © Mattel Inc 1966/ China

Model #: 1350 Name: Animal Lovin' Barbie Box Date: 1988 Hair Color: blonde & golden blonde Hairstyle: front & sides pulled back rest mid-back length, ends curled under, gold net scarf tied across forehead Face: blue eyes, brown brows, pink lips & blush Clothing: metallic gold halter top with pink sleeveless animal print vest, matching mini skirt with sewn in panties, pink dangle earrings & ring, plastic panda bear, pink hiking boots Extras: pink oval brush & sheet of cardboard punch outs Head: superstar Head Markings: inside or outside rim © Mattel Inc 1976 +/- country Arms: bent Body: tan tnt Body Markings: © Mattel Inc 1966/ Malaysia

Model #: 3022 Name: Cool Times Barbie Box Date: 1988 Hair Color: blonde Hairstyle: sides & front pulled back, rest waist length with bangs Face: lilac-blue eyes, blonde brows, pink lips & blush Clothing: white crop top T-shirt with sundae appliqué, hot pink satin mini skirt jumper with white tulle slip, matching bolero jacket, white knee-length pants with black dots, turquoise, white, hot pink leggings, blue & pink sundae, turquoise earrings & ring, turquoise scooter, white tennis shoes Extras: hot pink oval brush & sheet of cardboard punch outs Booklet: BWOF 1988 & instructions Head: superstar Head Markings: inside or outside rim © Mattel Inc 1976 +/- country Arms: bent Body: tan tnt Body Markings: © Mattel Inc 1966/ China

Model #: 1189 Name: Feeling Fun Barbie Box Date: 1988 Hair Color: blonde Hairstyle: front & sides pulled up in ponytail tied with pink satin ribbon, rest waist length crinkled Face: turquoise eyes, brown brows, hot pink lips & blush Clothing: white cotton T-shirt with pink, black & blue designs with glitter, light blue denim jacket with self fringe & silver dots, matching mini skirt with pink & silver lace overlay, rhinestone stud earrings & ring, pink fabric knee-high boots Extras: pink pearl oval brush Booklet: BWOF 1988 Head: superstar Head Markings: inside or outside rim © Mattel Inc 1976 +/- country Arms: bent Body: tan tnt Body Markings: © Mattel Inc 1966/ China

Model #: 1953 Name: Garden Party Barbie Box Date: 1988 Hair Color: blonde Hairstyle: sides & front pulled back, rest mid-back length, ends curled under Face: blue eyes, blonde brows, pink lips & blush Clothing: lilac mini dress with tulle overlay & iridescent v-neck bodice with white & lilac tulle accents at shoulders, matching overskirt, shortened in front, lilac flower choker, rhinestone stud earrings & ring, wide lilac pumps Extras: lilac oval brush & sheet of cardboard punch outs Booklet: BWOF 1988 Head: superstar Head Markings: inside or outside rim © Mattel Inc 1976 +/- country Arms: bent Body: tan tnt Body Markings: © Mattel Inc 1966/ Malaysia

Model #: 1205 Name: Gift Giving Barbie Box Date: 1988 Hair Color: blonde Hairstyle: waist length, ends curled under Face: lavender eyes, blonde brows, hot pink lips & blush Clothing: iridescent lilac short sleeve full-skirted mini dress with white lace bodice detail, pink panties, lilac earrings & ring, gift, pink charm, wide lilac bow pumps Extras: lilac oval brush, pink child size charm, sheet of cardboard punch outs & stickers Booklet: BWOF 1988 & instructions Head: superstar Head Markings: inside or outside rim © Mattel Inc 1976 +/- country Arms: bent Body: tan tnt Body Markings: © Mattel Inc 1966/ Malaysia

Model #: 1283 Name: Style Magic Barbie Box Date: 1988 Hair Color: 2 tone blonde Hairstyle: mid-back length, bangs, ends curled Face: lavender-blue eyes, blonde brows, hot pink lips & blush Clothing: aqua & pink halter bodysuit with sheer pink mini skirt & bodice trim of coral, aqua & white design, fuchsia hoop earrings & ring, wide fuchsia pumps Extras: half triangle, circle, half circle fuchsia comb, matching curlers & sheet of cardboard punch outs Booklet: BWOF 1988 & instructions Head: superstar Head Markings: inside or outside rim © Mattel Inc 1976 +/- country Arms: bent Body: tan tnt Body Markings: © Mattel Inc 1966/ Malaysia Notes: WondraCurl hair

Model #: 1604 Name: Superstar Barbie Box Date: 1988 Hair Color: blonde Hairstyle: wavy waist length Face: blue eyes, blonde brows, pink frosted lips & blush Clothing: pink nylon sleeveless top trimmed in silver with matching mini skirt, full tiered overskirt with silver stars, faux fur boa, clear & silver star drop earrings & ring, wide pink pumps Extras: square comb, child's pink bracelet, silver star charm & sheet of cardboard punch outs Booklet: BWOF 1988 Head: superstar Head Markings: inside or outside rim © Mattel Inc 1976 +/- country Arms: bent Body: tan tnt Body Markings: © Mattel Inc 1966/ China

Model #: 2751 Name: Barbie & the Beat Box Date: 1989 Hair Color: blonde Hairstyle: sides & front pulled back with pink barrette, waist length, bangs Face: blue-green eyes, brown brows, hot pink lips & blush Clothing: pink spaghetti strap top, matching slim mini skirt, acid washed blue & pink glitter long sleeve jacket, matching mini skirt, hot pink tulle underskirt, hot pink disk earrings & ring, lime green guitar with gold strap, hot pink boot tops, wide hot pink pumps Extras: lime green oval brush, Barbie & the Beat cassette, sheet of cardboard punch outs Booklet: BWOF 1988 Head: superstar Head Markings: inside or outside rim © Mattel Inc 1976 +/- country Arms: bent Body: tan tnt Body Markings: © Mattel Inc 1966/ China Notes: outfit has glow in dark glitter

Model #: 9099 Name: Barbie and the All Stars Box Date: 1989 Hair Color: blonde Hairstyle: front section & 1 side pulled into ponytail tied with pink fabric rest crinkled thigh length Face: light blue eyes, blonde brows, lilac lips & blush Clothing: white & pink leotard with blue metallic stars, pink footless tights, white & blue star leggings, pink tote bag converts to skirt, blue jump rope, dumb bells, leg weights, soda can, blue disk earrings & ring, wide hot pink pumps & tennis shoes Extras: hot pink oval brush Booklet: BWOF 1988 & instructions Head: superstar Head Markings: inside or outside rim © Mattel Inc 1976 +/- country Arms: bent Body: tan tnt Body Markings: © Mattel Inc 1966/ China

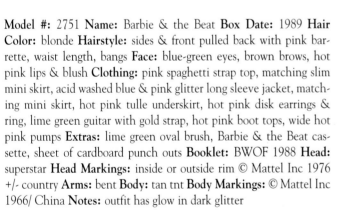

Model #: 3237 **Name:** Beach Blast Barbie **Box Date:** 1989 **Hair Color:** blonde **Hairstyle:** sides & front pulled back with hot pink barrette, attached color change hairpiece, rest thigh length crinkled, bangs **Face:** light blue eyes, blonde brows, pink lips & blush **Clothing:** 2-piece bikini with black trim, pink wraparound sunglasses, yellow visor & Frisbee **Extras:** hot pink seahorse comb **Booklet:** WOB 1988 **Head:** superstar **Head Markings:** inside or outside rim © Mattel Inc 1976 +/- country **Arms:** ptr **Body:** dark tan tnt **Body Markings:** © Mattel Inc 1966/ China **Notes:** may develop pale splotches on legs

Model #: 3509 **Name:** Dance Club Barbie **Box Date:** 1989 **Hair Color:** blonde **Hairstyle:** sides & front pulled back into 3 twisted ponytails tied with colored ribbons, rest waist length, ends turned under, curly bangs **Face:** blue eyes, light brown brows, hot pink lips & blush **Clothing:** black nylon crop top with 3 color fabric flowers, white vinyl jacket, hot pink mini skirt with sewn in panties, turquoise dangle earrings & ring, black wide brim hat with colored fabric flowers, hot pink nylon anklets, wide black pumps **Extras:** hot pink oval brush, Barbie Dance Club cassette & sheet of cardboard punch outs **Booklet:** BWOF 1988 **Head:** superstar **Head Markings:** inside or outside rim © Mattel Inc 1976 +/- country **Arms:** bent **Body:** tan tnt **Body Markings:** © Mattel Inc 1966/ China **Notes:** Child's World exclusive, doll packaged with cassette player

Model #: 4836 **Name:** Dance Magic Barbie **Box Date:** 1989 **Hair Color:** blonde **Hairstyle:** waist length, ends curled under **Face:** turquoise eyes, blonde brows, deep pink lips & blush **Clothing:** pink & iridescent bodysuit with white iridescent trim, tulle boa, long skirt with pink underskirt, iridescent fan, metallic pink drop earrings, choker, ring, white ballet slippers, wide pink pumps **Extras:** white oval brush, pink wash cloth, applicator to change lip color, sheet of cardboard punch outs **Booklet:** BWOF 1988 & instructions **Head:** superstar **Head Markings:** inside or outside rim © Mattel Inc 1976 +/- country **Arms:** bent **Body:** tan tnt **Body Markings:** © Mattel Inc 1966/ Malaysia **Notes:** also gift set with regular issue Barbie & Ken

Model #: 9584 **Name:** Flight Time Barbie **Box Date:** 1989 **Hair Color:** blonde **Hairstyle:** sides pulled back, rest waist length, ends curled under **Face:** blue eyes, blonde brows, pink lips & blush **Clothing:** white sleeveless blouse with gold tie, pink jacket, matching straight knee-length skirt, multicolor full mini skirt trimmed in gold, matching tie, pink briefcase, pink pilot's hat, gold stud earrings & ring, pink wrist accent, narrow pink pumps **Extras:** pink oval brush, child's pink Barbie wings, sheet of stickers, sheet of cardboard punch outs **Booklet:** BWOF 1988 & instructions **Head:** superstar **Head Markings:** inside or outside rim © Mattel Inc 1976 +/- country **Arms:** bent **Body:** tan tnt **Body Markings:** © Mattel Inc 1966/ Malaysia

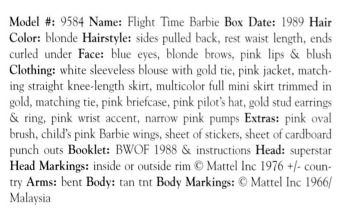

Model #: 7365 Name: Ice Capades Barbie Box Date: 1989 Hair Color: blonde Hairstyle: front & sides pulled up, rest waist length, ends curled under, iridescent teardrop hat with lilac, pink & turquoise sheer scarves Face: blue eyes, brown brows, hot pink lips & blush Clothing: pink & iridescent bodysuit with multi petal skirt of pink, turquoise & lilac glitter chiffon, gold ring, white ice skates Extras: pink-purple oval brush & sheet of cardboard punch outs Booklet: BWOF 1988 Head: superstar Head Markings: inside or outside rim © Mattel Inc 1976 +/- country Arms: bent Body: tan tnt Body Markings: © Mattel Inc 1966/ China

Model #: 1920 Name: UNICEF Barbie Box Date: 1989 Hair Color: blonde Hairstyle: 1 side & front pulled into ponytail, rest waist length, ends curled Face: blue eyes, brown brows, red lips & blush Clothing: strapless gown with white bodice, full skirt of blue tulle with metallic stars & purple underskirt, long white handless gloves, red & gold sash with star trim, light blue stud earrings, pendant, ring, wide royal blue pumps Extras: 2-piece clear stand & white oval brush Booklet: Rights of the Child Head: superstar Head Markings: inside or outside rim © Mattel Inc 1976 +/- country Arms: bent Body: tan tnt Body Markings: © Mattel Inc 1966/ China

Model #: 2125 Name: Wedding Fantasy Barbie Box Date: 1989 Hair Color: blonde Hairstyle: waist length, ends curled under Face: blue eyes, blonde brows, pink lips & blush Clothing: 2-piece gown, white satin top with iridescent trim at bodice and collar, lace leg of mutton sleeves, full white satin skirt with iridescent lace overlay, white tulle veil with white beaded halo, pearl stud earrings & ring, pink fabric flower & iridescent tulle bouquet, pantyhose with sewn in white panties, teddy, garter, wide white pumps Extras: 2-piece pearl stand, white oval brush & punch out Head: superstar Head Markings: inside or outside rim © Mattel Inc 1976 +/- country Arms: bent Body: tan tnt Body Markings: © Mattel Inc 1966/ China

Model #: 9932 Name: Western Fun Barbie Box Date: 1989 Hair Color: blonde Hairstyle: sides pulled to back of head, rest waist length Face: green-turquoise eyes, brown brows, pink lips & blush Clothing: turquoise crop top, multicolor mini skirt, pink fringe long sleeve short jacket, turquoise stretch pants, pink belt, hat with ribbon hatband, turquoise drop earrings, necklace, ring, belt, pink cowboy boots Extras: turquoise oval brush & sheet of cardboard punch outs Booklet: BWOF 1988 Head: superstar Head Markings: inside or outside rim © Mattel Inc 1976 +/- country Arms: bent Body: tan tnt Body Markings: © Mattel Inc 1966/ China Notes: also gift set with horse

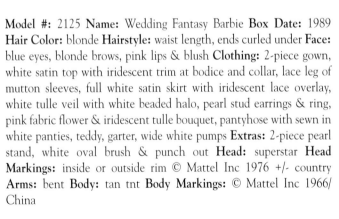

Model #: 4103 Name: Wet n' Wild Barbie Box Date: 1989 Hair Color: 2 tones of blonde Hairstyle: front section pulled back with pink snake tie, rest curly thigh length with bangs Face: blue eyes, blonde brows, deep pink lips & blush Clothing: 1-piece change-color swimsuit of pink & orange, blue snake bracelet & pink sunglasses Extras: blue oval brush Head: superstar Head Markings: inside or outside rim © Mattel Inc 1976 +/- country Arms: ptr Body: tan tnt Body Markings: © Mattel Inc 1966/ China

Model #: 9423 Name: All American Barbie Box Date: 1990 Hair Color: blonde Hairstyle: sides & front pulled back with turquoise snake-tie, rest crinkled mid-thigh length, bangs Face: blue eyes, dark blonde brows, hot pink lips & blush Clothing: pink scoop neck 3/4 length sleeve crop top, blue acid washed mini skirt with sewn in panties & flag pattern trim, matching vest, pink hoop earrings & ring, multicolor knee socks, 2 pair of Reeboks Extras: hot pink oval brush & sheet of cardboard punch outs Head: superstar Head Markings: inside or outside rim © Mattel Inc 1976 +/- country Arms: bent Body: tan tnt Body Markings: © Mattel Inc 1966/ Malaysia Notes: Toys R Us & Club gift set doll with horse

Model #: 9601 Name: Bathtime Fun Barbie Box Date: 1990 Hair Color: blonde Hairstyle: shoulder-length ponytail with blue foam rubber flower accent, ends curled under, bangs Face: blue eyes, light brown brows, pink lips & blush Clothing: stretch nylon 1-piece multicolor swimsuit of pink, yellow, aqua, white, foam rubber light blue scalloped skirt & bracelet, pink stud earrings & ring Extras: white oval brush, can of foam soap & sheet of cardboard punch outs Head: superstar Head Markings: inside or outside rim © Mattel Inc 1976 +/- country Arms: bent Body: tan tnt Body Markings: © Mattel Inc 1966/ Malaysia

Model #: 9404 Name: Benetton Barbie Box Date: 1990 Hair Color: blonde Hairstyle: sides & front pulled back with blue band, rest crinkled thigh length, bangs Face: blue eyes, brown brows, red lips & blush Clothing: yellow sleeveless turtleneck top with blue ribbon trim, red long sleeve coat with royal blue piping & ribbon trim, matching red mini skirt, blue floral stretch pants & matching tote bag, pink leggings, red felt hat, pink bandanna, blue hoop earrings & ring, red tennis shoes Extras: blue oval brush & sheet of cardboard punch outs Booklet: BFG 1991 Head: superstar Head Markings: inside or outside rim © Mattel Inc 1976 +/- country Arms: bent Body: tan tnt Body Markings: © Mattel Inc 1966/ China

Model #: 7123 **Name:** Costume Ball Barbie **Box Date:** 1990 **Hair Color:** blonde **Hairstyle:** front & sides loosely pulled back, waist length, ends curled under **Face:** blue-green eyes, blonde brows, deep pink lips & blush **Clothing:** mini dress with iridescent spaghetti strap bodice, pink tulle boa, pink overskirt with iridescent print accent, child's mask trimmed with rickrack, butterfly wings, pink metallic stud earrings & ring, pink scepter, mask holder, wide pink pumps **Extras:** pink oval brush, sheet of cardboard punch outs **Booklet:** IIB 1990 & instructions **Head:** superstar **Head Markings:** inside or outside rim © Mattel Inc 1976 +/- country **Arms:** bent **Body:** tan tnt **Body Markings:** © Mattel Inc 1966/ Malaysia

Model #: 7913 **Name:** Happy Birthday Barbie **Box Date:** 1990 **Hair Color:** blonde with glitter strands **Hairstyle:** waist length, ends curled under, bangs, 1 side pulled up & held with pink fabric flower & lilac ribbon **Face:** blue eyes, brown brows, deep pink lips & blush **Clothing:** 2-piece gown, solid pink bodice with pink multicolor puffed sleeves, large multicolor pink full skirt, Happy Birthday sash, silver stud earrings & ring, wide pink pearl pumps **Extras:** 2-piece pearl stand, pink pearl comb **Booklet:** IIB 1990 **Head:** superstar **Head Markings:** inside or outside rim © Mattel Inc 1976 +/- country **Arms:** bent **Body:** tan tnt **Body Markings:** © Mattel Inc 1966/ Malaysia

Model #: 5940 **Name:** Hawaiian Fun Barbie **Box Date:** 1990 **Hair Color:** blonde **Hairstyle:** side & front pulled back with pink band, section pulled back with yellow band, all thigh length **Face:** blue eyes, light brown brows, pink lips & blush **Clothing:** hot pink, yellow & green bikini, hot pink mini hula skirt, hot pink & black sunglasses **Extras:** green oval brush, bracelet for child **Booklet:** BFG 1991 & Hawaiian Luau kit offer **Head:** superstar **Head Markings:** inside or outside rim © Mattel Inc 1976 +/- country **Arms:** ptr **Body:** dark tan tnt **Body Markings:** © Mattel Inc 1966/ China **Notes:** Club gift set: Lots of Fashions doll & clothing

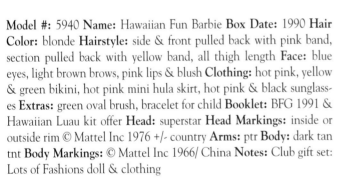

Model #: 2249 **Name:** Home Pretty Barbie **Box Date:** 1990 **Hair Color:** blonde **Hairstyle:** sides & front pulled back, rest waist length, ends curled under **Face:** blue eyes, blonde brows, hot pink lips & blush **Clothing:** pink crossover bodysuit with white & pink fabric flowers at shoulders, pink tulle multi layer knee-length skirt, white lace apron, silver stud earrings & ring, wide pink pumps **Extras:** lilac oval brush **Booklet:** BWOF 1988 **Head:** superstar **Head Markings:** inside or outside rim © Mattel Inc 1976 +/- country **Arms:** bent **Body:** tan tnt **Body Markings:** © Mattel Inc 1966/ Malaysia

Model #: 9847 **Name:** Ice Capades Barbie **Box Date:** 1990 **Hair Color:** blonde **Hairstyle:** pulled up to top of head, mid-back-length ponytail, purple & white hair ornament **Face:** blue eyes, brown brows, hot pink lips & blush **Clothing:** white & purple glitter splatter sleeveless turtleneck bodysuit with white glitter splatter & sheer purple fabric partial overskirt, gold ring, white ice skates **Extras:** white oval brush **Head:** superstar **Head Markings:** inside or outside rim © Mattel Inc 1976 +/- country **Arms:** bent **Body:** dark tan tnt **Body Markings:** © Mattel Inc 1966/ Malaysia

Model #: 9725 **Name:** Lights & Lace Barbie **Box Date:** 1990 **Hair Color:** blonde **Hairstyle:** sides pulled up & tied with pink lace & silver bow, rest waist length, ends curled, curly bangs **Face:** turquoise eyes, light brown brows, deep pink frosted lips & blush **Clothing:** spaghetti strap, sweetheart neck, full skirt pink & silver lace mini dress with matching bolero jacket & sewn in panties, pink & iridescent dangle earrings & ring, lighted belt, shoe top lace ruffles, pink microphone, pink cowboy boots **Extras:** pink hair pick & sheet of cardboard punch outs **Booklet:** BF&F 1991 & instructions **Head:** superstar **Head Markings:** inside or outside rim © Mattel Inc 1976 +/- country **Arms:** bent **Body:** tan tnt **Body Markings:** © Mattel Inc 1966/ China

Model #: 7027 **Name:** Summit Barbie **Box Date:** 1990 **Hair Color:** blonde **Hairstyle:** 1 side & front pulled up in band, rest waist length, ends curled under **Face:** blue eyes, brown brows, red lips & blush **Clothing:** gown with gold lamé bodice, full white skirt, white tulle & gold glitter overskirt, white bolero jacket with gold braid trim, gold stud earrings & ring, wide white pumps **Extras:** red oval brush, sheet of cardboard punch outs & Summit badge **Booklet:** 1st Summit 1990 **Head:** superstar **Head Markings:** inside or outside rim © Mattel Inc 1976 +/- country **Arms:** bent **Body:** tan tnt **Body Markings:** © Mattel Inc 1966/ China

Model #: 9608 **Name:** Wedding Day Barbie **Box Date:** 1990 **Hair Color:** blonde **Hairstyle:** curly bangs, rest waist length, ends curled under **Face:** lilac-blue eyes, blonde brows, hot pink lips & blush **Clothing:** pink sweetheart neck puffed sleeved gown of pink & white dotted swiss with lace bodice & wide pink satin belt, metallic pink stud earrings & ring, pink flower bouquet, wide pink pearl pumps **Extras:** pink pearl oval brush & sheet of cardboard punch outs **Head:** superstar **Head Markings:** inside or outside rim © Mattel Inc 1976 +/- country **Arms:** bent **Body:** tan tnt **Body Markings:** © Mattel Inc 1966/ Malaysia **Notes:** box available w/ open lattice or closed, also part of 6 doll gift set

Model #: 3137 Name: American Beauty Queen Barbie Box Date: 1991 Hair Color: blonde Hairstyle: waist length with ends curled under, silver tiara Face: blue eyes, blonde brows, hot pink lips & blush Clothing: off-the-shoulder silver, pink & blue gown, converts to silver swimsuit & ballet tutu, long silver handless gloves, silver stud earrings & ring, pearl ballet shoes, wide pearl pumps Extras: pearl oval brush & sheet of cardboard punch outs Booklet: 1991 PB Head: superstar Head Markings: inside or outside rim © Mattel Inc 1976 +/- country Arms: bent Body: tan tnt Body Markings: © Mattel Inc 1966/ China

Model #: 5274 Name: Bath Magic Barbie Box Date: 1991 Hair Color: blonde Hairstyle: sides pulled up into mid-back-length ponytail tied with hot pink ribbon, ends curled under, bangs Face: blue eyes, light brown brows, deep pink lips & blush Clothing: yellow & pink splatter nylon bodysuit, inverse pattern full mini skirt, hot pink stud earrings & ring Extras: hot pink oval brush & 3 color capsules containing foam rubber decorations Booklet: instructions Head: Teen Talk Barbie Head Markings: © 1991 Mattel Inc Arms: bent Body: tan tnt Body Markings: © Mattel Inc 1966/ Malaysia

Model #: 3679 Name: Birthday Surprise Barbie Box Date: 1991 Hair Color: blonde Hairstyle: sides & front pulled up & twisted, held with a peach satin ribbon, rest waist length, ends curled Face: blue eyes, light brown brows, peach lips & blush Clothing: peach gown with white iridescent accents on bodice & peach fabric flowers at neckline, tulle glitter skirt with pearl accents, sewn in panties, peach drop earrings & ring, wide peach pearl pumps Extras: 2-piece pearl stand & oval brush, gift=bracelet, earrings or necklace Booklet: 1991 PB Head: superstar Head Markings: inside or outside rim © Mattel Inc 1976 +/- country Arms: bent Body: tan tnt Body Markings: © Mattel Inc 1966/ Malaysia

Model #: 1623 Name: Dream Bride Barbie Box Date: 1991 Hair Color: blonde Hairstyle: waist length, ends curled under Face: blue eyes, brown brows, pink lips & blush Clothing: gown with white satin square neck bodice & iridescent appliqué trim, leg of mutton lace sleeves, separate large satin skirt with lace insert, matching veil, iridescent tulle bouquet with peach fabric flowers & ribbon streamers, lace teddy, white shimmering pantyhose, blue garter, pearl stud earrings, double row choker, ring, wide pearl pumps Extras: 2-piece pearl stand & oval brush Head: superstar Head Markings: inside or outside rim © Mattel Inc 1976 +/- country Arms: bent Body: tan tnt Body Markings: © Mattel Inc 1966/ China

Model #: 1434 Name: Mermaid Barbie Box Date: 1991 Hair Color: blonde with gold strands & streak of light blue Hairstyle: thigh length, sides & front pulled to top of head held with blue iridescent hair ornament Face: blue eyes, light brown brows, hot pink lips Clothing: iridescent blue top, matching mermaid skirt, blue stud earrings Extras: blue seahorse hair pick Head: superstar Head Markings: inside or outside rim © Mattel Inc 1976 +/- country Arms: ptr Body: tan tnt Body Markings: © Mattel Inc 1966/ China Notes: tan or pink tone body

Model #: 3248 Name: Rappin' Rockin' Barbie Box Date: 1991 Hair Color: blonde Hairstyle: crinkled thigh length with curly bangs Face: light blue eyes, blonde brows, hot pink lips & blush Clothing: hot pink hooded sleeveless bodysuit with black satin bolero jacket & black vinyl mini skirt, fuchsia & gold disk earrings, gold ring & pendant, lime green scrunch sock tops, hot pink high-top tennis shoes, hot pink boom box Extras: hot pink oval brush & sheet of cardboard punch outs Head: Teen Talk Barbie Head Markings: © 1991 Mattel Inc Arms: bent Body: tan tnt Body Markings: © Mattel Inc 1966/ China

Model #: 2214 Name: Rollerblades Barbie Box Date: 1991 Hair Color: blonde Hairstyle: 1 side twisted & tied with pink band, remainder held back with multicolor headband, thigh length, curly bangs Face: blue-lilac eyes, blonde brows, hot pink lips & blush Clothing: long sleeve white vinyl crop top with multicolor floral ruffle at scoop neck, matching shorts with hot pink fanny pack, hot pink knee pads, hot pink hoop earrings & ring, floral elbow pads, hot pink rollerblades Extras: hot pink oval brush Booklet: instructions Head: superstar Head Markings: inside or outside rim © Mattel Inc 1976 +/- country Arms: bent Body: tan tnt Body Markings: © Mattel Inc 1966/ China Notes: rollerblade sparks are fire hazard, Club gift set

Model #: 7511 Name: Ski Fun Barbie Box Date: 1991 Hair Color: blonde Hairstyle: waist-length ponytail divided & ends held with pink band, curled bangs, multicolor head scarf Face: blue eyes, blonde brows, pink lips & blush Clothing: 1-piece ski suit, multicolor bodice, remainder hot pink with gold piping, multicolor jacket with hot pink sleeves & gold collar, multicolor scrunches, foil ski ticket pendant, mittens, pink ski poles & skis, gold stud earrings & ring, wide hot pink pumps, hot pink ski boots, hot pink goggles Extras: hot pink oval brush & 2 trading cards Booklet: instructions Head: superstar Head Markings: inside or outside rim © Mattel Inc 1976 +/- country Arms: bent Body: tan tnt Body Markings: © Mattel Inc 1966/ China

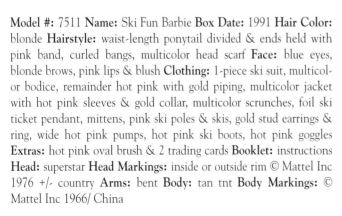

Model #: 3550 Name: Snap 'N Play Barbie Box Date: 1991 Hair Color: blonde Hairstyle: sides pulled up to small ponytail, rest waist length, ends curled, bangs Face: blue-green eyes, brown brows, deep pink lips & blush Clothing: yellow midi plastic top with fabric bow, tiered mini skirt of yellow vinyl & blue, white, black & pink pattern fabric, extra mini skirt different pattern same colors, extra top, pink plastic snap-on hair accessories, wide yellow pumps Extras: yellow oval brush Head: Teen Talk Head Markings: © 1991 Mattel Inc Arms: ptr Body: tan tnt, painted pink bra & panties Body Markings: © Mattel Inc 1966/ China

Model #: 2482 Name: Sparkle Eyes Barbie Box Date: 1991 Hair Color: blonde Hairstyle: sides pulled back, curly bangs, rest thigh length, ends curled under Face: blue rhinestone eyes, blonde brows, hot pink lips & blush Clothing: silver lamé fitted mini dress with sweetheart neck & spaghetti straps, pink glitter tulle full overskirt & matching boa, metallic pink drop earrings, choker, ring, pink Brazil pumps Extras: pink oval brush & sheet of cardboard punch outs Head: superstar Head Markings: inside or outside rim © Mattel Inc 1976 +/- country Arms: bent Body: tan tnt Body Markings: © Mattel Inc 1966/ China Notes: Club gift set exclusive doll, dressing room & fashion set

Model #: 1390 Name: Sun Sensation Barbie Box Date: 1991 Hair Color: blonde with iridescent streaks Hairstyle: 1 side pulled back with gold band, rest thigh length, ends turned under Face: blue eyes, blonde brows, frosted light red lips & blush Clothing: gold bikini, gold star earrings, 3 gold charm pendant Extras: pink oval brush Head: superstar Head Markings: inside or outside rim © Mattel Inc 1976 +/- country Arms: ptr Body: dark tan tnt Body Markings: © Mattel Inc.1966/ Indonesia Notes: Club gift set doll, swimming pool & extra outfits, also Club exclusive gift set: Deluxe 100 piece gift set

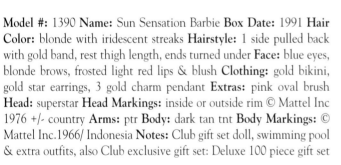

Model #: 5745 Name: Teen Talk Barbie Box Date: 1991 Hair Color: blonde Hairstyle: front & sides pulled back, rest waist length & curly Face: blue eyes, blonde brows, fuchsia lips & blush Clothing: pink, white & aqua top with spaghetti straps & sweetheart neck, matching jacket, sheer multicolor skirt, pink knee-high lace trim stretch pants, matching shorts, aqua hat with 3 rose trim, pink stud earrings & ring, matching bag, aqua tennis shoes, wide pink pumps Extras: pink oval brush, 2 batteries Booklet: instructions Head: Teen Talk Barbie Head Markings: © 1991 Mattel Inc Arms: bent Body: tan talker Body Markings: © Mattel Inc 1966/ China Notes: push button on back to talk, wide assortment of hair colors & styles, face paint, statements, outfit styles and combinations, most valuable version says "Math Class is Tough"

Model #: 1112 Name: Totally Hair Barbie Box Date: 1991 Hair Color: blonde Hairstyle: crimped floor length with back-swept bangs, pulled up with hot pink scarf Face: blue eyes, light brown brows, pink lips Clothing: scoop neck long sleeve straight mini dress with swirled multicolor pattern of pink, hot pink, purple, turquoise, light green & white, white panties, hot pink triangle earrings, ring, wide hot pink pumps Extras: hot pink hair pick, rubber bands, Dep styling gel, 4 hair ornaments Booklet: styling tips Head: superstar Head Markings: inside or outside rim © Mattel Inc 1976 +/- country Arms: bent Body: tan tnt Body Markings: © Mattel Inc 1966/ China

Model #: 1117 Name: Totally Hair Barbie Box Date: 1991 Hair Color: brunette Hairstyle: crimped floor length with back-swept bangs, pulled up with green scarf Face: blue-lavender eyes, light brown brows, hot pink lips & blush Clothing: scoop neck long sleeve straight mini dress with swirled multicolor pattern of turquoise, blue, hot pink, green & white, white panties, blue triangle earrings, ring, wide blue pumps Extras: blue hair pick, rubber bands, Dep styling gel, 4 hair ornaments Booklet: styling tips & 1991 PB Head: superstar Head Markings: inside or outside rim © Mattel Inc 1976 +/- country Arms: bent Body: tan tnt Body Markings: © Mattel Inc 1966/ Malaysia

Model #: 4159 Name: Bath Blast Barbie Box Date: 1992 Hair Color: blonde Hairstyle: right side pulled up into mid-back-length ponytail, ends curled under, bangs Face: turquoise eyes, light brown brows, fuchsia lips & blush Clothing: 1-piece nylon fuchsia swimsuit with white bubbles, yellow, blue & green dots, fuchsia stud earrings & ring Extras: fuchsia oval brush, can of blue foam & yellow flower shape decorative tip accessory Booklet: 1992 PB Head: superstar Head Markings: inside or outside rim © Mattel Inc 1976 +/- country Arms: bent Body: tan tnt Body Markings: © Mattel Inc 1966/ Malaysia

Model #: 3388 Name: Birthday Party Barbie Box Date: 1992 Hair Color: blonde with glitter strands Hairstyle: sides & top pulled back with gold-edged pink ribbon, bangs, waist length, ends curled Face: blue eyes, brown brows, deep pink lips & blush Clothing: aqua, pink, white gown with full skirt trimmed with ruffles, floral stencil & gold glitter, large puffed sleeves, aqua bodice, pink stud earrings, pendant, ring, birthday cake, wide pink pearl pumps Extras: 2-piece pink pearl stand Head: superstar Head Markings: inside or outside rim © Mattel Inc 1976 +/- country Arms: bent Body: tan tnt Body Markings: © Mattel Inc 1966/ Malaysia

Model #: 3157 Name: Caboodles Barbie Box Date: 1992 Hair Color: blonde Hairstyle: thigh length Face: blue-green eyes, light brown brows, pink lips & blush Clothing: hot pink scoop neck short sleeved flared skirt mini dress of pink, purple, turquoise & yellow, with silver glitter fabric, sewn in matching panties, matching baseball cap, hot pink stud earrings & ring, hot pink tennis shoes Extras: hot pink oval brush, caboodles case, heart shape blush, fragrance & lipstick Head: superstar Head Markings: inside or outside rim © Mattel Inc 1976 +/- country Arms: bent Body: tan tnt Body Markings: © Mattel Inc 1966/ China

Model #: 7014 Name: Earring Magic Barbie Box Date: 1992 Hair Color: blonde Hairstyle: waist length crinkled, bangs, sides pulled up to top of head, ponytail held with silver band Face: blue eyes, light brown brows, hot pink lips Clothing: hot pink vinyl mini dress with sheer bodice & long sleeves, silver hoop & sun dangle earrings & ring, silver belt with 2 dangle stars, wide hot pink pumps Extras: hot pink oval brush & pair of silver dangling heart clip-on earrings for child Booklet: BFG 1992 PB Head: superstar Head Markings: inside or outside rim © Mattel Inc 1976 +/- country Arms: bent Body: tan tnt Body Markings: © Mattel Inc 1966/ China Notes: Radio Shack exclusive packaged with 2 software programs

Model #: 10255 Name: Earring Magic Barbie Box Date: 1992 Hair Color: brunette Hairstyle: waist length crinkled, bangs, sides pulled up to top of head, ponytail held with gold band Face: dark blue eyes, light brown brows, mauve lips & blush Clothing: bright blue vinyl mini dress with sheer bodice & long sleeves, gold hoop & sun dangle earrings & ring, gold belt with 2 dangle stars, wide blue pumps Extras: blue oval brush & pair of gold dangling heart clip-on earrings for child Booklet: BFG 1992 PB Head: superstar Head Markings: inside or outside rim © Mattel Inc 1976 +/- country Arms: bent Body: tan tnt Body Markings: © Mattel Inc 1966/ Malaysia

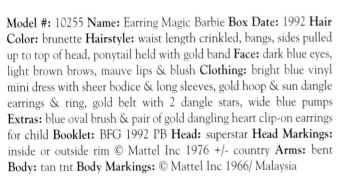

Model #: 3602 Name: Glitter Beach Barbie Box Date: 1992 Hair Color: 2 shades of blonde Hairstyle: thigh length, pulled back with multicolor glitter headband with bangs Face: blue eyes, brown brows, hot pink lips & blush Clothing: bikini of purple, hot pink, yellow, green fabric with glitter, silver stud earrings, beaded pendant Extras: hot pink oval brush & glitter lotion Head: superstar Head Markings: inside or outside rim © Mattel Inc 1976 +/- country Arms: ptr Body: dark tan tnt Body Markings: © Mattel Inc.1966/ Indonesia

Model #: 2308 Name: Hollywood Hair Barbie Box Date: 1992 Hair Color: blonde Hairstyle: ankle length pulled back with gold fabric tie, bangs Face: blue eyes, dark blonde brows, hot pink lips & blush Clothing: 1-piece halter-style mid-thigh bodysuit, gold at neckline and cuffs of shorts, white satin jacket with gold print sleeves & waistband with 4 gold stars, gold print mini skirt, gold dangle earrings, gold cowboy boots Extras: yellow star comb, hair mist Booklet: instructions Head: superstar Head Markings: inside or outside rim © Mattel Inc 1976 +/- country Arms: bent Body: tan tnt Body Markings: © Mattel Inc.1966/ Indonesia Notes: make pink stars appear in hair, Club exclusive gift set

Model #: 1861 Name: Romantic Bride Barbie Box Date: 1992 Hair Color: blonde Hairstyle: mid-back length with ends curled, bangs Face: blue eyes, light brown brows, deep pink lips & blush Clothing: long white gown with satin bodice & leg of mutton sleeves, tulle overskirt, pink tulle bouquet & trim, white tulle veil with pearl trim, white stud earrings & ring, wide white pumps Extras: pink oval brush Head: superstar Head Markings: inside or outside rim © Mattel Inc 1976 +/- country Arms: bent Body: tan tnt Body Markings: © Mattel Inc 1966/ China

Model #: 5471 Name: Sea Holiday Barbie Box Date: 1992 Hair Color: blonde Hairstyle: waist length, ends curled under Face: blue eyes, blonde brows, pale pink lips & blush Clothing: blue swimsuit with white & gold bodice, long blue skirt with wide gold waistband, blue multicolor satin bolero jacket, gold charm pendant, gold dangle earrings & ring, white vinyl hat with gold brim, Barbie fold-out pictures, wide white pumps Extras: hot pink oval brush & pink lip gloss, camera Head: superstar Head Markings: inside or outside rim © Mattel Inc 1976 +/- country Arms: bent Body: tan tnt Body Markings: © Mattel Inc 1966/ China

Model #: 7902 Name: Secret Hearts Barbie Box Date: 1992 Hair Color: blonde Hairstyle: front pulled back, rest waist length with ends turned under Face: blue eyes, blonde brows, frosted hot pink lips & blush Clothing: sleeveless iridescent gown with ruffle at v-neck, full skirt with white glitter tulle trimmed with white ribbon & pink change-color hearts, heart drop earrings, pendant, silver ring, wide white pumps Extras: pearl oval brush, heart water tray & iridescent heart ice cube holder Booklet: instructions Head: superstar Head Markings: inside or outside rim © Mattel Inc 1976 +/- country Arms: bent Body: tan tnt Body Markings: © Mattel Inc.1966/ Indonesia Notes: also in Club gift set variation - see gift sets

Model #: 10257 Name: Troll Barbie Box Date: 1992 Hair Color: blonde Hairstyle: 1 side & center front pulled back with faux fur purple ornament, other side twisted & pulled under hair, rest waist length, ends curled under with curly bangs Face: turquoise eyes, blonde brows, fuchsia lips & blush Clothing: long sleeve top with white body & black troll print sleeves, matching pants, pink dangle earrings & ring, tiny troll with 3 colors of interchangeable faux fur hair, pink string pendant, wide hot pink pumps Extras: hot pink oval brush Head: superstar Head Markings: inside or outside rim © Mattel Inc 1976 +/- country Arms: bent Body: tan tnt Body Markings: © Mattel Inc 1966/ China

Model #: 10610 Name: Angel Lights Barbie Box Date: 1993 Hair Color: blonde Hairstyle: top & part of sides pulled back, rest waist length, ends curled under, iridescent bead tiara Face: blue eyes, light brown brows, hot pink lips & blush Clothing: gown with white lace shaped like angel wings, v-neck top with pearl accents & iridescent glitter, full skirt with heavy iridescent glitter & lace hem, matching underskirt & hooped frame with filament lights, crystal drop earrings, silver ring Extras: tree attachments: cup, dowel, c support, AC adapter Booklet: instructions Head: superstar Head Markings: inside or outside rim © Mattel Inc 1976 +/- country Arms: bent Body: tan tnt, white legs Body Markings: © Mattel Inc 1966/ China Notes: lighted Christmas tree topper

Model #: 11079 Name: Bedtime Barbie Box Date: 1993 Hair Color: blonde Hairstyle: front & 1 side pulled into small ponytail, rest thigh length, ends curled under Face: blue eyes, brown brows, red lips & pink blush Clothing: pink flannel long nightgown with white lace trim & pink rose with green ribbon, pink wash cloth, pink toothbrush, sewn on slippers Extras: pink oval brush Head: superstar Head Markings: inside or outside rim © Mattel Inc 1976 +/- country Arms: soft Body: tan soft body Body Markings: cloth tag:© Mattel, Inc.1993/ El Segundo, CA 90245 U.S.A./ surface washable(repeated)/ Reg.No.PA-60/ All New Materials/ Consisting of Polyester Fibers/ Made in China Notes: painted eyes & mouth open & close with ice water & warm water, also Club exclusive gift set doll & bed

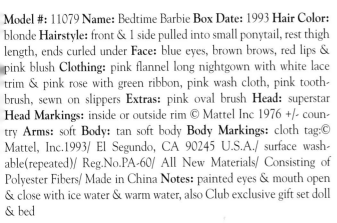

Model #: 11689 Name: Bicyclin' Barbie Box Date: 1993 Hair Color: blonde Hairstyle: sides & top pulled up to ponytail, rest thigh length, bangs Face: blue eyes, blonde brows, pink lips & blush Clothing: green & pink bicycling outfit: jacket, midi top & pants, purple sunglasses, pink helmet, pink stud earrings, multicolor bicycle with flag, pinwheel, water bottle & pump accessories, hot pink bicycle shoes Extras: hot pink oval brush Booklet: instructions Head: superstar Head Markings: inside or outside rim © Mattel Inc 1976 +/- country Arms: gymnast Body: tan gymnast Body Markings: © 1993 Mattel, Inc./ China:

Model #: 11333 **Name:** Birthday Barbie **Box Date:** 1993 **Hair Color:** blonde **Hairstyle:** front & sides pulled back with turquoise ribbon & fabric hair ornament, rest waist length, ends curled **Face:** turquoise eyes, blonde brows, deep pink lips & blush **Clothing:** turquoise gown with multicolor white, pink, coral, glitter full skirt with matching puffed sleeves, Happy Birthday sash, pearl stud earrings & ring, wide turquoise pumps **Extras:** hot pink oval brush & sheet of cardboard punch outs **Head:** superstar **Head Markings:** inside or outside rim © Mattel Inc 1976 +/- country **Arms:** bent **Body:** tan tnt **Body Markings:** © Mattel Inc 1966/ Malaysia

Model #: 11074 **Name:** Camp Fun Barbie **Box Date:** 1993 **Hair Color:** blonde **Hairstyle:** front section pulled into pink rubber band, rest waist length, curly bangs **Face:** blue eyes, blonde brows, bright pink lips & blush **Clothing:** white appliqué T-shirt, pink windbreaker, denim shorts, white anklets, pink backpack, yellow lantern & sunglasses, orange binoculars, turquoise stud earrings & ring, fuchsia hiking boots **Extras:** fuchsia oval brush **Booklet:** 1993 PB & instructions **Head:** superstar **Head Markings:** inside or outside rim © Mattel Inc 1976 +/- country **Arms:** bent **Body:** tan tnt **Body Markings:** © Mattel Inc 1966/ Malaysia **Notes:** hair changes color in sunlight

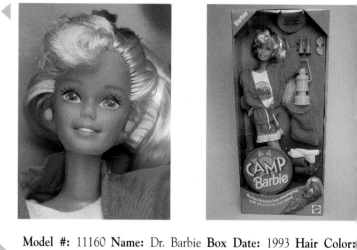

Model #: 11160 **Name:** Dr. Barbie **Box Date:** 1993 **Hair Color:** blonde **Hairstyle:** ponytail held with blue band, curly bangs **Face:** blue eyes, dark blonde brows, pink lips & blush **Clothing:** blue sleeveless mini dress with white lab coat, blue bow earrings & ring, pink stethoscope in chest, white medical bag, baby, wide royal blue pumps **Extras:** royal blue oval brush, 2 sheets of stickers, sheet of cardboard punch outs, light blue ear checker, reflex hammer, baby bottle, rattle, vitamin bottle, bandage box, clipboard, cough syrup bottle, syringe, baby food jar, blood pressure checker, beeper, pacifier, lotion bottle **Booklet:** instructions **Head:** superstar & baby **Head Markings:** Barbie=inside or outside rim © Mattel Inc 1976 +/- country Baby=© M.I. 1985 **Arms:** bent **Body:** tan tnt, baby **Body Markings:** Barbie=© Mattel Inc 1966/ Indonesia Baby=© 1973/ Mattel Inc/ Indonesia **Notes:** baby available in four varieties, Toys R Us exclusive in 1995 model #14309 packaged with 3 babies, brunette hair version Festival exclusive

Model #: 10393 **Name:** Fountain Mermaid Barbie **Box Date:** 1993 **Hair Color:** pink with iridescent strands **Hairstyle:** thigh length with bangs **Face:** blue-green eyes, blonde brows, pink lips & blush **Clothing:** hot pink satin spaghetti strap crop top with gold seashell & pearl ornament, matching mermaid skirt trimmed with iridescent pink & white glitter tulle & gold sequins, pink fountain crown, white stud earrings **Extras:** pink seahorse comb, fountain pump **Booklet:** instructions **Head:** superstar **Head Markings:** inside or outside rim © Mattel Inc 1976 +/- country **Arms:** ptr **Body:** tan tnt **Body Markings:** © Mattel Inc 1966/ China

Model #: 13965 **Name:** Glitter Hair Barbie **Box Date:** 1993 **Hair Color:** blonde **Hairstyle:** mid-calf length, curly bangs **Face:** blue eyes, blonde brows, deep pink lips & blush **Clothing:** sleeveless mini dress with appliquéd black top, black inset belt, pink glitter short skirt, pink dangle earrings & ring, pink visor, pink tennis shoes **Extras:** pink applicator comb & tube of pink glitter gel **Booklet:** instructions **Head:** superstar **Head Markings:** inside or outside rim © Mattel Inc 1976 +/- country **Arms:** bent **Body:** tan tnt, "B" panties **Body Markings:** © Mattel Inc.1966/ Indonesia

Model #: 10966 **Name:** Glitter Hair Barbie **Box Date:** 1993 **Hair Color:** brunette **Hairstyle:** mid-calf length, curly bangs **Face:** green eyes, brown brows, orange lips & blush **Clothing:** sleeveless mini dress with appliquéd orange top, black inset belt, yellow glitter short skirt, orange dangle earrings & ring, yellow visor, yellow tennis shoes **Extras:** yellow applicator comb & tube of yellow glitter gel **Booklet:** instructions **Head:** superstar **Head Markings:** inside or outside rim © Mattel Inc 1976 +/- country **Arms:** bent **Body:** tan tnt, white panties **Body Markings:** © Mattel Inc 1966/ China

Model #: 10968 **Name:** Glitter Hair Barbie **Box Date:** 1993 **Hair Color:** red **Hairstyle:** mid-calf length, curly bangs **Face:** blue eyes, reddish brows, pink lips & blush **Clothing:** sleeveless mini dress with appliquéd hot pink top, black inset belt, turquoise glitter short skirt, pink dangle earrings & ring, turquoise visor, turquoise tennis shoes **Extras:** pink applicator comb & tube of pink glitter gel **Booklet:** instructions **Head:** superstar **Head Markings:** inside or outside rim © Mattel Inc 1976 +/- country **Arms:** bent **Body:** tan tnt, white panties **Body Markings:** © Mattel Inc 1966/ Malaysia

Model #: 12127 **Name:** Gymnast Barbie **Box Date:** 1993 **Hair Color:** blonde **Hairstyle:** waist-length ponytail braided with hot pink ribbon, bangs **Face:** turquoise eyes, light brown brows, pink lips & blush **Clothing:** bodysuit with pink & gold glitter sleeves & half bodice, remainder yellow, orange, green & blue, hot pink footless tights, pair of white anklets, gold stud earrings & ring, 3 hair ribbons, gold medal, pink duffel bag with "B" monogram, 2 orange hand weights, hot pink high-top athletic shoes **Extras:** blue oval brush **Head:** superstar **Head Markings:** inside or outside rim © Mattel Inc 1976 +/- country **Arms:** gymnast **Body:** tan gymnast **Body Markings:** © 1993 Mattel, Inc./ China: **Notes:** brunette version Festival exclusive

Model #: 10963 **Name:** Locket Surprise Barbie **Box Date:** 1993 **Hair Color:** blonde **Hairstyle:** crinkled thigh length, side part **Face:** blue eyes, blonde brows, pink lips **Clothing:** pink elastic ruffle around bodice, pink glitter knee-length skirt with iridescent edging, gold filigree drop earrings, ring, wide pink pumps **Extras:** pink oval brush, heart locket lip gloss insert, photo of Ken, blush **Booklet:** instructions **Head:** superstar **Head Markings:** inside or outside rim © Mattel Inc 1976 +/- country **Arms:** bent **Body:** tan b/l, pink locket **Body Markings:** © Mattel Inc 1966/ China **Notes:** chest opens up for accessory storage

Model #: 10039 **Name:** Paint' n Dazzle Barbie **Box Date:** 1993 **Hair Color:** blonde **Hairstyle:** sides & front pulled back with pink band, rest mid-thigh length **Face:** blue eyes, blonde brows, hot pink lips & blush **Clothing:** pink top with matching full mini skirt, sewn in panties, white & hot pink pattern fabric insert, pink denim jacket with contrasting collar and waistband, all trimmed with silver rickrack, hot pink round earrings & ring, wide hot pink pumps **Extras:** hot pink oval brush, rhinestones, roses, 2 bottles Tulip fabric paint **Booklet:** instructions **Head:** superstar **Head Markings:** inside or outside rim © Mattel Inc 1976 +/- country **Arms:** bent **Body:** tan tnt **Body Markings:** © Mattel Inc 1966/ China **Notes:** Club gift set

Model #: 10059 **Name:** Paint' n Dazzle Barbie **Box Date:** 1993 **Hair Color:** brunette **Hairstyle:** sides & front pulled back with yellow band, rest mid-thigh length **Face:** lavender eyes, brown brows, hot pink lips & blush **Clothing:** yellow crop top with gold sequin neckline, purple denim pants, matching jacket with gold sequins & multicolor fabric insert, purple round earrings & ring, wide purple pumps **Extras:** purple oval brush, stars, pom-poms, 2 bottles Tulip fabric paint **Booklet:** instructions **Head:** superstar **Head Markings:** inside or outside rim © Mattel Inc 1976 +/- country **Arms:** bent **Body:** tan tnt **Body Markings:** © Mattel Inc 1966/ China

Model #: 10057 **Name:** Paint' n Dazzle Barbie **Box Date:** 1993 **Hair Color:** red **Hairstyle:** sides & front pulled back with blue band, rest mid-thigh length **Face:** turquoise eyes, brown brows, deep orange lips & blush **Clothing:** orange mini dress with lace trim at hem, denim jacket with floral fabric insert & sequin trim, matching floral print stretch pants, royal blue round earrings & ring, wide royal blue pumps **Extras:** royal blue oval brush, sequins, pearls, 2 bottles Tulip fabric paint **Booklet:** instructions **Head:** superstar **Head Markings:** inside or outside rim © Mattel Inc 1976 +/- country **Arms:** bent **Body:** tan tnt **Body Markings:** © Mattel Inc 1966/ Malaysia

Model #: 10953 Name: Sun Jewel Barbie Box Date: 1993 Hair Color: blonde Hairstyle: sides & part of front pulled to side, banded in hot pink, rest thigh length, ends curled under, partial bangs Face: blue eyes, blonde brows, hot pink lips & blush Clothing: hot pink 2-piece swimsuit with crystal jewel trim on bodice & waist, matching dangle earrings Extras: hot pink oval brush & stick-on jewels Head: superstar Head Markings: inside or outside rim © Mattel Inc 1976 +/- country Arms: ptr Body: dark tan tnt Body Markings: © Mattel Inc 1966/ China

Model #: 11505 Name: Swim 'n Dive Barbie Box Date: 1993 Hair Color: blonde Hairstyle: 1 section of hair above each ear twisted & tied in back, rest waist length, bangs Face: blue eyes, light brown brows, hot pink lips & blush Clothing: hot pink with silver glitter long sleeve 1-piece wetsuit, silver stud earrings, scuba mask, tanks that propel doll in water, flippers Extras: hot pink oval brush Booklet: instructions Head: superstar Head Markings: inside or outside rim © Mattel Inc 1976 +/- country Arms: gymnast Body: tan gymnast Body Markings: © 1993 Mattel, Inc./ Malaysia

Model #: 10390 Name: Twinkle Lights Barbie Box Date: 1993 Hair Color: blonde Hairstyle: front & sides in twisted ponytail, curly bangs, rest waist length, ends curled under Face: turquoise eyes, blonde brows, pink lips & blush Clothing: sleeveless gown with iridescent white bodice, pink glitter tulle full skirt with on/off belt, crystal drop earrings, pendant, ring, wide hot pink pumps Extras: pink oval brush & 2 batteries Booklet: instructions Head: superstar Head Markings: inside or outside rim © Mattel Inc 1976 +/- country Arms: bent Body: tan tnt fiber optic strands imbedded in chest, partial white painted bra Body Markings: front pelvis ©1966,1992/ Mattel, Inc/ China

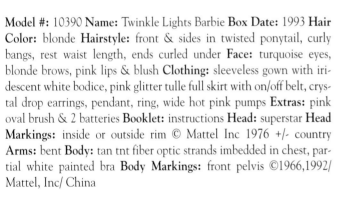

Model #: 10293 Name: Western Stampin' Barbie Box Date: 1993 Hair Color: blonde Hairstyle: side part, sides pulled to back of head, rest crinkled thigh length Face: blue eyes, blonde brows, hot pink lips & blush Clothing: silver top, turquoise & silver belt with white fringe, silver lamé mini skirt with white panties, turquoise long sleeve short jacket with silver trim, turquoise cowboy hat with silver trim, silver cowboy boot earrings, ring, turquoise cowboy boots with rolling stampers Extras: turquoise oval brush, ink pad, silver glitter & sheet of cardboard punch outs Booklet: instructions Head: superstar Head Markings: inside or outside rim © Mattel Inc 1976 +/- country Arms: bent Body: tan tnt Body Markings: © Mattel Inc 1966/ Malaysia Notes: #11020 Toys R Us & 2 Club gift sets — 1 with horse other with doll & extras

Model #: 13199 **Name:** Baywatch Barbie **Box Date:** 1994 **Hair Color:** blonde **Hairstyle:** thigh length **Face:** blue eyes, brown brows, light red lips & blush **Clothing:** white midi top, 1-piece red swimsuit with Baywatch insignia, red nylon jacket, blue, red & yellow life-guard shorts, blue stud earrings & ring, white tennis shoes, red Baywatch visor & silver whistle on black cord **Extras:** white oval brush, red Frisbee, yellow binoculars, gray & white "talking" dolphin, red flotation device **Head:** superstar **Head Markings:** inside or outside rim © Mattel Inc 1976 +/- country **Arms:** bent **Body:** tan tnt **Body Markings:** © Mattel Inc 1966/ Malaysia

Model #: 12954 **Name:** Birthday Barbie **Box Date:** 1994 **Hair Color:** blonde **Hairstyle:** top pulled back with pink fabric & light blue ribbon, bangs, rest waist length, ends curled under **Face:** blue eyes, blonde brows, hot pink lips & blush **Clothing:** white gown, full multicolor teal, coral, hot pink, glitter skirt with matching puffed sleeves, Happy Birthday blue sash, pink stud earrings & ring, wide white pumps **Extras:** hot pink oval brush & sheet of cardboard punch outs **Head:** superstar **Head Markings:** inside or outside rim © Mattel Inc 1976 +/- country **Arms:** bent **Body:** tan tnt, pink panties **Body Markings:** © Mattel Inc 1966/ Malaysia

Model #: 12443 **Name:** Bubble Angel Barbie **Box Date:** 1994 **Hair Color:** blonde **Hairstyle:** thigh-length crinkled ponytail with curly bangs **Face:** blue eyes, blonde brows, deep pink lips & blush **Clothing:** iridescent blue bodysuit with sewn in shimmery glitter pantyhose, iridescent fan bodice & overskirt, silver stud earrings, choker, ring, clear blue plastic wings to make bubbles, clear blue pointed flats **Extras:** blue oval brush, bubble solution, wand & tray **Booklet:** instructions **Head:** superstar **Head Markings:** inside or outside rim © Mattel Inc 1976 +/- country **Arms:** Shani **Body:** tan tnt **Body Markings:** © Mattel Inc 1966/ Malaysia

Model #: 13051 **Name:** Butterfly Princess Barbie **Box Date:** 1994 **Hair Color:** blonde **Hairstyle:** thigh length crinkled, bangs, sides pulled up with pink satin ribbon **Face:** light blue eyes, blonde brows, deep pink lips & blush **Clothing:** long full skirt gown with multicolor top and pink tulle overskirt with iridescent butterfly accents, sewn in panties, gold stud earrings & ring, pink & green magnetic flower magic wand to make butterflies move, wide pink pearl pumps **Extras:** pink pearl oval brush, butterfly princess fold-out pamphlet, ring for child **Booklet:** instructions **Head:** superstar **Head Markings:** inside or outside rim © Mattel Inc 1976 +/- country **Arms:** bent **Body:** tan tnt **Body Markings:** © Mattel Inc.1966/ Indonesia

Model #: 12639 Name: Cut and Style Barbie Box Date: 1994 Hair Color: blonde Hairstyle: ankle length, bangs, Velcro in back of head Face: blue eyes, light brown brows, hot pink lips & blush Clothing: pink vinyl vest with 3 gold buttons, full pink nylon mini skirt with sewn in panties & matching tulle slip, gold & black drop earrings, gold ring, black choker with gold pendant, wide hot pink pumps Extras: hot pink oval brush, matching safety scissors, length of blonde hair with Velcro, green headband, yellow headband, 2 fabric ribbons & 4 colored rubber bands Booklet: 2 instructions Head: superstar Head Markings: inside or outside rim © Mattel Inc 1976 +/- country Arms: bent Body: tan tnt Body Markings: © Mattel Inc.1966/ Indonesia

Model #: 12643 Name: Cut and Style Barbie Box Date: 1994 Hair Color: brunette Hairstyle: ankle length, bangs, Velcro in back of head Face: light brown eyes, brown brows, orange lips & blush Clothing: yellow-green vinyl vest with 3 gold buttons, full yellow-green nylon mini skirt with sewn in panties & matching tulle slip, gold & black drop earrings, gold ring, black choker & gold pendant, wide yellow-green pumps Extras: yellow-green oval brush, matching safety scissors, length of brunette hair with Velcro, hot pink headband, orange headband, 2 fabric ribbons & 4 colored rubber bands Booklet: 2 instructions & 1995 PB Head: superstar Head Markings: inside or outside rim © Mattel Inc 1976 +/- country Arms: bent Body: tan tnt Body Markings: © Mattel Inc 1966/ China

Model #: 12644 Name: Cut and Style Barbie Box Date: 1994 Hair Color: redhead Hairstyle: ankle length, bangs, Velcro in back of head Face: turquoise eyes, reddish brown brows, red lips & blush Clothing: lime green vinyl vest with 3 gold buttons, full lime green nylon mini skirt with sewn in panties & matching tulle slip, gold & black drop earrings, gold ring, black choker & gold pendant, wide lime green pumps Extras: lime green oval brush, matching safety scissors, length of red hair with Velcro, yellow headband, hot pink headband, 2 fabric ribbons & 4 colored rubber bands Booklet: 2 instructions Head: superstar Head Markings: inside or outside rim © Mattel Inc 1976 +/- country Arms: bent Body: tan tnt Body Markings: © Mattel Inc.1966/ Indonesia

Model #: 11902 Name: Dance 'N Twirl Barbie Box Date: 1994 Hair Color: blonde Hairstyle: front & sides pulled up to top of head, tied with 2 shades of pink satin ribbon, rest thigh length Face: blue eyes, blonde brows, hot pink lips & blush Clothing: pink & white pattern strapless full skirted gown with fringe at hem, silver & crystal bead drop earrings, ring & wide pink pumps Extras: pink oval brush, doll stand, dance base, radio controller to make doll dance Booklet: instructions Head: superstar Head Markings: inside or outside rim © Mattel Inc 1976 +/- country Arms: bent Body: tan tnt Body Markings: © Mattel Inc 1966/ China

Model #: 13083 Name: Dance Moves Barbie Box Date: 1994 Hair Color: blonde Hairstyle: hip length crinkled, sides pulled up to top of head held with hot pink band, bangs Face: blue eyes, light brown brows, hot pink lips Clothing: pink & silver metallic scoop neck long sleeve crop top, silver suspenders on metallic hot pink shorts, silver & hot pink metallic tights, silver hoop earrings & ring, black Jazzie flats Extras: hot pink oval brush, fake pink cassette player with headphones & boom box, black hand held microphone Booklet: instructions Head: superstar Head Markings: inside or outside rim © Mattel Inc 1976 +/- country Arms: bent Body: tan tnt with gymnast legs Body Markings: © Mattel Inc 1966/ China Notes: arms click into position

Model #: 13511 Name: Hot Skatin' Barbie Box Date: 1994 Hair Color: blonde Hairstyle: thigh-length ponytail with curled bangs Face: blue eyes, brown brows, deep pink lips & blush Clothing: 1-piece stretch multicolor bodysuit with silver glitter swirls, yellow vinyl belt with hot pink water bottle, yellow vinyl knee pads, yellow inline skates with hot pink wheels, pair of white ice skates, pink helmet, sheer pink glitter ice skating skirt, pink stud earrings Extras: hot pink oval brush Head: superstar Head Markings: inside or outside rim © Mattel Inc 1976 +/- country Arms: gymnast Body: tan gymnast Body Markings: © 1993 Mattel, Inc./ Malaysia

Model #: 12696 Name: Slumber Party Barbie Box Date: 1994 Hair Color: blonde Hairstyle: crinkled thigh length, curly bangs, light blue fabric headband with white stars & moons Face: blue eyes, light brown brows, pink lips & blush Clothing: 2-piece blue & white dot pajamas trimmed in lace Extras: light blue oval brush, white wash cloth, sheet of dayglo stickers, clear zipper carrying case Head: superstar Head Markings: inside or outside rim © Mattel Inc 1976 +/- country Arms: soft Body: tan soft body Body Markings: cloth tag: © Mattel Inc.1994/ El Segundo, CA 90245 U.S.A/ surface washable(repeated) Reg.No.Pa-60/ All new materials consisting of polyester fiber/ Made in Indonesia Notes: painted eyes open and close with ice water & warm water

Model #: 12290 Name: Super Talk Barbie Box Date: 1994 Hair Color: blonde Hairstyle: thigh length crinkled Face: blue lilac eyes, blonde brows, fuchsia lips & blush Clothing: white cotton bodysuit, blue denim long sleeve bolero jacket with gold cuffs & collar, jewel trim, blue denim mini skirt with gold ruffle, gold hoop earrings & ring, white scrunches, gold hiking boots Extras: white oval brush Booklet: instructions Head: superstar Head Markings: inside or outside rim © Mattel Inc 1976 +/- country Arms: bent Body: tan tnt supertalk Body Markings: © Mattel Inc 1966/ China Notes: in 1995 a Toys R Us exclusive, smaller box, model number #14308 & box dated 1995 see Super Talk black version, says over 100,000 things, press button on back to talk

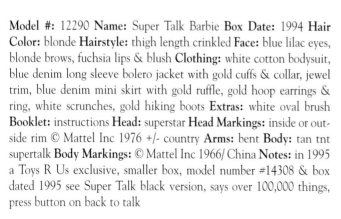

Model #: 12446 Name: Tropical Splash Barbie Box Date: 1994 Hair Color: blonde Hairstyle: front & sides pulled to 1 side & braided, rest waist length Face: blue eyes, blonde brows, deep pink lips & blush Clothing: black multicolor floral bikini with gold accents, gold seashell necklace, gold drop earrings Extras: hot pink oval brush, Barbie perfume Head: superstar Head Markings: inside or outside rim © Mattel Inc 1976 +/- country Arms: ptr Body: dark tan tnt Body Markings: © Mattel Inc 1966/ China Notes: perfume is same as used on Mackie's Masquerade doll, fabric pattern & earrings vary

Model #: 13516 Name: Winter Sport Barbie Box Date: 1994 Hair Color: blonde Hairstyle: waist-length ponytail at top of head, with bangs & multicolored headband Face: green eyes, brown brows, deep pink lips & blush Clothing: 1-piece multicolor bodysuit with silver glitter, pink, yellow & turquoise long sleeve jacket, hot pink with silver glitter skating skirt, hot pink skis & poles, orange snowboard, yellow-green knee pads, hot pink stud earrings, yellow & blue goggles, turquoise ski boots, white ice skates Extras: hot pink oval brush Head: superstar Head Markings: inside or outside rim © Mattel Inc 1976 +/- country Arms: gymnast Body: tan gymnast Body Markings: © 1993 Mattel, Inc./ China: Notes: Available at JCP, Toys R Us, FAO

Model #: 14024 Name: Oshogatsu Barbie Box Date: 1995 Hair Color: black Hairstyle: sides & front pulled into ponytail with gold & red hair ornament, bangs, thigh length Face: brown eyes, brown brows, red lips & blush Clothing: red kimono with gold flowers, gold & ivory obi, gold clutch purse, pearl ring, sleeveless white slip, white anklets, white & red zori sandals Extras: 2-piece black stand, gold oval brush Head: Steffie Head Markings: inside rim © 1971 Mattel Inc & country Arms: Shani Body: tan tnt Body Markings: © Mattel Inc 1966/ China Notes: doll commemorates New Year

Model #: 13611 Name: Pretty Dreams Barbie Box Date: 1995 Hair Color: blonde Hairstyle: sides & front pulled back with white iridescent bow, thigh-length hair Face: green eyes, blonde brows, fuchsia lips & blush Clothing: pink velour long sleeve nightgown trimmed with white iridescent lace Extras: pink oval brush Head: supersize Head Markings: © 1976 Mattel Inc Body: tan 18" soft body Body Markings: cloth tag:© Mattel, Inc.1993 or 94 or 95/El Segundo, CA 90245 U.S.A./ surface washable(repeated)/ Reg.No.PA-60/ All New Materials/ Consisting of Polyester Fibers/ Made in China

African American Barbies

Model #: 13914 **Name:** Teacher Barbie **Box Date:** 1995 **Hair Color:** blonde **Hairstyle:** top & sides pulled up with red band, bangs, rest thigh length, little girl has pigtails & bangs **Face:** blue eyes, blonde brows, red lips & blush **Clothing:** white long sleeve blouse with red ribbon tie, black school print short jumper, white stud earrings & ring, red glasses, 2 assorted little friends, girl wearing white & red playsuit, boy wearing blue & white playsuit with black suspenders, yellow & green desks, matching talking blackboard with clock, 2 books & pencils, eraser, chalk, sharpener **Extras:** red oval brush & cardboard punch out posters **Booklet:** instructions **Head:** superstar, girl & boy little friends **Head Markings:** Barbie=inside & outside rim © Mattel Inc 1976 +/- country girl=© Mattel Inc. 1976 boy=© Mattel 1995 **Arms:** 1 bent & 1 Shani **Body:** tan tnt, "B" panties **Body Marking:** Barbie=© Mattel Inc 1966/ Indonesia Kids: © 1976 Mattel Inc/ Indonesia **Notes:** little boy & girl available in white & black versions with different

Model #: 1293 **Name:** Black Barbie **Box Date:** 1979 **Hair Color:** black **Hairstyle:** short curly bouffant **Face:** brown eyes, black brows, light red lips & blush **Clothing:** red sparkle long sleeve scoop neck bodysuit, gold accent at neck, matching long wrap skirt, red earrings with dangle or hoops, pendant, ring, hair ornament, red ankle straps **Booklet:** BWOF 1979 **Head:** Steffie **Head Markings:** inside rim © 1971 Mattel Inc & country **Arms:** bent **Body:** dark brown tnt **Body Markings:** © Mattel Inc 1966/ Taiwan **Notes:** first black Barbie

Model #: 3989 **Name:** Magic Curl Barbie black version **Box Date:** 1981 **Hair Color:** brunette **Hairstyle:** pulled back into mass of small curls held with yellow ribbon **Face:** brown eyes, black brows, pink lips & blush **Clothing:** long yellow dress accented with yellow lace & wide yellow ribbon belt, square neck, puffed sleeves, wraparound towel, yellow mules **Extras:** white pointed brush & comb, purple brush & comb with handgrip, mirror, 2 barrettes, 2 hair ornaments, applicator bottle, magic mist packet, hand towel, vanity tray **Booklet:** BWOF 1981 & instructions **Head:** Steffie **Head Markings:** inside rim © 1971 Mattel Inc & country **Arms:** bent **Body:** dark brown tnt **Body Markings:** © Mattel Inc 1966/ Taiwan

Model #: 5723 **Name:** Twirley Curls Barbie black version **Box Date:** 1982 **Hair Color:** black **Hairstyle:** side part, mid-thigh-length side ponytail banded at nape of neck **Face:** brown eyes, black brows, hot pink lips & blush **Clothing:** hot pink halter-style bodysuit, matching long slim skirt with fabric ruffle & silver wide belt, rhinestone ring, hot pink mules **Extras:** pink pointed comb & brush, 4 white barrettes, 2 pink ribbons, purple chair with suction cups, pink twirley curler **Booklet:** instructions **Head:** Hispanic **Head Markings:** inside rim © Mattel Inc, 1983 **Arms:** bent **Body:** dark brown tnt **Body Markings:** © Mattel Inc 1966/ Taiwan

Model #: 4859 Name: Crystal Barbie black version Box Date: 1983 Hair Color: brunette Hairstyle: pulled back into 3 intertwined ponytails Face: brown eyes, brown brows, dark mauve lips & blush Clothing: white spaghetti strap opalescent gown with ruffle hem & matching boa, fuchsia & purple waistband, rhinestone drop earrings, pendant & ring, narrow clear silver glitter pumps Extras: white pointed comb & brush, crystal pendant for child Booklet: BWOF 1983 & instructions Head: Hispanic Head Markings: inside rim © Mattel Inc, 1983 Arms: bent Body: dark brown tnt Body Markings: © Mattel Inc 1966/ Taiwan

Model #: 7834 Name: Great Shapes Barbie black version Box Date: 1983 Hair Color: black Hairstyle: side part, side sections pulled back, rest mid-back curly Face: brown eyes, brown brows, pink lips & blush Clothing: turquoise 1-piece sleeveless full-length bodysuit, multi-striped leggings, pink sash, turquoise headband, pink workout bag & booklet, pink ankle strap ballet shoes Booklet: BWOF 1984 Head: Hispanic Head Markings: inside rim © Mattel Inc, 1983 Arms: ptr Body: dark brown tnt Body Markings: © Mattel Inc.1966/ Philippines Notes: next issue came with doll size walkman

Model #: 7745 Name: Sun Gold Malibu Barbie black version Box Date: 1983 Hair Color: brunette Hairstyle: side part, curly mid-back length Face: brown eyes, brown brows, peach lips & blush Clothing: gold 2-tone checked 1-piece swimsuit, pink, purple & black pairs of sunglasses, fold-out gold tote bag converts to blue mat Booklet: BWOF 1984 Head: Hispanic Head Markings: inside rim © Mattel Inc, 1983 Arms: ptr Body: dark brown tnt Body Markings: © Mattel Inc.1966/ Philippines

Model #: 7945 Name: Day-to-Night Barbie black version Box Date: 1984 Hair Color: black Hairstyle: side part with front sections pulled to back of head, rest waist length, ends curled under Face: brown eyes, black brows, hot pink lips & blush Clothing: spaghetti strap metallic hot pink bodysuit, pink chiffon scarf, pink jacket with white lapels & buttons, matching reversible skirt, white hat with pink & white hatband, white briefcase, rhinestone stud earrings & ring, white plastic clutch purse with pink strap, hot pink mules, narrow white & pink pumps Extras: pink pointed comb & brush, sheet of cardboard punch outs Booklet: BWOF 1984 & instructions Head: Hispanic Head Markings: inside rim © Mattel Inc, 1983 Arms: bent Body: dark brown tnt Body Markings: © Mattel Inc 1966/ Taiwan

Model #: 9516 **Name:** Peaches n' Cream Barbie black version **Box Date:** 1984 **Hair Color:** brown & red streaks **Hairstyle:** side part with sides pulled to back, waist length, ends curled under **Face:** light brown eyes, black brows, orange lips & blush **Clothing:** gown with spaghetti strap iridescent sweetheart bodice & full pink & orange chiffon skirt with ruffle hem, matching boa, orange chiffon belt, rhinestone stud earrings, pendant & ring, narrow peach pumps **Extras:** white pointed comb & brush, 2 orange barrettes, 2 hair combs, orange costume spinner & sheet of cardboard punch outs **Booklet:** BWOF 1984 & instructions **Head:** Hispanic **Head Markings:** inside rim © Mattel Inc, 1983 **Arms:** bent **Body:** dark brown tnt **Body Markings:** © Mattel Inc 1966/ Taiwan

Model #: 1207 **Name:** Astronaut Barbie black version **Box Date:** 1985 **Hair Color:** black **Hairstyle:** side part, curly mid-back length pulled to nape of neck, **Face:** brown eyes, black brows, hot pink lips & blush **Clothing:** metallic fuchsia & silver long sleeve turtleneck bodysuit with Barbie appliqué, matching pants with silver belt, matching pleated mini skirt, silver tights, wide fuchsia belt, silver purse, computer, clear helmet, silver backpack, flagpole, fuchsia over-the-knee boots **Extras:** pink pointed brush, sheet of stickers & sheet of cardboard punch outs **Booklet:** BWOF 1986 & instructions **Head:** Hispanic **Head Markings:** : inside rim © Mattel Inc, 1983 **Arms:** bent **Body:** dark brown tnt **Body Markings:** © Mattel Inc 1966/ Malaysia

Model #: 2422 **Name:** Dream Glow Barbie black version **Box Date:** 1985 **Hair Color:** brunette **Hairstyle:** middle part, sides pulled to back of head, rest thigh length **Face:** brown eyes, black brows, hot pink lips & blush **Clothing:** halter-style gown, hot pink bodice trimmed in silver lace, full skirt of sheer pink fabric with white dayglo stars & silver lace, matching stole, rhinestone earrings, pendant, ring, lilac plastic parasol, narrow lilac pumps **Extras:** white pointed brush **Booklet:** BWOF 1985 & instructions **Head:** Hispanic **Head Markings:** inside rim © Mattel Inc, 1983 **Arms:** bent **Body:** dark brown tnt **Body Markings:** © Mattel Inc.1966/ Philippines **Notes:** stars in outfit glow in dark

Model #: 2137 **Name:** Magic Moves Barbie black version **Box Date:** 1985 **Hair Color:** brunette **Hairstyle:** side part, banded in 2 long ponytails **Face:** hazel eyes, black brows, bright coral lips & blush **Clothing:** aqua halter gown with slim skirt, metallic top with silver collar & belt, matching cape with faux fur trim, rhinestone earrings & ring, narrow aqua pumps **Extras:** lavender pointed brush, fake hair dryer, small oval brush & comb, 2 sheets of cardboard punch outs **Booklet:** BWOF 1984 & instructions **Head:** Hispanic **Head Markings:** inside rim © Mattel Inc, 1983 **Arms:** bent **Body:** dark brown tnt **Body Markings:** © Mattel Inc 1966/ Taiwan **Notes:** box liner may be hot pink or metallic

Model #: 1022 **Name:** Tropical Barbie black version **Box Date:** 1985 **Hair Color:** red with black streaks **Hairstyle:** side part ponytail at nape of neck held with yellow fabric flower, twisted mid-thigh ponytail **Face:** light brown eyes, black brows, light red lips & blush **Clothing:** 1-piece off-the-shoulder navy, yellow, hot pink swimsuit **Extras:** yellow pointed brush **Head:** Hispanic **Head Markings:** inside rim © Mattel Inc, 1983 **Arms:** ptr **Body:** dark brown tnt **Body Markings:** © Mattel Inc 1966/ China

Model #: 1739 **Name:** Funtime Barbie black version **Box Date:** 1986 **Hair Color:** red brown **Hairstyle:** waist length, 1/2 of front section in ponytail at side, other 1/2 pulled back, ends curled under **Face:** brown eyes, black brows, hot pink lips & blush **Clothing:** pink metallic crop top with short sleeves, glitter disk in center of bodice with clock hands, matching pink shorts, pink disk earrings, pink watch, blue, lavender & coral knee socks, pink tennis shoes, pink metallic headband, pink wrap sunglasses **Extras:** pink oval brush, child's digital watch with pink band **Booklet:** BWOF 1987 & instructions **Head:** Hispanic **Head Markings:** inside rim © Mattel Inc, 1983 **Arms:** bent or ptr **Body:** dark brown tnt **Body Markings:** © Mattel Inc.1966/ Philippines **Notes:** Philippine dolls developing blotches on legs

Model #: 1756 **Name:** Jewel Secrets Barbie black version **Box Date:** 1986 **Hair Color:** brunette **Hairstyle:** side part, front section pulled to side, remainder sectioned into 3 with bands on ends, thigh length **Face:** brown eyes, brown brows, hot pink lips & blush **Clothing:** silver halter mini dress with full skirt, pink satin & silver glitter stripe bag for child which doubles as full skirt for doll, blue accent ruffle mini skirt, silver & pink jeweled choker, rhinestone stud earrings & ring, narrow clear silver glitter pumps **Extras:** pink oval brush & "The Secret of the Magic Jewels" book **Booklet:** BWOF 1986 & instructions **Head:** Hispanic **Head Markings:** inside rim © Mattel Inc, 1983 **Arms:** bent **Body:** dark brown tnt **Body Markings:** © Mattel Inc.1966/ Philippines

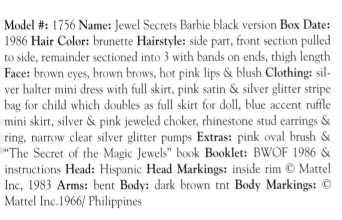

Model #: 3296 **Name:** Super Hair Barbie black version **Box Date:** 1986 **Hair Color:** brunette & red **Hairstyle:** partial topknot held with white curler in front, rest waist length with ends curled under **Face:** brown eyes, brown brows, deep pink lips & blush **Clothing:** 1-piece long sleeve high collar jumpsuit with gold & silver trim on bodice, wide silver belt, rhinestone stud earrings & ring, narrow white pumps **Extras:** purple oval brush & matching mirror, fake hair dryer, hair ornament, 4 barrettes, small comb & brush, assorted ribbons **Booklet:** BWOF 1986 & instructions **Head:** Hispanic **Head Markings:** inside rim © Mattel Inc, 1983 **Arms:** bent **Body:** dark brown tnt **Body Markings:** © Mattel Inc.1966/ Philippines

Model #: 4552 **Name:** Perfume Pretty Barbie black version **Box Date:** 1987 **Hair Color:** brownish red **Hairstyle:** sides & front pulled up with pink ribbon, rest mid-thigh length with bangs **Face:** lavender eyes, black brows, hot pink lips & blush **Clothing:** pink stretch halter gown with multi-layer tulle flared skirt at mid calf, pink bow detail on bodice, pink tulle bolero jacket, pink bow stud earrings & ring, clear & silver dot bow necklace, wide pink bow pumps **Extras:** pink oval brush, 1/2 circle comb, Barbie fragrance perfume & sheet of cardboard punch outs **Booklet:** Perfume Pretty Barbie Tips & instructions **Head:** Christie **Head Markings:** © Mattel Inc./ 1987 **Arms:** bent **Body:** dark brown tnt **Body Markings:** © Mattel Inc.1966/ Philippines

Model #: 1605 **Name:** Superstar Barbie black version **Box Date:** 1988 **Hair Color:** black **Hairstyle:** wavy waist length **Face:** light brown eyes, black brows, frosted pink lips & blush **Clothing:** pink nylon sleeveless top trimmed in silver with matching mini skirt, full tiered overskirt with silver stars, faux fur boa, clear & silver star drop earrings & ring, wide pink pumps **Extras:** square comb, child's pink bracelet, silver star charm & sheet of cardboard punch outs **Booklet:** BWOF 1988 **Head:** Christie **Head Markings:** © Mattel Inc./ 1987 **Arms:** bent **Body:** dark brown tnt **Body Markings:** © Mattel Inc 1966/ China

Model #: 4824 **Name:** Animal Lovin' Barbie black version **Box Date:** 1989 **Hair Color:** black **Hairstyle:** front & sides pulled back rest mid-back length, ends curled under, gold net scarf tied across forehead **Face:** brown eyes, black brows, hot pink lips & blush **Clothing:** metallic gold halter top with pink sleeveless animal print vest, matching mini skirt with sewn in panties, pink dangle earrings & ring, plastic panda bear, pink hiking boots **Extras:** pink oval brush & sheet of cardboard punch outs **Booklet:** BWOF 1988 **Head:** Christie **Head Markings:** © Mattel Inc./ 1987 **Arms:** bent **Body:** dark brown tnt **Body Markings:** © Mattel Inc 1966/ Malaysia

Model #: 7080 **Name:** Dance Magic Barbie black version **Box Date:** 1989 **Hair Color:** black **Hairstyle:** waist length, ends curled under **Face:** brown eyes, black brows, fuchsia lips & blush **Clothing:** pink & iridescent bodysuit with white iridescent trim, tulle boa, long skirt with pink underskirt, iridescent fan, metallic pink drop earrings, choker, ring, white ballet slippers, wide pink pumps **Extras:** white oval brush, pink wash cloth, applicator to change lip color, sheet of cardboard punch outs **Booklet:** BWOF 1988 & instructions **Head:** Christie **Head Markings:** © Mattel Inc./ 1987 **Arms:** bent **Body:** dark brown tnt **Body Markings:** © Mattel Inc 1966/ Malaysia

Model #: 9916 **Name:** Flight Time Barbie black version **Box Date:** 1989 **Hair Color:** black **Hairstyle:** sides pulled back, rest waist length, ends curled under **Face:** brown eyes, black brows, hot pink lips & blush **Clothing:** white sleeveless blouse with gold tie, pink jacket, matching straight knee-length skirt, multicolor full gold trimmed mini skirt & tie, pink briefcase, pink pilot's hat, gold stud earrings & ring, pink wrist accent, narrow pink pumps **Extras:** pink oval brush, child's pink Barbie wings, sheet of stickers, sheet of cardboard punch outs **Booklet:** BWOF 1988 & instructions **Head:** Christie **Head Markings:** © Mattel Inc./ 1987 **Arms:** bent **Body:** dark brown tnt **Body Markings:** © Mattel Inc 1966/ Malaysia

Model #: 7348 **Name:** Ice Capades Barbie black version **Box Date:** 1989 **Hair Color:** black **Hairstyle:** front & sides pulled up, rest waist length, ends curled under, iridescent teardrop hat with lilac, pink & turquoise sheer scarves **Face:** brown eyes, black brows, hot pink lips & blush **Clothing:** pink & iridescent bodysuit with multi-petal skirt of pink, turquoise & lilac glitter chiffon, gold ring, white ice skates **Extras:** pink-purple oval brush & sheet of cardboard punch outs **Booklet:** BWOF 1988 **Head:** Christie **Head Markings:** © Mattel Inc./ 1987 **Arms:** bent **Body:** dark brown tnt **Body Markings:** © Mattel Inc 1966/ Malaysia

Model #: 4770 **Name:** UNICEF Barbie black version **Box Date:** 1989 **Hair Color:** brunette **Hairstyle:** 1 side & front pulled into ponytail, rest waist length, ends curled **Face:** hazel eyes, black brows, red lips & blush **Clothing:** strapless gown with white bodice, full skirt of blue tulle with metallic stars & purple underskirt, long white handless gloves, red & gold sash with star trim, light blue stud earrings, pendant, ring, wide royal blue pumps **Extras:** 2-piece clear stand & white oval brush **Booklet:** Rights of the Child **Head:** Christie **Head Markings:** © Mattel Inc./ 1987 **Arms:** bent **Body:** dark brown tnt **Body Markings:** © Mattel Inc 1966/ China

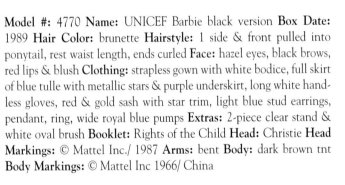

Model #: 7011 **Name:** Wedding Fantasy Barbie black version **Box Date:** 1989 **Hair Color:** black **Hairstyle:** waist length, ends curled under **Face:** lavender eyes, black brows, hot pink lips & blush **Clothing:** 2-piece gown, white satin top with iridescent trim at bodice and collar, lace leg of mutton sleeves, full white satin skirt with iridescent lace overlay, white tulle veil with white beaded halo, pearl stud earrings & ring, pink fabric flower & iridescent tulle bouquet, pantyhose with sewn in white panties, teddy, garter, wide white pumps **Extras:** 2-piece pearl stand, white oval brush & punch out **Head:** Christie **Head Markings:** © Mattel Inc./ 1987 **Arms:** bent **Body:** dark brown tnt **Body Markings:** © Mattel Inc 1966/ China

Model #: 2930 Name: Western Fun Barbie black version Box Date: 1989 Hair Color: brunette Hairstyle: sides pulled to back of head, rest waist length Face: brown eyes, black brows, hot pink lips & blush Clothing: turquoise crop top, multicolor mini skirt, pink fringe long sleeve short jacket, turquoise stretch pants, pink belt, hat with ribbon hatband, turquoise drop earrings, necklace, ring, belt, pink cowboy boots Extras: turquoise oval brush & sheet of cardboard punch outs Booklet: BWOF 1988 Head: Christie Head Markings: © Mattel Inc./ 1987 Arms: bent Body: dark brown tnt Body Markings: © Mattel Inc 1966/ Malaysia

Model #: 9603 Name: Bathtime Fun Barbie black version Box Date: 1990 Hair Color: black Hairstyle: shoulder-length ponytail with blue foam rubber flower accent, ends curled under, bangs Face: brown eyes, black brows, deep pink lips & blush Clothing: stretch nylon 1-piece multicolor swimsuit of pink, yellow, aqua, white, foam rubber light blue scalloped skirt & bracelet, pink stud earrings & ring Extras: white oval brush, can of foam soap & sheet of cardboard punch outs Head: Christie Head Markings: © Mattel Inc./ 1987 Arms: bent Body: dark brown tnt Body Markings: © Mattel Inc 1966/ Malaysia

Model #: 7134 Name: Costume Ball Barbie black version Box Date: 1990 Hair Color: black Hairstyle: front & sides loosely pulled back, waist length, ends curled under Face: brown eyes, black brows, deep pink lips & blush Clothing: mini dress with iridescent spaghetti strap bodice, pink tulle boa, pink overskirt with iridescent print accent, child's mask trimmed with rickrack, butterfly wings, pink metallic stud earrings & ring, pink scepter, mask holder, wide pink pumps Extras: pink oval brush, sheet of cardboard punch outs Booklet: IIB 1990 & instructions Head: Christie Head Markings: © Mattel Inc./ 1987 Arms: bent Body: dark brown tnt Body Markings: © Mattel Inc 1966/ Malaysia

Model #: 9561 Name: Happy Birthday Barbie black version Box Date: 1990 Hair Color: brunette Hairstyle: 1 side pulled up & held with pink fabric flower & lilac ribbon, bangs, rest waist length, ends curled under Face: brown eyes, black brows, hot pink lips & blush Clothing: 2-piece gown, solid pink bodice with pink multicolor puffed sleeves, large multicolor pink full skirt, Happy Birthday sash, silver stud earrings & ring, wide pink pearl pumps Extras: 2-piece pearl stand, pink pearl comb Booklet: IIB 1990 Head: Christie Head Markings: © Mattel Inc./ 1987 Arms: bent Body: dark brown tnt Body Markings: © Mattel Inc 1966/ Malaysia

Model #: 7028 **Name:** Summit Barbie black version **Box Date:** 1990 **Hair Color:** brunette **Hairstyle:** 1 side & front pulled up in band, rest waist length, ends curled under **Face:** brown eyes, black brows, red lips & blush **Clothing:** gown with gold lamé bodice, full white skirt, white tulle & gold glitter overskirt, white bolero jacket with gold braid trim, gold stud earrings & ring, wide white pumps **Extras:** red oval brush, sheet of cardboard punch outs & Summit badge **Booklet:** 1st Summit 1990 **Head:** Christie **Head Markings:** © Mattel Inc./ 1987 **Arms:** bent **Body:** dark brown tnt **Body Markings:** © Mattel Inc 1966/ China

Model #: 3245 **Name:** American Beauty Queen Barbie black version **Box Date:** 1991 **Hair Color:** black **Hairstyle:** waist length, ends curled under, silver tiara **Face:** brown eyes, black brows, hot pink lips & blush **Clothing:** off-the-shoulder silver, pink & blue gown, converts to silver swimsuit & ballet tutu, long silver handless gloves, silver stud earrings & ring, pearl ballet shoes, wide pearl pumps **Extras:** pearl oval brush & sheet of cardboard punch outs **Booklet:** 1991 PB **Head:** Christie **Head Markings:** © Mattel Inc./ 1987 **Arms:** bent **Body:** dark brown tnt **Body Markings:** © Mattel Inc 1966/ China

Model #: 7951 **Name:** Bath Magic Barbie black version **Box Date:** 1991 **Hair Color:** black **Hairstyle:** sides pulled up into mid-back-length ponytail tied with hot pink ribbon, ends curled under, bangs **Face:** brown eyes, black brows, hot pink lips & blush **Clothing:** yellow & pink splatter nylon bodysuit, inverse pattern full mini skirt, hot pink stud earrings & ring **Extras:** hot pink oval brush & 3 color capsules containing foam rubber decorations **Booklet:** instructions **Head:** Christie **Head Markings:** © Mattel Inc./ 1987 **Arms:** bent **Body:** dark brown tnt **Body Markings:** © Mattel Inc 1966/ Malaysia

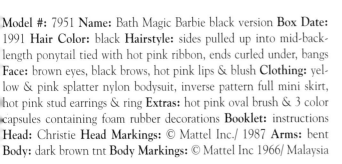

Model #: 4051 **Name:** Birthday Surprise Barbie black version **Box Date:** 1991 **Hair Color:** brunette **Hairstyle:** sides & front pulled up & twisted, held with a peach satin ribbon, rest waist length, ends curled **Face:** brown eyes, black brows, orange lips & blush **Clothing:** peach gown with white iridescent accents on bodice & peach fabric flowers at neckline, tulle glitter skirt with pearl accents, sewn in panties, peach drop earrings & ring, wide peach pearl pumps **Extras:** 2-piece pearl stand & pearl oval brush & gift=bracelet, earrings or necklace **Booklet:** 1991 PB **Head:** Christie **Head Markings:** © Mattel Inc./ 1987 **Arms:** bent **Body:** dark brown tnt **Body Markings:** © Mattel Inc 1966/ Malaysia

Model #: 3445 Name: Snap 'N Play Barbie black version Box Date: 1991 Hair Color: black Hairstyle: sides pulled up to small ponytail, rest waist length, ends curled with bangs Face: brown eyes, black brows, fuchsia lips & blush Clothing: yellow midi plastic top with fabric bow, tiered mini skirt of yellow vinyl & blue, white, black & pink pattern fabric, extra mini skirt different pattern same colors, extra top pink plastic snap-on hair accessories, wide yellow pumps Extras: yellow oval brush Head: Christie Head Markings: © Mattel Inc./ 1987 Arms: ptr Body: dark brown tnt, painted pink bra & panties Body Markings: © Mattel Inc 1966/ China

Model #: 5950 Name: Sparkle Eyes Barbie black version Box Date: 1991 Hair Color: brunette Hairstyle: sides pulled back, curly bangs, rest thigh length, ends curled under Face: green rhinestone eyes, black brows, frosted deep pink lips & blush Clothing: silver lamé fitted mini dress with sweetheart neck & spaghetti straps, pink glitter tulle full overskirt & matching boa, metallic pink drop earrings, choker, ring, pink Brazil pumps Extras: pink oval brush & sheet of cardboard punch outs Head: Christie Head Markings: © Mattel Inc./ 1987 Arms: bent Body: dark brown tnt Body Markings: © Mattel Inc 1966/ Malaysia

Model #: 1612 Name: Teen Talk Barbie black version Box Date: 1991 Hair Color: dark red Hairstyle: curly bangs, crinkled, mid-thigh length Face: lavender eyes, black brows, hot pink lips & blush Clothing: pink, white & aqua top with spaghetti straps & sweetheart neck, matching jacket, sheer multicolor skirt, pink knee-high lace trim stretch pants, matching shorts, aqua hat with 3 rose trim, pink stud earrings & ring, matching bag, aqua tennis shoes, wide pink pumps Extras: pink oval brush, 2 batteries Booklet: instructions Head: Christie Head Markings: © Mattel Inc./ 1987 Arms: bent Body: dark brown talker Body Markings: © Mattel Inc 1966/ China Notes: push button on back for talk, black or dark red hair colors, wide variations in statements, face paint, hairstyles, outfit styles and combinations

Model #: 5948 Name: Totally Hair Barbie black version Box Date: 1991 Hair Color: black Hairstyle: crimped floor length with back-swept bangs, pulled up with green scarf Face: lavender-green eyes, black brows, frosted coral lips Clothing: scoop neck long sleeve straight mini dress with swirled multicolor pattern of turquoise, blue, hot pink, green & white, white panties, blue triangle earrings, ring, wide blue pumps Extras: blue hair pick, rubber bands, Dep styling gel, 4 hair ornaments Booklet: styling tips Head: Christie Head Markings: © Mattel Inc./ 1987 Arms: bent Body: dark brown tnt Body Markings: © Mattel Inc 1966/ Malaysia

Model #: 3830 Name: Bath Blast Barbie black version Box Date: 1992 Hair Color: black Hairstyle: right side pulled up into ponytail, mid-back length, ends curled under, bangs Face: lavender eyes, black brows, pink lips & blush Clothing: 1-piece nylon fuchsia swimsuit with white bubbles & yellow, blue & green dots, fuchsia stud earrings & ring Extras: fuchsia oval brush, can of blue foam & yellow flower shape decorative tip accessory for foam Head: Christie Head Markings: © Mattel Inc./ 1987 Arms: bent Body: dark brown tnt Body Markings: © Mattel Inc 1966/ Malaysia

Model #: 7948 Name: Birthday Party Barbie black version Box Date: 1992 Hair Color: black Hairstyle: sides & top pulled back with gold-edged pink ribbon, bangs, waist length, ends curled Face: brown eyes, black brows, pink frosted lips & blush Clothing: aqua, pink, white gown with full skirt trimmed with ruffles, floral stencil & gold glitter, large puffed sleeves, aqua bodice, pink stud earrings, pendant, ring, birthday cake, wide pink pearl pumps Extras: 2-piece pink pearl stand Head: Christie Head Markings: © Mattel Inc./ 1987 Arms: bent Body: dark brown tnt Body Markings: © Mattel Inc 1966/ Malaysia

Model #: 2374 Name: Earring Magic Barbie black version Box Date: 1992 Hair Color: black Hairstyle: waist length crinkled, bangs, sides pulled up to top of head, ponytail held with silver band Face: lavender eyes, black brows, hot pink lips & blush Clothing: hot pink vinyl mini dress with sheer bodice & long sleeves, silver hoop & sun dangle earrings & ring, silver belt with 2 dangle stars, wide hot pink pumps Extras: hot pink oval brush & pair of silver dangling heart clip-on earrings for child Booklet: BFG 1992 PB Head: Christie Head Markings: © Mattel Inc./ 1987 Arms: bent Body: dark brown tnt Body Markings: © Mattel Inc 1966/ Malaysia

Model #: 11054 Name: Romantic Bride Barbie black version Box Date: 1992 Hair Color: black Hairstyle: mid-back length with ends curled, bangs Face: brown eyes, dark brown brows, pink lips & blush Clothing: long white gown with satin bodice & leg of mutton sleeves, tulle overskirt, pink tulle bouquet & trim, white tulle veil with pearl trim, white stud earrings & ring, wide white pumps Extras: pink oval brush Head: Christie Head Markings: © Mattel Inc./ 1987 Arms: bent Body: dark brown tnt Body Markings: © Mattel Inc 1966/ China

Model #: 3836 Name: Secret Hearts Barbie black version Box Date: 1992 Hair Color: brunette Hairstyle: front pulled back, rest waist length with ends turned under Face: brown eyes, black brows, hot pink lips & blush Clothing: sleeveless iridescent gown with ruffle at v-neck, full skirt with white glitter tulle trimmed with white ribbon & pink change-color hearts, heart drop earrings, pendant, silver ring, wide white pumps Extras: pearl oval brush, heart water tray & iridescent heart ice cube holder Booklet: instructions Head: Christie Head Markings: © Mattel Inc./ 1987 Arms: bent Body: dark brown tnt Body Markings: © Mattel Inc 1966/ China

Model #: 11184 Name: Bedtime Barbie black version Box Date: 1993 Hair Color: black Hairstyle: front & 1 side pulled into small ponytail, rest thigh length, ends curled under Face: brown eyes, black brows, deep pink lips Clothing: pink flannel long nightgown with white lace trim & pink rose with green ribbon, pink wash cloth, pink toothbrush, sewn on slippers Extras: pink oval brush Head: Christie Head Markings: © Mattel Inc./ 1987 Arms: soft Body: dark brown soft body Body Markings: cloth tag:© Mattel, Inc.1993/ El Segundo, CA 90245 U.S.A./ surface washable(repeated)/ Reg.No.PA-60/ All New Materials/ Consisting of Polyester Fibers/ Made in China Notes: painted eyes & mouth open & close with ice water & warm water

Model #: 11817 Name: Bicyclin' Barbie black version Box Date: 1993 Hair Color: black Hairstyle: sides & top pulled up to ponytail, rest thigh length, bangs Face: brown eyes, black brows, hot pink lips & blush Clothing: green & pink bicycling outfit: jacket, midi top & pants, purple sunglasses, pink helmet, pink stud earrings, multicolor bicycle with flag, pinwheel, water bottle & pump accessories, hot pink bicycle shoes Extras: hot pink oval brush Booklet: instructions Head: Christie Head Markings: © Mattel Inc./ 1987 Arms: gymnast Body: dark brown gymnast Body Markings: © 1993 Mattel, Inc./ China:

Model #: 11334 Name: Birthday Barbie black version Box Date: 1993 Hair Color: brunette Hairstyle: front & sides pulled back with turquoise ribbon & fabric hair ornament, rest waist length, ends curled under Face: hazel eyes, black brows, fuchsia lips & blush Clothing: turquoise gown, multicolor white, pink, coral, glitter full skirt with matching puffed sleeves, Happy Birthday sash, pearl stud earrings & ring, wide turquoise pumps Extras: hot pink oval brush & sheet of cardboard punch outs Head: Christie Head Markings: © Mattel Inc./ 1987 Arms: bent Body: dark brown tnt Body Markings: © Mattel Inc 1966/ Malaysia

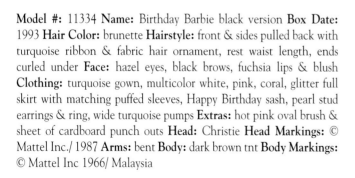

70

Model #: 11831 Name: Camp Fun Barbie black version Box Date: 1993 Hair Color: red Hairstyle: front section pulled into pink rubber band, rest waist length, curly bangs Face: green-brown eyes, black brows, hot pink lips & blush Clothing: white appliqué T-shirt, pink windbreaker, denim shorts, white anklets, pink backpack, yellow lantern & sunglasses, orange binoculars, turquoise stud earrings & ring, fuchsia hiking boots Extras: fuchsia oval brush Booklet: 1993 PB & instructions Head: Christie Head Markings: © Mattel Inc./ 1987 Arms: bent Body: dark tan tnt Body Markings: © Mattel Inc 1966/ China Notes: hair changes color in sunlight

Model #: 11814 Name: Dr. Barbie black version Box Date: 1993 Hair Color: black Hairstyle: ponytail held with blue band, curly bangs Face: brown eyes, black brows, deep pink lips & blush Clothing: blue sleeveless mini dress with white lab coat, blue bow earrings & ring, pink stethoscope in chest, white medical bag, baby, wide royal blue pumps Extras: royal blue oval brush, sheet of band aids, sheet of cardboard punch outs, light blue ear checker, reflex hammer, baby bottle, rattle, vitamin bottle, bandage box, clipboard, cough syrup bottle, syringe, baby food jar, blood pressure checker, beeper, pacifier, lotion bottle Booklet: instructions Head: Christie & baby Head Markings: Barbie=© Mattel Inc/ 1987 Baby= © M.I. 1985 Arms: bent Body: dark brown tnt Body Markings: Barbie=© Mattel Inc 1966/ China Baby=© 1973/ Mattel Inc/ China Notes: baby available in four varieties, Toys R Us exclusive in 1995 model #14315 packaged with 3 babies

Model #: 10522 Name: Fountain Mermaid Barbie black version Box Date: 1993 Hair Color: pink with iridescent strands Hairstyle: thigh length, bangs Face: brown eyes, black brows, hot pink lips & blush Clothing: hot pink satin spaghetti strap crop top with gold seashell & pearl ornament, matching mermaid skirt trimmed with iridescent pink & white glitter tulle & gold sequins, pink fountain crown, white stud earrings Extras: pink seahorse comb, fountain pump Booklet: instructions Head: Christie Head Markings: © Mattel Inc./ 1987 Arms: ptr Body: dark brown tnt Body Markings: © Mattel Inc 1966/ China

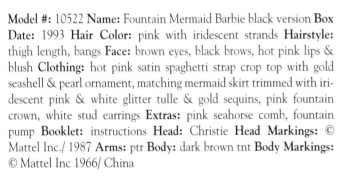

Model #: 11332 Name: Glitter Hair Barbie black version Box Date: 1993 Hair Color: black Hairstyle: mid-calf length, curly bangs Face: brown eyes, black brows, pink lips & blush Clothing: sleeveless mini dress with appliquéd hot pink top, black inset belt, turquoise glitter short skirt, pink dangle earrings & ring, pink visor, pink tennis shoes Extras: pink applicator comb & tube of pink glitter gel Booklet: instructions Head: Christie Head Markings: © Mattel Inc./ 1987 Arms: bent Body: dark brown tnt, "B" panties Body Markings: © Mattel Inc 1966/ China

Model #: 12153 Name: Gymnast Barbie black version Box Date: 1993 Hair Color: black Hairstyle: waist-length ponytail braided with hot pink ribbon, bangs Face: brown eyes, black brows, hot pink lips & blush Clothing: bodysuit with pink & gold glitter sleeves & half bodice, remainder yellow, orange, green & blue, hot pink footless tights, pair of white anklets, gold stud earrings & ring, 3 hair ribbons, gold medal, pink duffel bag with "B" monogram, 2 orange hand weights, hot pink high-top athletic shoes Extras: blue oval brush Head: Christie Head Markings: © Mattel Inc./ 1987 Arms: gymnast Body: dark brown gymnast Body Markings: © 1993 Mattel, Inc./ China:

Model #: 11224 Name: Locket Surprise Barbie black version Box Date: 1993 Hair Color: black Hairstyle: side part, crinkled thigh length Face: lavender-green eyes, black brows, deep pink lips & blush Clothing: pink elastic ruffle around bodice, pink glitter knee-length skirt with iridescent edging, gold filigree drop earrings, ring, wide pink pumps Extras: pink oval brush, heart locket lip gloss insert, photo of Ken, blush Booklet: instructions Head: Christie Head Markings: © Mattel Inc./ 1987 Arms: bent Body: dark brown b/l, pink locket Body Markings: © Mattel Inc.1966/ Indonesia Notes: chest opens for storage of small accessories

Model #: 10058 Name: Paint' n Dazzle Barbie black version Box Date: 1993 Hair Color: black Hairstyle: sides & front pulled back with blue band, rest mid-thigh length Face: brown eyes, black brows, deep orange lips & blush Clothing: orange mini dress with lace trim at hem, denim jacket with floral fabric insert & sequin trim, matching floral print stretch pants, royal blue round earrings & ring, wide royal blue pumps Extras: royal blue oval brush, sequins, pearls, 2 bottles Tulip fabric paint Booklet: instructions Head: Christie Head Markings: © Mattel Inc./ 1987 Arms: bent Body: dark brown tnt Body Markings: © Mattel Inc 1966/ China

Model #: 11734 Name: Swim 'n Dive Barbie black version Box Date: 1993 Hair Color: black Hairstyle: 1 section of hair above each ear twisted & tied in back, rest waist length, bangs Face: lavender eyes, black brows, hot pink lips & blush Clothing: hot pink with silver glitter long sleeve 1-piece wetsuit, silver stud earrings, scuba mask, tanks that really propel doll in water, flippers Extras: hot pink oval brush Booklet: instructions Head: Christie Head Markings: © Mattel Inc./ 1987 Arms: gymnast Body: dark brown gymnast Body Markings: © 1993 Mattel, Inc./ Malaysia

Model #: 10521 **Name:** Twinkle Lights Barbie black version **Box Date:** 1993 **Hair Color:** brunette **Hairstyle:** front & sides in twisted ponytail, curly bangs, rest waist length, ends curled under **Face:** brown eyes, black brows, hot pink lips & blush **Clothing:** sleeveless gown with iridescent white bodice, pink glitter tulle full skirt with on/off belt, crystal drop earrings, pendant, ring, wide hot pink pumps **Extras:** pink oval brush & 2 batteries **Booklet:** instructions **Head:** Christie **Head Markings:** © Mattel Inc./ 1987 **Arms:** bent **Body:** dark brown tone tnt fiber optic strands imbedded in chest, partial white painted bra **Body Markings:** front pelvis ©1966,1992/ Mattel, Inc/ China

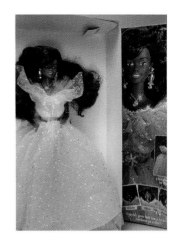

Model #: 10539 **Name:** Western Stampin' Barbie black version **Box Date:** 1993 **Hair Color:** brunette **Hairstyle:** parted on side, sides pulled to back of head, rest crinkled thigh length **Face:** lavender eyes, black brows, hot pink lips & blush **Clothing:** silver top, turquoise & silver belt with white fringe, silver lamé mini skirt with white panties, turquoise long sleeve short jacket with silver trim, turquoise cowboy hat with silver trim, silver cowboy boot earrings, ring, turquoise cowboy boots with rolling stampers **Extras:** turquoise oval brush, ink pad, silver glitter & sheet of cardboard punch outs **Booklet:** instructions **Head:** Christie **Head Markings:** © Mattel Inc./ 1987 **Arms:** bent **Body:** dark brown tnt **Body Markings:** © Mattel Inc 1966/ China

Model #: 13258 **Name:** Baywatch Barbie black version **Box Date:** 1994 **Hair Color:** black **Hairstyle:** thigh length **Face:** brown eyes, black brows, red lips & blush **Clothing:** white midi top, 1-piece red swimsuit with Baywatch lifeguard insignia, red nylon jacket, blue, red & yellow lifeguard shorts, blue stud earrings & ring, white tennis shoes, red Baywatch visor & silver whistle on black cord **Extras:** white oval brush, red Frisbee, yellow binoculars, gray & white "talking" dolphin, red flotation device **Head:** Christie **Head Markings:** © Mattel Inc./ 1987 **Arms:** bent **Body:** dark brown tnt **Body Markings:** © Mattel Inc 1966/ Malaysia

Model #: 12955 **Name:** Birthday Barbie black version **Box Date:** 1994 **Hair Color:** brunette **Hairstyle:** top pulled back with pink fabric & light blue ribbon, bangs, rest waist length, ends curled under **Face:** hazel eyes, black brows, fuchsia lips & blush **Clothing:** white gown, full multicolor teal, coral, hot pink, glitter skirt with matching puffed sleeves, Happy Birthday blue sash, pink stud earrings & ring, wide white pumps **Extras:** hot pink oval brush & sheet of cardboard punch outs **Head:** Christie **Head Markings:** © Mattel Inc./ 1987 **Arms:** bent **Body:** dark brown tnt, pink panties **Body Markings:** © Mattel Inc 1966/ Malaysia

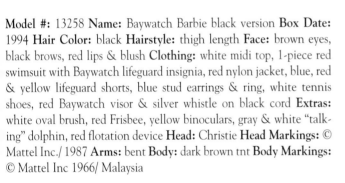

Model #: 12444 **Name:** Bubble Angel Barbie black version **Box Date:** 1994 **Hair Color:** brunette **Hairstyle:** thigh-length crinkled ponytail with curly bangs **Face:** brown eyes, black brows, red lips & blush **Clothing:** iridescent blue bodysuit with sewn in shimmery glitter pantyhose, iridescent fan bodice & overskirt, silver stud earrings, choker, ring, clear blue plastic wings to make bubbles, clear blue pointed flats **Extras:** blue oval brush, bubble solution, wand & tray **Booklet:** instructions **Head:** Christie **Head Markings:** © Mattel Inc./ 1987 **Arms:** Shani **Body:** dark brown tnt **Body Markings:** © Mattel Inc 1966/ Malaysia

Model #: 13052 **Name:** Butterfly Princess Barbie black version **Box Date:** 1994 **Hair Color:** black **Hairstyle:** thigh length crinkled, bangs, sides pulled up with pink satin ribbon **Face:** brown eyes, black brows, deep pink lips & blush **Clothing:** long full skirt gown with multicolor top and pink tulle overskirt with iridescent butterfly accents, sewn in panties, gold stud earrings & ring, pink and green flower magnetic magic wand makes butterflies move, wide pink pearl pumps **Extras:** pink pearl oval brush, butterfly princess fold-out pamphlet, ring for child **Booklet:** instructions **Head:** Christie **Head Markings:** © Mattel Inc./ 1987 **Arms:** bent **Body:** dark brown tnt **Body Markings:** © Mattel Inc.1966/ Indonesia

Model #: 12642 **Name:** Cut and Style Barbie black version **Box Date:** 1994 **Hair Color:** black **Hairstyle:** ankle length, bangs, Velcro in back of head **Face:** brown eyes, black brows, red lips & blush **Clothing:** orange vinyl vest with 3 gold buttons, full orange nylon mini skirt with sewn in panties & matching tulle slip, gold & black drop earrings, gold ring, black choker & gold pendant, wide orange pumps **Extras:** orange oval brush, matching safety scissors, length of black hair with Velcro, yellow headband, lime green headband, 2 fabric ribbons & 4 colored rubber bands **Booklet:** 2 instructions **Head:** Christie **Head Markings:** © Mattel Inc./ 1987 **Arms:** bent **Body:** dark brown tnt **Body Markings:** © Mattel Inc.1966/ Indonesia

Model #: 12143 **Name:** Dance 'N Twirl Barbie black version **Box Date:** 1994 **Hair Color:** brunette **Hairstyle:** front & sides pulled up to top of head, tied with 2 shades of pink satin ribbon, rest thigh length **Face:** brown eyes, black brows, deep pink lips & blush **Clothing:** pink & white pattern strapless full skirted gown with fringe at hem, silver & crystal bead drop earrings, ring & wide pink pumps **Extras:** pink oval brush, doll stand, dance base, radio controller to make doll dance **Booklet:** instructions **Head:** Christie **Head Markings:** © Mattel Inc./ 1987 **Arms:** bent **Body:** dark brown tnt **Body Markings:** © Mattel Inc 1966/ China

Model #: 13086 **Name:** Dance Moves Barbie black version **Box Date:** 1994 **Hair Color:** black **Hairstyle:** hip length crinkled, sides pulled up to top of head held with blue band, bangs **Face:** brown eyes, black brows, red lips & blush **Clothing:** blue & silver metallic scoop neck long sleeve crop top, silver suspenders on metallic blue shorts, silver & blue metallic tights, silver hoop earrings & ring, black Jazzie flats **Extras:** blue oval brush, fake blue cassette player with headphones & boom box, black hand held microphone **Booklet:** instructions **Head:** Christie **Head Markings:** © Mattel Inc./ 1987 **Arms:** bent **Body:** dark brown tnt with gymnast legs **Body Markings:** © Mattel Inc 1966/ Malaysia **Notes:** arms click into position

Model #: 13512 **Name:** Hot Skatin' Barbie Black **Box Date:** 1994 **Hair Color:** black **Hairstyle:** thigh-length ponytail with curled bangs **Face:** brown eyes, black brows, hot pink lips & blush **Clothing:** 1-piece stretch multicolor bodysuit with silver glitter swirls, yellow vinyl belt with purple water bottle, yellow vinyl knee pads, yellow inline skates with purple wheels, pair of white ice skates, purple helmet, sheer pink glitter ice skating skirt, pink stud earrings **Extras:** hot pink oval brush **Head:** Christie **Head Markings:** © Mattel Inc./ 1987 **Arms:** gymnast **Body:** dark brown gymnast **Body Markings:** © 1993 Mattel, Inc./ Malaysia

Model #: 12697 **Name:** Slumber Party Barbie black version **Box Date:** 1994 **Hair Color:** black **Hairstyle:** crinkled thigh length, curly bangs, light blue fabric headband with white stars & moons **Face:** lavender eyes, black brows, deep pink lips & blush **Clothing:** 2-piece blue & white dot pajamas trimmed in lace **Extras:** light blue oval brush, white wash cloth, sheet of dayglo stickers, clear zipper carrying case **Head:** Christie **Head Markings:** © Mattel Inc./ 1987 **Arms:** soft **Body:** dark brown soft body **Body Markings:** cloth tag:© Mattel, Inc.1993 or 94 or 95/El Segundo, CA 90245 U.S.A./ surface washable(repeated)/ Reg.No.PA-60/ All New Materials/ Consisting of Polyester Fibers/ Made in China **Notes:** painted eyes open and close with ice water & warm water

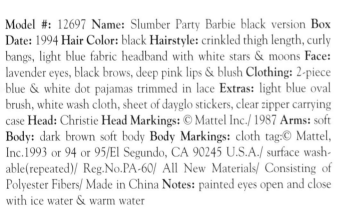

Model #: 12379 **Name:** Super Talk Barbie black version **Box Date:** 1994 **Hair Color:** black **Hairstyle:** thigh length crinkled **Face:** lilac-brown eyes, brown brows, hot pink lips & blush **Clothing:** white cotton bodysuit, blue denim long sleeve bolero jacket with gold cuffs & collar, jewel trim, blue denim mini skirt with gold ruffle, gold hoop earrings & ring, white scrunches, gold hiking boots **Extras:** white oval brush **Booklet:** instructions **Head:** Christie **Head Markings:** © Mattel Inc./ 1987 **Arms:** bent **Body:** dark brown tnt supertalk **Body Markings:** © Mattel Inc 1966/ China **Notes:** 1995 Toys R Us exclusive, smaller box, model number #14316 & 1995 box date (pictured, see caucasian version for larger box), says over 100,000 things, press button on back to talk

Model #: 13630 Name: Pretty Dreams Barbie black version Box Date: 1995 Hair Color: black Hairstyle: sides & front pulled back with white iridescent bow, thigh-length hair Face: brown eyes, black brows, deep pink lips & blush Clothing: pink velour long sleeve nightgown trimmed with white iridescent lace Extras: pink oval brush Head: supersize Head Markings: © 1976 Mattel Inc Body: dark brown 18" soft body Body Markings: cloth tag:© Mattel, Inc.1993 or 94 or 95/El Segundo, CA 90245 U.S.A./ surface washable(repeated)/ Reg.No.PA-60/ All New Materials/ Consisting of Polyester Fibers/ Made in China

Model #: 13915 Name: Teacher Barbie black version Box Date: 1995 Hair Color: black Hairstyle: top & sides pulled up with red band, bangs, rest thigh length, little girl has pigtails & bangs Face: brown eyes, black brows, red lips & blush Clothing: white long sleeve blouse with red ribbon tie, black school print short jumper, white stud earrings & ring, red glasses, 2 assorted little friends, girl wearing white & red playsuit, boy wearing blue & white playsuit with black suspenders, yellow & green desks, matching talking blackboard with clock, 2 books & pencils, eraser, chalk, sharpener Extras: red oval brush & cardboard punch out posters Booklet: instructions Head: Christie, girl & boy little friends Head Markings: Barbie=© Mattel Inc/ 1987 girl=© Mattel Inc 1976 boy=© Mattel 1995 Arms: 1 bent & 1 Shani Body: dark brown tnt, "B" panties Body Markings: Barbie=© Mattel Inc 1966/ Indonesia kids=© 1976 Mattel Inc/ Indonesia Notes: little boy & girl available in white & black with different hair colors

Hispanic Barbies

Model #: 1292 Name: Hispanic Barbie Box Date: 1979 Hair Color: black Hairstyle: mid-back length, middle part, cello on head Face: brown eyes, brown brows, peach lips & blush Clothing: knee-length dress with white scoop neck, long sleeved top, red full skirt with black & gold ribbon trim, wide black belt, black lace shawl, black & gold choker with red fabric rose, red hoop earrings & ring, extra red dangle earrings & necklace & hair ornament, black ankle straps Booklet: BWOF 1979 Head: Steffie Head Markings: inside rim © 1971 Mattel Inc & country Arms: bent Body: dark tan tnt Body Markings: © Mattel Inc 1966/ Taiwan

Model #: 5724 Name: Twirley Curls Barbie Hispanic version Box Date: 1982 Hair Color: black Hairstyle: side part, mid-thigh-length side ponytail banded at nape of neck Face: brown eyes, brown brows, rose lips & blush Clothing: hot pink halter-style bodysuit, matching long slim skirt with fabric ruffle & silver wide belt, rhinestone ring, hot pink mules Extras: pink pointed comb & brush, 4 white barrettes, 2 pink ribbons, purple chair with suction cups, pink twirley curler Booklet: instructions Head: Hispanic Head Markings: inside rim © Mattel Inc, 1983 Arms: bent Body: dark tan tnt Body Markings: © Mattel Inc 1966/ Taiwan

Model #: 4970 Name: Sun Gold Malibu Barbie Hispanic version Box Date: 1983 Hair Color: brunette Hairstyle: middle part, curly mid-back length Face: brown eyes, brown brows, rust lips & blush Clothing: gold 2-tone checked 1-piece swimsuit, pink, purple & black pairs of sunglasses, fold-out gold tote bag converts to blue mat Booklet: BWOF 1984 Head: Hispanic Head Markings: inside rim © Mattel Inc, 1983 Arms: ptr Body: dark tan tnt Body Markings: © Mattel, Inc. 1966/ Hong Kong

Model #: 4970 Name: Sunsational Malibu Barbie Hispanic version Box Date: 1983 Hair Color: black Hairstyle: middle part, sides pulled back, rest waist length Face: brown eyes, brown brows, rose lips & blush Clothing: turquoise 1-piece halter-style swimsuit with purple trim & flower appliqué, turquoise towel, purple mirror sunglasses Booklet: BWOF 1983 Head: Hispanic Head Markings: inside rim © Mattel Inc, 1983 Arms: ptr Body: dark tan tnt Body Markings: © Mattel, Inc. 1966/ Hong Kong

Model #: 7944 Name: Day-to-Night Barbie Hispanic version Box Date: 1984 Hair Color: brown & red streaked Hairstyle: side part with front sections pulled to back of head, rest waist length, ends curled under Face: green eyes, brown brows, dark mauve lips & blush Clothing: spaghetti strap metallic hot pink bodysuit, pink chiffon scarf, pink jacket with white lapels & buttons, matching reversible skirt, white hat with pink & white hatband, white briefcase, rhinestone stud earrings & ring, white plastic clutch purse with pink strap, hot pink mules, narrow white & pink pumps Extras: pink pointed comb, brush & sheet of cardboard punch outs Booklet: BWOF 1984 & instructions Head: Hispanic Head Markings: inside rim © Mattel Inc, 1983 Arms: bent Body: dark tan tnt Body Markings: © Mattel Inc 1966/ Taiwan

Model #: 1647 Name: Dream Glow Barbie Hispanic version Box Date: 1985 Hair Color: brunette Hairstyle: middle part, sides pulled back, rest thigh length Face: teal eyes, brown brows, pink lips & blush Clothing: halter-style gown with hot pink bodice trimmed in silver lace, full skirt of sheer pink fabric with white dayglo stars & silver lace, matching stole, rhinestone earrings, pendant, ring, pink plastic parasol, narrow pink pumps Extras: white pointed brush Booklet: BWOF 1985 & instructions Head: Hispanic Head Markings: inside rim © Mattel Inc, 1983 Arms: bent Body: dark tan tnt Body Markings: © Mattel Inc 1966/ Taiwan Notes: stars in outfit glow in the dark

Model #: 1646 Name: Tropical Barbie Hispanic version Box Date: 1985 Hair Color: brownish red Hairstyle: middle part, banded at nape of neck with yellow fabric flower, twisted mid-thigh ponytail Face: brown eyes, brown brows, peach lips & blush Clothing: 1-piece off-the-shoulder navy, yellow, hot pink swimsuit Extras: yellow pointed brush Booklet: BWOF 1986 Head: Hispanic Head Markings: inside rim © Mattel Inc, 1983 Arms: ptr Body: dark tan tnt Body Markings: © Mattel Inc 1966/ China

Model #: 2066 Name: Flight Time Barbie Hispanic version Box Date: 1989 Hair Color: brunette Hairstyle: sides pulled back, rest waist length, ends curled under Face: brown eyes, dark brown brows, deep pink lips & blush Clothing: white sleeveless blouse with gold tie, pink jacket, matching straight knee-length skirt, multicolor full gold trimmed mini skirt & tie, pink briefcase, pink pilot's hat, gold stud earrings & ring, pink wrist accent, narrow pink pumps Extras: pink oval brush, child's pink Barbie wings, sheet of stickers, sheet of cardboard punch outs Booklet: BWOF 1988 & instructions Head: Steffie Head Markings: inside rim © 1971 Mattel Inc & country Arms: bent Body: dark tan tnt Body Markings: © Mattel Inc 1966/ Malaysia

Model #: 4782 Name: UNICEF Barbie Hispanic version Box Date: 1989 Hair Color: brunette Hairstyle: 1 side & front pulled into ponytail, rest waist length, ends curled Face: brown eyes, black brows, red lips & blush Clothing: strapless gown with white bodice, full skirt of blue tulle with metallic stars & purple underskirt, long white handless gloves, red & gold sash with star trim, light blue stud earrings, pendant, ring, wide royal blue pumps Extras: 2-piece clear stand & white oval brush Booklet: Rights of the Child Head: Hispanic Head Markings: inside rim © Mattel Inc, 1983 Arms: bent Body: dark tan tnt Body Markings: © Mattel Inc 1966/ China

Model #: 7030 Name: Summit Barbie Hispanic version Box Date: 1990 Hair Color: brunette Hairstyle: 1 side & front pulled up in band, rest waist length, ends curled under Face: brown eyes, brown brows, red lips & blush Clothing: gown with gold lamé bodice, full white skirt, white tulle & gold glitter overskirt, white bolero jacket with gold braid trim, gold stud earrings & ring, wide white pumps Extras: red oval brush, sheet of cardboard punch outs & Summit badge Booklet: 1st Summit 1990 Head: Steffie Head Markings: inside rim © 1971 Mattel Inc & country Arms: bent Body: dark tan tnt Body Markings: © Mattel Inc 1966/ China

Model #: 13253 Name: Birthday Barbie Hispanic version Box Date: 1994 Hair Color: brunette Hairstyle: top pulled back with pink fabric & light blue ribbon, bangs, rest waist length, ends curled under Face: lavender eyes, brown brows, fuchsia lips & blush Clothing: white gown, full multicolor teal, coral, hot pink, glitter skirt with matching puffed sleeves, Happy Birthday blue sash, pink stud earrings & ring, wide white pumps Extras: hot pink oval brush & sheet of cardboard punch outs Head: Teresa Head Markings: © 1990, Mattel/ Inc Arms: bent Body: dark tan tnt, pink panties Body Markings: © Mattel Inc 1966/ Malaysia

Asian Barbies

Model #: 4774 Name: UNICEF Barbie Asian version Box Date: 1989 Hair Color: black Hairstyle: 1 side & front pulled into ponytail, rest waist length, ends curled Face: hazel eyes, black brows, red lips & blush Clothing: strapless gown with white bodice, full skirt of blue tulle with metallic stars & purple underskirt, long white handless gloves, red & gold sash with star trim, light blue stud earrings, pendant, ring, wide royal blue pumps Extras: 2-piece clear stand & white oval brush Booklet: Rights of the Child Head: Oriental Head Markings: © Mattel Inc 1980 Arms: bent Body: dark tan tnt Body Markings: © Mattel Inc 1966/ China

Model #: 7029 Name: Summit Barbie Asian version Box Date: 1990 Hair Color: black Hairstyle: 1 side & front pulled up in band, rest waist length, ends curled under Face: brown eyes, black brows, red lips & blush Clothing: gown with gold lamé bodice, full white skirt, white tulle & gold glitter overskirt, white bolero jacket with gold braid trim, gold stud earrings & ring, wide white pumps Extras: red oval brush, sheet of cardboard punch outs & Summit badge Booklet: 1st Summit 1990 Head: Oriental Head Markings: © Mattel Inc 1980 Arms: bent Body: tan tnt Body Markings: © Mattel Inc 1966/ China

Midge

Model #: 860 **Name:** Midge **Issue Date:** 1963-:66 **Box Date:** 1962 **Hair Color:** blonde titian brunette **Hairstyle:** middle part, chin to shoulder-length flip, bangs, cello on head **Face:** blue eyes, light brown brows, coral lips, sprinkle of light brown freckles **Clothing:** *blonde:* 2-piece swimsuit, light blue top, medium blue bottom, white mules & wrist tag *brunette:* light pink top, red bottom, white mules & wrist tag *titian:* yellow-green top, orange bottoms, white mules & wrist tag **Extras:** black or gold wire stand **Booklet:** B&K, BK&M white 1962, or EFBM Book 1 1963 **Head:** Midge **Arms:** reg **Body:** tan s/l with painted nails **Body Markings:** Midge T.M./ © 1962/ Barbie®/ © 1958/ by/ Mattel, Inc./ in 1964 add word "Patented" **Notes:** available with teeth, no freckles, side glance eyes, painted legs, box variation with blue headband, gift sets: Ensemble, Fashion Queen Barbie & Her Friends, Barbie's Wedding Party Gift Set, On Parade, rare Midge Mix and Match gift set

Model #: 1009 **Name:** Wig Wardrobe Midge **Box Date:** 1964 **Hair Color:** red paint **Face:** molded head with removable orange band, blue eyes, light reddish brows, coral lips **Extras:** 3 wigs: red pigtails with blue ribbons & bangs, blonde middle part pageboy, brunette top-knot, made in Japan **Head:** Midge molded **Head Markings:** © M.I **Notes:** high color variation, gift set: Color 'N Curl

Model #: 1080 **Name:** Midge bendable leg **Box Date:** 1964 **Hair Color:** blonde brownette titian **Hairstyle:** chin to shoulder-length pageboy, middle part with bangs & blue ribbon headband, cello on head **Face:** blue eyes, light brows, deep coral lips & blush, with light brown freckles **Clothing:** multicolor turquoise, yellow, red, orange, & blue striped 1-piece swimsuit with elastic waist, turquoise mules, wrist tag **Extras:** gold wire stand **Booklet:** BWOF 1965 **Head:** b/l Midge **Head Markings:** inside rim Copyr. © 1958 Mattel Inc **Arms:** reg **Body:** tan b/l with painted nails **Body Markings:** indented © 1958/ Mattel, Inc./ U.S. Patented/ U.S. Pat. Pend/ Made in/ Japan with last 2 lines raised, later issues same markings all raised

Model #: 4442 Name: California Midge Box Date: 1987 Hair Color: red Hairstyle: sides pulled back, curly bangs, rest curly mid-back length Face: green eyes, brown brows, hot pink lips & blush Clothing: pink bodysuit, blue sleeveless white dot jacket, yellow & white speckled mini skirt, white fake roller skates with pink centers & laces, knee pads, 1 yellow & 1 blue earring, blue visor & Frisbee Extras: light blue oval brush, sheet of glitter stickers, comic book Booklet: BWOF 1986 Head: Steffie Head Markings: inside rim © 1971 Mattel Inc & country Arms: ptr Body: tan tnt Body Markings: © Mattel Inc.1966/ Philippines Notes: may develop pale splotches on legs

Model #: 4442 Name: California Dream Midge Box Date: 1987 Hair Color: red Hairstyle: sides pulled back, curly bangs, curly mid-back length Face: green eyes, brown brows, hot pink lips & blush Clothing: pink bodysuit, blue & white dot sleeveless jacket, yellow & white splatter mini skirt, blue visor & Frisbee, 1 yellow & 1 blue earring, pair of white fake roller skates different mold from Calif.Midge Extras: light blue oval brush, sheet of glitter stickers & cardboard punch outs, comic book Booklet: BWOF 1986 Head: Steffie Head Markings: inside rim © 1971 Mattel Inc & country Arms: ptr Body: tan tnt Body Markings: © Mattel Inc.1966/ Philippines Notes: may develop pale splotches on legs

Model #: 3216 Name: Cool Times Midge Box Date: 1988 Hair Color: red Hairstyle: short tufted hair on top of head, bangs, ponytail below shoulders Face: blue eyes, brown brows, orange lips & blush Clothing: white long sleeve top with appliqué, blue mini skirt, pants with white & black dots, multicolor leggings, blue earrings & ring, yellow pogo stick, tub of popcorn, tennis shoes Extras: blue oval brush & sheet of cardboard punch outs Booklet: BWOF 1987 Head: Steffie Head Markings: inside rim © 1971 Mattel Inc & country Arms: bent Body: tan tnt Body Markings: © Mattel Inc 1966/ China

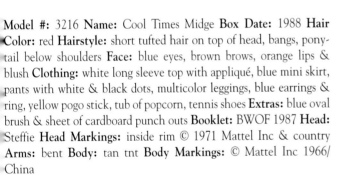

Model #: 9360 Name: Barbie and the All Stars Midge Box Date: 1989 Hair Color: red Hairstyle: curly hair pulled up on sides into long ponytail, bangs Face: green eyes, brown brows, pink lips & blush Clothing: white & purple baseball top & shorts, lilac round earrings, ring, purple bat & ball, sports bag converts to dress, white tennis shoes, wide purple pumps Extras: purple oval brush Head: Diva Head Markings: © 1985 Mattel Inc. Arms: bent Body: tan tnt Body Markings: © Mattel Inc 1966/ Malaysia

Model #: 2752 Name: Barbie & the Beat Midge Box Date: 1990 Hair Color: red Hairstyle: pulled back, curly bangs, curly waist length Face: green eyes, brown brows, orange lips & blush Clothing: orange crop top & mini skirt, jacket of orange, yellow, blue splotchy fabric with matching overskirt, orange guitar & gold strap, royal blue sunglasses, ring & earrings, wide royal blue pumps Extras: orange oval brush & cardboard punch outs Booklet: WOF 1989 Head: Diva Head Markings: © 1985 Mattel Inc. Arms: bent Body: tan tnt Body Markings: © Mattel Inc 1966/ China Notes: outfit had glow in dark glitter

Model #: 9606 Name: Wedding Day Midge Box Date: 1990 Hair Color: red Hairstyle: waist length, ends curled under Face: blue eyes, brown brows, deep pink lips & blush Clothing: white lace & dotted swiss gown with puffed sleeves, garter, gloves, rhinestone stud earrings, ring, pink & green bouquet, veil, purple satin jacket, wide white pumps Extras: cardboard punch out stand & white oval brush Head: Diva Head Markings: © 1985 Mattel Inc. Arms: bent Body: tan tnt Body Markings: © Mattel Inc 1966/ China Notes: box available w/ open lattice or closed, also part of 6 doll gift set

Model #: 10256 Name: Earring Magic Midge Box Date: 1992 Hair Color: red Hairstyle: crinkled, waist length, bangs, sides pulled up to top of head, ponytail held with copper band Face: blue eyes, light brown brows, red lips & blush Clothing: bright yellow vinyl mini dress with sheer bodice & sleeves, copper hoop & sun dangle earrings & ring, copper belt with 2 dangle stars, wide yellow pumps Extras: yellow oval brush & pair of copper dangling heart clip-on earrings for child Booklet: BFB 1992 PB Head: Diva Head Markings: © 1985 Mattel Inc. Arms: bent Body: tan tnt Body Markings: © Mattel Inc 1966/ China

Model #: 5476 Name: Sea Holiday Midge Box Date: 1992 Hair Color: reddish brown Hairstyle: waist length, ends curled under Face: green eyes, light brown brows, deep pink lips Clothing: yellow short sleeve midriff top, pink nylon swimsuit bottoms, long yellow nylon skirt, multicolor scarf tied around waist, matching print long sleeve shirt, gold star & binocular charm pendant, gold stud earrings & ring, large yellow straw hat, Barbie fold-out pictures, wide yellow pumps Extras: hot pink oval brush Head: Diva Head Markings: © 1985 Mattel Inc. Arms: bent Body: tan tnt Body Markings: © Mattel Inc 1966/ China

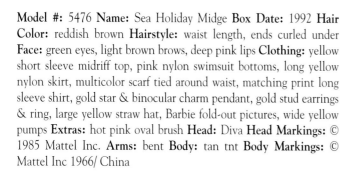  

Model #: 11077 Name: Camp Fun Midge Box Date: 1993 Hair Color: red Hairstyle: front section held with blue rubber band, rest waist length, curly bangs Face: blue eyes, light red brows, fuchsia lips & blush Clothing: yellow appliqué crop T-shirt, turquoise vest, light purple pants, backpack, orange coffee pot, fuchsia frying pan, yellow sunglasses, yellow stud earrings & ring, turquoise hiking boots Extras: yellow oval brush Booklet: instructions Head: Diva Head Markings: © 1985 Mattel Inc. Arms: bent Body: dark tan tnt Body Markings: © Mattel Inc.1966/ Indonesia Notes: hair changes color in sunlight

Model #: 13393 Name: Hot Skatin' Midge Box Date: 1994 Hair Color: red Hairstyle: thigh-length ponytail with curled bangs Face: green eyes, pale reddish brows, orange lips & blush Clothing: 1-piece stretch multicolor bodysuit with silver glitter swirls, hot pink vinyl belt with hot pink water bottle, hot pink vinyl knee pads, hot pink inline skates with yellow wheels, pair of white ice skates, yellow-green helmet, sheer blue glitter ice skating skirt, turquoise stud earrings Extras: turquoise oval brush Head: Diva Head Markings: © 1985 Mattel Inc. Arms: gymnast Body: tan gymnast Body Markings: © 1993 Mattel, Inc./ Malaysia

Model #: 13236 Name: Slumber Party Midge Box Date: 1994 Hair Color: red Hairstyle: crinkled thigh length, curly bangs, aqua fabric headband with white stars & moons Face: blue green eyes, reddish brown brows, fuchsia lips & blush Clothing: 2-piece aqua & white dot pajamas trimmed in lace Extras: aqua oval brush, white wash cloth, sheet of dayglo stickers, clear zipper carrying case Booklet: 1995 PB Head: Diva Head Markings: © 1985 Mattel Inc. Arms: soft Body: tan soft body Body Markings: cloth tag:© Mattel, Inc.1993 or 94 or 95/El Segundo, CA 90245 U.S.A./ surface washable(repeated)/ Reg.No.PA-60/ All New Materials/ Consisting of Polyester Fibers/ Made in China Notes: painted eyes open and close with ice water & warm water

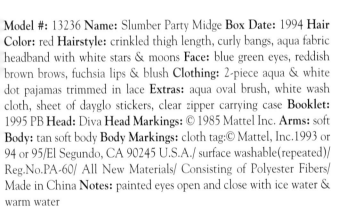

Model #: 13514 Name: Winter Sport Midge Box Date: 1994 Hair Color: red Hairstyle: waist-length ponytail at top of head, bangs & multicolored headband Face: green eyes, light brown brows, coral lips & blush Clothing: 1-piece multicolor bodysuit with silver glitter, yellow, green & turquoise long sleeve jacket, turquoise with silver glitter skating skirt, turquoise skis & poles, green snowboard, hot pink knee pads, turquoise stud earrings, orange & blue goggles, hot pink ski boots, white ice skates Extras: turquoise oval brush Booklet: 1994 PB Head: Diva Head Markings: © 1985 Mattel Inc. Arms: gymnast Body: light tan gymnast Body Markings: © 1993 Mattel, Inc./ China Notes: European issue but sold in Toys R Us

Model #: 1165 **Name:** Stacey twist & turn **Box Date:** 1967 **Hair Color:** blonde titian **Hairstyle:** side part hair pulled back at nape of neck with wide light red ribbon tied in a bow, hair waist length, pin curl on forehead & cheeks, cello on head **Face:** blue eyes, rooted lashes, light brown brows, light red lips & blush **Clothing:** 1-piece light red peek-a-boo swimsuit with 3 white buttons on bodice, wrist tag **Extras:** clear X stand **Booklet:** WOBF Book 1 1967 **Head:** Stacey **Head Markings:** inside rim © 1965 Mattel Inc & country **Arms:** reg **Body:** pink tnt, painted nails **Body Markings:** © 1966/ Mattel, Inc./ U.S. Patented/ U.S. Pat. Pend/ Made in/ Japan **Notes:** gift set: Stripes Are Happening

Model #: 1125 **Name:** Talking Stacey **Box Date:** 1968 **Hair Color:** blonde titian **Hairstyle:** waist-length side ponytail tied with green ribbon, bangs, cello on head **Face:** blue eyes, rooted lashes, light brown brows, deep pink lips & blush **Clothing:** multicolor pink, hot pink, pale pink, green, navy, white striped 2-piece swimsuit with gold buttons on left shoulder, wrist tag **Extras:** clear X stand **Head:** Stacey **Head Markings:** inside rim © 1965 Mattel Inc & country **Arms:** Mexico **Body:** pink talking Barbie **Body Markings:** ©1967/ Mattel, Inc./ U.S. & Foreign/ Pats.Pend./ Mexico **Notes:** speaks with British accent when string pulled, usually mute, limbs fall off, same doll & model # also available in slim clear box

Model #: 1118 **Name:** P.J. twist & turn **Box Date:** 1969 **Hair Color:** blonde **Hairstyle:** mid-back-length pigtails tied with multicolor seed beads, parted in middle with bangs & lilac round sunglasses, cello on head **Face:** brown eyes, rooted lashes, brown brows, deep pink lips & blush **Clothing:** 1-piece pink swimsuit with crochet lace trim, wrist tag **Extras:** clear X stand **Booklet:** LB 1969 **Head:** Midge **Head Markings:** inside rim © Mattel Inc. 1958 & country, date may be gone **Arms:** reg **Body:** pink tnt, painted nails **Body Markings:** © 1966/ Mattel, Inc./ U.S. Patented/ U.S. Pat. Pend/ Made in/ Japan **Notes:** Sears gift set: Swingin' in Silver

Model #: 1165 **Name:** Stacey twist & turn **Box Date:** 1969 **Hair Color:** blonde titian **Hairstyle:** nape of neck length flip, side part, cello on head **Face:** blue eyes, rooted lashes, brown brows, deep pink lips & blush **Clothing:** 1-piece swimsuit, blue & pink floral print with inverted background, wrist tag **Extras:** clear X stand **Booklet:** LB&S 1970 **Head:** Stacey **Head Markings:** inside rim © 1965 Mattel Inc & country **Arms:** reg **Body:** pink tnt, painted nails **Body Markings:** © 1966/ Mattel, Inc./ U.S. Patented/ U.S. Pat. Pend/ Made in/ Japan

Model #: 1165 Name: Stacey twist & turn Issue date: 1969 Box Date: 1967 Hair Color: blonde titian Hairstyle: nape of neck length flip, side part, cello on head Face: blue eyes, rooted lashes, brown brows, deep pink lips & blush Clothing: 1-piece knit swimsuit multi-color splotches of blue, hot pink, orange, yellow & green with white collar, wrist tag Extras: clear X stand Booklet: LB 1969 Head: Stacey Head Markings: inside rim © 1965 Mattel Inc & country Arms: reg Body: pink tnt, painted nails Body Markings: © 1966/ Mattel, Inc./ U.S. Patented/ U.S. Pat. Pend/ Made in/ Japan Notes: version issued with shorter hair in same suit & same model #, Sears gift set: Nite Lightning

Model #: 1113 Name: Talking P.J. Box Date: 1969 Hair Color: blonde Hairstyle: middle part, 2 below shoulder-length pigtails, tied with multicolor seed beads, bangs, round lavender sunglasses, cello on head Face: brown eyes, rooted lashes, light brown brows, orange lips & blush Clothing: mini dress, pink background with orange flowers and hot pink centers, orange nylon panties with white lace at legs, hot pink pilgrims, wrist tag Extras: clear X stand Head: Midge Head Markings: inside rim © Mattel Inc. 1958 & country, date may be gone Arms: Mexico Body: pink talking Barbie Body Markings: © 1967/ Mattel, Inc./ U.S. & Foreign/ Pats.Pend./ Hong Kong Notes: speaks when string pulled, usually mute, limbs fall off

Model #: 1125 Name: Talking Stacey Box Date: 1969 Hair Color: blonde titian Hairstyle: waist-length side ponytail tied with green ribbon, bangs, cello on head Face: blue eyes, rooted lashes, light brown brows, light orange lips & blush Clothing: 1-piece v-neck metallic blue & silver swimsuit, wrist tag Extras: clear X stand Head: Stacey Head Markings: inside rim © 1965 Mattel Inc & country Arms: Mexico Body: pink talking Barbie Body Markings: © 1967/ Mattel, Inc./ U.S. & Foreign/ Pats.Pend./ Hong Kong Notes: speaks with British accent when string pulled, usually mute, limbs fall off

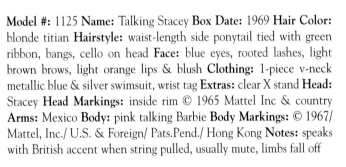

Model #: 1156 Name: Live Action P.J. Box Date: 1970 Hair Color: blonde Hairstyle: side part hair flipped up below shoulders, 2 small sections on either side of part braided and tied off with seed beads Face: brown eyes, rooted lashes, light brown brows, orange lips & blush Clothing: orange long sleeve mini dress with sewn in orange pantyhose & knee-high gold metallic boots, purple vest with fringe below knee, wrist tag Extras: clear touch 'n go stand Booklet: LB&S 1970 & instructions Head: Midge Head Markings: inside rim © Mattel Inc. 1958 & country, date may be gone Arms: living Body: tan live action Body Markings: © 1968 Mattel, Inc./ U.S. & Foreign Patented/ Patented in Canada 1967/ Other Patents pending/ Taiwan Notes: also available in Live Action on Stage # 1153 & Sears exclusive gift set: Fashion 'n Motion

Model #: 1187 Name: Sun Set Malibu P.J. Issue Date: 1972-77 Box Date: 1970 Hair Color: blonde Hairstyle: mid-back-length pigtails held with multicolor seed beads, side part, lilac clear plastic round sunglasses, cello on head Face: light blue eyes, dark brown brows, pale pink lips Clothing: 1-piece lilac nylon halter-style swimsuit with mint green beach towel Head: Steffie Head Markings: inside rim © 1971 Mattel Inc & country Arms: Francie Body: tan tnt Body Markings: © 1966/ Mattel, Inc./ U.S. Patented/ U.S. Pat.Pend./ Made in/ Korea Notes: during '70s doll made in Korea, Taiwan or Japan, with Mexico, regular or Francie arms, same doll with same model # issued in white box, also in pink box under the Malibu name, see Sun Set Ken 1974 for example of white box & Malibu Barbie 1975 for example of pink box, towel dropped in later issues

Model #: 3312 Name: Busy Steffie Box Date: 1971 Hair Color: brunette Hairstyle: shoulder-length flip Face: blue eyes, brown brows, pink lips & blush Clothing: spaghetti strap long gown of multicolor fabric, green square toe low heel shoes, wrist tag Extras: white X stand, brown princess telephone, TV, travel case, record player, record, tray, 2 glasses, stickers Booklet: LB&S 1970 & instructions Head: Steffie Head Markings: inside rim © 1971 Mattel Inc & country Arms: busy Body: pink tnt Body Markings: © 1966/ Mattel, Inc./ U.S. & Foreign/ Patented/ Other Pats/ Pending/ Made in/ U.S.A. or Hong Kong Notes: green spots may appear on arms, arms fall off

Model #: 1186 Name: Busy Talking Steffie Box Date: 1971 Hair Color: blonde Hairstyle: below shoulder length, curly ends gathered at nape of neck, curly bangs & pin curl on each cheek Face: light blue eyes, brown brows, pink lips & blush Clothing: 1-piece playsuit, pink & white checked long sleeve top with white buttons, turquoise shorts, brown & white small check belt with matching open back hat, pink & white knee-high spats, white square toe low heel shoes, wrist tag Extras: clear X stand, brown princess telephone, TV, travel case, record player, record, tray, 2 glasses, stickers Booklet: LB&S 1970 & instructions Head: Steffie Head Markings: inside rim © 1971 Mattel Inc & country Arms: busy Body: pink talking Body Markings: © 1967/ Mattel, Inc./ U.S. & Foreign/ Pats.Pend./ Hong Kong Notes: speaks when string on back pulled, usually mute, arms fall off

Model #: 1183 Name: Walk Lively Steffie Box Date: 1971 Hair Color: brunette Hairstyle: middle part, flipped up at nape of neck Face: brown eyes, rooted lashes, brown brows, peach lips & blush Clothing: sleeveless jumpsuit of pink, red, orange, white, navy print with sheer red sash, red pilgrims, wrist tag Extras: light brown round walking stand Booklet: LWOB 1971 & instructions Head: Steffie Head Markings: inside rim © 1971 Mattel Inc & country Arms: Mexico Body: pink walking Body Markings: © 1967 Mattel, Inc./ U.S. Pat.pend/ Taiwan

Model #: 4221 **Name:** Quick Curl Kelley **Box Date:** 1972 **Hair Color:** red **Hairstyle:** middle part, double flip at nape of neck, cello on head **Face:** brown eyes, brown brows, peach lips & blush **Clothing:** green & white dot gown with sheer sleeves, white satin collar, black ribbon accents, 2 ribbons, bobby pins, 3 bows, white low heel square toe shoes **Extras:** white X stand, pointed pink brush, comb & curler **Head:** Steffie **Head Markings:** inside rim © 1971 Mattel Inc & country **Arms:** Mexico **Body:** pink tnt **Body Markings:** © 1966/ Mattel, Inc./ U.S. & Foreign/ Patented/ Other pats/ Pending/ Made in/ Taiwan

Model #: 7808 **Name:** Yellowstone Kelley **Box Date:** 1973 **Hair Color:** red **Hairstyle:** middle part, mid-back length, cello on head **Face:** brown eyes, brown brows, peach lips & blush **Clothing:** red long sleeve blouse with white dots, blue & white striped shorts, matching pants, white knee-high socks, brown vinyl backpack, light & dark yellow vinyl sleeping bag, green camp stove, pot, frying pan, cup, plate, stickers for stove, white tennis shoes & wrist tag **Head:** Steffie **Head Markings:** inside rim © 1971 Mattel Inc & country **Arms:** Mexico **Body:** dark tan tnt **Body Markings:** © 1966/ Mattel, Inc./ U.S. & Foreign/ Patented/ Other pats/ Pending/ Made in/ Taiwan

Model #: 7281 **Name:** Free Moving P.J. **Box Date:** 1974 **Hair Color:** blonde **Hairstyle:** middle part, pulled into below shoulder pigtails, tied with light green ribbons, cello on head **Face:** brown eyes, blonde brows, peach lips & blush **Clothing:** 1-piece white playsuit with green insert at waist, long green skirt with white & black flowers, golf club, tennis racket, ball, white tennis shoes **Head:** Steffie **Head Markings:** inside rim © 1971 Mattel Inc & country **Arms:** Mexico **Body:** pink free moving **Body Markings:** © 1967/ Mattel, Inc./ Taiwan/ U.S.Pat.Pend. **Notes:** pull down lever on back of doll permits free movement

Model #: 7263 **Name:** Gold Medal Olympic P.J. Gymnast **Box Date:** 1974 **Hair Color:** blonde **Hairstyle:** side part, mid-back-length pigtails held with multicolor beads, cello on head **Face:** lavender eyes, blonde brows, peach lips & blush **Clothing:** blue, red & white bodysuit with red & white jacket, gold medal pendant **Extras:** 3-piece balance beam with leg or arm holder **Booklet:** instructions **Head:** Steffie **Head Markings:** inside rim © 1971 Mattel Inc & country **Arms:** Mexico **Body:** tan tnt **Body Markings:** © 1966/ Mattel, Inc./ U.S. & Foreign/ Patented/ Other pats/ Pending/ Made in/ Taiwan

Model #: 9218 Name: Deluxe Quick Curl P.J. Box Date: 1975 Hair Color: blonde Hairstyle: middle part, chin-length flip, cello on head Face: brown eyes, brown brows, peach lips & blush Clothing: orange sleeveless long cotton dress with ruffle at hem, white fringe shawl, long fall on orange headband, 2 ribbons, 2 colored bobby pins, orange pilgrims Extras: pointed white comb & brush Head: Steffie Head Markings: inside rim © 1971 Mattel Inc & country Arms: ptr Body: pink tnt Body Markings: © 1966/ Mattel, Inc./ U.S. & Foreign/ Patented/ Other pats/ Pending/ Made in/ Taiwan

Model #: 2323 Name: Fashion Photo P.J. Box Date: 1977 Hair Color: brunette Hairstyle: middle part, sides pulled to back of head, rest waist length Face: brown eyes, brown brows, peach lips & blush Clothing: silver spaghetti strap bodysuit, green, turquoise & yellow long chiffon skirt, turquoise pants, turquoise rhinestone earrings, pendant & ring, turquoise ankle straps Extras: 2-piece blue modeling stand & cable, pose changes by turning lens on black camera, preprinted photos Booklet: instructions Head: Steffie Head Markings: inside rim © 1971 Mattel Inc & country Arms: bent Body: pink tnt Body Markings: © Mattel Inc 1966/ Taiwan Notes: special leg joint allows greater flexibility at hip

Model #: 1187 Name: Sun Lovin' Malibu P.J. Box Date: 1978 Hair Color: blonde Hairstyle: side part, pulled into mid-back-length pigtails, held with multicolor seed beads Face: lilac eyes, black brows, peach lips & blush Clothing: purple bikini with "PJ" initials on hip, peach vinyl tote bag, purple mirror sunglasses Booklet: BWOF 1980 Head: Steffie Head Markings: inside rim © 1971 Mattel Inc & country Arms: bent Body: dark tan tnt, painted tan lines Body Markings: © Mattel Inc.1966/ Philippines

Model #: 1187 Name: Sunsational Malibu P.J. Box Date: 1981 Hair Color: blonde Hairstyle: side part, pulled into mid-back-length pigtails, held with multicolor seed beads Face: lilac eyes, black brows, peach lips & blush Clothing: 1-piece halter-style green swimsuit with light green trim & flower appliqué, purple, green, yellow striped towel, purple mirror sunglasses Booklet: BWOF 1980 Head: Steffie Head Markings: inside rim © 1971 Mattel Inc & country Arms: ptr Body: tan tnt Body Markings: © Mattel Inc.1966/ Philippines

Model #: 5869 Name: Dream Date P.J. Box Date: 1982 Hair Color: brown & blonde streaked Hairstyle: side part, pulled back at nape of neck, waist length, ends curled under Face: blue eyes, light brown brows, pink lips Clothing: blue sequin top, light blue satin long slim skirt with slit up side & matching sleeve detail, both edged in royal blue satin, royal blue satin belt with fabric rose, rhinestone stud earrings & ring, light blue mules Extras: small white comb, brush & mirror with handgrip, perfume bottle Booklet: instructions Head: Steffie Head Markings: inside rim © 1971 Mattel Inc & country Arms: bent Body: tan tnt Body Markings: © Mattel Inc 1966/ Taiwan

Model #: 4103 Name: Tracy Bride Box Date: 1982 Hair Color: brunette Hairstyle: middle part, sides pulled back, rest mid-back length, ends turned under Face: green eyes, brown brows, peach lips & blush Clothing: white gown with long sleeves, high neck lace bodice, white satin skirt with lace at hem, pink, purple & green plastic floral bouquet trimmed in lace & lilac ribbons, white tulle veil with lilac flowers, rhinestone stud earrings & ring, white mules Extras: 2-piece clear stand, lilac small oval brush, comb, mirror with handgrip, perfume bottle Booklet: BWOF 1981 Head: Steffie Head Markings: inside rim © 1971 Mattel Inc & country Arms: bent Body: tan tnt Body Markings: © Mattel Inc.1966/ Philippines

Model #: 1187 Name: Sun Gold Malibu P.J. Box Date: 1983 Hair Color: brown Hairstyle: middle part, mid-back length Face: blue-green eyes, blonde brows, peach lips & blush Clothing: silver halter-style 1-piece swimsuit, red mirror sunglasses, orange sunglasses, purple sunglasses, pink tote bag converts to mat Booklet: BWOF 1984 Head: Steffie Head Markings: inside rim © 1971 Mattel Inc & country Arms: ptr Body: dark tan tnt Body Markings: © Mattel, Inc. 1966/ Hong Kong

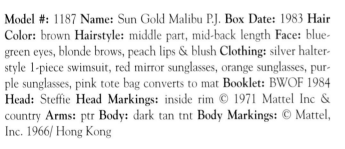

Model #: 7455 Name: Sweet Roses P.J. Box Date: 1983 Hair Color: brown Hairstyle: middle part, band at nape of neck, rest curly waist length Face: lavender eyes, blonde brows, rose lips & blush Clothing: rose & pink satin strapless long gown, skirt in gathered petals, rose fabric accents at neck, elbows, rhinestone ring, pink mules Extras: pointed pink brush & comb Booklet: BWOF 1984 Head: Steffie Head Markings: inside rim © 1971 Mattel Inc & country Arms: bent Body: ivory tnt Body Markings: © Mattel Inc.1966/ Philippines

Model #: 2427 Name: Rocker Diva Box Date: 1985 Hair Color: red Hairstyle: middle part, 2 shoulder-length curly pigtails, silver mesh scarf tied across forehead Face: blue eyes, pale reddish brows, radical turquoise & purple eyeshadow, pale pink lips Clothing: yellow halter top, lace front, metallic blue short sleeve jacket, fuchsia trim, metallic fuchsia pants, light green ribbon belt, clear orange buckle, yellow & neon orange dangle earrings & ring, orange snake bracelet, fuchsia faux fur headband, yellow Rockers T-shirt, yellow lace anklets, orange mules Extras: orange pointed brush, white microphone, 2 sheets of cardboard punch outs, 1 iron-on Rockers transfer Booklet: BWOF 1985 & instructions Head: Diva Head Markings: © 1985 Mattel Inc. Arms: bent Body: tan tnt Body Markings: © Mattel Inc.1966/ Philippines Notes: many different clothing combinations

Model #: 3179 Name: Jewel Secrets Whitney Box Date: 1986 Hair Color: brunette Hairstyle: middle part, banded at nape of neck, twisted thigh-length ponytail, silver tiara with turquoise jewels Face: lilac-green eyes, blonde brows, pink lips & blush Clothing: silver long sleeve top over a turquoise glitter spaghetti strap slim gown with wide silver belt, pleated silver cape/skirt, long handless metallic magenta gloves & matching purse, rhinestone stud earrings, ring, turquoise mules Extras: pink pearl oval brush, flickering picture, Whitney storybook "Secret of the Fashion Show" Booklet: BWOF 1986, instructions Head: Steffie Head Markings: inside rim © 1971 Mattel Inc & country Arms: bent Body: tan tnt Body Markings: © Mattel Inc.1966/ Philippines

Model #: 3159 Name: Rocker Diva 2nd issue Box Date: 1986 Hair Color: red Hairstyle: curly to shoulders portion of hair pulled into small ponytail at top of head, curly bangs Face: green eyes, light reddish brown brows, coral lips & blush Clothing: lime green tank top, orange tank top with gold stars & Rockers logo, lime green with fuchsia stars stretch pants, lime green cuff with long orange fringe, lime green dangle earrings & ring, lime green hair ornament, narrow lime green pumps Extras: lime green oval brush, sheet of cardboard punch outs, silver microphone Booklet: BWOF 1987 & instructions Head: Diva Head Markings: © 1985 Mattel Inc. Arms: bent Body: tan tnt Body Markings: © Mattel Inc.1966/ Philippines

Model #: 4405 Name: Nurse Whitney Box Date: 1987 Hair Color: brunette Hairstyle: side part pulled into waist-length ponytail at nape of neck Face: turquoise eyes, light brown brows, fuchsia lips Clothing: white long sleeve high collar pleated front blouse, white a-line knee-length skirt, iridescent lilac pleated ankle-length skirt, iridescent spaghetti strap top & nurse's hat, rhinestone earrings & ring, Dr.'s bag, cast, ear checker, clipboard, watch, adhesive strips, reflex hammer, blood pressure cord, scale, tray, bottles, notepad, labels, wide white pumps Extras: lilac oval brush & sheet of cardboard punch outs Booklet: BWOF 1987 & instructions Head: Steffie Head Markings: inside rim © 1971 Mattel Inc & country Arms: bent Body: tan tnt Body Markings: © Mattel Inc 1966/ Malaysia

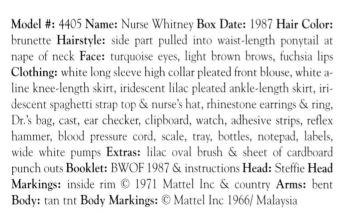

Model #: 4557 **Name:** Perfume Pretty Whitney **Box Date:** 1987 **Hair Color:** brunette **Hairstyle:** front & sides pulled up with light blue ribbon, rest waist length & curly **Face:** blue eyes, brown brows, deep pink lips & blush **Clothing:** light blue knee-length dress with detached tulle, flocked long sleeves, sheer tulle full skirt, dropped lace bodice, blue bow at neckline, pearl stud earrings, necklace, ring & wide blue pearl bow pumps **Extras:** blue pearl oval brush, matching pendant for child, ribbon for pendant & sheet of cardboard punch outs **Head:** Steffie **Head Markings:** inside rim © 1971 Mattel Inc & country **Arms:** bent **Body:** tan tnt **Body Markings:** © Mattel Inc.1966/ Philippines **Notes:** also available in high color version

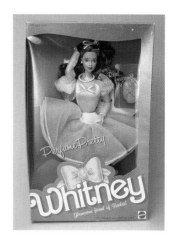

Model #: 4967 **Name:** Sensations Bopsy **Box Date:** 1987 **Hair Color:** reddish blonde **Hairstyle:** 2 mid-back-length pigtails with bangs **Face:** green eyes, blonde brows, fuchsia lips & blush **Clothing:** yellow-green metallic sleeveless top, turquoise metallic belt, yellow satin capri pants, turquoise & white vinyl jacket, turquoise drop earrings & ring, black microphone, pink & black glasses, white lace anklets, black and white saddle shoes **Extras:** turquoise oval brush & 2 sheets of cardboard punch outs **Booklet:** BWOF 1987 **Head:** Diva **Head Markings:** © 1985 Mattel Inc. **Arms:** bent **Body:** tan tnt **Body Markings:** © Mattel Inc 1966/ China

Model #: 1290 **Name:** Style Magic Whitney **Box Date:** 1988 **Hair Color:** brown & brunette **Hairstyle:** mid-back length, ends curled with bangs **Face:** teal eyes, brown brows, fuchsia lips & blush **Clothing:** off-the-shoulder turquoise bodysuit with sheer turquoise mini skirt & shoulder detail with white, red & yellow glitter paint pattern, turquoise hoop earrings & ring, wide turquoise pumps **Extras:** half triangle, circle, half circle turquoise comb, matching curlers & sheet of cardboard punch outs **Booklet:** BWOF 1988 & instructions **Head:** Steffie **Head Markings:** inside rim © 1971 Mattel Inc & country **Arms:** bent **Body:** dark tan tnt **Body Markings:** © Mattel Inc 1966/ Malaysia **Notes:** WondraCurl hair

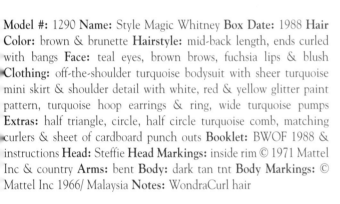

Model #: 3512 **Name:** Dance Club Kayla **Box Date:** 1989 **Hair Color:** red **Hairstyle:** waist-length hair with curly bangs **Face:** green eyes, brown brows, hot pink lips & blush **Clothing:** fuchsia jacket, white vinyl short top, green mini skirt & blue belt, green glitter scarf, neon green earrings & ring, white anklets with lace edge, wide black pumps **Extras:** yellow oval brush **Head:** Diva **Head Markings:** © 1985 Mattel Inc. **Arms:** bent **Body:** tan tnt **Body Markings:** © Mattel Inc 1966/ China

Model #: 11209 Name: Locket Surprise Kayla Box Date: 1993 Hair Color: red Hairstyle: side part, crinkled thigh length Face: green eyes, red brows, red lips & blush Clothing: turquoise elastic ruffle around bodice, turquoise glitter knee-length skirt with iridescent edging, silver filigree drop earrings, ring, wide turquoise pumps Extras: turquoise oval brush, heart locket lip gloss insert, photo of Barbie, blush Booklet: instructions Head: Teresa Head Markings: © 1990, Mattel/ Inc Arms: bent Body: tan b/l, turquoise locket Body Markings: © Mattel Inc 1966/ China Notes: chest opens up for storage of small accessories

Model #: 10295 Name: Western Stampin' Tara Lynn Box Date: 1993 Hair Color: black Hairstyle: thigh length Face: aqua eyes, black brows, red lips & blush Clothing: black & gold print top, red fringed vest, red & gold print mini dress with sewn in panties, gold belt buckle, fringed black & red armlets, gold drop earrings & ring, gold kerchief, red cowboy hat with gold accent, red cowboy boots with rolling stampers Extras: red oval brush, ink pad, gold glitter & sheet of cardboard punch outs Booklet: instructions Head: Steffie Head Markings: inside rim © 1971 Mattel Inc & country Arms: bent Body: tan tnt Body Markings: © Mattel Inc 1966/ China

Barbie's African American Friends

Model #: 1126 Name: Talking Christie Box Date: 1968 Hair Color: oxidized red or brunette Hairstyle: chin-length bouffant Face: brown eyes, rooted lashes, black brows, hot pink lips & blush Clothing: light green sleeveless knit top with green & pink yarn trim at hem, pink vinyl shorts, wrist tag Extras: clear X stand Head: vintage Christie Head Markings: inside rim © 1965 Mattel Inc & country Arms: Mexico Body: dark brown talking Body Markings: ©1967/ Mattel, Inc./ U.S. & Foreign/ Pats.Pend./ Mexico Notes: speaks when string pulled, usually mute, limbs fall off, same doll & model # also available in slim clear box

Model #: 1119 Name: Christie twist & turn Box Date: 1969 Hair Color: oxidized red or brunette Hairstyle: chin-length bouffant Face: brown eyes, rooted lashes, black brows, hot pink lips & blush Clothing: 1-piece v-neck swimsuit of solid hot pink & yellow, pink, yellow, white, orange print, wrist tag Extras: clear X stand Head: vintage Christie Head Markings: inside rim © 1965 Mattel Inc & country Arms: reg Body: dark brown tnt Body Markings: © 1966/ Mattel, Inc./ U.S. Patented/ U.S. Pat. Pend/ Made in/ Japan

Model #: 1126 Name: Talking Christie Box Date: 1969 Hair Color: oxidized red or brunette Hairstyle: chin-length bouffant Face: brown eyes, rooted lashes, black brows, orange lips & blush Clothing: orange vinyl bikini, multicolor yellow, light green, olive green, pink, orange v-neck short sleeve top, wrist tag Extras: clear X stand Booklet: LB Head: vintage Christie Head Markings: inside rim © 1965 Mattel Inc & country Arms: Mexico Body: dark brown talking Body Markings: ©1967/ Mattel, Inc./ U.S. & Foreign/ Pats.Pend./ Mexico Notes: speaks when string pulled, usually mute, limbs fall off

Model #: 1175 Name: Live Action Christie Box Date: 1970 Hair Color: black Hairstyle: middle part, mid-back length, held back with orange sheer scarf, cello on head Face: brown-orange eyes, rooted lashes, black brows, orange lips & blush Clothing: multicolor purple, lilac, orange, gold pattern crop top with long extended sleeve fringe, matching pants, fuchsia square toe low heel shoes, wrist tag Extras: clear touch 'n go stand Booklet: LB&S 1970 & instructions Head: Midge Head Markings: inside rim © Mattel Inc. 1958 & country, date may be gone Arms: living Body: dark brown live action Body Markings: © 1968 Mattel, Inc./ U.S. & Foreign Patented/ Patented in Canada 1967/ Other Patents pending/ Taiwan

Model #: 7745 Name: Sun Set Malibu Christie Issue Date: 1973-1977 Box Date: 1970 Hair Color: black Hairstyle: side part, mid-back length, cello on head Face: brown eyes, black brows, peach lips Clothing: 1-piece orange/red swimsuit with wrist tag, white towel, round lavender sunglasses Head: vintage Christie Head Markings: inside rim © 1965 Mattel Inc & country Arms: reg Body: dark brown tnt Body Markings: © 1966/ Mattel, Inc./ U.S. Patented/ U.S. Pat.Pend./ Made in/ Korea Notes: '70s dolls made in either Korea or Taiwan, regular, Mexico or Francie arms, some dolls have black painted sideburns, same doll with same model # issued in yellow swimsuit in white box & also issued in pink box under Malibu name, see Sun Set Ken 1974 for example of white box & Malibu Barbie 1975 for example of pink box , towel dropped in later issues

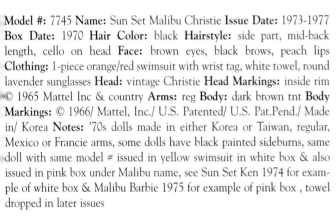

Model #: 7283 Name: Free Moving Cara Box Date: 1974 Hair Color: black Hairstyle: middle part, below shoulder length, sides pulled into small pigtails tied with orange ribbons, cello on head Face: brown eyes, black brows, dark orange lips & blush Clothing: 1-piece white playsuit with orange insert at waist, long orange skirt with white & black flowers, golf club, tennis racket, ball, white tennis shoes Head: Steffie Head Markings: inside rim © 1971 Mattel Inc & country Arms: ptr Body: dark brown free moving Body Markings: © 1967/ Mattel, Inc./ Taiwan/ U.S.Pat.Pend. Notes: pull down lever on back of doll permits free movement

Model #: 7291 **Name:** Quick Curl Cara **Box Date:** 1974 **Hair Color:** brunette **Hairstyle:** side part, ends turned under at nape of neck, cello on head **Face:** brown eyes, brown brows, peach lips **Clothing:** multicolor turquoise, green, hot pink, purple, yellow crop top tied in front, sheer turquoise sleeves and matching cuffs, matching long wrap skirt, white panties, 2 ribbons & 2 white barrettes, turquoise t-straps **Extras:** pointed white comb, brush, curler **Head:** Steffie **Head Markings:** inside rim © 1971 Mattel Inc & country **Arms:** Mexico **Body:** dark brown tnt **Body Markings:** © 1966/ Mattel, Inc./ U.S. & Foreign/ Patented/ Other pats/ Pending/ Made in/ Taiwan

Model #: 9528 **Name:** Ballerina Cara **Box Date:** 1975 **Hair Color:** black **Hairstyle:** parted in middle, sides pulled to back of head, shoulder-length ponytail, gold crown **Face:** brown eyes, black brows, pink lips **Clothing:** pink satin tutu with gold-edged pink tulle, 3 red plastic roses & green leaves, pink ankle strap ballet slippers **Extras:** 2-piece pink stand **Booklet:** instructions **Head:** Steffie **Head Markings:** inside rim © 1971 Mattel Inc & country **Arms:** ballerina **Body:** dark brown tnt **Body Markings:** © Mattel, Inc.1966/ U.S. Patent Pending/ Taiwan

Model #: 9220 **Name:** Deluxe Quick Curl Cara **Box Date:** 1975 **Hair Color:** brunette **Hairstyle:** middle part, nape of neck length flip, cello on head **Face:** light brown eyes, black brows, peach lips **Clothing:** yellow spaghetti strap long dress with ruffle hem, white fringe shawl, 2 white bobby pins, rubber band, 2 ribbons, brunette fall with yellow ribbon ties, white choker, yellow pilgrims **Extras:** white pointed brush, comb, curler **Head:** Steffie **Head Markings:** inside rim © 1971 Mattel Inc & country **Arms:** ptr **Body:** dark brown tnt **Body Markings:** © 1966/ Mattel, Inc./ U.S. & Foreign/ Patented/ Other pats/ Pending/ Made in/ Taiwan

Model #: 9839 **Name:** Supersize Christie **Box Date:** 1976 **Hair Color:** brunette **Hairstyle:** side part, waist length, cello on head **Face:** brown eyes, black brows, dark peach lips & blush **Clothing:** silver white & aqua bodysuit with matching long skirt & pants, rhinestone stud earrings, pendant, ring, aqua ankle straps **Extras:** 3-piece white star stand, white punch out jewelry for doll & child **Booklet:** instructions **Head:** supersize **Head Markings:** Taiwan/© 1976 Mattel, Inc. **Arms:** bent **Body:** dark brown tnt supersize **Body Markings:** © Mattel, Inc. 1976/ U.S.A. **Notes:** 18 inch body

Model #: 9950 Name: Superstar Christie Box Date: 1976 Hair Color: brunette & light red streaks Hairstyle: side part, waist length Face: brown eyes, black brows, light red lips & blush Clothing: yellow satin halter gown with yellow & silver ruffled lace boa, rhinestone stud earrings, pendant & ring, yellow ankle straps Extras: 2-piece star stand Head: superstar Head Markings: inside or outside rim © Mattel Inc 1976 +/- country Arms: bent Body: dark brown tnt Body Markings: © Mattel Inc 1966/ Taiwan

Model #: 2324 Name: Fashion Photo Christie Box Date: 1977 Hair Color: red with brunette streaks Hairstyle: middle part, sides pulled back, rest waist length Face: brown eyes, brown brows, peach lips & blush Clothing: gold spaghetti strap bodysuit with orange, neon orange & yellow chiffon long skirt, yellow pants, orange rhinestone stud earrings, pendant & ring, yellow ankle straps Extras: 2-piece pink modeling stand & cable, pose changes by turning lens on black camera, preprinted photos Booklet: instructions Head: superstar Head Markings: inside or outside rim © Mattel Inc 1976 +/- country Arms: bent Body: dark brown tnt Body Markings: © Mattel Inc 1966/ Taiwan Notes: special leg joint allows greater flexibility at hip

Model #: 2955 Name: Kissing Christie Box Date: 1978 Hair Color: brunette Hairstyle: curly below shoulder length, side part Face: brown eyes, black brows, coral lips Clothing: peach floral print chiffon long sleeve gown with inset waistband, pair of peach ankle straps, yellow, orange & green plastic flower bouquet Extras: 2-piece clear stand, pink liquid lipstick & sheet of cardboard punch outs Booklet: BWOF 1978 & instructions Head: Kissing Head Markings: © Mattel, Inc/ 1978 Taiwan Arms: bent Body: dark brown tnt Body Markings: © Mattel Inc 1966/ Taiwan Notes: press back panel for pucker & smack noise

Model #: 7745 Name: Sun Lovin' Malibu Christie Box Date: 1978 Hair Color: black Hairstyle: middle part, side pulled into pigtails, rest mid-back length Face: brown eyes, black brows, peach lips Clothing: peach bikini with "C" initial on hip, peach vinyl tote bag, purple mirror sunglasses Head: Steffie Head Markings: inside rim © 1971 Mattel Inc & country Arms: ptr Body: dark brown tnt, painted tan lines Body Markings: © Mattel Inc.1966/ Philippines

Model #: 1295 Name: Beauty Secrets Christie Box Date: 1979 Hair Color: black Hairstyle: waist-length ponytail with curled ends, curly bangs & sides Face: brown eyes, black brows, pink lips & blush Clothing: turquoise teddy with lace trim, short jacket, long slim skirt with slit in back, turquoise mules or ankle straps Extras: 2-piece clear stand, pink brush comb & mirror with handgrip, pink perfume bottle, large mirror, powder puff, wash cloth, pink toothbrush, hair dryer, compact, turquoise carryall Booklet: BWOF 1979 & instructions Head: superstar Head Markings: inside or outside rim © Mattel Inc 1976 +/- country Arms: Living Barbie Body: dark brown tnt Body Markings: © Mattel Inc 1979,/ Taiwan 1966 Notes: press panel on back & arms move

Model #: 3249 Name: Golden Dreams Christie Box Date: 1980 Hair Color: red & brunette Hairstyle: mid-back length, curly, parted in middle Face: light brown eyes, dark brown brows, peach lips & blush Clothing: metallic copper halter jumpsuit, white sheer & metallic copper stripe overskirt & long handless gloves, copper rhinestone earrings, pendant, ring, sheer tie on wrap, 2 combs, 2 barrettes, 2 rubber bands, clear ankle straps Extras: white with gold accent brush, comb, curler & clear hair arranger Booklet: BWOF 1979 & instructions Head: Steffie Head Markings: inside rim © 1971 Mattel Inc & country Arms: bent Body: dark brown tnt Body Markings: © Mattel Inc 1966/ Taiwan

Model #: 3554 Name: Pink n' Pretty Christie Box Date: 1981 Hair Color: brunette Hairstyle: shoulder-length ponytail at top of head ends curled under Face: brown eyes, black brows, mauve lips & blush Clothing: pink sleeveless blouse with silver dots, floor-length slim nylon pink skirt, matching pants, knee-length chiffon skirt with pale faux fur hem, matching stole, headband, clear rhinestone dangle earrings, pendant, ring, pale pink mules Extras: small lavender brush comb & mirror with handgrip Booklet: BWOF 1980 Head: Steffie Head Markings: inside rim © 1971 Mattel Inc & country Arms: bent Body: dark brown tnt Body Markings: © Mattel Inc 1966/ Taiwan

Model #: 7745 Name: Sunsational Malibu Christie Box Date: 1981 Hair Color: black Hairstyle: middle part, sides pulled back with yellow band, rest mid-back length, ends curled under Face: brown eyes, brown brows, light red lips & blush Clothing: 1-piece halter-style yellow swimsuit with red trim & flower appliqué, red towel, purple mirror sunglasses Booklet: BWOF 1980 Head: Steffie Head Markings: inside rim © 1971 Mattel Inc & country Arms: ptr Body: dark brown tnt Body Markings: © Mattel Inc.1966/ Philippines

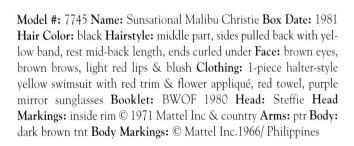

Model #: 1141 Name: Rocker Dee-Dee Box Date: 1985 Hair Color: black Hairstyle: front pulled back & tied with orange lace, rest mid-back length, curly Face: brown eyes, black brows, orange lips & blush Clothing: yellow-green & gold striped short sleeve top, black vinyl mini skirt, multicolor black, blue, purple, green, yellow, hot pink footless tights, yellow & orange dangle earrings, yellow ring, orange snake bracelet, blue purple & green faux fur headband, orange Rockers T-shirt, narrow orange pumps Extras: orange pointed brush, white microphone, 2 sheets of cardboard punch outs, 1 iron-on Rockers transfer Booklet: BWOF 1984 & instructions Head: Hispanic Head Markings: inside rim © Mattel Inc, 1983 Arms: bent Body: dark brown tnt Body Markings: © Mattel Inc.1966/ Philippines Notes: many different clothing combinations

Model #: 3160 Name: Rocker Dee-Dee 2nd issue Box Date: 1986 Hair Color: black Hairstyle: curly, below shoulder, sides form small ponytail, curly bangs Face: brown eyes, black brows, light orange lips & blush Clothing: orange turtleneck halter top with metallic blue stars & Rockers logo, blue mini skirt with fuchsia stars, orange lycra footed tights, orange cuff with yellow-green long fringe, lime green dangle earrings & ring, orange hair ornament, narrow orange pumps Extras: orange oval brush, sheet of cardboard punch outs, silver microphone Booklet: BWOF 1987 & instructions Head: Hispanic Head Markings: inside rim © Mattel Inc, 1983 Arms: bent Body: dark brown tnt Body Markings: © Mattel Inc.1966/ Philippines Notes: many different clothing combinations

Model #: 4443 Name: California Christie Box Date: 1987 Hair Color: black Hairstyle: sides & top pulled up into curly topknot, rest curly mid-back length Face: brown eyes, black brows, orange lips & blush Clothing: orange cotton crop top with clear plastic appliqué, yellow 1-piece swimsuit, yellow and white striped & polka dot mid-thigh shorts with yellow & white dot pocket, orange tie belt, orange disk earrings, yellow visor & Frisbee, orange knee socks, yellow high-top tennis shoes Extras: yellow oval brush, sheet of stickers & cardboard punch outs, comic book Booklet: BWOF 1987 & instructions Head: Christie Head Markings: © Mattel Inc./ 1987 Arms: ptr Body: dark brown tnt Body Markings: © Mattel Inc.1966/ Philippines

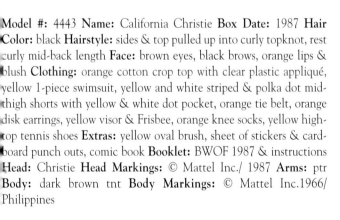

Model #: 4443 Name: California Dream Christie Box Date: 1987 Hair Color: black Hairstyle: sides and top pulled up into curly topknot, rest curly mid-back length Face: brown eyes, black brows, orange lips & blush Clothing: orange cotton crop top with clear plastic appliqué, yellow 1-piece swimsuit, yellow & white striped & polka dot mid-thigh shorts with orange & white dot pocket, orange tie belt, orange disk earrings, yellow visor & Frisbee, orange knee socks, yellow high-top tennis shoes Extras: yellow oval brush, sheet of stickers & cardboard punch outs, comic book Booklet: BWOF 1987 & instructions Head: Christie Head Markings: © Mattel Inc./ 1987 Arms: ptr Body: dark brown tnt Body Markings: © Mattel Inc 1966/ Malaysia

Model #: 4092 Name: Island Fun Christie Box Date: 1987 Hair Color: dark red & black streaks Hairstyle: side part, mid-thigh-length ponytail banded at nape of neck & split into 3 Face: brown eyes, black brows, pink lips & blush Clothing: 1-piece yellow swimsuit with orange Hawaiian print wrap skirt, orange & hot pink lei Extras: yellow seahorse comb Booklet: BWOF 1987 & instructions Head: Christie Head Markings: © Mattel Inc./ 1987 Arms: ptr Body: dark brown tnt Body Markings: © Mattel Inc.1966/ Philippines Notes: may have green splotches & stickiness on legs

Model #: 4976 Name: Sensations Belinda Box Date: 1987 Hair Color: brunette Hairstyle: shoulder-length side ponytail with curly bangs Face: brown eyes, blonde brows, orange lips & blush Clothing: orange metallic mini dress with neon orange satin & tulle flared skirt, sewn in panties, lime green satin & white vinyl sleeve jacket, orange drop earrings & ring, pink & black glasses, black microphone, white lace anklets, white & black saddle shoes Extras: orange oval brush & 2 sheets of cardboard punch outs Booklet: BWOF 1987 Head: Christie Head Markings: © Mattel Inc./ 1987 Arms: bent Body: dark brown tnt Body Markings: © Mattel Inc 1966/ China

Model #: 3217 Name: Cool Times Christie Box Date: 1988 Hair Color: brunette Hairstyle: sides & front pulled into topknot, rest pulled into side thigh-length crinkled ponytail Face: brown eyes, black brows, purple lips & blush Clothing: yellow crop top with appliqué, purple satin mini skirt with black & white suspenders, black & white striped pants, yellow dangle earrings & ring, multicolor scrunches, hot dog in bun, hot pink paddle ball, white tennis shoes Extras: yellow oval brush & sheet of cardboard punch outs Booklet: BWOF 1988 & instructions Head: Christie Head Markings: © Mattel Inc./ 1987 Arms: bent Body: dark brown tnt Body Markings: © Mattel Inc 1966/ China

Model #: 1288 Name: Style Magic Christie Box Date: 1988 Hair Color: red & brunette streaks Hairstyle: mid-back length, ends curled, bangs Face: lavender eyes, black brows, peach lips & blush Clothing: aqua & peach halter bodysuit with sheer peach mini skirt & bodice trim with coral, aqua & white design, peach hoop earrings & ring, wide peach pumps Extras: half triangle, circle, half circle peach comb, matching curlers & sheet of cardboard punch outs Booklet: BWOF 1988 & instructions Head: Christie Head Markings: © Mattel Inc./ 1987 Arms: bent Body: dark brown tnt Body Markings: © Mattel Inc 1966/ Malaysia Notes: WondraCurl hair

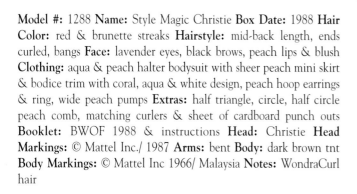

Model #: 2754 **Name:** Barbie & the Beat Christie **Box Date:** 1989 **Hair Color:** black **Hairstyle:** parted in middle, 1 side tied with band, other with barrette, curly bangs, rest curly waist length **Face:** brown eyes, black brows, hot pink lips & blush **Clothing:** yellow-green long sleeve crop top with hot pink ruffle, acid washed vest & mini skirt, yellow-green tulle underskirt, pink jewel at waist, yellow-green square earrings & ring, hot pink guitar & gold strap, yellow-green fake boot tops with pink lace edge, wide yellow-green pumps **Extras:** hot pink oval brush & sheet of cardboard punch outs **Booklet:** BWOF 1988 **Head:** Christie **Head Markings:** © Mattel Inc./ 1987 **Arms:** bent **Body:** dark brown tnt **Body Markings:** © Mattel Inc 1966/ China **Notes:** outfit has glow in dark glitter

Model #: 9352 **Name:** Barbie and the All Stars Christie **Box Date:** 1989 **Hair Color:** black **Hairstyle:** front section pulled back with orange fabric tie, rest crinkled thigh length **Face:** brown eyes, black brows, orange lips & blush **Clothing:** 1-piece white & orange body-suit with purple metallic stars, orange stretch footless tights, tote bag converts into dress, purple relay baton, running weight, soda can, orange disk earrings & ring, wide orange pumps, white tennis shoes **Extras:** orange oval brush & sheet of cardboard punch outs **Booklet:** BWOF 1988 & instructions **Head:** Christie **Head Markings:** © Mattel Inc./ 1987 **Arms:** bent **Body:** dark brown tnt **Body Markings:** © Mattel Inc 1966/ Malaysia

Model #: 3253 **Name:** Beach Blast Christie **Box Date:** 1989 **Hair Color:** black **Hairstyle:** sides & front pulled up in curly topknot, rest curly mid-back length, barrette with blond crinkle color-change hairpiece **Face:** light brown eyes, black brows, orange lips & blush **Clothing:** 1-piece swimsuit of yellow, lime green & black, pink wrap-around sunglasses, hot pink visor & Frisbee **Extras:** turquoise seahorse comb **Booklet:** BWOF 1988 **Head:** Christie **Head Markings:** © Mattel Inc./ 1987 **Arms:** ptr **Body:** dark brown tnt **Body Markings:** © Mattel Inc 1966/ China

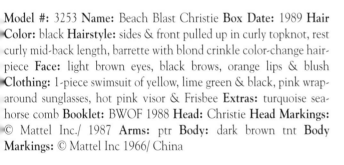

Model #: 3513 **Name:** Dance Club Devon **Box Date:** 1989 **Hair Color:** black **Hairstyle:** sides & front pulled back with turquoise fabric tie, rest waist length, ends curled under, curly bangs **Face:** brown eyes, black brows, hot pink lips & blush **Clothing:** multicolor black splotched crop top, turquoise vinyl short jacket, turquoise capri pants with sheer turquoise partial overskirt with black waistband & hot pink flower at waist, hot pink drop earrings & ring, white vinyl boot tops, pink sheer scarf, wide white pumps **Extras:** turquoise oval brush & sheet of cardboard punch outs **Booklet:** BWOF 1988 **Head:** Christie **Head Markings:** © Mattel Inc./ 1987 **Arms:** bent **Body:** dark brown tnt **Body Markings:** © Mattel Inc 1966/ China

Model #: 4121 **Name:** Wet n' Wild Christie **Box Date:** 1989 **Hair Color:** red & brown streaks **Hairstyle:** sides pulled to 1 side held with hot pink snake tie, rest crinkled mid-thigh length, spiky bangs **Face:** lavender eyes, black brows, orange lips & blush **Clothing:** 2-piece change-color bikini of orange & blue, pink sunglasses, orange snake bracelet **Extras:** blue oval brush **Head:** Christie **Head Markings:** © Mattel Inc./ 1987 **Arms:** ptr **Body:** dark brown tnt **Body Markings:** © Mattel Inc 1966/ China

Model #: 9425 **Name:** All American Christie **Box Date:** 1990 **Hair Color:** brunette **Hairstyle:** front & sides pulled up with orange snake tie, rest crinkled thigh length **Face:** brown eyes, black brows, orange lips & blush **Clothing:** orange crop top & matching mini skirt, acid washed denim jacket with red & white stripe collar & cuffs, white panties, multicolor socks, green hoop earrings & ring, 2 pair of Reeboks **Extras:** lime green oval brush & sheet of cardboard punch outs **Head:** Christie **Head Markings:** © Mattel Inc./ 1987 **Arms:** bent **Body:** dark brown tnt **Body Markings:** © Mattel Inc 1966/ Malaysia

Model #: 9407 **Name:** Benetton Christie **Box Date:** 1990 **Hair Color:** black **Hairstyle:** side part with 2 pigtails tied with red bands each split into 3 pigtails tied with multicolor bands **Face:** brown eyes, black brows, red lips & blush **Clothing:** sleeveless multicolor turtle neck & matching purse, white long sleeve hooded coat with multi color stripes, pink stretch pants, red leggings, yellow scarf, hot pink hoop earrings & ring, yellow tennis shoes **Extras:** hot pink oval brush & sheet of cardboard punch outs **Head:** Christie **Head Markings:** © Mattel Inc./ 1987 **Arms:** bent **Body:** dark brown tnt **Body Markings** © Mattel Inc 1966/ China

Model #: 5944 **Name:** Hawaiian Fun Christie **Box Date:** 1990 **Hair Color:** black with red streaks **Hairstyle:** front & sides pulled to 1 side with different color bands twisted, mid-back length with curly bangs **Face:** brown eyes, black brows, orange lips & blush **Clothing:** light green, yellow & red bikini, green mini hula skirt, green & black sunglasses **Extras:** neon yellow oval brush, bracelet for child **Head:** Christie **Head Markings:** © Mattel Inc./ 1987 **Arms:** ptr **Body:** dark brown tnt **Body Markings:** © Mattel Inc 1966/ Malaysia

Model #: 9728 Name: Lights & Lace Christie **Box Date:** 1990 **Hair Color:** black **Hairstyle:** sides pulled up & tied with yellow lace & silver bow, rest waist length, ends curled, curly bangs **Face:** brown eyes, black brows, pink frosted lips & blush **Clothing:** yellow & silver mini dress with spaghetti straps, sweetheart neck, full skirt, sewn in panties & matching bolero jacket, green & iridescent dangle earrings & ring, lighted belt, shoe top lace ruffles, green microphone, green cowboy boots **Extras:** green hair pick & sheet of cardboard punch outs **Booklet:** BF&F 1991 & instructions **Head:** Christie **Head Markings:** © Mattel Inc./ 1987 **Arms:** bent **Body:** dark brown tnt **Body Markings:** © Mattel Inc 1966/ Malaysia

Model #: 3265 Name: Rappin' Rockin' Christie **Box Date:** 1991 **Hair Color:** black **Hairstyle:** crinkled thigh-length ponytail held with yellow band, curly bangs **Face:** brown eyes, black brows, orange lips & blush **Clothing:** lime green sleeveless mid-thigh stretch bodysuit, orange satin hooded long sleeve jacket, green & gold disk earrings, gold ring & pendant, orange boom box, yellow scrunch sock tops, orange high-top tennis shoes **Extras:** yellow oval brush **Head:** Christie **Head Markings:** © Mattel Inc./ 1987 **Arms:** bent **Body:** dark brown tnt **Body Markings:** © Mattel Inc 1966/ China

Model #: 2217 Name: Rollerblades Christie **Box Date:** 1991 **Hair Color:** black **Hairstyle:** crinkled thigh length with yellow-green ribbon headband, curly bangs **Face:** lilac-green eyes, black brows, pink lips & blush **Clothing:** purple sleeveless bodysuit with chartreuse mid-thigh shorts trimmed in purple, multicolor fanny pack, hot pink triangle earrings & ring, purple knee pads, chartreuse elbow pads, lilac rollerblades **Extras:** chartreuse oval brush **Booklet:** instructions **Head:** Christie **Head Markings:** © Mattel Inc./ 1987 **Arms:** bent **Body:** dark brown tnt **Body Markings:** © Mattel Inc 1966/ China **Notes:** rollerblade sparks are fire hazard

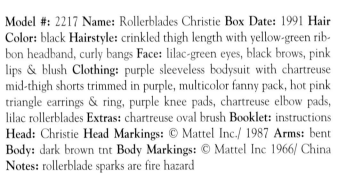

Model #: 1394 Name: Sun Sensation Christie **Box Date:** 1991 **Hair Color:** black with reddish brown streaks **Hairstyle:** sides divided in 2, tied with metallic turquoise bands, rest thigh length, ends curled under, curly bangs **Face:** light brown, black brows, frosted red lips & blush **Clothing:** metallic blue halter top bikini, gold star earrings, 3 charm gold pendant **Extras:** lilac oval brush **Head:** Christie **Head Markings:** © Mattel Inc./ 1987 **Arms:** ptr **Body:** dark brown tnt **Body Markings:** © Mattel Inc 1966/ Malaysia

Model #: 4907 **Name:** Glitter Beach Christie **Box Date:** 1992 **Hair Color:** brunette with reddish streaks **Hairstyle:** crinkled thigh length, pulled back with multicolor glitter headband **Face:** lavender-green eyes, black brows, hot pink lips & blush **Clothing:** 2-piece swimsuit of light green, orange, hot pink with silver glitter, silver stud earrings, beaded pendant **Extras:** orange oval brush **Head:** Christie **Head Markings:** © Mattel Inc./ 1987 **Arms:** ptr **Body:** dark brown tnt **Body Markings:** © Mattel Inc 1966/ Malaysia

Model #: 10958 **Name:** Sun Jewel Shani **Box Date:** 1993 **Hair Color:** black **Hairstyle:** sides pulled to 1 side & banded, rest thigh length, ends curled **Face:** green eyes, black brows, orange lips & blush **Clothing:** orange 2-piece swimsuit with crystal jewel bodice trim, matching dangle earrings, orange ring **Extras:** green oval brush & stick on jewels **Head:** Shani **Head Markings:** © 1990/ Mattel Inc **Arms:** Shani **Body:** dark brown tnt **Body Markings:** © Mattel Inc 1966/ Malaysia

Model #: 12451 **Name:** Tropical Splash Christie **Box Date:** 1994 **Hair Color:** brunette **Hairstyle:** sides & front pulled back into braided ponytail, rest thigh length **Face:** brown eyes, black brows, hot pink lips & blush **Clothing:** black, gold, light blue, green halter-style bikini with matching large gold earrings, gold seashell pendant **Extras:** royal blue oval brush & Barbie perfume **Booklet:** 1994 PB **Head:** Christie **Head Markings:** © Mattel Inc./ 1987 **Arms:** ptr **Body:** dark brown tnt **Body Markings:** © Mattel Inc 1966/ Malaysia **Notes:** perfume is same as used on Mackie's Masquerade doll, fabric pattern & earrings vary

Barbie's Hispanic Friends

Model #: 5503 **Name:** California Dream Teresa **Box Date:** 1987 **Hair Color:** reddish brown **Hairstyle:** side ponytail with bangs **Face:** brown eyes, brown brows, deep pink lips & blush **Clothing:** yellow & white dot & stripe crop top with matching ruffle shorts & long sleeve jacket, yellow dangle earrings, visor, Frisbee, white & yellow anklets, yellow high-top tennis shoes **Extras:** yellow oval brush, comic book, sheet of cardboard punch outs **Booklet:** BWOF 1987 **Head:** Hispanic **Head Markings:** inside rim © Mattel Inc, 1983 **Arms:** ptr **Body:** dark tan tnt **Body Markings:** © Mattel Inc 1966/ China **Notes:** no information on whether doll ever issued as California Teresa

Model #: 4117 **Name:** Island Fun Teresa **Box Date:** 1987 **Hair Color:** black **Hairstyle:** middle part, mid-thigh ponytail banded at nape of neck & split in 3 **Face:** brown eyes, black brows, orange lips & blush **Clothing:** 1-piece orange swimsuit with turquoise Hawaiian print wrap skirt, pink & orange lei **Extras:** turquoise seahorse comb **Booklet:** BWOF 1987 & instructions **Head:** Hispanic **Head Markings:** inside rim © Mattel Inc, 1983 **Arms:** ptr **Body:** dark tan tnt **Body Markings:** © Mattel, Inc. 1966/ Hong Kong

Model #: 3249 **Name:** Beach Blast Teresa **Box Date:** 1988 **Hair Color:** brunette **Hairstyle:** front & sides pulled back with barrette & attached blond crinkle color-change hairpiece, rest mid-back length with ends curled under **Face:** brown eyes, brown brows, hot pink lips & blush **Clothing:** 1-piece high neck swimsuit of turquoise, black & yellow, pink wraparound sunglasses, hot pink visor & Frisbee **Extras:** hot pink seahorse comb **Booklet:** BWOF 1988 **Head:** Hispanic **Head Markings:** inside rim © Mattel Inc, 1983 **Arms:** ptr **Body:** dark tan tnt **Body Markings:** © Mattel Inc 1966/ China

Model #: 3218 **Name:** Cool Times Teresa **Box Date:** 1988 **Hair Color:** brownish red **Hairstyle:** side ponytail divided in 2 with half twisted, rest waist length, curly bangs **Face:** brown eyes, brown brows, orange lips & blush **Clothing:** white with black & white stripe crop trop, hamburger appliqué, light orange satin mini skirt jumper, black & white checked pants with orange & turquoise leggings, hot pink dangle earrings & ring, hamburger jump rope, hamburger, white tennis shoes **Extras:** turquoise oval brush & sheet of cardboard punch outs **Booklet:** BWOF 1988 & instructions **Head:** Hispanic **Head Markings:** inside rim © Mattel Inc, 1983 **Arms:** bent **Body:** dark tan tnt **Body Markings:** © Mattel Inc 1966/ China

Model #: 9353 **Name:** Barbie and the All Stars Teresa **Box Date:** 1989 **Hair Color:** brunette & red **Hairstyle:** front & side pulled into 3 sections, 2 held with blue bands, 1 with red ribbon, rest crinkled thigh length **Face:** brown eyes, brown brows, pink lips & blush **Clothing:** red, white & gold star halter-style bodysuit, white pleated tennis skirt with gold band, white tennis racket, 3 red balls, tote bag converts to matching jacket, red hoop earrings & ring, wide red pumps, white tennis shoes **Extras:** red oval brush & sheet of cardboard punch outs **Booklet:** BWOF 1988 & instructions **Head:** Steffie **Head Markings:** inside rim © 1971 Mattel Inc & country **Arms:** bent **Body:** dark tan tnt **Body Markings:** © Mattel Inc 1966/ Malaysia

Model #: 4136 Name: Wet n' Wild Teresa Box Date: 1989 Hair Color: brunette Hairstyle: 1 side pulled back with blue snake tie & braided, rest mid-thigh length, spiky bangs Face: brown eyes, black brows, deep pink lips & blush Clothing: 1-piece change-color swimsuit of yellow, green & turquoise, turquoise sunglasses, orange snake bracelet Extras: orange oval brush Head: Steffie Head Markings: inside rim © 1971 Mattel Inc & country Arms: ptr Body: dark tan tnt Body Markings: © Mattel Inc 1966/ China

Model #: 9426 Name: All American Teresa Box Date: 1990 Hair Color: reddish brown Hairstyle: sides & front pulled to 1 side held with neon green snake tie, rest waist length with ends curled under, spiky bangs Face: green eyes, brown brows, orange lips & blush Clothing: green T-shirt with orange cuff sleeves, acid washed blue overalls with flag bodice detail, orange bandanna, orange hoop earrings & ring, 2 pair of Reeboks Extras: orange oval brush & sheet of cardboard punch outs Head: Steffie Head Markings: inside rim © 1971 Mattel Inc & country Arms: bent Body: dark tan tnt Body Markings: © Mattel Inc 1966/ Malaysia

Model #: 9727 Name: Lights & Lace Teresa Box Date: 1990 Hair Color: brunette Hairstyle: sides pulled up & tied with turquoise lace & silver bow, rest waist length, ends curled, curly bangs Face: brown eyes, black brows, purple lips & blush Clothing: turquoise & silver lace mini dress with spaghetti straps, sweetheart neck, full skirt, matching bolero jacket & sewn in panties, purple & iridescent dangle earrings & ring, lighted belt, shoe top lace ruffles, purple microphone, purple cowboy boots Extras: purple hair pick & sheet of cardboard punch outs Booklet: BF&F 1991 & instructions Head: Steffie Head Markings: inside rim © 1971 Mattel Inc & country Arms: bent Body: dark tan tnt Body Markings: © Mattel Inc 1966/ Malaysia

Model #: 3270 Name: Rappin' Rockin' Teresa Box Date: 1991 Hair Color: brown & red Hairstyle: front & sides sectioned in 3 pigtails on 1 side tied with different color bands, rest thigh length crinkled Face: brown eyes, brown brows, pink lips & blush Clothing: yellow spaghetti strap full skirted mini dress with matching mid-thigh shorts, turquoise long sleeved crop top jacket with collar, blue & gold disk earrings, gold ring & pendant, yellow boom box, hot pink scrunch sock tops, yellow high-top tennis shoes Extras: orange oval brush Booklet: 1991 PB Head: Teresa Head Markings: © 1990, Mattel/ Inc Arms: bent Body: dark tan tnt Body Markings: © Mattel Inc 1966/ China

Model #: 2216 Name: Rollerblades Teresa Box Date: 1991 Hair Color: brunette Hairstyle: pink headband, thigh length, curly bangs Face: brown eyes, light brown brows, hot pink lips & blush Clothing: orange short sleeve crop top, hot pink lace mid-thigh shorts with orange sewn in panties & mini skirt, lime green fanny pack, orange elbow pads & knee pads, yellow heart shaped earrings & ring, light orange rollerblades Extras: hot pink oval brush Booklet: instructions Head: Teresa Head Markings: © 1990, Mattel/ Inc Arms: bent Body: dark tan tnt Body Markings: © Mattel Inc 1966/ China Notes: rollerblade sparks are fire hazard

Model #: 4921 Name: Glitter Beach Teresa Box Date: 1992 Hair Color: reddish brown Hairstyle: thigh length pulled back with multicolor glitter headband, ends curled under, bangs Face: green eyes, brown brows, frosted deep pink lips & blush Clothing: 1-piece yellow, purple, pink, turquoise swimsuit with glitter & yellow trim, silver stud earrings, beaded pendant Extras: lilac oval brush Head: Teresa Head Markings: © 1990, Mattel/ Inc Arms: ptr Body: dark tan tnt Body Markings: © Mattel Inc 1966/ Malaysia

Model #: 2316 Name: Hollywood Hair Teresa Box Date: 1992 Hair Color: blonde with brown streaks Hairstyle: ankle length, sides pulled back & tied with orange & gold fabric tie, bangs Face: brown-green eyes, black brows, orange lips & blush Clothing: halter-style bodysuit of gold & orange, sleeveless orange jacket with gold & orange collar, mini skirt with gold waistband, orange & gold print skirt, gold slip, gold dangle earrings & ring, wide orange pumps Extras: orange star comb & hair mist Booklet: 1992 PB & instructions Head: Teresa Head Markings: © 1990, Mattel/ Inc Arms: bent Body: dark tan tnt Body Markings: © Mattel Inc 1966/ Malaysia Notes: make pink stars appear in hair

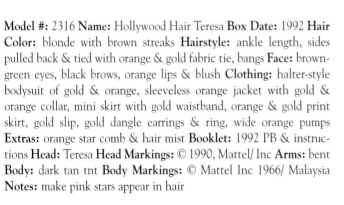

Model #: 11078 Name: Camp Fun Teresa Box Date: 1993 Hair Color: brown Hairstyle: front section pulled into pink rubber band, rest waist length with curly bangs Face: brown eyes, brown brows, hot pink lips & blush Clothing: denim bra top, blue windbreaker, yellow knee-high pants, yellow anklets, backpack, sunglasses, hot pink pot, 2 pink cups, hot pink hiking boots Extras: hot pink oval brush Booklet: instructions Head: Teresa Head Markings: © 1990, Mattel/ Inc Arms: bent Body: dark tan tnt Body Markings: © Mattel Inc 1966/ Malaysia Notes: hair changes color in sunlight

Model #: 10957 **Name:** Sun Jewel Teresa **Box Date:** 1993 **Hair Color:** brunette **Hairstyle:** sides pulled back with clear band, thigh length, ends curled under **Face:** lavender-green eyes, dark brown brows, orange lips & blush **Clothing:** lime green 1-piece halter-style swimsuit with crystal jewel trim on bodice & matching dangle earrings **Extras:** turquoise oval brush & stick on jewels **Head:** Teresa **Head Markings:** © 1990, Mattel/ Inc **Arms:** ptr **Body:** dark tan tnt **Body Markings:** © Mattel Inc 1966/ Malaysia

Model #: 13201 **Name:** Baywatch Teresa **Box Date:** 1994 **Hair Color:** brunette **Hairstyle:** thigh length **Face:** brown eyes, light brown brows, red lips & blush **Clothing:** blue hooded long sleeve midriff top with Baywatch insignia, matching below knee blue stretch pants with yellow stripe on side of leg, red 1-piece swimsuit, yellow visor, yellow tennis shoes, yellow stud earrings & ring, silver whistle on black cord **Extras:** yellow oval brush, yellow Frisbee, red binoculars, red flotation device, yellow windup surf board **Head:** Teresa **Head Markings:** © 1990, Mattel/ Inc **Arms:** bent **Body:** tan tnt **Body Markings:** © Mattel Inc 1966/ Malaysia **Notes:** foreign issue doll available in some U.S. stores

Model #: 13238 **Name:** Butterfly Princess Teresa **Box Date:** 1994 **Hair Color:** brunette **Hairstyle:** thigh length crinkled, bangs, sides pulled up with pink satin ribbon **Face:** hazel eyes, brown brows, deep pink lips & blush **Clothing:** long full skirt gown with multicolor top and lilac tulle overskirt with iridescent butterfly accents, sewn in panties, gold stud earrings & ring, green & lilac magnetic flower magic wand to make butterflies move, wide lilac pearl pumps **Extras:** lilac pearl oval brush, butterfly princess fold out pamphlet, ring for child **Booklet:** instructions **Head:** Teresa **Head Markings:** © 1990, Mattel/ Inc **Arms:** bent **Body:** dark tan tnt **Body Markings:** © Mattel Inc.1966/ Indonesia

Model #: 13084 **Name:** Dance Moves Teresa **Box Date:** 1994 **Hair Color:** brunette **Hairstyle:** hip length crinkled, sides pulled up to top of head held with purple band, bangs **Face:** green eyes, light brown brows, light purple lips & blush **Clothing:** purple & silver metallic scoop neck long sleeve crop top, silver suspenders on metallic purple shorts, silver & purple metallic tights, silver hoop earrings & ring, black Jazzie flats **Extras:** purple oval brush, fake purple cassette player with headphones & boom box, black hand held microphone **Booklet:** instructions **Head:** Teresa **Head Markings:** © 1990, Mattel/ Inc **Arms:** bent **Body:** tan tnt with gymnast legs **Body Markings:** © Mattel Inc 1966/ China **Notes:** arms click into position

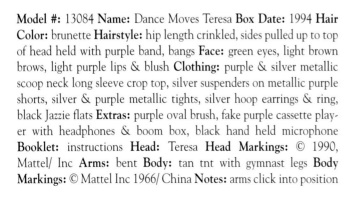

Model #: 13235 Name: Slumber Party Teresa Box Date: 1994 Hair Color: brunette Hairstyle: crinkled thigh length, curly bangs, pink fabric headband with white stars & moons Face: blue eyes, brown brows, hot pink lips & blush Clothing: 2-piece pink & white dot pajamas trimmed in lace Extras: pink oval brush, white wash cloth, sheet of dayglo stickers, clear zipper carrying case Booklet: 1995 PB Head: Teresa Head Markings: © 1990, Mattel/ Inc Arms: soft Body: tan soft body Body Markings: cloth tag:© Mattel, Inc.1993 or 94 or 95/El Segundo, CA 90245 U.S.A./ surface washable(repeated)/ Reg.No.PA-60/ All New Materials/ Consisting of Polyester Fibers/ Made in China Notes: painted eyes open and close with ice water & warm water

Model #: 12450 Name: Tropical Splash Teresa Box Date: 1994 Hair Color: brunette Hairstyle: top & 1 side pulled back & braided, rest thigh length Face: brown-green eyes, light brown brows, deep pink lips & blush Clothing: black, hot pink, purple, green strapless tie front bikini with large matching gold earrings, gold starfish pendant Extras: purple oval brush & Barbie perfume Head: Teresa Head Markings: © 1990, Mattel/ Inc Arms: ptr Body: dark tan tnt Body Markings: © Mattel Inc 1966/ Malaysia Notes: perfume is same as used on Mackie's Masquerade doll, fabric pattern & earrings vary

Barbie's Asian Friends

Model #: 1196 Name: Rocker Dana Box Date: 1985 Hair Color: black Hairstyle: mid-back ponytail held with orange lace scarf Face: brown eyes, black brows, bright 2-tone blue eyeshadow, orange lips & blush Clothing: orange lace tank top, white vinyl 3/4 sleeve jacket with triangles of blue, yellow & orange, blue lycra footless tights, wide blue belt with silver buckle, orange and yellow glitter dangle earrings, orange ring, blue faux fur headband, orange snake bracelet, white Rockers T-shirt, narrow orange pumps Extras: orange pointed brush, white microphone, 2 sheets of cardboard punch outs, 1 iron-on Rockers transfer Booklet: BWOF 1985 & instructions Head: Oriental Head Markings: © Mattel Inc 1980 Arms: bent Body: tan tnt Body Markings: © Mattel Inc.1966/ Philippines Notes: many different clothing combinations

Model #: 2056 Name: Tropical Miko Box Date: 1985 Hair Color: black Hairstyle: pulled back to nape of neck with yellow fabric flower, twisted mid-thigh-length ponytail Face: brown eyes, dark brown brows, orange lips & blush Clothing: 1-piece off-the-shoulder green, purple, hot pink swimsuit Extras: yellow pointed brush Booklet: BWOF 1986 Head: Oriental Head Markings: © Mattel Inc 1980 Arms: ptr Body: dark tan tnt Body Markings: © Mattel, Inc. 1966/ Hong Kong Notes: head turning greasy

Model #: 3158 Name: Rocker Dana 2nd issue Box Date: 1986 Hair Color: black Hairstyle: mid-back length, ends curled, sides pulled up in ponytail, curly bangs Face: brown eyes, black brows, turquoise eye-shadow, hot pink lips & blush Clothing: turquoise midi length T-shirt with gold stars & Rockers logo & fuchsia cuffs at sleeves, silver pants with suspenders, turquoise dangle earrings & ring, turquoise cuff with hot pink long fringe, turquoise hair ornament & narrow hot pink pumps Extras: turquoise oval brush, sheet of cardboard punch outs, silver microphone Booklet: BWOF 1987 & instructions Head: Oriental Head Markings: © Mattel Inc 1980 Arms: bent Body: tan tnt Body Markings: © Mattel Inc 1966/ Taiwan

Model #: 4065 Name: Island Fun Miko Box Date: 1987 Hair Color: black Hairstyle: middle part, mid-thigh-length ponytail banded at nape of neck & split in 3 Face: brown eyes, brown brows, deep pink lips & blush Clothing: 1-piece hot pink swimsuit, yellow Hawaiian print wrap skirt, pink & yellow lei Extras: hot pink seahorse comb Booklet: BWOF 1987 & instructions Head: Oriental Head Markings: © Mattel Inc 1980 Arms: ptr Body: dark tan tnt Body Markings: © Mattel Inc 1966/ Malaysia

Model #: 4977 Name: Sensations Becky Box Date: 1987 Hair Color: black Hairstyle: very curly ponytail with curly bangs Face: brown eyes, black brows, hot pink lips & blush Clothing: green metallic halter-style mini dress with lime green satin flared skirt & sewn in panties, purple satin & white vinyl jacket, green drop earrings & ring, black microphone, pink & black glasses, white anklets, black & white saddle shoes Extras: lime green oval brush & 2 sheets of cardboard punch outs Booklet: BWOF 1987 Head: Oriental Head Markings: © Mattel Inc 1980 Arms: bent Body: dark tan tnt Body Markings: © Mattel Inc 1966/ China

Model #: 1352 Name: Animal Lovin' Nikki Box Date: 1988 Hair Color: brown & black streaks Hairstyle: parted in middle, front and sides divided & pulled into small pigtails, rest mid-back length, ends curled under Face: brown eyes, black brows, pink lips & blush Clothing: lilac animal print crop top, matching mini skirt with sewn in panties & gold waistband, lilac kerchief, plastic lion cub, pink dangle earrings & ring, pink hiking boots Extras: pink oval brush & sheet of cardboard punch outs Booklet: BWF 1988 Head: Oriental Head Markings: © Mattel Inc 1980 Arms: bent Body: tan tnt Body Markings: © Mattel Inc 1966/ Malaysia

Model #: 3244 Name: Beach Blast Miko Box Date: 1988 Hair Color: black Hairstyle: front & sides pulled back, pink barrette holds blonde crinkle color-change hairpiece, rest mid-back length, curly bangs Face: brown eyes, brown brows, deep pink lips & blush Clothing: 1-piece swimsuit of pink, lime green & black, pink wrap-around sunglasses, turquoise visor & Frisbee Extras: yellow seahorse comb Booklet: BWOF 1988 Head: Oriental Head Markings: © Mattel Inc 1980 Arms: ptr Body: dark tan tnt Body Markings: © Mattel Inc 1966/ Malaysia

Model #: 9933 Name: Western Fun Nia Box Date: 1989 Hair Color: black Hairstyle: pulled back in waist-length braid, curly bangs Face: teal eyes, brown brows, deep pink lips & blush Clothing: white long sleeve bodysuit with turquoise ribbon trimmed vest, 2 tiered multicolor mini skirt of blue, light blue, white, yellow & hot pink, turquoise felt hat with ribbon trim, turquoise dangle earrings, belt buckle, ring, pink belt, turquoise cowboy boots Extras: pink oval brush & sheet of cardboard punch outs Booklet: BWOF 1988 Head: Oriental Head Markings: © Mattel Inc 1980 Arms: bent Body: dark tan tnt Body Markings: © Mattel Inc 1966/ Malaysia

Model #: 4120 Name: Wet n' Wild Kira Box Date: 1989 Hair Color: black Hairstyle: sides & front pulled back with orange snake tie, rest mid-thigh length, spiky bangs Face: brown eyes, brown brows, orange lips & blush Clothing: 1-piece change-color swimsuit of pink & light green, turquoise snake bracelet & pink sunglasses Extras: hot pink oval brush Head: Oriental Head Markings: © Mattel Inc 1980 Arms: ptr Body: dark tan tnt Body Markings: © Mattel Inc.1966/ Malaysia

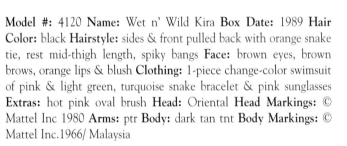

Model #: 9427 Name: All American Kira Box Date: 1990 Hair Color: black Hairstyle: sides & front pulled into pink snake tie, rest crinkled mid-thigh length Face: teal eyes, black brows, pink lips & blush Clothing: yellow-green sleeveless T-shirt, acid washed shorts with v-neck attached straps in flag design, matching acid washed bolero jacket, yellow hoop earrings & ring, multicolor knee socks, 2 pair of Reeboks Extras: yellow oval brush & sheet of cardboard punch outs Head: Oriental Head Markings: © Mattel Inc 1980 Arms: bent Body: dark tan tnt Body Markings: © Mattel Inc 1966/ Malaysia

Model #: 9409 Name: Benetton Kira **Box Date:** 1990 **Hair Color:** black **Hairstyle:** front & sides pulled back with red band, majority of hair draping to mid-back with ends tied in red band, swept back bangs **Face:** brown eyes, black brows, orange lips & blush **Clothing:** turquoise sleeveless turtleneck, long sleeve yellow faux fur short jacket, red striped pleated mini skirt, fuchsia scarf, yellow stretch pants, red leggings, orange bandanna, red tote bag, silver baseball hat, red hoop earrings & ring, fuchsia tennis shoes **Extras:** red oval brush & sheet of cardboard punch outs **Head:** Oriental **Head Markings:** © Mattel Inc 1980 **Arms:** bent **Body:** tan tnt **Body Markings:** © Mattel Inc 1966/ China

Model #: 5943 **Name:** Hawaiian Fun Kira **Box Date:** 1990 **Hair Color:** black **Hairstyle:** front & sides pulled to 1 side held with bands, ponytail twisted to waist, rest of hair pulled back with yellow band to top of thigh, bangs **Face:** brown eyes, dark brown brows, orange lips & blush **Clothing:** yellow, orange & teal 1-piece swimsuit, orange mini hula skirt, orange & black sunglasses **Extras:** hot pink oval brush, bracelet for child **Head:** Oriental **Head Markings:** © Mattel Inc 1980 **Arms:** ptr **Body:** dark tan tnt **Body Markings:** © Mattel Inc 1966/ Malaysia

Model #: 2218 **Name:** Rollerblades Kira **Box Date:** 1991 **Hair Color:** black **Hairstyle:** thigh length, pulled back with purple headband, bangs **Face:** brown-green eyes, brown brows, hot pink lips & blush **Clothing:** turquoise shorts, chartreuse belt & crop top with ribbon around neck, purple fanny pack, matching knee & elbow pads, yellow round earrings & ring, chartreuse rollerblades **Extras:** chartreuse oval brush **Booklet:** instructions **Head:** Oriental **Head Markings:** © Mattel Inc 1980 **Arms:** bent **Body:** dark tan tnt **Body Markings:** © Mattel Inc 1966/ China **Notes:** rollerblade sparks are a fire hazard

Model #: 1447 **Name:** Sun Sensation Kira **Box Date:** 1991 **Hair Color:** black with red streaks **Hairstyle:** sides & front pulled back with purple metallic band, rest thigh length, ends curled under **Face:** lilac-green eyes, dark brown brows, frosted light red lips & blush **Clothing:** metallic purple bikini with gold star earrings, 3 gold charm pendant **Extras:** aqua oval brush **Head:** Oriental **Head Markings:** © Mattel Inc 1980 **Arms:** ptr **Body:** dark tan tnt **Body Markings:** © Mattel Inc.1968/ Malaysia

Model #: 4924 Name: Glitter Beach Kira Box Date: 1992 Hair Color: black with red streaks Hairstyle: thigh length, pulled back with multicolor glitter headband Face: brown eyes, black brows, frosted orange lips & blush Clothing: 1-piece multicolor swimsuit with silver glitter & orange insert & straps, silver stud earrings, beaded pendant Extras: blue oval brush Head: Oriental Head Markings: © Mattel Inc 1980 Arms: ptr Body: dark tan tnt Body Markings: © Mattel Inc 1966/ Malaysia

Model #: 10956 Name: Sun Jewel Kira Box Date: 1993 Hair Color: black Hairstyle: thigh length, ends curled under Face: brown-lavender eyes, black brows, red lips & blush Clothing: 1-piece high neck purple swimsuit with crystal jewel trim on bodice & matching dangle earrings Extras: yellow oval brush & stick on jewels Head: Oriental Head Markings: © Mattel Inc 1980 Arms: ptr Body: tan tnt Body Markings: © Mattel Inc.1966/ Indonesia

Model #: 12449 Name: Tropical Splash Kira Box Date: 1994 Hair Color: black Hairstyle: front & 1 side pulled back & braided, remaining sides banded, rest thigh length Face: green eyes, black brows, deep pink lips & blush Clothing: black, gold, turquoise, yellow strapless bikini, gold sun necklace, large multicolor gold earrings Extras: aqua oval brush & Barbie perfume Head: Oriental Head Markings: © Mattel Inc 1980 Arms: ptr Body: dark tan tnt Body Markings: © Mattel Inc.1966/ Indonesia Notes: perfume is same as used on Mackie's Masquerade doll, fabric pattern & earrings vary

Chapter 4

Skipper, Francie, Tutti Dolls and Other Like-Sized Friends 1964-1995

Skipper

Model #: 950 **Name:** Skipper **Issue Date:** 1964-66 **Box Date:** 1963 **Hair Color:** shades of blonde, brunette or titian **Hairstyle:** middle part, waist length with bangs, brass headband, cello on head **Face:** blue eyes, reddish brows, coral lips **Clothing:** 1-piece red & white sailor suit style swimsuit with white trim, red flats, wrist tag **Extras:** black or gold wire stand, small white brush & comb **Booklet:** Skipper 1963 or JES 1964 **Head:** Skipper **Body:** tan s/l **Body Markings:** Skipper/ © 1963/ Mattel, Inc. **Notes:** later issue eliminated Skipper name from markings, gift sets: Party Time & Wedding Party part of 4 dressed doll set

Model #: 1030 **Name:** Skipper bendable leg **Box Date:** 1964 **Hair Color:** shades of blonde, brunette or titian **Hairstyle:** middle part with bangs, waist length, brass headband, cello on head **Face:** turquoise eyes, light brown brows, peach/yellow lips **Clothing:** 1-piece navy stretch swimsuit with white & red striped bib shaped insert with anchor design, red flats, wrist tag **Extras:** gold wire stand, small white brush & comb **Booklet:** EFBM Book 1, 1964 **Head:** Skipper **Head Markings:** inside rim Copyr. © 1963 Mattel, Inc **Body:** tan b/l **Body Markings:** © 1963/ Mattel, Inc. **Notes:** also pink lips gift set: Holiday Party

Model #: 1105 **Name:** Skipper twist & turn **Box Date:** 1968 **Hair Color:** blonde brunette titian **Hairstyle:** waist length held back with turquoise headband, parted in middle with bangs, cello on head **Face:** blue eyes, rooted lashes, brown brows, deep pink lips & blush **Clothing:** pink & turquoise striped 1-piece swimsuit & wrist tag **Extras:** clear X stand **Booklet:** WOBF 1968 **Head:** Skipper **Head Markings:** inside rim Copyr. © 1963 Mattel, Inc **Body:** pink tnt **Body Markings:** © 1967 Mattel, Inc./ U.S. Patd./ U.S. Pats.Pend./ Made in Taiwan **Notes:** variations in swimsuit fabric, Sears gift sets: Perfectly Pretty & Wow! What a Cool Outfit

Model #: 1117 **Name:** Dramatic New Living Skipper **Box Date:** 1969 **Hair Color:** blonde **Hairstyle:** side part pulled into 2 pigtails tied with pink ribbons, ends turned up, pin curl on forehead **Face:** blue eyes, rooted lashes, light brown brows, deep pink lips & blush **Clothing:** 1-piece green, turquoise, hot pink stripe swimsuit with self fabric tie held with small hot pink ring, wrist tag **Extras:** clear X stand **Booklet:** LB&S 1970 **Head:** Skipper **Head Markings:** inside rim Copyr. © 1963 Mattel, Inc **Arms:** living **Body:** pink living **Body Markings:** © 1969 Mattel, Inc./ Taiwan/ U.S.& for. Patd/ other Pats. Pend./ Patd. in Canada 1967 **Notes:** Sears gift set: Very Best Velvet

Model #: 1105 Name: Skipper twist & turn Box Date: 1969 Hair Color: blonde brunette Hairstyle: mid-back-length banana curl pigtails with orange bows, bangs Face: blue eyes, rooted lashes, brown brows, deep pink lips & blush Clothing: orange & pink check 1-piece swimsuit with purple lines, wrist tag Extras: clear X stand Booklet: BWBSN Head: Skipper Head Markings: inside rim Copyr. © 1963 Mattel, Inc Body: pink tnt Body Markings: © 1967 Mattel, Inc./ U.S. Patd./ U.S. Pats.Pend./ Made in Taiwan Notes: gift set: Bright 'N Breezy

Model #: 1105 Name: Skipper twist & turn Box Date: 1969 Hair Color: blonde brunette Hairstyle: long sausage curl pigtails tied with orange ribbons, bangs, cello on head Face: blue eyes, rooted lashes, light brown brows, deep pink lips & blush Clothing: orange 2-piece vinyl swimsuit with orange & yellow cover-up, wrist tag Extras: clear X stand Booklet: WOBF 1968 Head: Skipper Head Markings: inside rim Copyr. © 1963 Mattel, Inc Body: tan tnt Body Markings: © 1967 Mattel, Inc./ U.S. Patd./ U.S. Pats.Pend./ Made in Taiwan

Model #: 1117 Name: Living Skipper Box Date: 1970 Hair Color: blonde Hairstyle: shoulder-length pigtails tied with orange ribbons Face: blue eyes, rooted lashes, deep pink lips & blush Clothing: seersucker 2-piece yellow swimsuit with yellow & metallic tulle, orange or yellow skateboard, wrist tag Extras: clear X stand Booklet: LB&S 1970 Head: Skipper Head Markings: inside rim Copyr. © 1963 Mattel, Inc Arms: living Body: pink living Body Markings: © 1969 Mattel, Inc./ Taiwan/ U.S.& for. Patd/ other Pats. Pend./ Patd. in Canada 1967

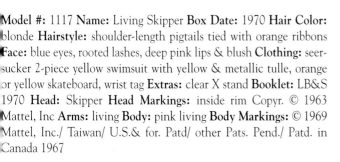

Model #: 1147 Name: Skipper Trade-in Box Date: 1970 Hair Color: blonde Hairstyle: short pigtails with ends curled up, tied with pink ribbons, parted on side with pin curl on forehead Face: blue eyes, rooted lashes, pink lips & blush, brown eyebrows Clothing: green, orange & blue swimsuit, wrist tag Extras: clear X stand Booklet: LB&S 1970 Head: Skipper Head Markings: inside rim Copyr. © 1963 Mattel, Inc Body: pink living Body Markings: © 1969 Mattel, Inc./ Taiwan/ U.S.& for. Patd/ other Pats. Pend./ Patd. in Canada 1967

Model #: 950 **Name:** Skipper reissue **Issue Date:** 1970 **Box Date:** 1963 **Hair Color:** blonde brunette titian **Hairstyle:** middle part, waist length, with bangs, brass headband, cello on head **Face:** blue eyes, brown brows, deep pink lips & blush **Clothing:** red & white 1-piece swimsuit, red flats, wrist tag **Extras:** clear X stand, small white brush & comb **Booklet:** LB&S 1970 **Head:** Skipper **Head Markings:** inside rim Copyr. © 1963 Mattel, Inc **Body:** pink s/l **Body Markings:** © 1963/ Mattel, Inc. **Notes:** illustrations on original s/ box updated

Model #: 1069 **Name:** Sun Set Malibu Skipper **Issue Date:** 1971-1977 **Box Date:** 1970 **Hair Color:** blonde **Hairstyle:** waist length, middle part with bangs, cello on head **Face:** blue eyes, brown brows, peach lips **Clothing:** 2-piece orange nylon swimsuit with blue beach towel **Head:** Skipper **Head Markings:** inside rim Copyr. © 1963 Mattel, Inc **Arms:** Skipper **Body:** tan tnt **Body Markings:** © 1967 Mattel, Inc./ U.S.Patd/ U.S.Pats.Pend/ Made in Korea **Notes:** dolls made in either Japan or Korea, same doll with same model # issued in white box or pink box under the Malibu name, see Sun Set Ken 1974 for example of white box & Malibu Barbie 1975 for example of pink box, towel dropped in later editions

Model #: 4223 **Name:** Quick Curl Skipper **Box Date:** 1972 **Hair Color:** blonde **Hairstyle:** side part, shoulder-length pageboy, with turquoise bow in hair, cello on head **Face:** turquoise eyes, brown brows, pink lips, brown freckles **Clothing:** turquoise & white gingham long dress with solid turquoise bodice, black ribbon, bow at waist, lace at neck and hem, 3 white barrettes, 4 ribbons, rubber band, wrist tag, white flats **Extras:** white X stand & hot pink pointed comb, brush, curler **Booklet:** BWOB 1973 **Head:** Skipper **Head Markings:** inside rim Copyr. © 1963 Mattel, Inc **Body:** pink tnt **Body Markings:** © 1967 Mattel, Inc./ U.S. Patd./ U.S. Pats.Pend. Made in Taiwan **Notes:** box available in several styles

Model #: 1117 **Name:** Skipper Pose 'N Play/baggie **Box Date:** 1973 **Hair Color:** blonde or red **Hairstyle:** short pigtails tied with blue ribbons, pin curls at ears, bangs, cello on head **Face:** blue eyes, brown brows, pale pink lips **Clothing:** blue & white sleeveless playsuit/swimsuit with blue buttons & wrist tag **Head:** Skipper **Head Markings:** inside rim Copyr. © 1963 Mattel, Inc **Arms:** living with swing action **Body:** pink living **Body Markings:** © 1969 Mattel, Inc./ Taiwan/ U.S.& for. Patd/ other Pats. Pend./ Patd. in Canada 1967 **Notes:** also packaged in 1971 with gym playset model #1179

Model #: 7259 **Name:** Growing Up Skipper **Box Date:** 1974 **Hair Color:** blonde **Hairstyle:** mid-back length, middle part, red ribbon headband, cello on head **Face:** blue eyes, light brown brows, peach lips & blush **Clothing:** red bodysuit with blue collar, red & white houndstooth mini skirt with blue waistband, matching long skirt, blue scarf, red knee socks, white platform sandals, red flats **Head:** Skipper **Head Markings:** inside rim Copyr. © 1963 Mattel, Inc **Arms:** straight **Body:** pink growing up **Body Markings:** © 1967/ Mattel/ Inc./ Hong Kong/ U.S. & For. Pat. **Notes:** turn arm & gains height & chest

Model #: 1069 **Name:** Sun Lovin' Malibu Skipper **Box Date:** 1978 **Hair Color:** blonde **Hairstyle:** middle part with bangs, waist length, cello on head **Face:** turquoise eyes, brown brows, peach lips & blush **Clothing:** turquoise bikini, turquoise vinyl tote bag, purple mirror sunglasses **Booklet:** BWOF 1979 **Head:** Skipper **Head Markings:** inside rim Copyr. © 1963 Mattel, Inc **Arms:** slight bend **Body:** dark tan tnt, painted tan lines **Body Markings:** © Mattel, Inc./ 1967/ Philippines

Model #: 2756 **Name:** Super Teen Skipper **Box Date:** 1978 **Hair Color:** blonde **Hairstyle:** waist length, banded at nape of neck, ends curled under, curly bangs **Face:** blue eyes, blonde brows, pink lips & blush **Clothing:** hot pink bodysuit trimmed with purple lace, purple shorts with pink trim, long purple skirt with lace trim, yellow skateboard with orange wheels, hot pink knee & elbow pads, white crash helmet, square pink mirror & brush with handgrip, clear ankle grip for skateboard, pink platform sandals with ankle strap **Booklet:** instructions **Head:** 1978 Skipper **Head Markings:** © 1978 Mattel Inc/ & country **Arms:** bent **Body:** pink tnt **Body Markings:** © Mattel, Inc. 1978/ © Mattel, Inc. 1967/Philippines

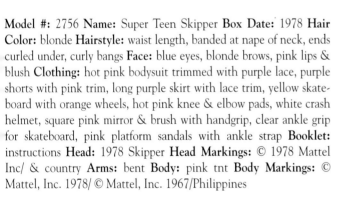

Model #: 1069 **Name:** Sunsational Malibu Skipper **Box Date:** 1981 **Hair Color:** blonde **Hairstyle:** middle part, waist length with bangs, cello on head **Face:** turquoise eyes, dark brown brows, peach lips & blush **Clothing:** 1-piece halter-style fuchsia swimsuit with pink trim & flower appliqué, pink towel, purple sunglasses **Booklet:** BWOF 1981 **Head:** Skipper **Head Markings:** inside rim Copyr. © 1963 Mattel, Inc **Arms:** slight bend **Body:** tan tnt **Body Markings:** © Mattel, Inc./ 1967/ Philippines

115

Model #: 5029 Name: Western Skipper Box Date: 1981 Hair Color: blonde Hairstyle: side part, double banded waist-length pigtails Face: blue eyes, blonde brows, peach lips & blush Clothing: red long sleeve cowboy shirt with white fringe, white jeans with black top-stitching & silver buckle, brown ring & matching lasso, white cowboy hat & cowboy boots Booklet: instructions Head: 1978 Skipper Head Markings: © 1978 Mattel Inc/ & country Arms: bent Body: pink tnt Body Markings: © Mattel, Inc. 1978/ © Mattel, Inc. 1967/Philippines

Model #: 5029 Name: Horse Lovin' Skipper Box Date: 1982 Hair Color: blonde Hairstyle: mid-back-length side part pigtails with double rubber band Face: turquoise eyes, blonde brows, peach lips & blush Clothing: cream & red pattern shirt, red vinyl jeans, fake shearling vest, brown ring, brown plastic lasso, tan cowboy hat & matching boots Booklet: BWOF 1982 & instructions Head: 1978 Skipper Head Markings: © 1978 Mattel Inc/ & country Arms: bent Body: pink tnt Body Markings: © Mattel, Inc. 1978/ © Mattel, Inc. 1967/Philippines

Model #: 7417 Name: Great Shapes Skipper Box Date: 1983 Hair Color: blonde Hairstyle: waist-length ponytail, ends curled, curl bangs Face: olive green eyes, light brown brows, peach lips & blush Clothing: pink leotard with ruffle trim at armholes, turquoise sash, pink & blue striped tights, turquoise tote bag, pink tennis shoes Booklet: BWOF 1984 Head: Skipper Head Markings: inside rim Copyr. © 1963 Mattel, Inc Arms: straight Body: tan tnt Body Markings: © Mattel, Inc./ 1967/ Philippines

Model #: 1069 Name: Sun Gold Malibu Skipper Box Date: 1983 Hair Color: blonde Hairstyle: side part, banded at nape of neck, split into 2 twisted mid-thigh-length ponytails Face: blue eyes, blonde brows, peach frosted lips & blush Clothing: 1-piece halter neck swimsuit, gold checked on top, solid turquoise bottom with turquoise bag that converts to mat, turquoise mirror sunglasses, lilac & pink sunglasses Booklet: BWOF 1984 Head: Skipper Head Markings: inside rim Copyr. © 1963 Mattel, Inc Arms: slight bend Body: dark tan tnt Body Markings: © Mattel, Inc./ 1967/ Philippines

Model #: 7927 Name: Hot Stuff Skipper Box Date: 1984 Hair Color: blonde Hairstyle: side part, 1 side pulled into ponytail rest banded at nape of neck, curly waist length Face: blue eyes, blonde brows, peach lips & blush Clothing: pink sleeveless bodysuit white tights, red mini skirt, turquoise headband & long sleeve high neck shirt, pink & turquoise leggings, pink mirror sunglasses, yellow tennis shoes, pink tennis shoes Extras: yellow pointed brush & comb Booklet: BWOF 1984 Head: 1984 Skipper Head Markings: © 1984/ Mattel Inc Arms: bent Body: tan tnt Body Markings: © Mattel, Inc. 1978 Notes: box says Philippines but not indicated on body

Model #: 1021 Name: Tropical Skipper Box Date: 1985 Hair Color: 2 tones of blonde Hairstyle: middle part, banded at nape of neck with yellow fabric flower twisted knee-length ponytail Face: turquoise eyes, blonde brows, peach lips Clothing: 1-piece off-the-shoulder navy, purple, yellow, green pattern swimsuit Extras: yellow pointed brush Booklet: BWOF 1986 Head: 1984 Skipper Head Markings: © 1984/ Mattel Inc Arms: slight bend Body: dark tan tnt Body Markings: © Mattel Inc 1967 Notes: box says China, but no country on doll

Model #: 3133 Name: Jewel Secrets Skipper Box Date: 1986 Hair Color: blonde Hairstyle: front & sides pulled back with red fabric bow, rest in ringlets to waist, curly bangs Face: turquoise eyes, blonde brows, deep pink lips & blush Clothing: sleeveless turtleneck halter-style red glitter bodysuit with matching mini skirt, white vinyl jacket, red sheer pantyhose, red vinyl duffel bag, red hair ornament, fake black camera, round red sunglasses, clear glitter flats Extras: sheet of cardboard punch outs & "A Ghost of a Secret" book Booklet: BWOF 1986 & instructions Head: 1984 Skipper Head Markings: © 1984/ Mattel Inc Arms: bent Body: tan tnt Body Markings: © Mattel, Inc. 1978 Notes: box says made in Hong Kong but not indicated on body

Model #: 4064 Name: Island Fun Skipper Box Date: 1987 Hair Color: 2 shades of blonde Hairstyle: middle part, mid-thigh ponytail banded at nape of neck, pulled in 3 curly ponytails Face: turquoise eyes, blonde brows, peach lips & blush Clothing: 1-piece orange swimsuit, blue Hawaiian print wrap skirt, hot pink & orange lei Extras: orange seahorse comb Booklet: BWOF 1987 & instructions Head: 1984 Skipper Head Markings: © 1984/ Mattel Inc Arms: straight Body: tan tnt Body Markings: © Mattel Inc 1967 Notes: box says China but not indicated on body

Model #: 5893 Name: Teen Fun Skipper Cheerleader Box Date: 1987 Hair Color: blonde & brown streaked Hairstyle: mid-back-length pigtails & bangs Face: light brown eyes, blonde brows, pink lips & blush Clothing: silver sleeveless leotard with white & silver glitter dot footless tights, pink satin mini skirt with silver glitter stars, silver star on bodice, 2 pink & white pom poms, tiara, baton, megaphone, hot pink tennis shoes Extras: hot pink oval brush, sheet of stickers, sheet of cardboard punch outs & teen scrapbook Booklet: BWOF 1988 & instructions Head: 1987 Skipper Head Markings: © Mattel Inc./ 1987 Arms: slight bend Body: tan tnt Body Markings: © Mattel, Inc.1987/ China

Model #: 5899 Name: Teen Fun Skipper Party Teen Box Date: 1987 Hair Color: blonde Hairstyle: sides & front pulled back, rest thigh length, ends curled under, curly bangs Face: lavender eyes, blonde brows, pink lips & blush Clothing: turtleneck long sleeve top of white & teal stripes, matching knee-length pants, white pantyhose with black & turquoise dots, turquoise & pink dotted tulle mini skirt, pink towel, 2 lilac sodas, 2 soft drinks, tray, turquoise bow flats Extras: lilac oval brush, sheet of stickers & sheet of cardboard punch outs Booklet: instructions Head: 1987 Skipper Head Markings: © Mattel Inc./ 1987 Arms: slight bend Body: tan tnt Body Markings: © Mattel, Inc.1987/ China

Model #: 5889 Name: Teen Fun Skipper Workout Box Date: 1987 Hair Color: blonde Hairstyle: front & sides pulled back, rest curly mid-back length, curly bangs Face: green eyes, blonde brows, deep pink lips & blush Clothing: yellow & white striped sleeveless crop top, gold leotard with ruffle at hip, white wrist bands, yellow footless tights, white & gold striped leggings, white headband, leg weights, jump rope, dumb bells, white towel, foam mat, yellow tennis shoes Extras: light green oval brush, sheet of stickers, sheet of cardboard punch outs & teen scrapbook Booklet: instructions Head: 1987 Skipper Head Markings: © Mattel Inc./ 1987 Arms: slight bend Body: tan tnt Body Markings: © Mattel, Inc.1987/ China

Model #: 4855 Name: Teen Sweetheart Skipper Box Date: 1987 Hair Color: blonde Hairstyle: sides & front pulled back, rest mid-thigh length, ends curled under, bangs Face: turquoise eyes, blonde brows, pink lips & blush Clothing: white sleeveless with glitter tulle mini dress with flower design on bodice, long skirt of pink dotted tulle & white fabric, white stockings with pink dots, pink necklace, white glitter gloves, silver tiara, drawstring purse, corsage, pink pearl flats Extras: pink pearl oval brush & sheet of cardboard punch outs Head: 1987 Skipper Head Markings: © Mattel Inc./ 1987 Arms: slight bend Body: tan tnt Body Markings: © Mattel, Inc.1987/ China

Model #: 1950 **Name:** Homecoming Queen Skipper **Box Date:** 1988 **Hair Color:** blonde **Hairstyle:** middle part, thigh length, ends curled under, tied back with pink ribbon headband with 3 pink fabric roses **Face:** blue eyes, blonde brows, pink lips & blush **Clothing:** white sleeveless gown with gold iridescent tulle, white ruffle detail on top, pink fabric flower detail on bodice & skirt, white purse with pink bow, pearl necklace, white pearl flats **Extras:** pink pearl oval brush, sheet of cardboard punch outs & teen scrapbook **Booklet:** instructions **Head:** 1987 Skipper **Head Markings:** © Mattel Inc./ 1987 **Arms:** slight bend **Body:** tan tnt **Body Markings:** © Mattel, Inc.1987/ China

Model #: 1951 **Name:** Teen Time Skipper **Box Date:** 1988 **Hair Color:** blonde **Hairstyle:** sides & front pulled back with pink & white dot fabric band, rest crinkled waist length, curly bangs **Face:** blue eyes, blonde brows, pink lips & blush **Clothing:** blue denim top with appliqué, pink & white stripe jacket, pink & white dots mini skirt converts to baby doll pajama top, matching panties, socks, clock, pencil, notebook, cordless phone, soda can, overnight case, white tennis shoes, pink fuzzy slippers **Extras:** yellow oval brush, sheet of stickers, sheet of cardboard punch outs & teen scrapbook **Booklet:** instructions **Head:** 1987 Skipper **Head Markings:** © Mattel Inc./ 1987 **Arms:** slight bend **Body:** tan tnt **Body Markings:** © Mattel, Inc.1987/ China

Model #: 3242 **Name:** Beach Blast Skipper **Box Date:** 1989 **Hair Color:** blonde **Hairstyle:** sides & front pulled back, attached barrette with color-change crimped hairpiece, rest waist length with curly bangs **Face:** lavender eyes, blonde brows, pink lips & blush **Clothing:** 1-piece swimsuit of hot pink, black & yellow, pink sunglasses, yellow Frisbee & visor **Extras:** yellow seahorse comb **Booklet:** BWOF 1988 **Head:** 1987 Skipper **Head Markings:** © Mattel Inc./ 1987 **Arms:** slight bend **Body:** tan tnt **Body Markings:** © Mattel, Inc.1987/ China

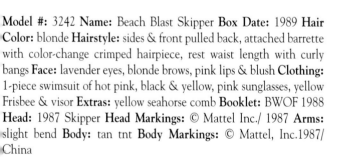

Model #: 4989 **Name:** Cool Tops Skipper **Box Date:** 1989 **Hair Color:** blonde **Hairstyle:** sides & front pulled back with pink snake tie, ponytail split into 3 & twisted, curly bangs, rest mid-thigh length **Face:** blue eyes, blonde brows, pink lips & blush **Clothing:** turquoise T-shirt, pink crop top with appliqué, yellow & white multicolor mini skirt, pink mid-calf stretch pants, yellow T-shirt holder, banana split charm, watch, purple purse & 2 T-shirt holders, pink flats **Extras:** pink oval brush, T-shirt decal, sheet of cardboard punch outs & decal for child's T-shirt **Booklet:** Skipper 1988 & instructions **Head:** 1987 Skipper **Head Markings:** © Mattel Inc./ 1987 **Arms:** slight bend **Body:** tan tnt **Body Markings:** © Mattel, Inc.1987/ China

Model #: 4138 Name: Wet n' Wild Skipper Box Date: 1989 Hair Color: blonde Hairstyle: sides & front pulled back with blue snake tie, rest mid-thigh length, spiky bangs Face: blue eyes, light brown brows, pink lips & blush Clothing: 1-piece pink & yellow color-changing swimsuit, blue sunglasses, clear snake bracelet Extras: orange oval brush Head: 1987 Skipper Head Markings: © Mattel Inc./ 1987 Arms: slight bend Body: tan tnt Body Markings: © Mattel, Inc.1987/ China

Model #: 9433 Name: Babysitter Skipper Box Date: 1990 Hair Color: blonde Hairstyle: sides & front pulled back with hot pink ribbon, rest thigh length, ends curled, bangs Face: blue eyes, blonde brows, pink lips & blush Clothing: white short sleeve crop top with orange dots, hot pink & white dot ruffle at neck, matching mini skirt with sewn in panties, pink boom box, rattle, bottle, soap, tray, jar, ribbon, blanket, baby's doll, baby in turquoise romper with pink ribbon, hot pink flats Extras: pink oval brush & sheet of cardboard punch outs Head: 1987 Skipper & baby Head Markings: Skipper=© Mattel Inc./ 1987 baby=© M.I. 1985 Arms: slight bend Body: tan tnt, baby Body Markings: Skipper=© Mattel, Inc. 1987/ Malaysia baby=© 1973/ Mattel Inc/ Malaysia

Model #: 5492 Name: Hawaiian Fun Skipper Box Date: 1990 Hair Color: blonde Hairstyle: sides & front pulled back with yellow band part pulled back with orange band, rest to top of thigh, ends turned under with bangs Face: blue eyes, blonde brows, pink lips & blush Clothing: 1-piece yellow-green & multicolor swimsuit, yellow mini hula skirt, yellow & black sunglasses Extras: orange oval brush & child's bracelet Head: 1987 Skipper Head Markings: © Mattel Inc./ 1987 Arms: slight bend Body: tan tnt Body Markings: © Mattel, Inc.1987/ Malaysia

Model #: 2709 Name: Pet Pals Skipper Box Date: 1991 Hair Color: blonde Hairstyle: sides & front pulled back with hot pink ribbon, rest crinkled mid-thigh length, curly bangs Face: blue eyes, blonde brows, deep pink lips & blush Clothing: hot pink & white print short sleeve shirt, sleeveless mini dress of white, black, hot pink & yellow-green with cat appliqué, yellow-green knee-high stretch pants, white dog with hot pink bow, pink collar with tag, bone, ball, can, 2 section food dish, leash, hot pink flats Extras: cardboard dog carrier Booklet: 1991 PB & instructions Head: 1987 Skipper Head Markings: © Mattel Inc./ 1987 Arms: bent Body: tan tnt Body Markings: © Mattel, Inc.1987/ Malaysia

Model #: 1446 **Name:** Sun Sensation Skipper **Box Date:** 1991 **Hair Color:** blonde with brown streaks **Hairstyle:** 1 side pulled back with metallic fuchsia tie, waist length, ends curled under, bangs **Face:** blue eyes, light brown brows, frosted pink lips & blush **Clothing:** metallic fuchsia bikini, gold stud earrings, gold sailboat pendant **Extras:** chartreuse oval brush **Head:** 1987 Skipper **Head Markings:** © Mattel Inc./ 1987 **Arms:** slight bend **Body:** tan tnt **Body Markings:** © Mattel, Inc.1987/ Malaysia

Model #: 3931 **Name:** Baton Twirler Skipper **Box Date:** 1992 **Hair Color:** blonde **Hairstyle:** mid-thigh length, ends curled under with bangs **Face:** blue eyes, light brown brows, pink lips & blush **Clothing:** long sleeve turtleneck orange & hot pink mini skirted twirling uniform with sewn in panties, pink hat with silver strap, silver baton with streamers, hot pink ankle high boots with orange & hot pink streamers **Extras:** hot pink oval brush **Head:** 1987 Skipper **Head Markings:** © Mattel Inc./ 1987 **Arms:** slight bend **Body:** tan tnt **Body Markings:** © Mattel, Inc.1987/ Malaysia

Model #: 4920 **Name:** Glitter Beach Skipper **Box Date:** 1992 **Hair Color:** blonde **Hairstyle:** crinkled thigh length, pulled back with glitter band, partial bangs **Face:** blue eyes, blonde brows, fuchsia lips & blush **Clothing:** 2-piece turquoise & multicolor glitter swimsuit, silver stud earrings, beaded pendant **Extras:** yellow oval brush **Head:** 1987 Skipper **Head Markings:** © Mattel Inc./ 1987 **Arms:** slight bend **Body:** tan tnt **Body Markings:** © Mattel, Inc.1987/ Malaysia

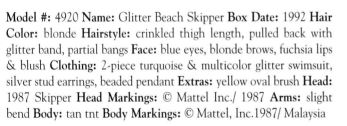

Model #: 2309 **Name:** Hollywood Hair Skipper **Box Date:** 1992 **Hair Color:** blonde **Hairstyle:** ankle length, sides & front pulled back with gold & turquoise fabric tie, bangs **Face:** blue eyes, light brown brows, hot pink lips & blush **Clothing:** turquoise & gold print short sleeve crop top with gold collar, matching turquoise capri pants, gold mini skirt, turquoise flats **Extras:** turquoise star comb & hair mist **Booklet:** 1992 PB & instructions **Head:** 1987 Skipper **Head Markings:** © Mattel Inc./ 1987 **Arms:** slight bend **Body:** tan tnt **Body Markings:** © Mattel, Inc.1987/ Malaysia **Notes:** make pink stars appear in hair

Model #: 11076 **Name:** Camp Fun Skipper **Box Date:** 1993 **Hair Color:** blonde **Hairstyle:** mid-thigh length with bangs **Face:** teal eyes, blonde brows, red lips & blush **Clothing:** white sleeveless T-shirt with appliqué, shirt sewn to orange knee-high stretch shorts, purple short sleeve jacket, orange baseball hat, white socks, yellow sunglasses, 2 hot pink cups, orange pot, orange backpack converts to sleeping bag, yellow stud earrings, orange flower flats **Extras:** yellow oval brush **Booklet:** instructions **Head:** 1987 Skipper **Head Markings:** © Mattel Inc./ 1987 **Arms:** slight bend **Body:** tan tnt **Body Markings:** © Mattel, Inc.1987/ Malaysia **Notes:** hair changes color in sunlight

Model #: 11179 **Name:** Cool & Crimp Skipper **Box Date:** 1993 **Hair Color:** blonde **Hairstyle:** side part, partial front & 1 side pulled back, partial bangs, rest thigh length **Face:** lavender eyes, blonde brows, deep pink lips & blush **Clothing:** blue T-shirt with contrasting cuffs & collarband, blue, white & pink knee-length overalls, pink pacifier earrings & pendant, 2 heart shaped crimpers, 2 wave crimpers, pink bottle, small comb, pink & white high-top tennis shoes **Extras:** pink oval brush & sheet of cardboard punch outs **Booklet:** 1993 PB & instructions **Head:** 1987 Skipper **Head Markings:** © Mattel Inc./ 1987 **Arms:** slight bend **Body:** tan tnt **Body Markings:** © Mattel, Inc.1987/ Malaysia

Model #: 10506 **Name:** Mermaid Skipper & Sea Twins **Box Date:** 1993 **Hair Color:** blonde **Hairstyle:** sides & front pulled back rest mid-thigh length crinkled with bangs **Face:** purple eyes, blonde brows, deep orange lips & blush **Clothing:** orange iridescent 2-piece mermaid costume with purple iridescent jewel at bodice & purple iridescent fins at ankles, white stud earrings & fuzzy wristband, 2 blonde babies with orange bows in crinkled ponytail wearing purple iridescent mermaid costumes **Extras:** orange seahorse comb **Booklet:** instructions **Head:** 1987 Skipper **Head Markings:** Skipper=© Mattel Inc/ 1987 twins=© 1993 M.I. **Arms:** slight bend **Body:** tan tnt, babies **Body Markings:** Skipper=© Mattel Inc 1987/ Malaysia twins=© 1973/ Mattel Inc/ Malaysia

Model #: 10955 **Name:** Sun Jewel Skipper **Box Date:** 1993 **Hair Color:** blonde **Hairstyle:** sides & front pulled back with clear band, rest mid-thigh length, partial curly bangs **Face:** blue eyes, blonde brows, pink lips & blush **Clothing:** yellow 2-piece swimsuit with crystal trim on bodice & matching dangle earrings **Extras:** hot pink oval brush & stick on jewels **Head:** 1987 Skipper **Head Markings:** © Mattel Inc./ 1987 **Arms:** slight bend **Body:** tan tnt **Body Markings:** © Mattel, Inc.1987/ Malaysia

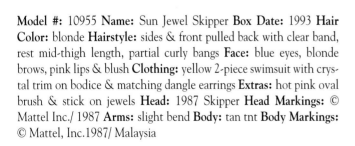

Model #: 12071 Name: Babysitter Skipper Box Date: 1994 Hair Color: blonde Hairstyle: 1 side & top pulled back with pink band, rest thigh length, ends curled under, bangs Face: lilac eyes, blonde brows, fuchsia lips & blush Clothing: white long sleeve sweatshirt top with multicolor pastel trim & bear appliqué, mauve pants, 3 assorted babies in yellow, aqua, pink buntings, yellow diaper pail, 2 bottles, divided dish, talc, rattle, doll, bar of soap, square dish, spoon, aqua tennis shoes Extras: aqua oval brush & cardboard chart Head: skipper 1987, babies Head Markings: Skipper=© Mattel Inc./ 1987 babies=© 1993 M.I. Arms: straight Body: tan tnt, babies Body Markings: Skipper=© Mattel, Inc. 1987/ China babies=© 1973/ Mattel Inc/ China

Model #: 12920 Name: Pizza Party Skipper Box Date: 1994 Hair Color: blonde Hairstyle: front & 1 side pulled back with red band rest mid-thigh length, bangs Face: blue eyes, light brown brows, rose lips & blush Clothing: long sleeve white with black dot Pizza Hut crop top, red mini skirt with sewn in panties, red stud earrings, white & black dot socks, 2 red napkins, 2 yellow plates, 6 slices of pizza, pizza cutter, spatula, large pizza with silver pizza plate, small pizza box, 2 forks & knives, 2 glasses, silver salt & pepper shakers, black oxford shoes Extras: red oval brush & sheet of stickers Booklet: 1994 PB Head: 1993 Skipper Head Markings: © Mattel Inc 1993 Arms: slight bend Body: tan tnt Body Markings: © Mattel, Inc.1987/ Indonesia

Model #: 12448 Name: Tropical Splash Skipper Box Date: 1994 Hair Color: blonde Hairstyle: front & sides pulled back into pony-tail, rest mid-thigh length with partial bangs Face: green eyes, brown brows, hot pink lips & blush Clothing: strapless 2-piece swimsuit of black, orange, yellow, gold with matching large gold earrings & gold seashell pendant Extras: orange oval brush & Barbie perfume Head: 1987 Skipper Head Markings: © Mattel Inc./ 1987 Arms: slight bend Body: dark tan tnt Body Markings: © Mattel, Inc.1987/ Indonesia Notes: perfume is same as used on Mackie's Masquerade doll, fabric pattern & earrings vary

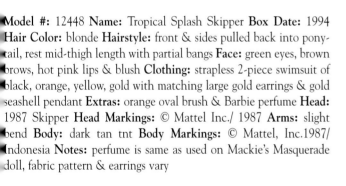

African American Skipper

Model #: 2390 Name: Homecoming Queen Skipper black version Box Date: 1988 Hair Color: black Hairstyle: middle part, thigh length, ends curled under, pulled back with pink ribbon with 3 pink fabric roses Face: gray-brown eyes, black brows, hot pink lips & blush Clothing: white sleeveless gown with gold iridescent tulle, white ruffle detail on top, pink fabric flower detail on bodice & skirt, white purse with pink bow, pearl necklace, white pearl flats Extras: pink pearl oval brush, sheet of cardboard punch outs & teen scrapbook Booklet: instructions Head: 1987 Skipper Head Markings: © Mattel Inc./ 1987 Arms: slight bend Body: dark brown tnt Body Markings: © Mattel, Inc.1987/ China Notes: this is the first black Skipper doll

Model #: 5441 Name: Cool Tops Skipper black version Box Date: 1989 Hair Color: brunette Hairstyle: sides & front pulled back with pink snake tie, ponytail split into 3 & twisted, curly bangs, rest mid-thigh length Face: gray eyes, black brows, pink lips & blush Clothing: turquoise T-shirt, pink crop top with appliqué, yellow & white multicolor mini skirt, pink mid-calf stretch pants, yellow T-shirt holder, banana split charm, watch, purple purse & 2 T-shirt holders, pink flats Extras: pink oval brush, T-shirt decal & sheet of cardboard punch outs Booklet: Skipper 1988 & instructions Head: 1987 Skipper Head Markings: © Mattel Inc./ 1987 Arms: slight bend Body: dark brown tnt Body Markings: © Mattel, Inc.1987/ China

Model #: 1599 Name: Babysitter Skipper black version Box Date: 1990 Hair Color: black Hairstyle: sides & front pulled back with hot pink ribbon, rest thigh length, ends curled, bangs Face: brown eyes, black brows, hot pink lips & blush Clothing: white short sleeve crop top with orange dots, hot pink & white dot ruffle at neck, matching mini skirt with sewn in panties, pink boom box, rattle, bottle, soap, tray, jar, ribbon, blanket, baby's doll, baby in turquoise romper with pink ribbon, hot pink flats Extras: pink oval brush & sheet of cardboard punch outs Head: 1987 Skipper Head Markings: © Mattel Inc./ 1987 baby=© M.I. 1985 Arms: slight bend Body: dark brown tnt, baby Body: tan tnt, baby Body Markings: Skipper=© Mattel, Inc. 1987/ Malaysia baby=© 1973/ Mattel Inc/ Malaysia

Model #: 4049 Name: Pet Pals Skipper black version Box Date: 1991 Hair Color: black Hairstyle: sides & front pulled back with hot pink ribbon, rest crinkled mid-thigh length, bangs Face: brown eyes, black brows, hot pink lips & blush Clothing: hot pink & white print short sleeve shirt, sleeveless mini dress of white, black, hot pink & yellow-green with cat appliqué, yellow-green knee-high stretch pants, white dog with hot pink bow, pink collar with tag, bone, ball, can, 2 section food dish, leash, hot pink flats Extras: cardboard dog carrier Booklet: 1991 PB & instructions Head: 1987 Skipper Head Markings: © Mattel Inc./ 1987 Arms: bent Body: dark brown tnt Body Markings: © Mattel, Inc.1987/ Malaysia

Model #: 7498 Name: Baton Twirler Skipper black version Box Date: 1992 Hair Color: black Hairstyle: mid-thigh length, ends curled under with bangs Face: brown-lilac eyes, black brows, hot pink lips & blush Clothing: long sleeve turtleneck orange & hot pink mini skirted twirling uniform with sewn in panties, pink hat with silver strap, silver baton with streamers, hot pink ankle high boots with orange & hot pink streamers Extras: hot pink oval brush Head: 1987 Skipper Head Markings: © Mattel Inc./ 1987 Arms: slight bend Body: dark brown tnt Body Markings: © Mattel, Inc.1987/ Malaysia

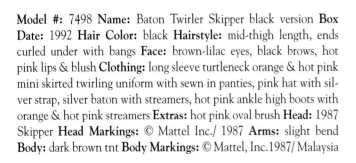

Model #: 12072 Name: Babysitter Skipper black version Box Date: 1994 Hair Color: black Hairstyle: 1 side & top pulled back with pink band, rest thigh length, ends curled under, bangs Face: lilac eyes, black brows, pink lips Clothing: white long sleeve sweatshirt top in multicolor pastel trim & bear appliqué, mauve pants, 3 assorted African American babies in yellow, aqua, pink buntings, yellow diaper pail, 2 bottles, divided dish, talc, rattle, doll, bar of soap, square dish, spoon, aqua tennis shoes Extras: aqua oval brush & cardboard chart Head: Skipper 1987, babies Head Markings: Skipper=© Mattel Inc./ 1987 babies=© 1993 M.I. Arms: straight Body: dark brown tnt, babies Body Markings: Skipper=© Mattel, Inc 1987/ China babies=© 1973/ Mattel Inc/ China

Model #: 11547 Name: Cool & Crimp Skipper black version Box Date: 1994 Hair Color: black Hairstyle: side part, partial front & 1 side pulled back, partial bangs, rest thigh length Face: brown eyes, black brows, light red lips & blush Clothing: blue T-shirt with contrasting cuffs & collarband, blue, white & pink knee-length overalls, pink pacifier earrings & pendant, 2 heart shaped crimpers, 2 wave crimpers, pink bottle, small comb, pink & white high-top tennis shoes Extras: pink oval brush & sheet of cardboard punch outs Booklet: 1993 PB & instructions Head: 1987 Skipper Head Markings: © Mattel Inc./ 1987 Arms: slight bend Body: dark brown tnt Body Markings: © Mattel, Inc.1987/ Malaysia

Model #: 12942 Name: Pizza Party Skipper black version Box Date: 1994 Hair Color: brunette Hairstyle: front & 1 side pulled back with red band, rest mid-thigh length, bangs Face: lavender eyes, black brows, red lips & blush Clothing: long sleeve white with black dot Pizza Hut crop top, red mini skirt with sewn in panties, red stud earrings, white & black dot socks, 2 red napkins, 2 yellow plates, 6 slices of pizza, pizza cutter, spatula, large pizza with silver pizza plate, small pizza box, 2 forks & knives, 2 glasses, silver salt & pepper shakers, black oxford shoes Extras: red oval brush & sheet of stickers Booklet: 1994 PB Head: 1993 Skipper Head Markings: © Mattel Inc 1993 Arms: slight bend Body: dark brown tnt Body Markings: © Mattel, Inc.1987/ Indonesia

Skipper's Female Friends

Model #: 1040 Name: Skooter Issue Date: 1965 Box Date: 1964 Hair Color: blonde brunette titian Hairstyle: middle part, pulled into 2 shoulder-length pigtails with ends curled up tied with red ribbons, bangs Face: brown eyes, brown brows, pink lips, blush & sprinkle of brown freckles Clothing: 2-piece swimsuit top red & white stripe, bottom solid red with white elastic waistband, optional silver metal trim may be in center waist, red flats & wrist tag Extras: gold wire stand, small white comb & brush Booklet: JES 1964 Head: Skooter Head Markings: inside rim Copyr. © 1963 Mattel, Inc. Body: tan or pink s/l Body Markings: © 1963/ Mattel, Inc. Notes: early issues are tan, pink may pale, gift set: Cut'N Button Costumes

Model #: 1120 Name: Skooter bendable leg Issue Date: 1966 Box Date: 1965 Hair Color: titian blonde brunette Hairstyle: middle part pulled into shoulder-length pigtails that curl up & are tied with red ribbons, bangs Face: brown eyes, light brown brows, pink lips, blush & sprinkle of light brown freckles Clothing: red & white dot sleeveless crop top with ruffle, blue denim shorts, red flats, wrist tag Extras: gold wire stand, small white brush & comb Booklet: EFBM Book 1, 1964 Head: Skooter Head Markings: inside rim Copyr. © 1963 Mattel, Inc. Body: tan or pink b/l Body Markings: © 1963/ Mattel, Inc. Notes: first issue was tan, pink tone may pale

Model #: 1143 Name: Fluff Box Date: 1970 Hair Color: blonde Hairstyle: shoulder-length pigtails tied with orange ribbons, ends curled under, pin curls on cheeks, curly bangs Face: brown eyes, brown brows, peach lips & blush Clothing: 1-piece playsuit yellow, orange, green stripe on top and solid orange on bottom, 2 yellow buttons, yellow or orange skateboard & wrist tag Extras: 2-piece clear stand Booklet: instructions Head: Fluff Head Markings: inside rim © 1969 Mattel Inc. Taiwan Arms: living Body: pink living Body Markings: © 1969 Mattel, Inc./ Taiwan/ U.S.& for. Patd/ other Pats. Pend./ Patd. in Canada 1967 Notes: Sears gift set: Sunshine Special

Model #: 1199 Name: Tiff Pose 'N Play Box Date: 1971 Hair Color: red Hairstyle: middle part, mid-back length, cello on head Face: brown eyes, brown brows, pink lips & blush Clothing: white sleeveless tee-shirt w/stop sign sticker, blue jeans with stickers, white tennis shoes with red stripes & orange skateboard Head: Fluff Head Markings: inside rim © 1969 Mattel Inc. Taiwan Arms: living with swing action Body: pink living Body Markings: © 1969 Mattel, Inc. Taiwan/ U.S.& for. Patd/ other Pats. Pend./ Patd. in Canada 1967

Model #: 9222 Name: Growing Up Ginger Box Date: 1975 Hair Color: brunette Hairstyle: waist length, side part, cello on head Face: brown eyes, brown brows, peach lips & blush Clothing: turquoise sleeveless bodysuit with pink collar, turquoise with white dot mini skirt with pink waistband, matching long skirt, pink scarf, pink anklets, white platform sandals, turquoise flats Head: Skipper Head Markings: inside rim Copyr. © 1963 Mattel, Inc Arms: straight Body: pink growing up Body Markings: © 1967/ Mattel/ Inc./ Hong Kong/ U.S. & For. Pat. Notes: turn arm & gains height & chest

Model #: 1952 **Name:** Teen Time Courtney **Box Date:** 1988 **Hair Color:** brunette **Hairstyle:** sides & front pulled back with red fabric ribbon rest curly mid-back length **Face:** brown eyes, light brown brows, light red lips & blush **Clothing:** red & white stripe 3/4 length sleeve T-shirt, blue denim vest, white with red dots skirt that converts to baby doll nightgown, matching panties, red round sunglasses, palette, paintbrush, art case, soda can, white tennis shoes, white fuzzy slippers **Extras:** red oval brush, sheet of stickers, sheet of cardboard punch outs & teen scrapbook **Booklet:** instructions **Head:** 1987 Skipper **Head Markings:** © Mattel Inc./ 1987 **Arms:** slight bend **Body:** tan tnt **Body Markings:** © Mattel, Inc.1987/ China

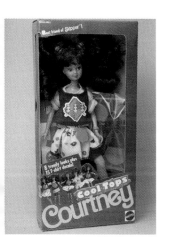 

Model #: 7079 **Name:** Cool Tops Courtney **Box Date:** 1989 **Hair Color:** brunette **Hairstyle:** middle part, sectioned into 4 with red snake ties, bangs, rest curly waist length **Face:** olive green eyes, light brown brows, peach lips & blush **Clothing:** yellow T-shirt, red tank top with appliqué, white multicolor baggy shorts, red knee-high stretch shorts, turquoise T-shirt holder, apple charm, watch, green purse & T-shirt holder, red flats **Extras:** red oval brush, T-shirt decal & sheet of cardboard punch outs **Booklet:** Skipper 1988 & instructions **Head:** 1987 Skipper **Head Markings:** © Mattel Inc./ 1987 **Arms:** slight bend **Body:** tan tnt **Body Markings:** © Mattel, Inc.1987/ China

Model #: 9434 **Name:** Babysitter Courtney **Box Date:** 1990 **Hair Color:** brunette **Hairstyle:** pigtails tied with lime green ribbon, waist length, bangs **Face:** green eyes, brown brows, deep pink lips & blush **Clothing:** white top with green splatters & pink & white with green sleeves, pink & white matching mini skirt with sewn in panties, fake cassette player with headphones, bottle, rattle, soap, tray, jar, blanket, baby's doll, lime green flats **Extras:** lime green oval brush & sheet of cardboard punch outs **Head:** 1987 Skipper **Head Markings:** Skipper=© Mattel Inc/ 1987 baby=© M.I. 1985 **Arms:** slight bend **Body:** tan tnt, baby **Body Markings:** Skipper=© Mattel, Inc. 1987/ Malaysia baby=© 1973 Mattel Inc/ Malaysia

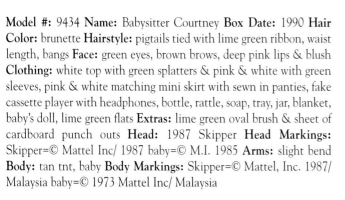  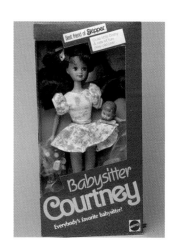

Model #: 2710 **Name:** Pet Pals Courtney **Box Date:** 1991 **Hair Color:** brunette **Hairstyle:** pulled back with purple ribbon, crinkled mid-thigh length with bangs **Face:** teal eyes, brown brows, red lips & blush **Clothing:** white, black, yellow, green, purple print short sleeve shirt, matching mini dress with orange & white bodice & cat appliqué, purple stretch knee-high shorts, orange cat with khaki face with purple bow, lilac collar with tag, bone, ball, can, leash, 2 section food dish, purple flats **Extras:** cardboard cat carrier **Booklet:** instructions **Head:** 1987 Skipper **Head Markings:** © Mattel Inc./ 1987 **Arms:** bent **Body:** tan tnt **Body Markings:** © Mattel, Inc.1987/ Malaysia

Model #: 3933 Name: Cheerleading Courtney Box Date: 1992 Hair Color: brunette Hairstyle: sides & front pulled back with turquoise ribbon, bangs, rest curly mid-thigh length Face: green eyes, dark brown brows, hot pink lips & blush Clothing: purple short sleeve top with silver collar & appliqué, turquoise & purple with silver glitter mini skirt with sewn in panties, turquoise & purple pom poms, turquoise anklets, purple tennis shoes Extras: purple oval brush Head: 1987 Head Markings: © Mattel Inc./ 1987 Arms: slight bend Body: tan tnt Body Markings: © Mattel, Inc.1987/ Malaysia

Model #: 11548 Name: Cool & Crimp Courtney Box Date: 1993 Hair Color: brunette Hairstyle: front & sides pulled back, bangs, rest thigh length Face: gray eyes, brown brows, deep pink lips & blush Clothing: short sleeve aqua crop top with lace at neck, white & aqua below knee pants with cuffs, lilac pacifier earrings & pendant, 2 lilac star crimpers, 2 wave crimpers, bottle, small comb, lilac & white high-top tennis shoes Extras: lilac oval brush & sheet of cardboard punch outs Booklet: instructions Head: 1987 Skipper Head Markings: © Mattel Inc./ 1987 Arms: slight bend Body: tan tnt Body Markings: © Mattel, Inc.1987/ Malaysia

Model #: 12943 Name: Pizza Party Courtney Box Date: 1994 Hair Color: brunette Hairstyle: thigh length with ends curled under, bangs, pulled back with blue band Face: green eyes, brown brows, rose lips & blush Clothing: white long sleeve Pizza Hut crop top, multicolor fabric sleeves, acid washed denim mini skirt with sewn in panties, red stud earrings, white anklets, red napkin, 3 sections of sub sandwich, ketchup, mustard, silver salt & pepper shakers, red carving knife, 2 yellow plates & glasses, 2 forks, 2 knives, black oxford shoes Extras: red oval brush & sheet of stickers Head: 1993 Skipper Head Markings: © Mattel Inc 1993 Arms: slight bend Body: tan tnt Body Markings: © Mattel, Inc.1987/ Malaysia

Skipper's Male Friends

Model #: 1090 Name: Ricky Issue Date: 1965 Box Date: 1964 Hair Color: painted red Face: blue eyes, reddish brows, peach lips, blush & sprinkle of light brown freckles Clothing: blue, red, light blue, dark blue stripe beach jacket with white terry cloth collar, blue swim trunks, red cork sandals, wrist tag Extras: black wire stand Booklet: JES Head: Ricky Head Markings: inside rim Copr.© 1963 Mattel, Inc. Body: tan or pink s/l Body Markings: © 1963/ Mattel, Inc. Notes: first issue tan, pink may pale

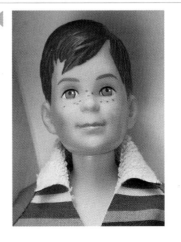

Model #: 1019 Name: Scott Box Date: 1979 Hair Color: brown Hairstyle: curly chin length Face: blue eyes, blonde brows, pink lips Clothing: tank top of yellow, navy, purple, matching shorts & jacket, blue jeans, navy tennis shoes, yellow, black & purple roller skates Head: Scott Head Markings: © Mattel Inc 1970 Arms: 1 ptr & 1 bent Body: pink Scott Body Markings: 2200-2109/ © Mattel Inc/ 1968

Model #: 9351 Name: Cool Tops Kevin Box Date: 1990 Hair Color: painted light brown & blonde Face: blue eyes, light brown brows, peach lips Clothing: long sleeve white T-shirt, turquoise & iridescent print vest, gray pleated pants, gray topsiders Extras: sheet of cardboard punch outs Booklet: BWOF 1988 Head: Kevin Head Markings: © Mattel 1989 Arms: ptr Body: tan b/l Body Markings: © Mattel, Inc.1968/ China

Model #: 9325 Name: Kevin Box Date: 1990 Hair Color: painted light brown & blonde Face: turquoise eyes, light brown brows, mauve lips Clothing: turquoise T-shirt, contrasting turquoise & black splatter sleeves & collarband, pink appliqué, yellow satin knee-length shorts, black pants, hot pink baseball hat, white socks, turquoise & black splatter fabric tennis shoes Extras: sheet of cardboard punch outs Head: Kevin Head Markings: © Mattel 1989 Arms: ptr Body: tan b/l Body Markings: © Mattel, Inc.1968/ China

Model #: 2711 Name: Pet Pals Kevin Box Date: 1991 Hair Color: painted brown Face: blue eyes, light brown brows, peach lips Clothing: black T-shirt with white erratic print, white shorts with black erratic print, yellow tank top with appliqué, Dalmatian dog with red satin bow, yellow dog dish, bone, ball, collar with tag, leash, can, food dish, black topsiders Extras: cardboard dog house Booklet: instructions Head: Kevin Head Markings: © Mattel 1989 Arms: ptr Body: tan b/l Body Markings: © Mattel, Inc.1968/ China

Model #: 4713 **Name:** Basketball Kevin **Box Date:** 1992 **Hair Color:** painted two tone blonde **Face:** blue eyes, blonde brows, peach lips **Clothing:** white T-shirt, jacket of orange satin, silver lamé & black with silver trim cuffs, collar, waistband, matching shorts, blue acid washed pants, white socks, basketball, black high-top athletic shoes **Extras:** sheet of stickers **Head:** Kevin **Head Markings:** © Mattel 1989 **Arms:** ptr **Body:** tan b/l **Body Markings:** © Mattel, Inc.1968/ China

Model #: 11549 **Name:** Cool & Crimp Kevin **Box Date:** 1993 **Hair Color:** painted two tone blonde **Face:** lilac-turquoise eyes, blonde brows, peach lips **Clothing:** short sleeve orange hooded top with appliqué & contrasting cuffs, purple denim baggy shorts with orange glitter trim, matching hat, star crimper, heart crimper, orange anklets, blue & white high-top tennis shoes **Extras:** sheet of cardboard punch outs **Booklet:** instructions **Head:** Kevin **Head Markings:** © Mattel 1989 **Arms:** ptr **Body:** tan b/l **Body Markings:** © Mattel, Inc.1968/ China

Model #: 12944 **Name:** Pizza Party Kevin **Box Date:** 1994 **Hair Color:** painted blonde **Face:** turquoise eyes, light brown brows, dark mauve lips **Clothing:** short sleeve Pizza Hut red T-shirt, blue acid washed knee-high shorts, red sock tops, blue crash helmet, bottle of Pepsi, 2 Pizza Hut cups, Pizza Hut pizza box, plastic pizza, yellow skateboard, 2 red napkins, black & white high-top tennis shoes **Head:** Kevin **Head Markings:** © Mattel 1989 **Arms:** ptr **Body:** tan b/l **Body Markings:** © Mattel, Inc.1968/ China

Francie

Model #: 1130 **Name:** Francie bendable leg **Box Date:** 1965 **Hair Color:** blonde brunette **Hairstyle:** loose flip to shoulders with bangs, middle part, cello on head **Face:** brown eyes, rooted lashes, light brown brows, deep pink lips & blush **Clothing:** 1-piece swimsuit with white background top of hot pink & green squares & daisy flowers with solid green bottoms, white or pink eyelash brush, wrist tag **Extras:** Barbie size gold wire stand **Booklet:** WOBF 1965 **Head:** Francie **Head Markings:** inside rim © 1965 Mattel Inc +/- country **Arms:** Francie **Body:** pink b/l **Body Markings:** © 1965/ Mattel, Inc./ U.S. Patented or Patd/ U.S. Pat. Pend./ Made in Japan **Notes:** swimsuit may be entirely made of patterned material with white or blue background, body may pale, Sears gift set: Francie and her Swingin' Separates, JCPenney gift set: Sportin' Set

Model #: 1140 **Name:** Francie straight leg **Box Date:** 1965 **Hair Color:** blonde brunette **Hairstyle:** soft shoulder-length flip with bangs, middle part, cello on head **Face:** brown eyes, blonde brows, deep pink lips & blush **Clothing:** 2-piece swimsuit white with red dot top & red & white diagonal check bottoms with white lace-up bow at waist, soft red pointed heels, wrist tag **Extras:** gold Barbie size wire stand **Booklet:** Francie 1965 **Head:** Francie **Head Markings:** inside rim © 1965 Mattel Inc +/- country **Arms:** Francie **Body:** pink s/l **Body Markings:** © 1965/ Mattel, Inc./ U.S. Patented or Patd/ U.S. Pat. Pend./ Made in Japan **Notes:** swimsuit bottom may have small or large checks and may have pink eyelash brush although no lashes

Model #: 1170 **Name:** Francie twist & turn **Box Date:** 1965 **Hair Color:** blonde brunette **Hairstyle:** loose flip to shoulders with bangs, middle part, cello on head **Face:** brown eyes, rooted lashes, light brown brows, deep pink lips & blush **Clothing:** 1-piece swimsuit with vertical multicolor stripe top, solid pink vinyl bottom with green sewn on belt with gold buckle, wrist tag **Extras:** clear X stand **Booklet:** WOBF Book 1 1967 **Head:** Francie **Head Markings:** inside rim © 1965 Mattel Inc +/- country **Arms:** Francie **Body:** pink tnt **Body Markings:** © 1966/ Mattel, Inc./ U.S. Patented/ U.S. Pat. Pend/ Made in/ Japan **Notes:** skin tone may pale

Model #: 1100 **Name:** Francie 1st "colored" black version light **Box Date:** 1965 **Hair Color:** red **Hairstyle:** below shoulder length with slight flip on ends, parted in middle with bangs, cello on head **Face:** light brown eyes, rooted lashes, black brows, deep pink lips **Clothing:** multicolor floral or abstract pattern bikini with sheer white top attached at hips & shoulders, wrist tag **Extras:** clear X stand & eyelash brush **Booklet:** WOBF Book 1 1966 **Head:** Francie **Head Markings:** inside rim © 1965 Mattel Inc +/- country **Arms:** Francie **Body:** dark brown tnt **Body Markings:** © 1966/ Mattel, Inc./ U.S. Patented/ U.S. Pat. Pend/ Made in/ Japan

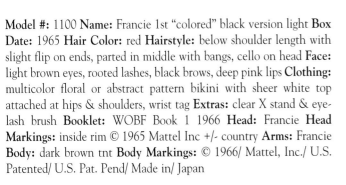

Model #: 1100 **Name:** Francie 2nd "colored" black version **Box Date:** 1965 **Hair Color:** dark brown **Hairstyle:** below shoulder length with slight flip at ends, parted in middle with bangs, cello on head **Face:** brown eyes, rooted lashes, black brows, deep pink lips **Clothing:** multicolor floral or abstract print bikini with sheer white top attached at hips & shoulders, wrist tag **Extras:** clear X stand & eyelash brush **Booklet:** WOBF Book 1 1966 or 67 **Head:** Francie **Head Markings:** inside rim © 1965 Mattel Inc +/- country **Arms:** Francie **Body:** dark brown tnt **Body Markings:** © 1966/ Mattel, Inc./ U.S. Patented/ U.S. Pat. Pend/ Made in/ Japan

Model #: 1122 **Name:** Francie Hair Happenin's **Box Date:** 1969 **Hair Color:** blonde **Hairstyle:** chin-length hair, parted in middle with bangs & blue ribbon headband **Face:** brown eyes, rooted lashes, light brown brows, deep pink lips & blush **Clothing:** turquoise mini dress with sewn in panties, white crochet lace sleeves & bodice insert, wrist tag, clear turquoise soft pointed heels **Extras:** clear X stand, Hairpieces: mini curls = topknot with large curls, swingy swirl = headband with double flip curls on either end with orange ribbon, twisty twirls = braid on headband with 2 banana curls on either side with pink yarn bows, fluffy whirl = headband green ribbon in center with short curls on either end **Booklet:** LB&S 1970 **Head:** Francie **Head Markings:** inside rim © 1965 Mattel Inc +/- country **Arms:** Francie **Body:** pink tnt **Body Markings:** © 1966/ Mattel, Inc./ U.S. Patented/ U.S. Pat. Pend/ Made in/ Japan

Model #: 1170 **Name:** Francie no bangs **Box Date:** 1969 **Hair Color:** blonde brunette **Hairstyle:** long flip to shoulders combed away from forehead with orange stretchy headband **Face:** brown eyes, brown brows, rooted lashes, coral lips & blush **Clothing:** orange pleated halter mini dress trimmed in white vinyl with orange panties, white soft buckle shoes & wrist tag **Extras:** clear X stand **Booklet:** BWB&B **Head:** Francie **Head Markings:** inside rim © 1965 Mattel Inc +/- country **Arms:** Francie **Body:** pink tnt **Body Markings:** © 1966/ Mattel, Inc./ U.S. Patented/ U.S. Pat. Pend/ Made in/ Japan

Model #: 1170 **Name:** Francie twist & turn **Issue Date:** 1969 **Box Date:** 1965 **Hair Color:** blonde brunette **Hairstyle:** short curly flip at nape of neck parted in middle with bangs & pink elastic headband for blondes, yellow for brunettes, cello on head **Face:** brown eyes, rooted lashes, brown brows, deep pink lips & blush **Clothing:** pink & yellow striped 1-piece swimsuit with 2 gold buttons & sewn in yellow vinyl belt at bodice, wrist tag **Extras:** clear X stand **Booklet:** BWB&B **Head:** Francie **Head Markings:** inside rim © 1965 Mattel Inc +/- country **Arms:** Francie **Body:** pink tnt **Body Markings:** © 1966/ Mattel, Inc./ U.S. Patented/ U.S. Pat. Pend/ Made in/ Japan

Model #: 1170 **Name:** Francie twist & turn **Issue Date:** 1970 **Box Date:** 1965 **Hair Color:** blonde brunette **Hairstyle:** short curly flip at nape of neck parted in middle with bangs & pink elastic headband for blondes, yellow for brunettes, cello on head **Face:** brown eyes, rooted lashes, brown brows, deep pink lips & blush **Clothing:** pink, white, yellow floral front wrap empire style spaghetti strap top, trimmed in lace, pink vinyl or nylon shorts & wrist tag **Extras:** clear X stand **Booklet:** LB&S 1970 **Head:** Francie **Head Markings:** inside rim © 1965 Mattel Inc +/- country **Arms:** Francie **Body:** pink tnt **Body Markings:** © 1966/ Mattel, Inc./ U.S. Patented/ U.S. Pat. Pend/ Made in/ Japan

Model #: 1129 **Name:** Francie with Growin' Pretty Hair **Box Date:** 1970 **Hair Color:** blonde **Hairstyle:** pulled up into bun with grow hair retractable ponytail, bangs, pin curls on each cheek **Face:** brown eyes, rooted lashes, light brown brows, deep pink lips & blush **Clothing:** sleeveless mini dress with pink metallic top and satin skirt with pink tulle & silver dots with silver trim waistband & bow, sewn in panties, soft pink pointed heels, wrist tag **Extras:** clear X stand, 2nd version has hairpieces: long 2 strand braid with pink bow on end, bob parted in middle ends curled under chin length, accessories: small white brush & comb, 2 white flowers, 8 bobby pins **Booklet:** Instructions **Head:** Francie **Head Markings:** inside rim © 1965 Mattel Inc +/- country **Arms:** 1st issue: reg 2nd: Mexico **Body:** pink tnt **Body Markings:** © 1966/ Mattel, Inc./ U.S. Pat. other/ Pats. Pend./ Pat. Canada/ 1967/ Japan **Notes:** 1st issue model # 1129 had no hairpieces, 2nd issue model # changed to 1074 included hairpieces, Sears exclusive gift set: Rise' N Shine

Model #: 1068 **Name:** Sun Set Malibu Francie **Issue Date:** 1971-77 **Box Date:** 1970 **Hair Color:** blonde **Hairstyle:** side part, mid-back length, cello on head **Face:** blue eyes, blonde brows, peach lips **Clothing:** 1-piece pink, red swimsuit with yellow vinyl belt, round lavender sunglasses, foil wrist tag, light orange towel **Head:** Casey **Head Markings:** inside rim © 1966 Mattel Inc & country **Arms:** Francie **Body:** tan tnt **Body Markings:** © 1966/ Mattel, Inc./ U.S. Patented/ U.S. Pat.Pend./ Made in/ Korea **Notes:** same doll & model # made through 1977 packaged in either a white box or pink box, made either in Japan or Korea, see Sun Set Ken 1974 for example of white box & Malibu Barbie 1975 for example of pink box, towel dropped in later issues

Model #: 3313 **Name:** Busy Francie **Box Date:** 1971 **Hair Color:** blonde **Hairstyle:** part on side, trimmed around face, rest shoulder length & tied with 2 light green ribbons **Face:** brown eyes, light brown brows, peach lips & blush **Clothing:** green ribbed hip long tank top, blue jean bell bottoms, red vinyl belt with gold buckle, square green low heels, wrist tag **Extras:** clear X stand, brown princess telephone, TV, travel case, record player, record, tray, 2 glasses, stickers **Booklet:** instructions **Head:** Francie **Head Markings:** inside rim © 1965 Mattel Inc +/- country **Arms:** busy **Body:** pink busy Francie **Body Markings:** © 1966/ Mattel, Inc./ Hong Kong/ U.S. & Foreign/ Patented/ Other Pats/ Pending

Model #: 4222 **Name:** Quick Curl Francie **Box Date:** 1972 **Hair Color:** brunette **Hairstyle:** shoulder-length flip, side part, cello on head **Face:** brown eyes, light brown brows, pink lips **Clothing:** yellow & white dot long dress with scoop neck & sheer sleeves, black ribbon detail at neckline and sleeves, 3 white barrettes, 4 ribbons, 4 rubber bands, wrist tag, square white low heels **Extras:** white X stand & hot pink pointed comb, brush, curler **Booklet:** LB&S 1970 **Head:** Francie **Head Markings:** inside rim © 1965 Mattel Inc +/- country **Arms:** Mexico **Body:** pink tnt **Body Markings:** © 1966/ Mattel, Inc./ Taiwan/ U.S. & Foreign/ Patented/ Other Pats/ Pending

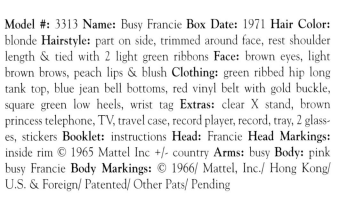

Model #: 1180 Name: Casey Box Date: 1966 Hair Color: brunette blonde titian Hairstyle: chin length or a bit longer, part on side, ends may be curled under, cello on head Face: blue eyes, rooted lashes, light brown brows, deep pink lips & blush Clothing: 1-piece swimsuit gold & white net on top and solid gold bottom with matching belt at hipline, single gold triangle earring in left ear, & foil wrist tag Extras: clear X stand Booklet: WOBF 1966 Head: Casey Head Markings: inside rim © 1966 Mattel Inc & country Arms: Francie Body: pink tnt Body Markings: © 1966/ Mattel, Inc./ U.S. Patented/ U.S. Pat. Pend/ Made in/ Japan Notes: gift set: Casey Goes Casual

Model #: 9000 Name: Casey Baggie Box Date: 1974 Hair Color: blonde Hairstyle: waist length, part on side Face: blue eyes, brown brows, pale pink lips Clothing: pink, red or rose 2-piece swimsuit Head: Francie Head Markings: inside rim © 1965 Mattel Inc +/- country Arms: Mexico Body: pink s/l thin hollow body Body Markings: © 1966/ Mattel, Inc./ Taiwan Notes: see last chapter for brunette Baggie Francie

Model #: 3698 Name: Chelsie High School Box Date: 1988 Hair Color: red Hairstyle: front & 1 side pulled up with hot pink snake tie into topknot, bangs, rest waist length Face: green eyes, reddish brows, pink lips & blush Clothing: white crop top with appliqué, light blue jacket with turquoise trim, matching mini skirt, turquoise mid-thigh stretch shorts, pink tennis shoes Extras: orange hair pick & sheet of cardboard punch outs Head: Chelsie/Tracey 1979 Head Markings: © Mattel Inc/ 1979 Arms: bent Body: tan Jazzie Body Markings: © Mattel, Inc. 1975/ Malaysia Notes: Tracey is a 1970s unaffiliated Mattel doll

Model #: 3637 Name: Dude High School Box Date: 1988 Hair Color: painted brown & blonde Face: blue eyes, brown brows, pink lips Clothing: pink & white T-shirt, acid washed denim jacket & knee-high shorts, white tennis shoes Extras: sheet of cardboard punch outs Head: Derek Head Markings: © Mattel Inc. 1985 Arms: bent Body: tan tnt Body Markings: © Mattel, Inc. 1968/ Malaysia

Model #: 3635 Name: Jazzie High School Box Date: 1988 Hair Color: blonde Hairstyle: top & side pulled into 4 sections, banded with yellow, rest waist length, bangs Face: blue eyes, blonde brows, hot pink lips & blush Clothing: white T-shirt with black & white check waistband, hot pink mini skirt with black & white waistband & black suspenders, white knee-high stretch shorts, denim jacket with white splatter yoke, light blue tennis shoes Extras: orange hair pick & sheet of cardboard punch outs Head: Starr/Jazzie Head Markings: © Mattel Inc/ 1979 Body: tan Jazzie Body Markings: © Mattel, Inc. 1975/ Malaysia Notes: Starr is a 1970s unaffiliated Mattel doll

Model #: 3634 Name: Jazzie Teen Dance Box Date: 1988 Hair Color: blonde Hairstyle: front & side section pulled into hot pink snake tie, very curly ends, rest waist length, curly bangs Face: blue eyes, blonde brows, pink lips & blush Clothing: black mini dress with 3 tiered hot pink, turquoise and lime green full mini skirt with matching bow, hot pink snake choker & blue snake bracelet, black pantyhose, multicolor wrist decoration, hot pink flats Extras: hot pink hair pick & sheet of cardboard punch outs Head: Starr/Jazzie Head Markings: © Mattel Inc/ 1979 Body: tan Jazzie Body Markings: © Mattel, Inc. 1975/ Malaysia Notes: Starr is a 1970s unaffiliated Mattel doll

Model #: 3631 Name: Jazzie Teen Looks Cheerleader Box Date: 1988 Hair Color: blonde Hairstyle: top & sides split into 2 sections, 1 tied with yellow band, 1 with yellow snake tie, rest waist crinkled length, bangs Face: blue eyes, blonde brows, pink lips & blush Clothing: turquoise short sleeve crop top, hot pink mini skirt with lime green suspenders, lime green mid-thigh stretch shorts, lime green & pink pom pom, pink tennis shoes Extras: turquoise hair pick Head: Starr/Jazzie Head Markings: © Mattel Inc/ 1979 Body: tan Jazzie Body Markings: © Mattel, Inc. 1975/ Malaysia Notes: Starr is a 1970s unaffiliated Mattel doll

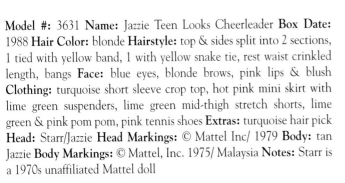

Model #: 3632 Name: Jazzie Teen Looks Swimsuit Box Date: 1988 Hair Color: 2 shades of blonde Hairstyle: side sections pulled back with orange snake tie & braided, bangs, rest waist length Face: brown eyes, blonde brows, hot pink lips & blush Clothing: pink swimsuit top with yellow straps & hot pink armlets, lime green swimsuit bottom with orange mini skirt wrap, yellow snake bangle bracelet Extras: turquoise hair pick Booklet: IIB 1990 Head: Starr/Jazzie Head Markings: © Mattel Inc/ 1979 Body: tan Jazzie Body Markings: © Mattel, Inc. 1975/ Malaysia Notes: Starr is a 1970s unaffiliated Mattel doll

Model #: 3633 Name: Jazzie Teen Looks Workout Box Date: 1988 Hair Color: blonde Hairstyle: front & sides sectioned into 3, 2 banded with yellow, 1 with blue snake tie, rest crinkled waist length, bangs Face: lilac eyes, blonde brows, hot pink lips & blush Clothing: turquoise sleeveless mid-thigh unitard with orange tank top & yellow shorts, orange snake bracelet, yellow tennis shoes Extras: turquoise hair pick Head: Starr/Jazzie Head Markings: © Mattel Inc/ 1979 Body: tan Jazzie Body Markings: © Mattel, Inc. 1975/ Malaysia Notes: Starr is a 1970s unaffiliated Mattel doll

Model #: 3636 Name: Stacie High School Box Date: 1988 Hair Color: black Hairstyle: front & sides sectioned in 2, 1 held with blue snake tie, 1 held with pink, rest thigh length, bangs Face: brown eyes, black brows, hot pink lips & blush Clothing: white sweatshirt style top, pink satin jacket with black and white checks, collar, cuffs and waistband, hot pink stretch mid-thigh shorts, black fanny pack, white tennis shoes Extras: orange hair pick & sheet of cardboard punch outs Head: Steffie Head Markings: inside rim © 1971 Mattel Inc & country Arms: bent Body: dark brown Jazzie Body Markings: © Mattel, Inc. 1975/ Malaysia

Model #: 9294 Name: Hawaiian Fun Jazzie Box Date: 1990 Hair Color: blonde Hairstyle: parted in middle, sides pulled back with colored band & braided, rest thigh length with bangs Face: turquoise eyes, blonde brows, hot pink lips & blush Clothing: yellow, hot pink, blue, light green 2-piece swimsuit, blue mini hula skirt, blue & black sunglasses Extras: neon yellow oval brush, bracelet for child Head: Starr/Jazzie 1979 Head Markings: © Mattel Inc/ 1979 Body: tan Jazzie Body Markings: © Mattel, Inc. 1975/ Malaysia Notes: Starr is a 1970s unaffiliated Mattel doll

Model #: 4088 Name: Jazzie Sun Lovin' Box Date: 1990 Hair Color: blonde Hairstyle: middle part, 1 side twisted into 3 pigtails other side 1 ponytail, curly bangs Face: blue eyes, blonde brows, pink lips & blush Clothing: pink oversize tank top with appliqué, white splatter mid-thigh cuffed shorts, hot pink & yellow 2-piece swimsuit, orange visor & Frisbee, yellow hoop earrings, hot pink tennis shoes Extras: hot pink oval brush & sheet of stickers & press on nails for child Booklet: BWOF 1988 Head: Starr/Jazzie Head Markings: © Mattel Inc/ 1979 Body: tan Jazzie Body Markings: © Mattel, Inc. 1975/ Malaysia Notes: Starr is a 1970s unaffiliated Mattel doll

Model #: 5507 **Name:** Jazzie Teen Scene **Box Date:** 1990 **Hair Color:** blonde **Hairstyle:** front & sides pulled up to topknot, small section of hair pulled back with yellow hair band, mid-back length, ends curled under **Face:** blue eyes, blonde brows, peach lips & blush **Clothing:** pink sleeveless top with black & gold bra on outside, black bolero jacket, black tulle with gold glitter mini skirt, black stretch pants with gold detail, orange hoop earrings & 3 bangle bracelets, 2 black, 1 orange, black bowler hat, gold hatband, black flats **Extras:** orange hair pick & cardboard fold out pictures **Head:** Starr/Jazzie **Head Markings:** © Mattel Inc/ 1979 **Body:** tan Jazzie **Body Markings:** © Mattel, Inc. 1975/ Malaysia **Notes:** Starr is a 1970s unaffiliated Mattel doll

Model #: 5473 **Name:** Sun Sensation Jazzie **Box Date:** 1991 **Hair Color:** 2 shades of blonde **Hairstyle:** sides pulled into pigtails with gold bands rest thigh length, ends turned under, bangs **Face:** lilac-blue eyes, blonde brows, frosted orange lips & blush **Clothing:** metallic blue bikini with gold stud earrings & gold ship's wheel charm pendant **Extras:** hot pink oval brush **Head:** Starr/Jazzie 1979 **Head Markings:** © Mattel Inc/ 1979 **Body:** tan Jazzie **Body Markings:** © Mattel, Inc. 1975/ Malaysia **Notes:** Starr is a 1970s unaffiliated Mattel doll

Model #: 4935 **Name:** Glitter Beach Jazzie **Box Date:** 1992 **Hair Color:** 2 shades of blonde **Hairstyle:** thigh length pulled back with multicolor glitter headband **Face:** lilac eyes, blonde brows, hot pink lips **Clothing:** 2-piece multicolor hot pink, turquoise, purple, yellow glitter bikini, silver stud earrings, beaded pendant **Extras:** neon green oval brush **Head:** Starr/Jazzie 1979 **Head Markings:** © Mattel Inc/ 1979 **Body:** tan Jazzie **Body Markings:** © Mattel, Inc. 1975/ Malaysia **Notes:** Starr is a 1970s unaffiliated Mattel doll

Tutti

Model #: 3550 **Name:** Tutti **Box Date:** 1965 **Hair Color:** blonde brunette **Hairstyle:** waist length, side part with bangs, pink ribbon headband, cello on head **Face:** blue eyes, light brown brows, deep pink lips & blush **Clothing:** pink & white check sleeveless sunsuit with white ruffle hem, flower appliqué at shoulder & hem, matching hat, white bow flats & wrist tag **Extras:** small pink comb & brush **Booklet:** Tutti 1965 **Head:** Tutti **Head Markings:** inside rim © Mattel Inc Japan **Body:** pink bendable **Body Markings:** © 1965/ Mattel, Inc./ Japan **Notes:** head may pale & body may develop green from internal wires

Model #: 3580 **Name:** Tutti **Box Date:** 1965 **Hair Color:** blonde brunette **Hairstyle:** waist length with bangs, pink ribbon headband, cello on head **Face:** blue eyes, light brown brows, deep pink lips & blush **Clothing:** dress with multicolor pink, yellow, green & white bodice, solid pink skirt & yellow bow with matching multicolor sewn in shorts, white bow flats & wrist tag **Extras:** small pink comb & brush **Booklet:** LB 1969 **Head:** Tutti **Head Markings:** inside rim © Mattel Inc Japan **Body:** pink bendable **Body Markings:** © 1965/ Mattel, Inc./ Japan **Notes:** head may pale & body may develop green stains from internal wires

Model #: 3580 **Name:** Tutti **Box Date:** 1965 **Hair Color:** blonde brunette **Hairstyle:** waist length, parted on side with bangs, pink ribbon headband, cello on head **Face:** blue eyes, light brown brows, deep pink lips & blush **Clothing:** sleeveless dress with solid pink bodice & floral multicolor skirt of white, green, pink & yellow, white ribbon bow at center bodice with matching sewn in shorts, white bow flats & wrist tag **Extras:** small pink comb & brush **Booklet:** WOBF 1966 **Head:** Tutti **Head Markings:** inside rim © Mattel Inc Japan **Body:** pink bendable **Body Markings:** © 1965/ Mattel, Inc./ Japan **Notes:** head may pale & body may develop green stains from internal wires

Model #: 3559 **Name:** Tutti Cookin' Goodies **Box Date:** 1965 **Hair Color:** brunette **Hairstyle:** bun on top of head with bangs **Face:** blue eyes, light brown brows, deep pink lips & blush **Clothing:** orange print dress with white bow & apron, orange shorts, white anklets, orange bow flats **Extras:** small white comb & brush, white stove trimmed in pink, black frying pan with 2 eggs, larger frying pan, & small orange saucepan **Booklet:** WOBF 1965 or 1966 **Head:** Tutti **Head Markings:** inside rim © Mattel Inc Japan **Body:** pink bendable **Body Markings:** © 1965/ Mattel, Inc./ Japan **Notes:** dress may be trimmed in yellow with yellow shorts, head may pale & body may develop green from internal wires

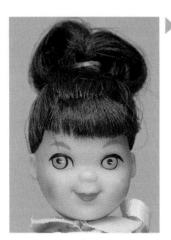

Model #: 3554 **Name:** Tutti Me n' My Dog **Box Date:** 1965 **Hair Color:** brunette **Hairstyle:** side part held with red bow rest thigh length **Face:** blue eyes, light brown brows, deep pink lips & blush **Clothing:** white fake fur hood hat tied under chin, red felt coat with white buttons & stitching with faux fur at collar & cuffs, red leash attached to large white dog with black eyes, nose & red tongue, red & white striped tights, white tennis shoes **Extras:** small white brush & comb **Booklet:** WOBF 1965 **Head:** Tutti **Head Markings:** inside rim © Mattel Inc Japan **Body:** pink bendable **Body Markings:** © 1965/ Mattel, Inc./ Japan **Notes:** head may pale & body may develop green from internal wires

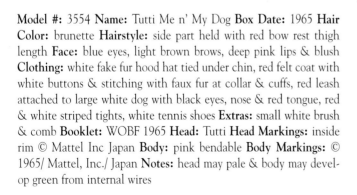

Model #: 3555 **Name:** Tutti Melody in Pink **Box Date:** 1965 **Hair Color:** blonde **Hairstyle:** short pigtails tied with pink bows turned up ends & bangs **Face:** blue eyes, light brown brows, deep pink lips & blush **Clothing:** pale pink lace dress & panties, white anklets, pale pink bow flats **Extras:** small orange "baby grand" style piano & bench, tiny pink brush & comb **Booklet:** WOBF 1965 **Head:** Tutti **Head Markings:** inside rim © Mattel Inc Japan **Body:** pink bendable **Body Markings:** © 1965/ Mattel, Inc./ Japan **Notes:** dress variation with bright pink bodice, head may pale & body may develop green from internal wires

 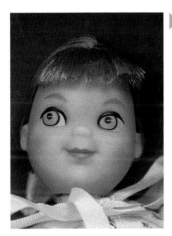

Model #: 3553 **Name:** Tutti Night-Night Sleep Tight! **Box Date:** 1965 **Hair Color:** titian **Hairstyle:** ponytail at nape of neck tied with pink ribbon, rest waist length with bangs **Face:** blue eyes, light brown brows, deep pink lips & blush **Clothing:** pink floral robe with solid pink nightgown, pink felt slippers with white lace trim, white plastic bed with bedspread made of robe material **Extras:** small pink brush & comb **Booklet:** WOBF 1965 **Head:** Tutti **Head Markings:** inside rim © Mattel Inc Japan **Body:** pink bendable **Body Markings:** © 1965/ Mattel, Inc./ Japan **Notes:** head may pale & body may develop green from internal wires

Model #: 3560 **Name:** Tutti Swing-A-Ling **Box Date:** 1965 **Hair Color:** blonde **Hairstyle:** middle part, waist length, bangs, green headband w/orange flower at each ear **Face:** blue eyes, blonde brows, hot pink lips & blush **Clothing:** yellow dress with lace long sleeves and overskirt, teal ribbon waistband with orange flower & pearl accent, yellow panties, yellow anklets & white bow flats **Extras:** small white brush & comb, metal white swing with red seat with hearts design cut outs **Booklet:** WOBF 1966 **Head:** Tutti **Head Markings:** inside rim © Mattel Inc Japan **Body:** pink bendable **Body Markings:** © 1965/ Mattel, Inc./ Japan **Notes:** head may pale & body may develop green from internal wires

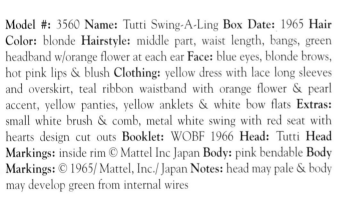

Model #: 3552 **Name:** Tutti Walkin' My Dolly **Box Date:** 1965 **Hair Color:** blonde **Hairstyle:** middle part, waist length with bangs **Face:** blue eyes, brown brows, deep pink lips & blush **Clothing:** solid skirt with red & white dot top & shorts, straw hat with red ribbons with flowers on ends, red bow flats, pink & white baby buggy with solid baby with light brown hair, blue bow, white blanket **Extras:** small pink brush & comb **Booklet:** WOBF 1965 **Head:** Tutti **Head Markings:** inside rim © Mattel Inc Japan **Body:** pink bendable **Body Markings:** © 1965/ Mattel, Inc./ Japan **Notes:** head may pale & body may develop green from internal wires

Model #: 3556 **Name:** Tutti and Todd Sundae Treat Set **Box Date:** 1965 **Hair Color:** titian **Hairstyle:** TU=sides pulled back with navy ribbon, bangs, rest mid-back length TO=side part short cut **Face:** TU= blue eyes, light red brows, deep pink lips & blush TO= brown eyes, light reddish brows, deep pink lips & blush **Clothing:** TU=red & white stripe dress with white bib trimmed in navy with navy buttons & shorts, white anklets & red bow flats, wrist tag TO=red & white striped jacket with white shirt, navy shorts, navy knee socks & white tennis shoes, wrist tag **Extras:** small white comb & brush, pink plastic table with 2 attached matching chairs, 2 silver metal spoons, 1 chocolate & 1 strawberry sundae **Booklet:** WOBF 1965 **Head:** Tutti **Head Markings:** inside rim © Mattel Inc Japan **Body:** pink bendable **Body Markings:** © 1965/ Mattel, Inc./ Japan **Notes:** head may pale & body may develop green from internal wires

Tutti-Sized Female Friends and Family

Model #: 3570 **Name:** Chris **Box Date:** 1966 **Hair Color:** blonde brunette titian **Hairstyle:** waist length with bangs, 2 green ribbon bows & 1 small oval green barrette, cello on head **Face:** brown eyes & brows, pink lips and cheek blush **Clothing:** yellow, orange, green & magenta mini dress with green shorts, pair of orange bow flats & wrist tag. 2 green bows in hair, 1 green oval barrette **Extras:** small pink brush & comb **Booklet:** WOBF 1966 **Head:** Tutti **Head Markings:** inside rim © Mattel Inc Japan **Body:** pink bendable **Body Markings:** © 1965/ Mattel, Inc./ Japan **Notes:** head may pale & body may develop green from internal wires, Sears gift set: Fun-Timers

Model #: 4240 **Name:** Stacie **Box Date:** 1991 **Hair Color:** blonde **Hairstyle:** crinkled thigh length with bangs **Face:** blue eyes, light brown brows, pink lips & blush **Clothing:** light green sleeveless turtleneck top, pink floral mini skirt with matching pink sleeveless top, hot pink vinyl long sleeve jacket with floral insert, floral backpack, hot pink knee-high shorts, black hat with floral hatband, hot pink stud earrings, lilac anklets, black flower flats with fabric bow **Extras:** hot pink oval brush & sheet of cardboard punch outs **Head:** 1991 Stacie **Head Markings:** © Mattel Inc./ 1991 **Body:** tan b/l **Body Markings:** Malaysia

Model #: 5411 **Name:** Party' N Play Stacie **Box Date:** 1992 **Hair Color:** blonde **Hairstyle:** waist length, ends curled under with bangs **Face:** blue eyes, blonde brows, deep pink lips & blush **Clothing:** white with black dots sleeveless bodysuit, black & white houndstooth jacket, contrasting collar & waistband, sheer hot pink mini skirt, black ribbon waistband & edging, v-neck sleeveless white T-shirt with black & hot pink trim, black shorts, soccer ball, hot pink studs & hat, black hatband, white anklets, black & white checked scarf, black high-top athletic shoes, hot pink flower flats **Extras:** hot pink oval brush **Head:** 1991 Stacie **Head Markings:** © Mattel Inc./ 1991 **Body:** tan b/l **Body Markings:** Malaysia

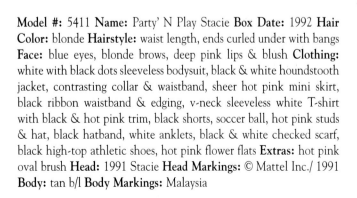

Model #: 4115 **Name:** Party' N Play Stacie black version **Box Date:** 1992 **Hair Color:** brunette **Hairstyle:** waist length with bangs **Face:** brown eyes, black brows, hot pink lips & blush **Clothing:** white with black dots sleeveless bodysuit, black & white houndstooth jacket, contrasting collar & waistband, sheer hot pink mini skirt with black ribbon waistband & edging, v-neck sleeveless white T-shirt with black & hot pink trim, black shorts, soccer ball, hot pink studs & hat, black hatband, white anklets, black & white checked scarf, black high-top athletic shoes, hot pink flower flats **Extras:** hot pink oval brush **Head:** 1991 Stacie **Head Markings:** © Mattel Inc./ 1991 **Body:** dark brown b/l **Body Markings:** Malaysia

Model #: 11477 **Name:** Happy Meal Janet **Box Date:** 1993 **Hair Color:** brunette **Hairstyle:** ponytail with blue band split in 3, 2 smaller ponytails twisted & tied with blue band, rest thigh length with bangs **Face:** brown eyes, black brows, orange lips & blush **Clothing:** turquoise & white striped T-shirt with hamburger appliqué, turquoise & white dots knee-length shorts & matching socks, orange & turquoise baseball cap, turquoise stud earrings, red tray, french fries, hamburger, drink, small happy meal box, orange high-top tennis shoes **Extras:** orange oval brush & happy meal box & child's jewelry **Head:** 1991 Stacie **Head Markings:** © Mattel Inc./ 1991 **Body:** dark brown b/l **Body Markings:** Malaysia

Model #: 11474 **Name:** Happy Meal Stacie **Box Date:** 1993 **Hair Color:** blonde **Hairstyle:** waist length **Face:** turquoise eyes, blonde brows, light red lips & blush **Clothing:** red top with appliqué & long sleeve red & white striped, blue high collar, red with white dots knee shorts, red hat with blue ribbon, red tray, french fries, hamburger, drink, small happy meal box, blue socks, red high-top athletic shoes **Extras:** red oval brush & happy meal box & child's jewelry **Head:** 1991 Stacie **Head Markings:** © Mattel Inc./ 1991 **Body:** tan b/l **Body Markings:** Malaysia

Model #: 11476 **Name:** Happy Meal Whitney **Box Date:** 1993 **Hair Color:** red **Hairstyle:** sides & front pulled back with pink band, rest crinkled thigh length with partial bangs **Face:** aqua lilac eyes, reddish brows, deep pink lips & blush **Clothing:** purple top with hot pink collar & short sleeves with white dots, appliqué, purple pants, pink stud earrings, purple heart shaped glasses, red tray, french fries, hamburger, drink, small happy meal box, hot pink high-top athletic shoes **Extras:** purple oval brush & happy meal box & child's jewelry **Booklet:** 1993 PB **Head:** 1991 Stacie **Head Markings:** © Mattel Inc./ 1991 **Body:** tan b/l **Body Markings:** Malaysia

Model #: 12984 **Name:** Polly Pocket Janet **Box Date:** 1994 **Hair Color:** brunette **Hairstyle:** sides & front pulled to 1 side with red band, rest crinkled mid-thigh length, partial bangs **Face:** brown eyes, black brows, red lips & blush **Clothing:** dress with split skirt, white top trimmed in red, multicolor black & white checked with red rose & green flowers, 3 clear pockets, 3 Polly Pocket dolls, red backpack converts to house for Polly Pocket, red stud earrings, lace anklets, red flower flats **Extras:** red oval brush **Head:** 1991 Stacie **Head Markings:** © Mattel Inc./ 1991 **Body:** dark brown b/l **Body Markings:** Malaysia

Model #: 12982 **Name:** Polly Pocket Stacie **Box Date:** 1994 **Hair Color:** blonde **Hairstyle:** sides & front pulled back with hot pink band, rest crinkled knee length, partial bangs **Face:** turquoise-lilac eyes, light brown brows, hot pink lips & blush **Clothing:** white bodysuit trimmed in pink, multicolor pink plaid full skirt with 2 clear pockets, blue denim vest with 2 clear pockets, hot pink stud earrings, lace anklets, hot pink backpack converts into house for Polly Pocket, 3 Polly Pocket dolls, hot pink flower flats **Extras:** hot pink oval brush **Head:** 1991 Stacie **Head Markings:** © Mattel Inc./ 1991 **Body:** tan b/l **Body Markings:** Malaysia **Notes:** JCPenney gift set regular doll & extra Polly Pocket dolls

Model #: 12983 **Name:** Polly Pocket Whitney **Box Date:** 1994 **Hair Color:** red **Hairstyle:** front & sides pulled to 1 side with green band, rest thigh length, partial bangs **Face:** lilac-turquoise eyes, reddish brows, pink lips & blush **Clothing:** white top with lilac edging, multicolor jumper with sewn in panties & 3 clear pockets, lilac heart shaped glasses & stud earrings, purple backpack converts to house for Polly Pocket, 3 Polly Pocket dolls, lace anklets, lilac flower flats **Extras:** lilac oval brush **Head:** 1991 Stacie **Head Markings:** © Mattel Inc./ 1991 **Body:** tan b/l **Body Markings:** Malaysia

Tutti-Sized Male Family

Model #: 3590 **Name:** Todd **Box Date:** 1965 **Hair Color:** titian **Hairstyle:** side part, short cut **Face:** brown eyes, brown brows, deep pink lips & blush **Clothing:** red, white & blue houndstooth hat, shorts & solid blue short sleeve shirt with button front, white cotton anklets, wrist tag, red tennis shoes **Booklet:** WOFB book 1 1966 **Head:** Tutti **Head Markings:** inside rim © Mattel Inc Japan **Body:** pink bendable **Body Markings:** © 1965/ Mattel, Inc./ Japan **Notes:** head may pale & body may develop green from internal wires

Model #: 7903 **Name:** Party' N Play Todd **Box Date:** 1992 **Hair Color:** brunette **Hairstyle:** short fuzzy **Face:** dark blue eyes, brown brows, mauve lips & blush **Clothing:** lime green T-shirt, black acid washed jeans, black jacket with multicolor check trim & turquoise accent at cuffs & waistband, white v-neck T-shirt with black & turquoise stripes, turquoise shorts, soccer ball, white socks, black high-top athletic shoes **Head:** 1990 Todd **Head Markings:** © 1990/ Mattel Inc. **Body:** tan b/l **Body Markings:** Malaysia

Model #: 11475 **Name:** Happy Meal Todd **Box Date:** 1993 **Hair Color:** brunette **Hairstyle:** fuzzy cropped **Face:** turquoise eyes, brown brows, mauve lips **Clothing:** white T-shirt with black sleeves & red collarband with McDonald's appliqué, black knee-high shorts, black baseball cap with red brim, red tray, french fries, hamburger, drink, small happy meal box, red socks, black high-top athletic shoes **Extras:** happy meal box & child's jewelry **Head:** 1990 Todd **Head Markings:** © 1990/ Mattel Inc. **Body:** tan b/l **Body Markings:** Malaysia

Baby-Sized Sister

Model #: 12489 **Name:** Kelly **Box Date:** 1994 **Hair Color:** blonde **Hairstyle:** curly bangs sides pulled up to small ponytail tied with pink ribbon rest thigh length **Face:** blue eyes, light brown brows, pink lips & blush **Clothing:** pink 1-piece sleeper trimmed in lace, black velvet dress trimmed in lace, white lace tights, diaper, baby bottle, divided dish & spoon, baby food, pacifier, rattle, bunny toy, blanket, black flat shoes with strap **Extras:** hot pink round brush & comb, white crib, hot pink mobile, sheet of cardboard punch outs **Booklet:** instructions **Head:** Kelly **Head Markings:** © 1994 Mattel Inc **Body:** light tan **Body Markings:** © 1994/ Mattel, Inc./ China **Notes:** doll smells like baby powder

Model #: 13256 **Name:** Kelly black version **Box Date:** 1994 **Hair Color:** brunette **Hairstyle:** curly bangs, sides pulled up to small ponytail tied with pink ribbon, rest thigh length **Face:** brown eyes, black brows, dark mauve lips & blush **Clothing:** pink 1-piece sleeper trimmed in lace, black velvet dress trimmed in lace, white lace tights, diaper, baby bottle, divided dish & spoon, baby food, pacifier, rattle, bunny toy, blanket, black flat shoes with strap **Extras:** hot pink round brush & comb, white crib, hot pink mobile, sheet of cardboard punch outs **Booklet:** instructions **Head:** Kelly **Head Markings:** © 1994 Mattel Inc **Body:** dark brown **Body Markings:** © 1994/ Mattel, Inc./ China **Notes:** doll smells like baby powder

Chapter 5 Ken Dolls and Other Like-Sized Friends Regular Issue 1961-1995

Model #: 750 **Name:** Ken flocked hair **Box Date:** 1961 **Hair Color:** blonde or brunette **Hairstyle:** flocked **Face:** blue eyes, brown brows, mauve lips **Clothing:** solid red knit trunks or red cotton or red cotton with white stripe on each side, optional yellow towel, optional red & white striped jacket with sewn in white terry cloth facing on late issues, red cork sandals, wrist tag **Extras:** black wire stand **Booklet:** B&K 1961 **Head:** Flocked Ken **Arms:** pts **Body:** tan s/l **Body Markings:** Ken T.M./ Pats.Pend/ © MCMLX/ by/ Mattel/ Inc. **Notes:** reddish brown hair available in JCPenney catalog, some bodies & heads turn white like the early Barbie dolls, rare painted legs, gift set: Barbie & Ken

Model #: 750 **Name:** Ken painted hair **Issue Date:** 1962 **Box Date:** 1961 **Hair Color:** painted blonde or brunette **Face:** turquoise eyes, brown brows, peach lips **Clothing:** red & white stripe beach jacket with either bonded or sewn in white terry cloth facing, red cotton trunks either solid or with white stripe trim on side, red cork sandals, wrist tag **Extras:** black wire stand **Booklet:** B&K 1962 **Head:** Painted Ken **Arms:** pts **Body:** tan s/l **Body Markings:** Ken T.M./ Pats.Pend/ © MCMLX/ by/ Mattel/ Inc. **Notes:** different shades of paint used for hair, booklets vary, some mint dolls have very loose limbs, heftier leg mold used in later issues, gift sets: On Parade, Wedding Party, Little Theatre, FQ Barbie & Her Friends, FQ Barbie & Ken Trousseau Set, Barbie & Ken Gift Set

Model #: 750 **Name:** Ken painted hair shortie **Box Date:** 1962 **Hair Color:** painted blonde or brunette **Face:** turquoise eyes, brown brows, peach lips **Clothing:** red & white striped jacket with terry cloth bonded collar & facing, red cotton trunks either solid or with red & white stripe on side, red cork sandals, wrist tag **Extras:** black wire stand **Booklet:** B&K 1962 **Head:** Painted Ken **Arms:** pts **Body:** tan s/l **Body Markings:** Ken®/ ©1960/ by/ Mattel, Inc./ Hawthorn/ Calif. U.S.A. **Notes:** body shorter than other Kens, heftier legs, shoulder & leg joints are loose

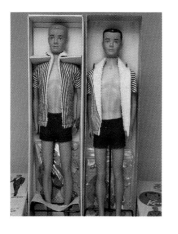

Model #: 1020 **Name:** Ken bendable leg **Issue Date:** 1965 **Box Date:** 1964 **Hair Color:** painted blonde or brunette **Face:** turquoise eyes, brown brows, peach lips, cello bag over head held with rubberband **Clothing:** navy & red short sleeve beach jacket with initial "K" & matching red trunks, red cork sandals, wrist tag **Extras:** black wire stand **Booklet:** EFBMl Book 1, 1964 **Head:** Painted Ken **Arms:** pts **Body:** tan b/l **Body Markings:** © 1960/ by/ Mattel, Inc/ Hawthorn/ Calif. U.S.A. **Notes:** later issues available with gold wire stand

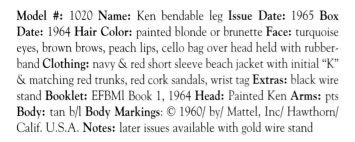

Model #: 1111 **Name:** Talking Ken Spanish **Box Date:** 1968 **Hair Color:** painted brown **Face:** blue eyes, brown brows, peach lips **Clothing:** orange swim trunks, short sleeve orange & turquoise trimmed beach jacket, wrist tag **Extras:** clear X stand **Head:** 1968 Ken **Head Markings:** © 1968 Mattel Inc **Arms:** pts **Body:** pink talking **Body Markings:** © 1968/ Mattel, Inc./ U.S. & For. Patd/ Other Pats/ Pending/ Mexico **Notes:** speaks in Spanish when string pulled, usually mute

Model #: 1124 **Name:** New Good Lookin' Ken **Box Date:** 1969 **Hair Color:** painted brown **Face:** blue eyes, brown brows, pink lips **Clothing:** mustard yellow nylon short sleeve pullover top with shorts in shades of red, orange & green, wrist tag **Extras:** clear X stand **Booklet:** LB 1969 **Head:** 1968 Ken **Head Markings:** © 1968 Mattel Inc **Arms:** pts **Body:** pink b/l **Body Markings:** © 1968/ Mattel, Inc./ U.S. & For. Patd/ Other Pats/ Pending/ Mexico **Notes:** Sears gift set: Red, White and Wild

Model #: 1111 **Name:** Talking Ken **Box Date:** 1968 **Hair Color:** painted reddish brown **Face:** blue eyes, reddish brows, pink lips **Clothing:** red short sleeve nehru style jacket with bronze color buttons, matching shorts, wrist tag **Extras:** clear X stand **Head:** 1968 Ken **Head Markings:** © 1968 Mattel Inc **Arms:** pts **Body:** pink talking **Body Markings:** © 1968/ Mattel, Inc./ U.S. & For. Patd/ Other Pats/ Pending/ Mexico **Notes:** speaks when string pulled, usually mute

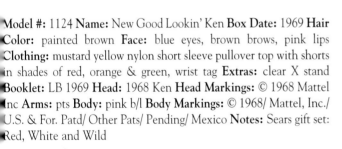

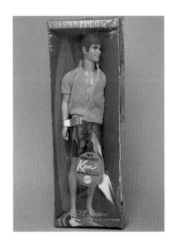

Model #: 1111 **Name:** Talking Ken **Box Date:** 1969 **Hair Color:** painted brown **Face:** blue eyes, brown brows, peach lips **Clothing:** orange swim trunks, short sleeve turquoise shirt with orange trim, wrist tag **Extras:** clear X stand **Booklet:** LB **Head:** 1968 Ken **Head Markings:** © 1968 Mattel Inc **Arms:** pts **Body:** pink talking **Body Markings:** © 1968/ Mattel, Inc./ U.S. & For.Patd/ Other Pats /Pending/ Hong Kong **Notes:** speaks when string pulled, usually mute

Model #: 1159 Name: Live Action Ken Box Date: 1970 Hair Color: painted brown Face: blue eyes, brown brows, peach lips Clothing: multicolor turquoise, purple, blue, green & gold long sleeve shirt, open in front with a hook & eye closure, yellow gold satin pants, brown fringe vest, brown loafers, wrist tag Extras: clear touch 'n go stand Booklet: instructions Head: 1968 Ken Head Markings: © 1968 Mattel Inc Arms: pts Body: pink live action Body Markings: © 1968/ Mattel, Inc./ Taiwan/ U.S. & For.Patd./ Patented in/ Canada 1967/ Other Pats/ Pending Notes: also available in Live Action on Stage # 1172

Model #: 1088 Name: Sun Set Malibu Ken Box Date: 1970 Hair Color: painted yellow Face: aqua eyes, brown brows, peach lips Clothing: orange nylon swim trunks, turquoise towel, wrist tag Head: 1968 Ken Head Markings: © 1968 Mattel Inc Arms: pts Body: dark tan b/l Body Markings: © 1968/ Mattel, Inc./ U.S. & For.Patd/ Other Pats /Pending/ Hong Kong Notes: also issued in pink box in under the Malibu, same model #, light green trunks, made in Hong Kong or Taiwan with pts or ptr arms Sears gift set: Surf's Up, see Malibu Barbie 1975 for example of pink box

Model #: 3314 Name: Busy Ken Box Date: 1971 Hair Color: painted brown Face: blue eyes, dark brown brows, pink lips Clothing: orange stretch tank top with brown vinyl belt with gold buckle, blue jeans, tennis shoes, wrist tag Extras: clear X stand, brown princess telephone, TV, travel case, record player, record, tray, 2 glasses, stickers Booklet: LB&S 1970 & instructions Head: 1968 Ken Head Markings: © 1968 Mattel Inc Arms: busy Body: pink b/l Body Markings: © 1968/ Mattel, Inc./ U.S. & For.Patd/ Other Pat /Pending/ Hong Kong

Model #: 1196 Name: Busy Talking Ken Box Date: 1971 Hair Color: painted brown Face: blue eyes, brown brows, peach lips Clothing: blue & red pattern short sleeve sport shirt with blue buttons & brown vinyl belt with gold buckle, red corduroy bell bottoms, dark brown loafers, wrist tag Extras: clear X stand, brown princess telephone, TV, travel case, record player, record, tray, 2 glasses, stickers Booklet: LB&S 1970 & instructions Head: 1968 Ken Head Markings: © 1968 Mattel Inc Arms: busy Body: pink talking Body Markings: © 1968/ Mattel, Inc./ U.S. & For.Patd/ Other Pats /Pending/ Hong Kong

Model #: 1184 **Name:** Walk Lively Ken **Box Date:** 1971 **Hair Color:** painted brown **Face:** blue eyes, brown brows, mauve lips **Clothing:** blue short sleeve knit sport shirt with blue, white, yellow & light brown plaid pants, light brown loafers, wrist tag **Extras:** brown round walking stand **Booklet:** LWOB 1971 & instructions **Head:** 1968 Ken **Head Markings:** © 1968 Mattel Inc **Arms:** pts **Body:** pink walking **Body Markings:** © 1968 Mattel, Inc./ U.S. Pat.Pend/ Taiwan

Model #: 4224 **Name:** Mod Hair Ken **Box Date:** 1972 **Hair Color:** brunette **Hairstyle:** collar length side part, cello on head **Face:** blue eyes, brown brows, pink lips **Clothing:** white turtleneck dickey, brown & white checked jacket, tan pants, brown flocked sheet with beard, mustache, sideburns, wrist tag, brown tennis shoes **Extras:** white X stand **Booklet:** BWOB 1973 **Head:** 1972 Ken **Head Markings:** © 1972 Mattel Inc. Hong Kong **Arms:** pts **Body:** pink b/l **Body Markings:** © 1968/ Mattel, Inc./ U.S. & For.Patd/ Other Pats /Pending/ Hong Kong **Notes:** Montgomery Ward sold this doll in a special blue brocade & black tuxedo

Model #: 7809 **Name:** Sun Valley Ken **Box Date:** 1973 **Hair Color:** painted blonde **Face:** blue eyes, brown brows, peach lips **Clothing:** red turtleneck top with blue stripes, navy ski jacket with matching pants, blue ski poles, red skis, red goggles & ski boots **Head:** 1968 Ken **Head Markings:** © 1968 Mattel Inc **Arms:** pts **Body:** dark tan b/l **Body Markings:** © 1968/ Mattel, Inc./ U.S. & For.Patd/ Other Pats/ Pending/ Taiwan

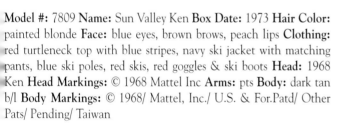

Model #: 7280 **Name:** Free Moving Ken **Box Date:** 1974 **Hair Color:** painted brown **Face:** blue eyes, brown brows, pink lips **Clothing:** 1-piece playsuit with red & white stripe top, white collar & solid white shorts, golf club, tennis racket, ball, white socks, white tennis shoes **Head:** 1968 Ken **Head Markings:** © 1968 Mattel Inc **Arms:** pts **Body:** pink free moving **Body Markings:** © 1968 Mattel, Inc./ Taiwan/ U.S.Patent/ Pending **Notes:** pull down lever on back of doll permits free movement

Model #: 7261 Name: Gold Medal Olympic Skier Ken Box Date: 1974 Hair Color: painted blonde Face: blue eyes, brown brows, peach lips Clothing: 1-piece red, white & blue turtleneck long sleeve ski outfit with blue vinyl belt, gold medal, red ski cap & goggles, blue skis & poles, navy #9 on yellow entry vest, red ski boots Head: 1968 Ken Head Markings: © 1968 Mattel Inc Arms: pts Body: dark tan b/l Body Markings: © 1968/ Mattel, Inc./ U.S. & For.Patd/ Other Pats/ Pending/ Taiwan

Model #: 1088 Name: Sun Set Malibu Ken Box Date: 1974 Hair Color: painted yellow Face: blue eyes, brown brows, peach lips Clothing: light green nylon swim trunks Head: 1968 Ken Head Markings: © 1968 Mattel Inc Arms: pts Body: dark tan b/l Body Markings: © 1968/ Mattel, Inc./ U.S. & For.Patd/ Other Pats/ Pending/ Taiwan Notes: also issued in pink box, same model #, under Malibu name, see Malibu Barbie 1975 for example of box, made in Taiwan & Hong Kong with either pts or ptr arms

Model #: 9342 Name: Now Look Ken Box Date: 1975 Hair Color: brunette Hairstyle: side part, nape of neck or shoulder length, cello on head Face: blue eyes, black brows, mauve lips Clothing: tan 2-piece casual suit, button front snap closure at waist, turquoise scarf brown flocked sheet of mustaches, beard and sideburns, brown loafers Extras: pointed brown brush Head: 1972 Ken Head Markings: © 1972 Mattel Inc. Hong Kong Arms: pts or ptr Body: pink b/l Body Markings: © 1968/ Mattel, Inc./ U.S. & For.Patd/ Other Pats /Pending/ Hong Kong Notes: Hong Kong or Taiwan, hard or soft head

Model #: 2211 Name: Superstar Ken Box Date: 1977 Hair Color: blonde painted Face: blue eyes, brown brows, peach lips Clothing: 1-piece navy blue long sleeve pantsuit with sewn in red scarf, wine vinyl belt with silver buckle, silver ID bracelet, watch & ring with red stone, red & silver sunglasses, black loafers Extras: 2-piece clear stand Head: superstar Head Markings: inside rim © Mattel Inc.1977 Arms: bent Body: tan tnt Body Markings: © Mattel, Inc 1968./ Hong Kong Notes: also 2 doll gift set with Barbie & Ken

Model #: 2960 **Name:** Hawaiian Ken **Box Date:** 1978 **Hair Color:** painted black **Face:** brown eyes, black brows, pink lips **Clothing:** white multicolor swim trunks, brown bead necklace, floral lei, orange towel, pink surfboard with floral pattern sticker **Head:** 1968 Ken **Head Markings:** © 1968 Mattel Inc **Arms:** ptr **Body:** dark tan b/l **Body Markings:** 1088 0500/ © Mattel/ Inc.1968/ Hong Kong

Model #: 1088 **Name:** Sun Lovin' Malibu Ken **Box Date:** 1978 **Hair Color:** painted blonde **Face:** blue eyes, brown brows, dark peach lips **Clothing:** turquoise & purple trimmed swim trunks with 'K' initial on hip, turquoise vinyl tote bag, turquoise mirror sunglasses **Head:** superstar **Head Markings:** inside rim © Mattel Inc.1977 **Arms:** ptr **Body:** tan b/l, painted tan lines **Body Markings:** 1088 0500/ © Mattel/ Inc.1968/ Hong Kong

Model #: 1294 **Name:** Sport & Shave Ken **Box Date:** 1979 **Hair Color:** brown rooted **Hairstyle:** side part, chin length **Face:** turquoise eyes, brown brows, mauve lips **Clothing:** white T-shirt with navy edging, yellow trunks with navy & white edging, navy pants, toothpaste, shaving mug, toothbrush, tennis racket, cologne, hair dryer, brush, 2 shavers, comb, watch, brown marking pen, blue & white tennis shoes **Booklet:** instructions **Head:** rooted superstar **Head Markings:** inside rim © Mattel Inc.1977 **Arms:** jointed wrists, bendable elbows & 1 fist **Body:** tan tnt **Body Markings:** © Mattel, Inc.1968/ Taiwan

 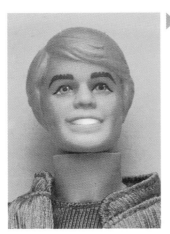

Model #: 1881 **Name:** Roller Skating Ken **Box Date:** 1980 **Hair Color:** painted blonde **Face:** blue eyes, brown brows, peach lips **Clothing:** red tee shirt, purple satin jacket, black trunks, red socks, white roller skates with red rollers **Head:** superstar **Head Markings:** inside rim © Mattel Inc.1977 **Arms:** ptr **Body:** tan b/l **Body Markings:** © Mattel, Inc 1968./ Hong Kong

Model #: 3600 Name: Western Ken Box Date: 1980 Hair Color: painted brunette Face: turquoise eyes, black brows, mauve lips Clothing: white western shirt with black cuffs, collar & yoke, black ribbon tie at neck, black vinyl jeans, white cowboy hat, black cowboy boots Booklet: BWOF 1980 Head: superstar Head Markings: inside rim © Mattel Inc.1977 Arms: bent Body: pink tnt Body Markings: © Mattel, Inc.1968/ Taiwan

Model #: 3553 Name: All Star Ken Box Date: 1981 Hair Color: painted brown Face: blue eyes, brown brows, peach lips Clothing: blue T-shirt, yellow & royal blue accents, blue shirt with yellow accents, silver muscle band, dumbbells, jump rope handles, racquet, weight bar, 10 lb., 5 lb., 25 lb. weights, jump rope string, light blue socks, royal blue tennis shoes Booklet: instructions Head: superstar Head Markings: inside rim © Mattel Inc.1977 Arms: jointed wrists, bendable elbows, grip hands Body: tan tnt Body Markings: © Mattel, Inc.1968/ Taiwan

Model #: 5316 Name: Fashion Jeans Ken Box Date: 1981 Hair Color: painted blonde Face: blue eyes, brown brows, pink lips Clothing: pink v-neck short sleeve T-shirt with collar, blue jeans, blue vinyl belt, black cowboy boots Head: superstar Head Markings: inside rim © Mattel Inc.1977 Arms: ptr Body: tan b/l Body Markings: © Mattel, Inc 1968./ Hong Kong

Model #: 1088 Name: Sunsational Malibu Ken Box Date: 1981 Hair Color: painted blonde Face: blue eyes, brown brows, deep peach lips Clothing: fuchsia & pink trimmed swim trunks, purple, yellow, green striped towel, turquoise mirror sunglasses Head: superstar Head Markings: inside rim © Mattel Inc.1977 Arms: ptr Body: tan b/l Body Markings: © Mattel, Inc 1968./ Hong Kong

Model #: 4077 Name: Dream Date Ken Box Date: 1982 Hair Color: painted black Face: dark blue eyes, brown brows, pale pink lips Clothing: black suit coat with hot pink flower, 1-piece bodysuit white top, hot pink cummerbund, gray slacks & black bow tie, black loafers Booklet: BWOF 1981 Head: superstar Head Markings: inside rim © Mattel Inc.1977 Arms: bent Body: tan tnt Body Markings: © Mattel, Inc.1968/ Taiwan

Model #: 3600 Name: Horse Lovin' Ken Box Date: 1982 Hair Color: painted brunette Face: blue eyes, black brows, mauve lips Clothing: red & cream patterned shirt, fake tan shearling vest, red vinyl jeans, red kerchief, tan cowboy hat & cowboy boots Booklet: BWOF 1981 Head: superstar Head Markings: inside rim © Mattel Inc.1977 Arms: bent Body: pink tnt Body Markings: © Mattel, Inc.1968/ Taiwan

Model #: 4898 Name: Crystal Ken Box Date: 1983 Hair Color: painted black Face: blue eyes, black brows, mauve lips Clothing: white 1-piece sleeveless jumpsuit with satin pants, white shirt, white vinyl collar & purple tie, iridescent vest, white jacket with purple buttons & flower, white socks & loafers Booklet: BWOF 1984 Head: 1983 Ken Head Markings: © 1983 Mattel Inc Arms: bent Body: tan tnt Body Markings: © Mattel, Inc.1968/ Taiwan

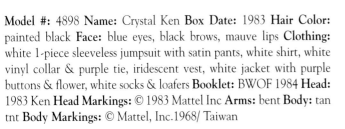

 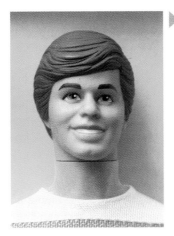

Model #: 7310 Name: Great Shapes Ken Box Date: 1983 Hair Color: painted brown Face: blue eyes, brown brows, mauve lips Clothing: white T-shirt with turquoise & yellow stripes, turquoise parachute pants & matching tote bag, white tennis shoes Booklet: BWOF 1983 Head: 1983 Ken Head Markings: © 1983 Mattel Inc Arms: ptr Body: tan b/l Body Markings: © Mattel, Inc 1968./ Hong Kong Notes: next issue came with doll size walkman

151

Model #: 7495 Name: Hawaiian Ken Box Date: 1983 Hair Color: painted black Face: brown eyes, brown brows, pink lips Clothing: Hawaiian shirt & matching trunks in fuchsia, orange & green pattern, white surfboard with sunset decal Booklet: BWOF 1984 Head: Hispanic Head Markings: © 1983 Mattel Inc Arms: ptr Body: tan b/l Body Markings: © Mattel, Inc 1968./ Hong Kong

Model #: 1088 Name: Sun Gold Malibu Ken Box Date: 1983 Hair Color: painted blonde Face: blue eyes, brown brows, mauve lips Clothing: light blue trunks with gold trim, pairs of pink, purple & black sunglasses, blue towel Booklet: BWOF 1984 Head: Ken 83 Head Markings: © 1983 Mattel Inc Arms: ptr Body: tan b/l Body Markings: © Mattel, Inc 1968./ Hong Kong

Model #: 9019 Name: Day-to-Night Ken Box Date: 1984 Hair Color: painted brunette Face: blue eyes, brown brows, peach lips Clothing: navy blazer, 1-piece blue & white tweed vest & pants, white shirt, pink & white striped tie, iridescent pink cummerbund & blue socks, black loafers Extras: sheet of cardboard punch outs Booklet: BWOF 1984 & instructions Head: Ken 1983 Head Markings: © 1983 Mattel Inc Arms: bent Body: tan tnt Body Markings: © Mattel, Inc.1968/ Taiwan

Model #: 2250 Name: Dream Glow Ken Box Date: 1985 Hair Color: painted brown Face: blue eyes, brown brows, peach lips Clothing: 1-piece jumpsuit with sleeveless white shirt, white vinyl high collar, hot pink bow tie, pink vest with white dayglo stars, gray pants, gray jacket, pink & white corsage, gray socks, gray loafers Booklet: BWOF 1985 Head: 1983 Ken Head Markings: © 1983 Mattel Inc Arms: bent Body: tan tnt Body Markings: © Mattel, Inc.1968/ Taiwan

Model #: 1020 **Name:** Tropical Ken **Box Date:** 1985 **Hair Color:** painted yellow **Face:** blue eyes, brown brows, peach lips **Clothing:** patterned swim trunks of navy, turquoise, yellow & hot pink, yellow lei **Booklet:** BWOF 1984 **Head:** Ken 1983 **Head Markings:** © 1983 Mattel Inc **Arms:** ptr **Body:** tan b/l **Body Markings:** © Mattel, Inc 1968./ Hong Kong

Model #: 1719 **Name:** Jewel Secrets Ken **Box Date:** 1986 **Hair Color:** brunette **Hairstyle:** side part, collar length **Face:** brown eyes, brown brows, peach lips **Clothing:** 1-piece sleeveless silver lamé jumpsuit with silver striped shirt, solid silver collar, blue iridescent bow tie & cummerbund, silver pants, silver argyle pattern tuxedo with tails, silver glitter socks, 3 color bracelet for Barbie, blue jewelry box, gray loafers **Extras:** turquoise oval brush & "Mystery at Sea" storybook **Booklet:** BWOF 1986 & instructions **Head:** 1986 Ken **Head Markings:** © 1986 Mattel Inc **Arms:** bent **Body:** tan tnt **Body Markings:** © Mattel Inc.1968/ Malaysia

Model #: 3131 **Name:** Rocker Ken **Box Date:** 1986 **Hair Color:** blonde **Hairstyle:** nape of neck length with curly bangs **Face:** blue eyes, blonde brows, pale pink lips **Clothing:** ankle-length silver coat & matching kerchief, silver sleeveless T-shirt with hot pink stars & Rockers logo, silver belt, silver vinyl pants, right hand pink star fingerless glove & matching socks, silver tennis shoes **Extras:** silver oval brush, pink guitar, sticker for guitar, pink guitar strap **Booklet:** BWOF 1985 & instructions **Head:** 1986 Ken **Head Markings:** © 1986 Mattel Inc **Arms:** bent **Body:** tan tnt **Body Markings:** © Mattel, Inc.1968/ Taiwan

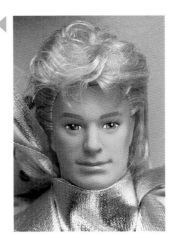

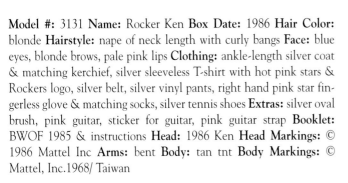

Model #: 4441 **Name:** California Ken **Box Date:** 1987 **Hair Color:** painted blonde **Face:** turquoise eyes, brown brows, peach lips **Clothing:** yellow & white striped sleeveless shirt with multicolor pattern, orange vinyl tie, white shorts with orange & white dot pattern, orange visor & Frisbee, soda can, orange X sandals **Extras:** comic book & sheet of cardboard punch outs & stickers **Booklet:** instructions **Head:** 1983 Ken **Head Markings:** © 1983 Mattel Inc **Arms:** ptr **Body:** tan b/l **Body Markings:** © Mattel Inc.1968/ Malaysia

153

Model #: 4441 **Name:** California Dream Ken **Box Date:** 1987 **Hair Color:** painted blonde **Face:** turquoise eyes, brown brows, peach lips **Clothing:** yellow & white striped sleeveless shirt with multicolor pattern, orange vinyl tie, white shorts with orange & white dot pattern, orange visor & Frisbee, soda can, orange X sandals **Extras:** comic book sheet of cardboard punch outs & stickers **Booklet:** BWOF 1988 & instructions **Head:** 1983 Ken **Head Markings:** © 1983 Mattel Inc **Arms:** ptr **Body:** tan b/l **Body Markings:** © Mattel Inc.1968/ Malaysia

Model #: 4118 **Name:** Doctor Ken **Box Date:** 1987 **Hair Color:** painted brunette **Face:** green eyes, brown brows, pink lips **Clothing:** 1-piece sleeveless jumpsuit with high collar, white top with lace front & blue bow tie, blue pants, reversible white satin Dr's coat, royal blue socks, white Dr. bag, stethoscope, 2 bottles, blood pressure cord, x-ray frame, beeper, reflex hammer, microscope, watch, ear checker, clipboard, notepads, royal blue loafers **Extras:** sheet of stickers & cardboard punch outs **Booklet:** BWOF 1987 & instructions **Head:** 1983 Ken **Head Markings:** © 1983 Mattel Inc **Arms:** bent **Body:** tan tnt **Body Markings:** © Mattel Inc.1968/ Malaysia

Model #: 4060 **Name:** Island Fun Ken **Box Date:** 1987 **Hair Color:** painted blonde **Face:** blue eyes, dark blonde brows, peach lips **Clothing:** turquoise Hawaiian print swim trunks & multicolor lei **Booklet:** BWOF 1987 **Head:** 1983 Ken **Head Markings:** © 1983 Mattel Inc **Arms:** ptr **Body:** dark tan b/l **Body Markings:** © Mattel Inc.1968/ Malaysia **Notes:** may develop light blotches on legs & stickiness

Model #: 4554 **Name:** Perfume Giving Ken **Box Date:** 1987 **Hair Color:** painted black **Face:** blue eyes, black brows, pink lips **Clothing:** 1-piece jumpsuit white shirt, gray pants, iridescent pink bow tie & cummerbund, silver gray jacket with dark gray lapels & pink flower, perfume bottle, white socks, gray loafers **Extras:** pink bow shaped notepad, sheet of cardboard punch outs **Booklet:** Perfume Pretty Barbie Tips & instructions **Head:** 1983 Ken **Head Markings:** © 1983 Mattel Inc **Arms:** bent **Body:** tan tnt **Body Markings:** © Mattel Inc.1968/ Malaysia

154

Model #: 1351 Name: Animal Lovin' Ken Box Date: 1988 Hair Color: painted brown Face: blue eyes, light brown brows, peach lips Clothing: blue animal print short sleeve shirt with gold belt, light blue cuffed pleated shorts, light blue kerchief, plastic monkey, gray topsiders Extras: sheet of cardboard punch outs Booklet: BWF 1988 Head: 1983 Ken Head Markings: © 1983 Mattel Inc Arms: bent Body: tan tnt Body Markings: © Mattel Inc.1968/ Malaysia

Model #: 3238 Name: Beach Blast Ken Box Date: 1988 Hair Color: painted yellow Face: blue eyes, light brown brows, peach lips Clothing: 1-piece short sleeve wetsuit in turquoise & black with pink trim, hot pink visor & Frisbee, yellow boom box Booklet: BWOF 1988 Head: 1983 Ken Head Markings: © 1983 Mattel Inc Arms: ptr Body: tan b/l Body Markings: © Mattel Inc.1968/ Malaysia

Model #: 3215 Name: Cool Times Ken Box Date: 1988 Hair Color: painted blonde Face: brown-blue eyes, brown brows, mauve lips Clothing: yellow T-shirt with orange sleeves & pizza appliqué, black pants with black & white stripes up sides & black & white square suspenders, pizza kite, piece of pizza, white tennis shoes Extras: sheet of cardboard punch outs Booklet: BWOF 1988 & instructions Head: 1983 Ken Head Markings: © 1983 Mattel Inc Arms: bent Body: tan tnt Body Markings: © Mattel Inc.1968/ Malaysia

Model #: 1535 Name: Superstar Ken Box Date: 1988 Hair Color: painted brown Face: blue eyes, brown brows, pink lips Clothing: 1-piece white jumpsuit with silver stars on shirt, silver collar, pink bow tie & cummerbund, silver lamé tails tuxedo jacket, silver trophy, white socks & loafers Extras: sheet of cardboard punch outs Booklet: BWOF 1988 Head: 1983 Ken or 1988 Ken Head Markings: © 1983 Mattel Inc or © M.I. 1988 Arms: bent Body: tan tnt Body Markings: © Mattel Inc. 1968/ Malaysia

Model #: 9361 **Name:** Barbie and the All Stars Ken **Box Date:** 1989 **Hair Color:** painted blonde **Face:** blue eyes, brown brows, mauve lips **Clothing:** white tank top with purple metallic stars, turquoise shorts, tote bag converts to turquoise pants, white knee socks, basketball hoop, soda can, basketball, white tennis shoes **Extras:** 3 sheets of cardboard punch outs **Booklet:** BWOF 1988 & instructions **Head:** 1983 Ken **Head Markings:** © 1983 Mattel Inc **Arms:** bent **Body:** tan tnt **Body Markings:** © Mattel Inc.1968/ Malaysia

Model #: 3511 **Name:** Dance Club Ken **Box Date:** 1989 **Hair Color:** painted light & medium brown **Face:** blue eyes, brown brows, mauve lips **Clothing:** 1-piece jumpsuit: hot pink T-shirt with "B" initial & black denim pants with cuffs, white vinyl jacket, black & silver belt, white socks, black tennis shoes **Extras:** sheet of cardboard punch outs **Booklet:** BWOF 1988 **Head:** 1983 Ken **Head Markings:** © 1983 Mattel Inc **Arms:** bent **Body:** tan tnt **Body Markings:** © Mattel Inc.1968/ Malaysia

Model #: 7081 **Name:** Dance Magic Ken **Box Date:** 1989 **Hair Color:** painted red **Face:** turquoise eyes, red brows, pink lips **Clothing:** 1-piece long sleeve white jumpsuit with vinyl collar & iridescent pink tie, iridescent white vest, white sleeveless jacket with iridescent white lapels, white socks, pink sash, purple wash cloth, white lace-up dance shoes **Extras:** purple applicator for changing color of hair, sheet of cardboard punch outs **Booklet:** BWOF 1988 & instructions **Head:** 1988 Ken **Head Markings:** © M.I. 1988 **Arms:** bent **Body:** tan tnt **Body Markings:** © Mattel Inc.1968/ Malaysia **Notes:** also gift set with regular issue Barbie & Ken

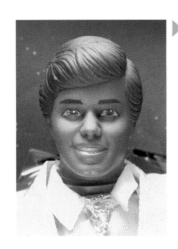

Model #: 9600 **Name:** Flight Time Ken **Box Date:** 1989 **Hair Color:** painted blonde **Face:** blue eyes, dark blonde brows, pink lips **Clothing:** jumpsuit: white shirt with gold airplane print & blue pants, white vinyl dickey with collar & gold tie, double breasted blue coat, blue socks, blue collar with gold ties, red jewel, blue pilot's hat, blue briefcase & loafers **Extras:** 2 sheets of cardboard punch outs & sheet of stickers **Booklet:** BWOF 1988 **Head:** 1983 Ken **Head Markings:** © 1983 Mattel Inc **Arms:** bent **Body:** tan tnt **Body Markings:** © Mattel Inc.1968/ Malaysia

Model #: 7375 **Name:** Ice Capades Ken **Box Date:** 1989 **Hair Color:** painted blonde **Face:** blue eyes, blonde brows, mauve lips **Clothing:** 1-piece jumpsuit: sleeveless halter top with pink glitter dots & white iridescent bow tie, high collar & aqua suspender pants, white short jacket with iridescent lapels, aqua ice skates **Extras:** sheet of cardboard punch outs **Booklet:** BWOF 1988 **Head:** 1983 Ken **Head Markings:** © 1983 Mattel Inc **Arms:** bent **Body:** tan tnt **Body Markings:** © Mattel Inc.1968/ Malaysia

Model #: 9934 **Name:** Western Fun Ken **Box Date:** 1989 **Hair Color:** painted brown **Face:** turquoise eyes, light brown brows, mauve lips **Clothing:** 1-piece jumpsuit: turquoise T-shirt, turquoise & purple splatter pants, purple & silver belt with turquoise buckle, turquoise kerchief, purple short jacket, purple boot spats & purple loafers **Extras:** sheet of cardboard punch outs **Booklet:** BWOF 1988 **Head:** 1988 Ken **Head Markings:** © M.I. 1988 **Arms:** bent **Body:** tan tnt **Body Markings:** © Mattel, Inc. 1968/ Mexico **Notes:** back of box shows hat, but not included

Model #: 4104 **Name:** Wet n' Wild Ken **Box Date:** 1989 **Hair Color:** painted blonde **Face:** blue eyes, dark blonde brows, peach lips **Clothing:** light green sleeveless crop top, change-color knee-length swim trunks of turquoise, yellow, hot pink & orange **Head:** 1983 Ken **Head Markings:** © 1983 Mattel Inc **Arms:** ptr **Body:** tan b/l **Body Markings:** © Mattel Inc.1968/ Malaysia

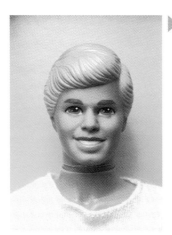

Model #: 9424 **Name:** All American Ken **Box Date:** 1990 **Hair Color:** painted blonde **Face:** blue eyes, brown brows, mauve lips **Clothing:** yellow T-shirt with pink cuffs & sign appliqué, blue acid washed pants with red & white waistband detailing, pair of high-top blue Reeboks **Extras:** sheet of cardboard punch outs **Booklet:** BFG 1991 **Head:** 1988 Ken **Head Markings:** © M.I. 1988 **Arms:** bent **Body:** tan tnt **Body Markings:** © Mattel Inc.1968/ Malaysia

Model #: 7154 Name: Costume Ball Ken Box Date: 1990 Hair Color: painted blonde Face: green eyes, brown brows, mauve lips Clothing: white shirt, orange cummerbund, black pants, white jacket, eye patch, mask, black bow tie, orange scarf, black socks, pink vest, white turban, black loafers Extras: sheet of cardboard punch outs Booklet: IIB 1990 Head: 1988 Ken Head Markings: © M.I. 1988 Arms: bent Body: tan tnt Body Markings: © Mattel Inc.1968/ Malaysia

Model #: 5941 Name: Hawaiian Fun Ken Box Date: 1990 Hair Color: painted 2-tone blonde Face: turquoise eyes, brown brows, mauve lips Clothing: yellow-green sleeveless crop top with appliqué, swim trunks in hot pink, turquoise, yellow-green & black, hot pink Frisbee, turquoise visor, green boom box Booklet: BFG 1991 Head: 1988 Ken Head Markings: © M.I. 1988 Arms: ptr Body: tan b/l Body Markings: © Mattel Inc.1968/ Malaysia

Model #: 9609 Name: Wedding Day Ken Box Date: 1990 Hair Color: painted blonde Face: blue eyes, brown brows, peach lips Clothing: black tuxedo with tails, gray vest, pink shirt w/white turned up collar, pink flower in lapel, black pin stripe pants, black socks & loafers Head: 1988 Ken Head Markings: © M.I. 1988 Arms: bent Body: tan tnt Body Markings: © Mattel Inc.1968/ Malaysia Notes: box available w/ open lattice or closed, also part of 6 doll gift set

Model #: 4903 Name: Rappin' Rockin' Ken Box Date: 1991 Hair Color: painted brown Face: blue eyes, brown brows, mauve lips Clothing: long sleeve hooded purple windbreaker, turquoise parachute pants, purple baseball hat, turquoise boom box, gold pendant, black loafers Extras: sheet of cardboard punch outs Head: modified Alan Head Markings: © 1991 Mattel Inc Arms: bent Body: tan tnt Body Markings: © Mattel Inc.1968/ Malaysia Notes: head mold Alan or modified Alan

Model #: 2215 **Name:** Rollerblades Ken **Box Date:** 1991 **Hair Color:** painted 2-tone blonde **Face:** turquoise eyes, brown brows, mauve lips **Clothing:** lime green tank top, black & multicolor mid-thigh shorts, turquoise fanny pack, black elbow pads, lime green & black knee pads, lime green rollerblades **Booklet:** instructions **Head:** Alan or modified Alan **Head Markings:** © 1990 Mattel Inc or © 1991 Mattel Inc **Arms:** bent **Body:** tan tnt **Body Markings:** © Mattel Inc.1968/ Malaysia **Notes:** rollerblade sparks are a fire hazard

Model #: 7512 **Name:** Ski Fun Ken **Box Date:** 1991 **Hair Color:** painted 2-tone blonde **Face:** blue eyes, brown brows, mauve lips **Clothing:** yellow, green, purple multicolor T-shirt, matching jacket & pants, gold mittens, orange headband, orange snowboard, purple goggles & ski boots **Extras:** sheet of cardboard punch outs **Booklet:** instructions **Head:** 1988 Ken **Head Markings:** © M.I. 1988 **Arms:** bent **Body:** tan tnt **Body Markings:** © Mattel Inc.1968/ Malaysia

Model #: 1392 **Name:** Sun Sensation Ken **Box Date:** 1991 **Hair Color:** painted 2-tone blonde **Face:** turquoise eyes, brown brows, pink lips **Clothing:** gold net crop T-shirt with yellow-green swim trunks **Head:** 1988 Ken **Head Markings:** © M.I. 1988 **Arms:** ptr **Body:** tan b/l **Body Markings:** © Mattel Inc.1968/ Malaysia

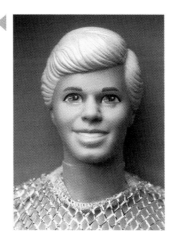

Model #: 1115 **Name:** Totally Hair Ken **Box Date:** 1991 **Hair Color:** brown **Hairstyle:** combed back from face, nape of neck length **Face:** blue eyes, brown brows, pale mauve lips **Clothing:** long sleeve multicolor swirl pattern shirt in pink, mauve, white, light green, turquoise, lavender parachute fabric pants with Ken label, white loafers **Extras:** purple hair pick & Dep styling gel **Booklet:** styling tips & 1991 PB **Head:** Totally Hair two versions **Head Markings:** © 1991 Mattel, Inc **Arms:** bent **Body:** tan tnt **Body Markings:** © Mattel Inc.1968/ Malaysia **Notes:** either white loafers or white jazz shoes, two different head molds used, both dated 1991, very similar but one has deeper dimple in chin & larger nose

Model #: 2290 **Name:** Earring Magic Ken **Box Date:** 1992 **Hair Color:** painted 2-tone blonde **Face:** blue eyes, light brown brows, peach lips **Clothing:** lavender vinyl vest with sheer short sleeve T-shirt, black jeans, silver earring left ear, silver hoop medallion, black oxford shoes **Extras:** silver hoop clip-on earrings for child 1 with Ken & 1 with Barbie **Head:** modified Alan **Head Markings:** © 1991 Mattel Inc **Arms:** bent **Body:** tan tnt **Body Markings:** © Mattel Inc. 1968/ China

Model #: 4904 **Name:** Glitter Beach Ken **Box Date:** 1992 **Hair Color:** painted 2-tone blonde **Face:** blue eyes, light brown brows, mauve lips **Clothing:** purple sleeveless crop top, swim trunks in hot pink, teal, purple glitter, hot pink surfer pendant **Head:** modified Alan **Head Markings:** © 1991 Mattel Inc **Arms:** ptr **Body:** tan b/l **Body Markings:** © Mattel Inc. 1968/ Malaysia

Model #: 4829 **Name:** Hollywood Hair Ken **Box Date:** 1992 **Hair Color:** painted blonde with lilac stars **Face:** blue eyes, light brown brows, mauve lips **Clothing:** white waist-length short sleeve T-shirt with rolled up sleeves, gold collarband, appliqué, black parachute pants with gold stars & gold waistband, gold high-top athletic shoes **Extras:** fuchsia applicator with white terry cloth **Head:** modified Alan **Head Markings:** © 1991 Mattel Inc **Arms:** bent **Body:** tan tnt **Body Markings:** © Mattel Inc. 1968/ Malaysia **Notes:** make stars in hair disappear

Model #: 5474 **Name:** Sea Holiday Ken **Box Date:** 1992 **Hair Color:** painted brunette **Face:** blue eyes, brown brows, mauve lips **Clothing:** white short jacket with gold lapels, matching white pants, navy blue, white & gold pattern short sleeve shirt with gold bow tie, white vinyl captain's hat with gold trim, blue, gold, white & black cotton swimsuit trunks, Barbie fold-out pictures, white loafers **Head:** modified Alan **Head Markings:** © 1991 Mattel Inc **Arms:** bent **Body:** tan tnt **Body Markings:** © Mattel Inc 1968/ China

Model #: 7988 **Name:** Secret Hearts Ken **Box Date:** 1992 **Hair Color:** painted brunette **Face:** blue eyes, brown brows, peach lips **Clothing:** waist-length pink tuxedo coat, white shirt with pink shimmering bow tie, pink & white heart cummerbund, 3 flower bouquet, white pants, white socks & lace-up oxfords **Extras:** pink tray with 3 hearts & heart for ice to change colors on outfit **Head:** 1991 Ken **Head Markings:** © 1991 Mattel Inc **Arms:** bent **Body:** tan tnt **Body Markings:** © Mattel Inc. 1968/ China

Model #: 3149 **Name:** Sparkle Surprise Ken **Box Date:** 1992 **Hair Color:** painted 2-tone brown **Face:** turquoise eyes, brown brows, pink lips **Clothing:** pink & silver striped sleeveless shirt with pink flocked collar, iridescent bow tie, black iridescent V insert, iridescent cummerbund, black iridescent suit, black iridescent tie, pink rose, gift box with bracelet, black oxford shoes **Extras:** sheet of cardboard punch outs **Head:** Alan or modified Alan **Head Markings:** © 1990 Mattel Inc or © 1991 Mattel Inc **Arms:** bent **Body:** tan tnt **Body Markings:** © Mattel Inc.1968/ Malaysia

Model #: 11075 **Name:** Camp Fun Ken **Box Date:** 1993 **Hair Color:** painted 2-tone blonde **Face:** blue eyes, blonde brows, pink lips **Clothing:** turquoise appliquéd T-shirt, flannel plaid shirt, denim shorts, turquoise baseball cap, yellow sunglasses, white socks, turquoise backpack, orange coffee pot & frying pan, black ankle high athletic shoes **Booklet:** instructions **Head:** Alan **Head Markings:** © 1990 Mattel Inc **Arms:** bent **Body:** tan tnt **Body Markings:** © Mattel Inc.1968/ Malaysia

Model #: 10964 **Name:** Locket Surprise Ken **Box Date:** 1993 **Hair Color:** painted 2-tone brown **Face:** teal brown eyes, brown brows, peach lips **Clothing:** pink high collar shirt, multicolor floral vest, gold lamé jacket, iridescent teal pants, teal socks & loafers **Extras:** gold heart shaped box with heart fragrance **Head:** Alan **Head Markings:** © 1990 Mattel Inc **Arms:** bent **Body:** tan tnt **Body Markings:** © Mattel Inc.1968/ Malaysia

Model #: 10954 Name: Sun Jewel Ken Box Date: 1993 Hair Color: painted blonde Face: turquoise eyes, light brown brows, mauve lips Clothing: swim trunks in hot pink & black with iridescent trim Extras: stick on jewels Head: modified Alan Head Markings: © 1991 Mattel Inc Arms: ptr Body: tan b/l Body Markings: © Mattel Inc.1968/ Malaysia

Model #: 10294 Name: Western Stampin' Ken Box Date: 1993 Hair Color: painted 2-tone brown Face: blue eyes, brown brows, peach lips Clothing: white long sleeve cowboy shirt with silver & black detailing & black fringe & cuffs, silver pendant, blue jeans with fake black chaps sewn in front, black belt with silver buckle, white cowboy hat with silver detail, black cowboy boots with rolling stampers Extras: ink pad, purple glitter & sheet of cardboard punch outs Booklet: instructions Head: Alan Head Markings: © 1990 Mattel Inc Arms: bent Body: tan tnt Body Markings: © Mattel Inc.1968/ Malaysia

Model #: 13200 Name: Baywatch Ken Box Date: 1994 Hair Color: painted brunette Face: blue eyes, brown brows, light mauve lips Clothing: white T-shirt, red & black nylon windbreaker, red nylon swim trunks with Baywatch lifeguard insignia, white Baywatch visor, silver whistle on black cord, white tennis shoes Extras: black boom box, red binoculars, white Frisbee, red flotation device, yellow WaveRunner Booklet: instructions Head: Alan Head Markings: © 1990 Mattel Inc Arms: bent Body: tan tnt Body Markings: © Mattel Inc. 1968/ China

Model #: 13513 Name: Hot Skatin' Ken Box Date: 1994 Hair Color: painted brunette Face: blue eyes, dark brown brows, light mauve lips Clothing: 1-piece stretch bodysuit in hot pink, black, yellow & orange, yellow knee pads, orange helmet, yellow inline skates with orange blades, black ice skates Head: Alan Head Markings: © 1990 Mattel Inc Arms: hot skatin Body: tan Hot Skatin' Ken Body Markings: © 1975 Mattel, Inc/ China Notes: original body mold used in 1970s on unaffiliated Mattel doll

Model #: 12956 Name: Shaving Fun Ken Box Date: 1994 Hair Color: brown Hairstyle: nape of neck length Face: green eyes, light brown brows, matching beard & mustache, peach lips Clothing: multicolor striped hooded short sleeve T-shirt, blue jean knee-length shorts, matching tote bag, green water bottle, blue visor & small handgrip brush, shaving cream, shaver, Frisbee, white socks, black high-top athletic shoes Extras: royal blue oval brush Booklet: instructions Head: 1990 new Ken head mold Head Markings: © 1991 Mattel Inc Arms: bent Body: tan tnt Body Markings: © Mattel Inc. 1968/ China Notes: make beard disappear & reappears

Model #: 12447 Name: Tropical Splash Ken Box Date: 1994 Hair Color: painted blonde Face: lilac eyes, blonde brows, peach lips Clothing: swim trunks in black, hot pink, green & gold with green towel Extras: Barbie perfume Booklet: 1994 PB Head: 1991 modified Alan Head Markings: © 1991 Mattel Inc Arms: ptr Body: tan b/l Body Markings: © Mattel, Inc. 1968/ Indonesia Notes: perfume is same as used on Mackie's Masquerade doll, fabric pattern & towel colors vary

Model #: 13515 Name: Winter Sport Ken Box Date: 1994 Hair Color: painted brunette Face: blue eyes, brown brows, mauve lips Clothing: 1-piece long sleeve turtleneck bodysuit in yellow, orange, black & hot pink, yellow-green & fuchsia jacket, yellow snowboard, orange skis & poles, yellow & black goggles, fuchsia ski boots, black ice skates Head: Alan Head Markings: © 1990 Mattel Inc Arms: hot skating Body: hot skating Ken Body Markings: © 1975 Mattel, Inc/ China Notes: Available at JCP, Toys R Us, FAO, original body mold used in 1970s on unaffiliated Mattel doll

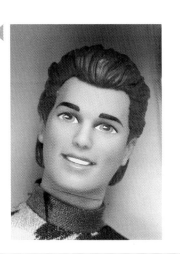 

African American and Hispanic Ken

Model #: 3849 Name: Sunsational Malibu Ken black version Box Date: 1981 Hair Color: black Hairstyle: curly to nape of neck Face: brown eyes, black brows, dark mauve lips Clothing: yellow & orange print swim trunks, purple, green & yellow striped towel, turquoise mirror sunglasses Booklet: BWOF 1981 Head: 1981 black Ken Head Markings: © 1981 Mattel Inc Arms: ptr Body: dark brown b/l Body Markings: © Mattel, Inc 1968./ Hong Kong

Model #: 9036 Name: Crystal Ken black version Box Date: 1983 Hair Color: painted black Face: brown eyes, black brows, pink lips Clothing: white 1-piece sleeveless jumpsuit with satin pants, white shirt, white vinyl collar & purple tie, iridescent vest, white jacket with purple buttons & flower, white socks & loafers Booklet: BWOF 1984 Head: 1983 black Ken Head Markings: © 1983 Mattel Inc Arms: bent Body: dark brown tnt Body Markings: © Mattel, Inc.1968/ Taiwan

Model #: 3849 Name: Sun Gold Malibu Ken black version Box Date: 1983 Hair Color: painted black Face: brown eyes, black brows, light red lips Clothing: light blue trunks with gold trim, pairs of pink, purple & black sunglasses, blue towel Booklet: BWOF 1984 Head: black 1983 Head Markings: © 1983 Mattel Inc Arms: ptr Body: dark brown b/l Body Markings: © Mattel, Inc 1968./ Hong Kong

Model #: 9018 Name: Day-to-Night Ken black version Box Date: 1984 Hair Color: painted black Face: brown eyes, black brows, light red lips Clothing: 1-piece navy blue tweed pants & white shirt with pink & hot pink striped tie, matching tweed vest, navy blue blazer, navy socks, pink iridescent cummerbund, black loafers Extras: sheet of cardboard punch outs Booklet: BWOF 1984 & instructions Head: 1983 black Ken Head Markings: © 1983 Mattel Inc Arms: bent Body: dark brown tnt Body Markings: © Mattel, Inc.1968/ Taiwan

Model #: 2421 Name: Dream Glow Ken black version Box Date: 1985 Hair Color: painted black Face: brown eyes, black brows, deep pink lips Clothing: 1-piece jumpsuit with sleeveless white shirt, white vinyl high collar, hot pink bow tie, pink vest with white dayglo stars, gray pants, gray jacket, pink & white corsage, gray socks, gray loafers Booklet: BWOF 1985 Head: 1983 black Ken Head Markings: © 1983 Mattel Inc Arms: bent Body: dark brown tnt Body Markings: © Mattel, Inc.1968/ Taiwan

164

Model #: 1023 Name: Tropical Ken black version Box Date: 1985 Hair Color: painted black Face: brown eyes, black brows, light red lips Clothing: swim trunks of navy, turquoise, yellow, hot pink & yellow lei Booklet: BWOF 1984 Head: 1983 black Ken Head Markings: © 1983 Mattel Inc Arms: ptr Body: dark brown b/l Body Markings: © Mattel, Inc 1968./ Hong Kong Notes: face may turn greasy

Model #: 3232 Name: Jewel Secrets Ken black version Box Date: 1986 Hair Color: painted black Face: brown eyes, black brows, pink-red lips Clothing: 1-piece sleeveless silver lamé jumpsuit with silver striped shirt, solid silver collar, blue iridescent bow tie & cummerbund, silver pants, silver argyle pattern tuxedo with tails, silver glitter socks, 3 color bracelet for Barbie, blue jewelry box, gray loafers Extras: turquoise oval brush & "Mystery at Sea" book Booklet: BWOF 1986 & instructions Head: 1983 black Ken Head Markings: © 1983 Mattel Inc Arms: bent Body: dark brown tnt Body Markings: © Mattel Inc.1968/ Malaysia

Model #: 4555 Name: Perfume Giving Ken black version Box Date: 1987 Hair Color: painted brunette Face: brown eyes, black brows & mustache, dark mauve lips Clothing: 1-piece jumpsuit: white shirt, gray pants, iridescent pink bow tie & cummerbund, silver gray jacket with dark gray lapels & pink flower, perfume bottle, white socks, gray loafers Extras: pink bow shaped notepad, sheet of cardboard punch outs Booklet: Perfume Pretty Barbie Tips & instructions Head: 1987 black Ken Head Markings: © Mattel Inc 1987 Arms: bent Body: dark brown tnt Body Markings: © Mattel Inc.1968/ Malaysia

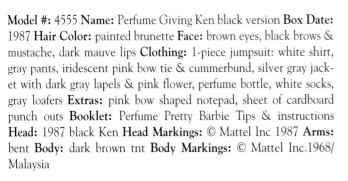

Model #: 1550 Name: Superstar Ken black version Box Date: 1988 Hair Color: painted brunette Face: brown eyes, black brows & mustache, dark mauve lips Clothing: 1-piece white jumpsuit with silver stars on shirt, silver collar, pink bow tie & cummerbund, silver lamé tails tuxedo jacket, silver trophy, white socks & loafers Extras: sheet of cardboard punch outs Booklet: BWOF 1988 Head: 1987 black Ken Head Markings: © Mattel Inc 1987 Arms: bent Body: dark brown tnt Body Markings: © Mattel Inc.1968/ Malaysia

Model #: 7082 **Name:** Dance Magic Ken black version **Box Date:** 1989 **Hair Color:** painted brunette **Face:** brown eyes, brown brows, black mustache, pink lips **Clothing:** 1-piece long sleeve white jumpsuit with vinyl collar & iridescent pink tie, iridescent white vest, white sleeveless jacket with iridescent white lapels, white socks, pink sash, purple wash cloth, white lace-up dance shoes **Extras:** purple applicator for changing color of hair, sheet of cardboard punch outs **Booklet:** BWOF 1988 & instructions **Head:** 1987 black Ken **Head Markings:** © Mattel Inc 1987 **Arms:** bent **Body:** dark brown tnt **Body Markings:** © Mattel Inc.1968/ Malaysia

Model #: 7160 **Name:** Costume Ball Ken black version **Box Date:** 1990 **Hair Color:** painted brunette **Face:** brown eyes, black brows, dark mauve lips **Clothing:** white shirt, orange cummerbund, black pants, white jacket, eye patch, mask, black bow tie, orange scarf, black socks, pink vest, white turban, black loafers **Extras:** sheet of cardboard punch outs **Booklet:** IIB 1990 **Head:** 1987 black Ken **Head Markings:** © Mattel Inc 1987 **Arms:** bent **Body:** dark brown tnt **Body Markings:** © Mattel Inc.1968/ Malaysia

Model #: 13259 **Name:** Baywatch Ken black version **Box Date:** 1994 **Hair Color:** painted black **Face:** brown eyes, black brows, pink-brown lips **Clothing:** white T-shirt, red & black nylon windbreaker, red nylon swim trunks with Baywatch lifeguard insignia, white Baywatch visor, silver whistle on black cord, white tennis shoes **Extras:** black boom box, red binoculars, white Frisbee, red flotation device, yellow WaveRunner **Booklet:** instructions **Head:** 1987 black Ken **Head Markings:** © Mattel Inc 1987 **Arms:** bent **Body:** dark brown tnt **Body Markings:** © Mattel Inc. 1968/ China

Model #: 4971 **Name:** Sun Gold Malibu Ken Hispanic version **Box Date:** 1983 **Hair Color:** painted brunette **Face:** brown eyes, brown brows, light pink lips **Clothing:** light blue trunks with gold trim, pairs of pink, purple & black sunglasses, towel **Booklet:** BWOF 1984 **Head:** Hispanic **Head Markings:** © 1983 Mattel Inc **Arms:** ptr **Body:** dark tan b/l **Body Markings:** © Mattel, Inc 1968./ Hong Kong

Model #: 1000 **Name:** Allan **Issue Date:** 1964 **Box Date:** 1963 **Hair Color:** painted red-brown **Face:** brown eyes, reddish brows, peach lips **Clothing:** multicolor horizontal stripe beach jacket with white terry cloth facing bonded to collar, blue swim trunks, blue cork sandals & wrist tag **Extras:** black wire stand **Booklet:** EFBM Book 1 1963 **Head:** Allan **Arms:** pts **Body:** tan s/l **Body Markings:** © 1960/ by/ Mattel, Inc/ Hawthorn/ Calif U.S.A. **Notes:** jacket also available with vertical stripes

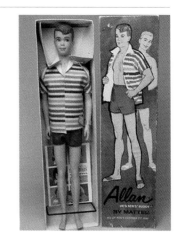

Model #: 1010 **Name:** Allan bendable leg **Issue Date:** 1965 **Box Date:** 1964 **Hair Color:** painted red-brown **Face:** brown eyes, reddish brows, peach lips, cello bag over head secured with rubberband **Clothing:** short sleeve red beach jacket with initial 'A' & multicolor stripe fabric accent, blue swim trunks, blue cork sandals, wrist tag **Extras:** black or gold wire stand **Booklet:** EFBM Book 1 1964 **Head:** Allan **Arms:** pts **Body:** tan b/l **Body Markings:** © 1960/ by/ Mattel, Inc/ Hawthorn/ Calif. U.S.A.

Model #: 4253 **Name:** Todd Groom **Box Date:** 1982 **Hair Color:** painted black **Face:** brown eyes, black brows, peach lips **Clothing:** 1-piece jumpsuit with white halter shirt, ruffled front, white vinyl high collar, purple tie, purple vinyl cummerbund & gray pants, purple tuxedo tails jacket, gray loafers **Booklet:** BWOF 1981 **Head:** superstar **Head Markings:** inside rim © Mattel Inc.1977 **Arms:** bent **Body:** tan tnt **Body Markings:** © Mattel, Inc.1968/ Taiwan

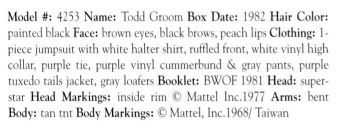

Model #: 2428 **Name:** Rocker Derek **Box Date:** 1985 **Hair Color:** painted brown & black **Face:** blue eyes, dark brown brows, pale pink lips **Clothing:** yellow-green sleeveless shirt with yellow-green vinyl collar, black satin tie, metallic fuchsia cummerbund, multicolor coat with tails in pink, turquoise, blue, white, green, black vinyl pants, white Rockers T-shirt, yellow-green nylon socks, white tennis shoes **Extras:** white microphone, 2 sheets of cardboard punch outs, 1 iron-on Rockers transfer **Booklet:** BWOF 1985 & instructions **Head:** Derek **Head Markings:** © Mattel Inc.1985 **Arms:** bent **Body:** tan tnt **Body Markings:** © Mattel, Inc.1968/ Taiwan **Notes:** many different clothing combinations

Model #: 3173 **Name:** Rocker Derek 2nd issue **Box Date:** 1986 **Hair Color:** painted brown & black **Face:** blue eyes, black brows, peach lips **Clothing:** yellow-green sleeveless T-shirt with gold stars & Rockers logo, metallic gold 3/4 length sleeve short jacket with orange handkerchief, copper colored belt, gold pants, right hand yellow-green fingerless glove, orange socks, silver tennis shoes **Extras:** yellow guitar, sticker for guitar, metallic guitar strap, silver microphone, sheet of cardboard punch outs **Booklet:** BWOF 1985 & instructions **Head:** Derek **Head Markings:** © Mattel Inc.1985 **Arms:** bent **Body:** tan tnt **Body Markings:** © Mattel, Inc.1968/ Taiwan

Model #: 9607 **Name:** Wedding Day Alan **Box Date:** 1990 **Hair Color:** painted red/brown **Face:** blue eyes, brown brows, peach lips **Clothing:** white tuxedo with tails & pants, gray vest, silver ascot, pink shirt with white turned up collar, pink flower in lapel, pink & white dot bow tie, white socks & loafers or lace-up oxfords **Extras:** cardboard punch outs **Head:** Alan **Head Markings:** © 1990 Mattel Inc **Arms:** bent **Body:** tan tnt **Body Markings:** © Mattel Inc.1968/ Malaysia **Notes:** available w/ open lattice work or closed, also part of 6 doll gift set

Ken's African American Friends

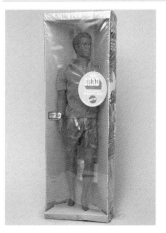 

Model #: 1142 **Name:** Brad **Box Date:** 1969 **Hair Color:** painted black **Face:** brown eyes, black brows, peach lips **Clothing:** orange nylon short sleeve pullover top with wild print in shades of orange & green, wrist tag **Extras:** clear X stand **Booklet:** LB 1970 **Head:** Brad **Head Markings:** © 1968 Mattel Inc **Arms:** pts **Body:** dark brown b/l **Body Markings:** © 1968/ Mattel, Inc./ U.S. & For Patd/ Other Pats/ Pending/ Hong Kong

Model #: 1114 **Name:** Talking Brad **Box Date:** 1969 **Hair Color:** painted black **Face:** brown eyes, black brows, dark mauve lips **Clothing:** multicolor low v-neck short sleeve top of yellow, mustard, fuchsia, olive green, hot pink & orange, orange trunks & wrist tag **Extras:** clear X stand **Head:** Brad **Head Markings:** © 1968 Mattel Inc **Arms:** pts **Body:** dark brown talking **Body Markings:** © 1968/ Mattel, Inc./ U.S. & For Patd/ Other Pats/ Pending/ Hong Kong **Notes:** speaks when string pulled, usually mute

Model #: 7282 Name: Free Moving Curtis Box Date: 1974 Hair Color: painted black Face: brown eyes, black brows, dark mauve lips Clothing: 1-piece playsuit with orange & white stripe short sleeve top with white collar and shorts, white socks, golf club, tennis racket, ball, white tennis shoes Head: Brad Head Markings: © 1968 Mattel Inc Arms: pts Body: dark brown free moving Body Markings: © 1968 Mattel, Inc./ Taiwan/ U.S.Patent/ Pending Notes: pull down lever on back of doll permits free movement

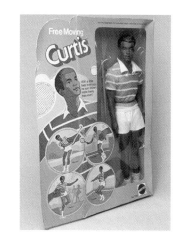

Model #: 4093 Name: Island Fun Steven Box Date: 1987 Hair Color: painted brunette Face: brown eyes, dark brown brows, dark mauve lips Clothing: hot pink Hawaiian print swim trunks & multicolor lei Booklet: BWOF 1988 Head: 1987 black Ken Head Markings: © Mattel Inc 1987 Arms: ptr Body: dark brown b/l Body Markings: © Mattel Inc.1968/ Malaysia Notes: may develop light splotches on legs & stickiness

Model #: 3251 Name: Beach Blast Steven Box Date: 1988 Hair Color: painted brunette Face: brown eyes, brown brows, dark mauve lips Clothing: mid-thigh swim trunks of hot pink, yellow & black, turquoise visor & Frisbee, hot pink boom box Booklet: BWOF 1988 Head: 1987 black Ken Head Markings: © Mattel Inc 1987 Arms: ptr Body: dark brown b/l Body Markings: © Mattel Inc.1968/ Malaysia

Model #: 4137 Name: Wet n' Wild Steven Box Date: 1989 Hair Color: painted brunette Face: brown eyes, dark brown brows, dark mauve lips Clothing: turquoise sleeveless crop top, change-color swim trunks of orange, yellow, green & blue Head: 1987 black Ken Head Markings: © Mattel Inc 1987 Arms: ptr Body: dark brown b/l Body Markings: © Mattel Inc.1968/ Malaysia

Model #: 5945 **Name:** Hawaiian Fun Steven **Box Date:** 1990 **Hair Color:** painted brunette **Face:** brown eyes, brown brows, dark mauve lips **Clothing:** orange sleeveless crop top with appliqué, swim trunks of yellow, green, purple, hot pink & orange, orange visor, yellow Frisbee, turquoise boom box **Head:** 1987 black Ken **Head Markings:** © Mattel Inc 1987 **Arms:** ptr **Body:** dark brown b/l **Body Markings:** © Mattel Inc.1968/ Malaysia

Model #: 1396 **Name:** Sun Sensation Steven **Box Date:** 1991 **Hair Color:** painted brunette **Face:** brown eyes, brown brows, dark mauve lips **Clothing:** silver net crop T-shirt & orange trunks **Head:** 1987 black Ken **Head Markings:** © Mattel Inc 1987 **Arms:** ptr **Body:** dark brown b/l **Body Markings:** © Mattel Inc.1968/ Malaysia

Model #: 4918 **Name:** Glitter Beach Steven **Box Date:** 1992 **Hair Color:** painted black **Face:** brown eyes, black brows, dark mauve lips **Clothing:** light green sleeveless crop top, swim trunks in orange, green, blue with glitter, orange surfer pendant **Head:** 1987 black Ken **Head Markings:** © Mattel Inc 1987 **Arms:** ptr **Body:** dark brown b/l **Body Markings:** © Mattel Inc.1968/ Malaysia

Model #: 10959 **Name:** Sun Jewel Steven **Box Date:** 1993 **Hair Color:** painted black **Face:** hazel eyes, dark brown brows, dark mauve lips **Clothing:** swim trunks in orange, black & light green with iridescent trim **Extras:** stick on jewels **Head:** 1987 black Ken **Head Markings:** © Mattel Inc 1987 **Arms:** ptr **Body:** dark brown b/l **Body Markings:** © Mattel Inc.1968/ Malaysia

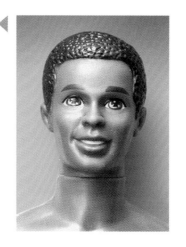

Model #: 12452 Name: Tropical Splash Steven Box Date: 1994 Hair Color: painted black Face: brown eyes, black brows, light red lips Clothing: swim trunks in black, hot pink, green & gold with green towel Extras: Barbie perfume Booklet: 1994 PB Head: 1987 black Ken Head Markings: © Mattel Inc 1987 Arms: ptr Body: dark brown b/l Body Markings: © Mattel, Inc. 1968/ Indonesia Notes: perfume is same as used on Mackie's Masquerade doll, fabric pattern & towel colors vary

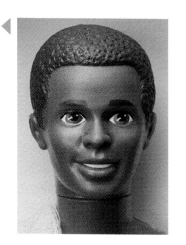
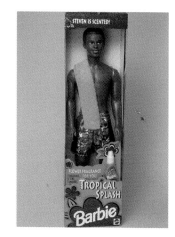

Chapter 6 Series Dolls

American Beauty Series

Model #: 4930 **Name:** American Beauty Mardi Gras **Box Date:** 1987 **Hair Color:** blonde **Hairstyle:** sides & front pulled into curly ponytail, top & sides tied with black hair ornament, rest pulled into curly ponytail to nape of neck, ringlets over each ear **Face:** light blue eyes, blonde brows, pink lips & blush **Clothing:** halter style full skirted gown, black bodice & lilac jewel, metallic lilac skirt with black dots & small black accent bow, matching short jacket with large bow in back, rhinestone stud earrings & ring, lilac glitter mask, black satin evening bag, pink pantyhose, wide lilac pumps **Extras:** 2-piece clear stand **Head:** superstar **Head Markings:** inside or outside rim © Mattel Inc 1976 +/- country **Arms:** bent **Body:** tan tnt **Body Markings:** © Mattel Inc 1966/ China **Notes:** 2nd doll issued was Army Barbie, which is customarily grouped with the Stars & Stripes series

American Stories Series

Model #: 12578 **Name:** American Stories Series Colonial **Box Date:** 1994 **Hair Color:** blonde **Hairstyle:** pulled back to nape of neck, mid-back-length ringlets **Face:** blue-gray eyes, blonde brows, red lips & blush **Clothing:** navy satin gown with white lace insert, collar, & sleeves with red bow accent, matching white hat, cross-stitch frame with appliqué, white pearl ring, black pointed flats **Extras:** 2-piece pearl stand, pearl oval brush & "The Messenger Quilt" storybook **Head:** superstar **Head Markings:** inside or outside rim © Mattel Inc 1976 +/- country **Arms:** bent **Body:** pink tnt **Body Markings:** © Mattel Inc 1966/ China

Model #: 12577 **Name:** American Stories Series Pilgrim **Box Date:** 1994 **Hair Color:** brunette **Hairstyle:** curled under at shoulders **Face:** blue eyes, light brown brows, red lips & blush **Clothing:** wine long sleeve dress with long full skirt, muslin cuffs, sewn on apron, hat, capelet with wine satin bow trim, tan basket with 3 ears of corn, gold ring, black pointed flats **Extras:** 2-piece pearl stand, wine oval brush, "Feast of Friendship" storybook **Head:** superstar **Head Markings:** inside or outside rim © Mattel Inc 1976 +/- country **Arms:** bent **Body:** pink tnt **Body Markings:** © Mattel Inc 1966/ Malaysia

Model #: 12680 **Name:** American Stories Series Pioneer **Box Date:** 1994 **Hair Color:** red **Hairstyle:** pulled back, mid-back-length ringlets **Face:** green eyes, reddish brows, red lips & blush **Clothing:** long sleeve high neck long dress of green, pink & light green calico print with off-white bib, collar & cuffs, ruffle at hem, peach ribbon accents, calico, peach & off-white bonnet, ring, brown plastic basket with red apples, black pointed flats **Extras:** 2-piece ivory stand, peach oval brush & "Western Promise" storybook **Head:** superstar **Head Markings:** inside or outside rim © Mattel Inc 1976 +/- country **Arms:** bent **Body:** pink tnt, pink panties **Body Markings:** © Mattel Inc.1966/ Indonesia

Ballroom Beauties

Model #: 14070 **Name:** Ballroom Beauties Collection Starlight Waltz **Box Date:** 1995 **Hair Color:** blonde **Hairstyle:** side pulled back into ponytail with silver jeweled hair ornament, mid-back length, ends curled under **Face:** blue eyes, rooted lashes, brown brows, fuchsia lips & blush **Clothing:** sleeveless full skirt gown, fuchsia satin bodice with white faux fur neckline, silver jeweled ornament at waist, metallic pink, gold, silver & green design, white net petticoat, white shimmer stockings with built in white panties, pink satin bag, teardrop crystal earrings & silver ring, wide hot pink pumps **Extras:** hot pink oval brush **Head:** superstar **Head Markings:** inside or outside rim © Mattel Inc 1976 +/- country **Arms:** bent **Body:** tan tnt **Body Markings:** © Mattel Inc 1966/ Malaysia **Notes:** brunette version a Disney show exclusive

Children's Collector Series

Model #: 13016 **Name:** Children's Collector Series Rapunzel **Box Date:** 1994 **Hair Color:** blonde **Hairstyle:** beyond floor-length side braided ponytail with bangs **Face:** blue eyes, light brown brows, pink lips **Clothing:** long gown of aqua & pink gold glitter chiffon with long sleeve pink, gold & metallic bodice, gold dunce style hat, aqua sewn in panties, gold stud earrings & ring, gold choker with pink stone, wide gold pumps **Extras:** 2-piece white stand, lavender oval brush **Head:** superstar **Head Markings:** inside or outside rim © Mattel Inc 1976 +/- country **Arms:** Shani **Body:** tan tnt **Body Markings:** © Mattel Inc 1966/ China

Designer Series

Model #: 13168 **Name:** Christian Dior **Box Date:** 1995 **Hair Color:** blonde **Hairstyle:** pulled into chignon **Face:** lavender eyes, light brown brows, red lips & blush **Clothing:** 2-piece brocade gown of black, red & gold heavily beaded long sleeves with bead work down front of top, long slim skirt, gold leaf drop earrings & ring, gold Brazil pumps **Extras:** 2-piece black stand with Barbie logo in gold **Booklet:** Dior 1995 **Head:** superstar **Head Markings:** inside or outside rim © Mattel Inc 1976 +/- country **Arms:** Shani **Body:** pink tnt **Body Markings:** © Mattel Inc 1966/ China

Classique Series

Model #: 1521 **Name:** Classique Benefit Ball **Box Date:** 1992 **Hair Color:** red **Hairstyle:** gently curled shoulder-length side ponytail with curly bangs **Face:** blue eyes, rooted lashes, light brown brows, hot pink lips & blush **Clothing:** metallic dark turquoise & gold slim gown with matching circular cape wrap, gold dangle earrings, gold & blue jewel pendant, gold ring, wide turquoise pumps **Extras:** 2-piece black stand **Booklet:** story **Head:** superstar **Head Markings:** inside or outside rim © Mattel Inc 1976 +/- country **Arms:** bent **Body:** tan tnt **Body Markings:** © Mattel Inc 1966/ China

Model #: 10149 **Name:** Classique City Style **Box Date:** 1993 **Hair Color:** blonde **Hairstyle:** nape of neck length bob **Face:** blue eyes, brown brows, deep pink lips & blush **Clothing:** empire mini dress: gold bodice & white waffle fabric skirt, matching jacket with gold trim, white pantyhose, white stud earrings, gold ring, white purse with gold chain shoulder strap, pearl & gold chain long necklaces, white hat with gold hatband, white "B" shopping bag, wide white pumps **Extras:** 2-piece white stand, gold oval brush **Booklet:** story **Head:** superstar **Head Markings:** inside or outside rim © Mattel Inc 1976 +/- country **Arms:** bent **Body:** tan tnt **Body Markings:** © Mattel Inc 1966/ Malaysia

Model #: 11622 **Name:** Classique Evening Extravaganza **Box Date:** 1993 **Hair Color:** blonde **Hairstyle:** very full & curly ponytail on top of head off to one side **Face:** lilac-blue eyes, rooted lashes, light brown brows, pink lips & blush **Clothing:** pink mirror trimmed off-the-shoulder fitted gown with pink pleated fan wrap, crystal & pink bead drop earrings, matching necklace, long hot pink gloves, hot pink wide pumps **Extras:** 2-piece pearl stand **Head:** superstar **Head Markings:** inside or outside rim © Mattel Inc 1976 +/- country **Arms:** Shani **Body:** tan tnt **Body Markings:** © Mattel Inc 1966/ China

Model #: 11638 **Name:** Classique Evening Extravaganza black version **Box Date:** 1993 **Hair Color:** brunette **Hairstyle:** very full & curly ponytail on top of head off to one side **Face:** brown eyes, rooted lashes, black brows, frosted dark pink lips & blush **Clothing:** gold mirror trimmed off-the-shoulder fitted gown, with yellow pleated fan wrap, crystal & yellow bead drop earrings, matching necklace, long yellow gloves, gold wide pumps **Extras:** 2-piece pearl stand **Head:** Christie **Head Markings:** © Mattel Inc./ 1987 **Arms:** Shani **Body:** dark brown tnt **Body Markings:** © Mattel Inc 1966/ China

Model #: 12999 **Name:** Classique Midnight Gala **Box Date:** 1995 **Hair Color:** blonde **Hairstyle:** thigh-length twisted ponytail with black velvet & sequin band at top of head **Face:** lilac-blue eyes, rooted lashes, dark blonde brows, wine color lips & blush, black beauty mark **Clothing:** black velvet strapless slim gown trimmed with multicolor sequins, seed beads & iridescent gold glitter swirls, matching long cape, gold dangle earrings with multicolor sequin trim, gold ring, wide black pumps **Extras:** 2-piece black stand **Head:** superstar **Head Markings:** inside or outside rim © Mattel Inc 1976 +/- country **Arms:** Shani **Body:** tan tnt **Body Markings:** © Mattel Inc 1966/ China

Model #: 10148 **Name:** Classique Opening Night **Box Date:** 1993 **Hair Color:** black **Hairstyle:** mid-back length with pink satin, tulle & silver tear drop shaped hat **Face:** lilac eyes, rooted lashes, black brows, deep pink lips & blush **Clothing:** 2-piece gown: silver long sleeve top trimmed in purple & hot pink sequins with pearl accents, full hot pink satin skirt trimmed with silver at hem, hot pink lace panties, silver & pink crystal drop earrings, silver ring, hot pink wide pumps **Extras:** 2-piece black stand, purple oval brush **Booklet:** story **Head:** superstar **Head Markings:** inside or outside rim © Mattel Inc 1976 +/- country **Arms:** bent **Body:** tan tnt **Body Markings:** © Mattel Inc 1966/ China

Model #: 11623 **Name:** Classique Uptown Chic **Box Date:** 1993 **Hair Color:** blonde **Hairstyle:** short bob **Face:** blue eyes, rooted lashes, pink coral lips & blush **Clothing:** white vinyl 2-piece pantsuit, matching overcoat with lace trim, gold buttons, pearl & gold drop earrings, choker, & ring, wide pearl pumps **Extras:** 2-piece pearl stand **Head:** superstar **Head Markings:** inside or outside rim © Mattel Inc 1976 +/- country **Arms:** Shani **Body:** tan tnt **Body Markings:** © Mattel Inc 1966/ Malaysia **Notes:** snaps on outfit may disintegrate

Enchanted Seasons Collection

Model #: 11875 **Name:** Enchanted Seasons Collection Snow Princess **Box Date:** 1994 **Hair Color:** blonde **Hairstyle:** shoulder-length ponytail with iridescent sequin & white feather hat **Face:** blue eyes, dark blonde brows, deep pink lips & blush **Clothing:** white long sleeve high neck gown of white heavily decorated with iridescent fabric, sequins, & feathers, crystal drop earrings, white ring, white panties, wide white pumps **Extras:** 2-piece white stand **Booklet:** COA **Head:** superstar **Head Markings:** inside or outside rim © Mattel Inc 1976 +/- country **Arms:** Shani **Body:** tan tnt **Body Markings:** © Mattel Inc 1966/ China **Notes:** 1st in series, original earrings stained face, dolls returned to Mattel given new heads & returned, some dolls had white legs, brunette version Festival exclusive

Model #: 12989 **Name:** Enchanted Seasons Collection Spring Bouquet **Box Date:** 1994 **Hair Color:** blonde **Hairstyle:** below shoulder length, soft curls at ends **Face:** green eyes, light brown brows, fuchsia frosted lips **Clothing:** long gown of pastel multicolor lace, large puffed sleeves to elbow, glitter flower trim on bodice, large pink straw hat trimmed in blue with flowers in the hatband, white wicker basket with glitter flower bouquet, gold stud earrings & ring, wide pale pink pumps **Extras:** 2-piece pink pearl stand & pink oval brush **Head:** superstar **Head Markings:** inside or outside rim © Mattel Inc 1976 +/- country **Arms:** Shani **Body:** pink tnt **Body Markings:** © Mattel Inc 1966/ Malaysia **Notes:** 2nd in series

Model #: 10776 **Name:** Dress 'n Fun **Box Date:** 1993 **Hair Color:** blonde **Hairstyle:** 1 side pulled back, rest waist length, ends curled under **Face:** blue green eyes, dark blonde brows, hot pink lips & blush **Clothing:** sleeveless v-neck multicolor white, purple, green, yellow, red & pink playsuit with pink vinyl belt, wide hot pink pumps **Extras:** hot pink oval brush **Head:** superstar **Head Markings:** inside or outside rim © Mattel Inc 1976 +/- country **Arms:** ptr **Body:** tan tnt **Body Markings:** © Mattel Inc.1966/ Indonesia **Black version:** model #11103 **Hair Color:** black **Face:** brown eyes, black brows, hot pink lips & blush **Head:** Christie **Head Markings:** © Mattel Inc. 1987 **Body:** dark brown tnt **Hispanic Version:** model #: 11102 **Hair Color:** brunette **Face:** brown eyes, brown brows, hot pink lips & blush **Head:** Teresa **Head Markings:** © 1990, Mattel/ Inc **Body:** dark tan tnt

Model #: 9629 **Name:** Fashion Play **Box Date:** 1990 **Hair Color:** blonde **Hairstyle:** 1 side pulled back with lavender fabric flower, rest mid-back length, ends curled under bangs **Face:** blue eyes, blonde brows, deep pink lips & blush **Clothing:** white teddy with lilac lace insert **Extras:** lilac oval brush **Head:** superstar **Head Markings:** inside or outside rim © Mattel Inc 1976 +/- country **Arms:** ptr **Body:** tan tnt **Body Markings:** © Mattel Inc 1966/ Malaysia **Notes:** Dream Wardrobe gift set doll & outfits, Club exclusive gift set: 100 Piece Deluxe Gift Set doll, fashions & accessories **Black Version:** model # 5953 **Hair Color:** black **Face:** brown eyes, black brows, pink lips & blush **Head:** Christie **Head Markings:** © Mattel Inc./ 1987 **Body:** dark brown tnt **Body Markings:** © Mattel Inc 1966/ China **Hispanic Version:** model #: 5954 **Hair Color:** brunette **Face:** lavender eyes, dark brown brows, bright pink lips **Head:** Steffie **Head Markings:** inside rim © 1971 Mattel Inc & country **Body:** dark tan tnt **Body Markings:** © Mattel Inc 1966/ China

Model #: 2370 **Name:** Fashion Play **Box Date:** 1991 **Hair Color:** blonde **Hairstyle:** sides & front pulled into topknot, rest mid-back length, ends curled under **Face:** blue eyes, blonde brows, hot pink lips & blush **Clothing:** halter-style crossover bodysuit to mid-thigh in hot pink, purple & light green splotches with hot pink sash, wide hot pink pumps **Extras:** hot pink oval brush **Head:** superstar **Head Markings:** inside or outside rim © Mattel Inc 1976 +/- country **Arms:** ptr **Body:** tan tnt **Body Markings:** © Mattel Inc 1966/ China **Black Version:** model #: 3842 **Hair Color:** black **Face:** brown eyes, black brows, mauve lips & blush **Head:** Christie **Head Markings:** © Mattel Inc./ 1987 **Body:** dark brown tnt **Body Markings:** © Mattel Inc 1966/ Malaysia **Hispanic Version:** model #: 3860 **Hair Color:** brunette **Face:** brown eyes, brown brows, deep pink lips & blush **Head:** Steffie **Head Markings:** inside rim © 1971 Mattel Inc & country **Body:** dark tan tnt **Body Markings:** © Mattel Inc 1966/ Malaysia

Model #: 4558 **Name:** Fun to Dress **Box Date:** 1987 **Hair Color:** blonde **Hairstyle:** middle part, sides pulled into pigtails rest mid-back length **Face:** turquoise eyes, blonde brows, pink lips & blush **Clothing:** white & pink splatter print bra & panties **Head:** superstar **Head Markings:** inside or outside rim © Mattel Inc 1976 +/- country **Arms:** ptr **Body:** tan tnt **Body Markings:** © Mattel Inc.1966/ Philippines **Black Version:** model #: 7668 **Hair Color:** black **Face:** brown eyes, black brows, hot pink lips & blush **Head:** Christie **Head Markings:** © Mattel Inc./ 1987 **Arms:** ptr **Body:** dark brown tnt **Body Markings:** © Mattel Inc 1966/ China

Model #: 1372 **Name:** Fun to Dress **Box Date:** 1988 **Hair Color:** blonde **Hairstyle:** front & sides pulled to back, rest mid-back length, ends curled under **Face:** blue eyes, blonde brows, fuchsia lips & blush **Clothing:** pink teddy with white lace trim **Head:** superstar **Head Markings:** inside or outside rim © Mattel Inc 1976 +/- country **Arms:** ptr **Body:** tan tnt **Body Markings:** © Mattel Inc 1966/ China **Black Version:** model #: 1373 **Hair Color:** brunette **Face:** lavender eyes, black brows, hot pink lips & blush **Head:** Christie **Head Markings:** © Mattel Inc./ 1987 **Arms:** ptr **Body:** dark brown tnt

Model #: 4808 **Name:** Fun to Dress **Box Date:** 1989 **Hair Color:** blonde **Hairstyle:** shoulder-length ends turned under **Face:** blue eyes, light brown brows, pink lips & blush **Clothing:** pink camisole with matching panties trimmed in white lace **Head:** superstar **Head Markings:** inside or outside rim © Mattel Inc 1976 +/- country **Arms:** ptr **Body:** tan tnt **Body Markings:** © Mattel Inc 1966/ Malaysia **Black Version:** model #: 4939 **Hair Color:** brunette **Face:** lavender eyes, black brows, hot pink lips & blush **Head:** Christie **Head Markings:** © Mattel Inc./ 1987 **Body:** dark brown tnt **Body Markings:** © Mattel Inc 1966/ China **Hispanic Version:** model #: 7373 **Hair Color:** brunette **Face:** brown eyes, brown brows, pink lips & blush **Head:** Hispanic **Head Markings:** inside rim © Mattel Inc, 1983 **Body:** dark tan tnt **Body Markings:** © Mattel Inc 1966/ China

Model #: 3240 **Name:** Fun to Dress **Box Date:** 1992 **Hair Color:** blonde **Hairstyle:** shoulder-length side ponytail tied with hot pink band **Face:** turquoise eyes, blonde brows, deep pink lips & blush **Clothing:** turquoise towel wrap with white lace trim, white stud earrings **Extras:** white oval brush **Head:** superstar **Head Markings:** inside or outside rim © Mattel Inc 1976 +/- country **Arms:** ptr **Body:** tan tnt, white panties **Body Markings:** © Mattel Inc 1966/ China **Notes:** also a Fun To Dress Fashion Gift Set with 2 extra outfits **Black Version:** model #: 2570 **Hair Color:** black **Face:** brown eyes, black brows, wine lips & blush **Head:** Christie **Head Markings:** © Mattel Inc./ 1987 **Body:** dark brown tnt, white panties **Body Markings:** © Mattel Inc 1966/ Malaysia **Hispanic Version:** model #: 2763 **Hair Color:** brunette **Face:** lilac-green eyes, black brows, deep pink lips & blush **Head:** Teresa **Head Markings:** © 1990, Mattel/ Inc **Body:** dark tan tnt, white panties **Body Markings:** © Mattel Inc 1966/ Malaysia

Model #: 12433 **Name:** Ruffle Fun **Box Date:** 1994 **Hair Color:** blonde **Hairstyle:** front section pulled back with hot pink band, rest mid-back length, ends curled under, bangs **Face:** light blue eyes, blonde brows, hot pink lips & blush **Clothing:** hot pink print spaghetti strap mini dress with yellow-green ruffle at neckline, hot pink stud earrings, wide hot pink pumps **Head:** superstar **Head Markings:** inside or outside rim © Mattel Inc 1976 +/- country **Arms:** ptr **Body:** tan tnt, pink panties **Body Markings:** © Mattel Inc 1966/ China **Black Version:** model #: 12434 **Hair Color:** black **Face:** green-brown eyes, brown brows, fuchsia lips & blush **Head:** Christie **Head Markings:** © Mattel Inc./ 1987 **Body:** dark brown tnt, pink panties **Body Markings:** © Mattel Inc.1966/ Indonesia **Hispanic Version:** model #: 12435 **Hair Color:** brunette **Face:** green eyes, black brows, hot pink lips & blush **Head:** Teresa **Head Markings:** © 1990, Mattel/ Inc **Body:** dark tan tnt, pink panties **Body Markings:** © Mattel Inc.1966/ Indonesia

Great Eras Series

Model #: 11397 **Name:** Great Eras Egyptian Queen **Box Date:** 1994 **Hair Color:** black **Hairstyle:** shoulder length **Face:** brown eyes, rooted lashes, dark brown brows, red lips & blush **Clothing:** aqua, gold & white chiffon egyptian outfit with metallic trim, headdress with ruby accent, gold flat slippers **Extras:** 2-piece white stand, white oval brush **Head:** superstar **Head Markings:** inside or outside rim © Mattel Inc 1976 +/- country **Arms:** ballerina cut fingers **Body:** tan tnt **Body Markings:** © Mattel Inc 1966/ China **Notes:** volume 3

Model #: 12792 Name: Great Eras Elizabethan Queen Box Date: 1994 Hair Color: red Hairstyle: pulled up on top of head with roll of hair curled back from forehead framing face Face: green eyes, tiny reddish brows, rooted lashes, deep red lips & pale blush Clothing: long gown of quilted gold & multicolor diamond pattern fabric, gold & white pattern top with lace stand-up collar and red velvet crown, white panties, pearl choker with gold cross, pearl ring, gold glitter flats Extras: 2-piece white stand Head: superstar Head Markings: inside or outside rim © Mattel Inc 1976 +/- country Arms: Shani Body: pink tnt Body Markings: © Mattel Inc.1966/ Indonesia Notes: volume 6

Model #: 4063 Name: Great Eras Flapper Box Date: 1993 Hair Color: blonde Hairstyle: curly chin-length bob with gold jeweled headband across forehead Face: blue eyes, rooted lashes, light brown brows, red lips & blush Clothing: scoop neck sleeveless flapper dress with white & gold brocade top, gold braid & gold bugle & seed bead skirt, white faux fur trimmed gold wrap, white panties, long strand of pearls, gold & white lace fan, white stocking rolled down to mid-thigh, white wide pumps with attached white cloth ankle straps Extras: 2-piece pearl stand Head: superstar Head Markings: inside or outside rim © Mattel Inc 1976 +/- country Arms: ballerina cut fingers Body: tan tnt Body Markings: © Mattel Inc 1966/ China Notes: volume 2

Model #: 3702 Name: Great Eras Gibson Girl Box Date: 1993 Hair Color: brunette Hairstyle: partial bangs, rest piled on top of head with a ringlet at each ear Face: light blue eyes, rooted lashes, brown brows, deep pink lips & blush Clothing: 2-piece long dress: high neck white satin top, leg of mutton sleeves with attached blue on blue satin caplet, pink jewel at throat, full skirt of blue on blue satin, straw hat with fuchsia & blue ribbon trimmed hatband, white parasol w/multicolor ribbons, white panties & slip, blue cloth boots w/silver buttons Extras: 2-piece white stand Head: superstar Head Markings: inside or outside rim © Mattel Inc 1976 +/- country Arms: ballerina cut fingers Body: tan tnt Body Markings: © Mattel Inc 1966/ China Notes: volume 1

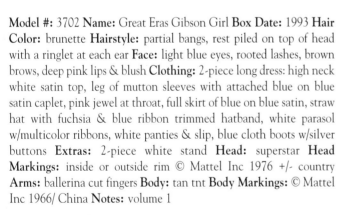

Model #: 12791 Name: Great Eras Medieval Lady Box Date: 1994 Hair Color: blonde Hairstyle: pigtails tucked into hat Face: blue eyes, light brown brows, rooted lashes, red lips & blush Clothing: dark blue velour long gown with white faux fur at boat style neckline, multicolor lined sleeves, gold braid trim at neck & belt, gold & white hat with purple train, white panties, gold plastic flats with turned up toes Extras: 2-piece black stand Head: superstar Head Markings: inside or outside rim © Mattel Inc 1976 +/- country Arms: Shani Body: tan tnt Body Markings: © Mattel Inc.1966/ Indonesia Notes: volume 5

Model #: 11478 **Name:** Great Eras Southern Belle **Box Date:** 1993 **Hair Color:** brunette **Hairstyle:** pulled back from face with ringlets to shoulder, hair held with blue & pink floral band **Face:** dark blue eyes, dark brown brows, pink lips & blush **Clothing:** long pink chiffon gown with full skirt & blue insert in bodice, blue & pink flower trim with pearl garland, pearl choker & ring, white panties, plastic hoop for skirt, white flats **Extras:** 2-piece white stand & pink oval brush **Head:** Mackie **Head Markings:** © 1991 Mattel Inc **Arms:** Shani **Body:** tan tnt **Body Markings:** © Mattel Inc 1966/ China **Notes:** volume 4

Happy Holiday Series

Model #: 1703 **Name:** Happy Holidays **Box Date:** 1988 **Hair Color:** blonde **Hairstyle:** side part with front section pulled back with band of silver ribbon & holly trim, waist length, ends curled **Face:** blue eyes, light brown brows, red lips & blush **Clothing:** red gown with velour bodice & red tulle with silver glitter clusters at shoulders, full tiered long skirt of same tulle, silver ribbon with holly trim at waist, rhinestone stud earrings & ring, white plastic & silver paint bow necklace, wide red bow shoes **Extras:** 2-piece stand **Head:** superstar **Head Markings:** inside or outside rim © Mattel Inc 1976 +/- country **Arms:** bent **Body:** tan tnt **Body Markings:** © Mattel Inc 1966/ China **Notes:** 1st in series

Model #: 3253 **Name:** Happy Holidays **Box Date:** 1989 **Hair Color:** blonde **Hairstyle:** front & sides pulled up, tied with red ribbon, snowflake & faux fur hair ornament, rest waist length, ends curled under **Face:** blue eyes, brown brows, red lips & blush **Clothing:** white gown trimmed with iridescent trim, faux fur, white glitter tulle & satin skirt, faux fur stole, red stud earrings, pendant & ring, wide white pumps **Extras:** 2-piece pearl stand, pearl oval brush, iridescent snowflake ornament & 8x10 picture of doll **Booklet:** BWOF 1988 **Head:** superstar **Head Markings:** inside or outside rim © Mattel Inc 1976 +/- country **Arms:** bent **Body:** tan tnt **Body Markings:** © Mattel Inc 1966/ China **Notes:** 2nd in series

Model #: 4098 **Name:** Happy Holidays **Box Date:** 1990 **Hair Color:** blonde **Hairstyle:** front & 1 side pulled back with hot pink tulle & bead star hair ornament, curly bangs, rest waist length, ends curled under **Face:** blue eyes, blonde brows, fuchsia lips & blush **Clothing:** fuchsia & silver gown with full tulle & silver skirt & neckline, green stud earrings, pendant & ring, wide pink pumps **Extras:** 2-piece pink stand, pink oval brush, silver & pink star ornament, 8x10 picture of doll **Booklet:** IIB 1990 **Head:** superstar **Head Markings:** inside or outside rim © Mattel Inc 1976 +/- country **Arms:** bent **Body:** tan tnt **Body Markings:** © Mattel Inc 1966/ China **Black Version:** model **#:** 4543 **Hair Color:** brunette **Face:** brown eyes, black brows, fuchsia lips & blush **Head:** Christie **Head Markings:** © Mattel Inc./ 1987 **Body:** dark brown tnt **Notes:** 3rd in series

Model #: 1871 **Name:** Happy Holidays **Box Date:** 1991 **Hair Color:** blonde **Hairstyle:** front & sides pulled back with green velvet sequin trimmed bow, rest waist length, ends curled **Face:** green eyes, light brown brows, red lips & blush **Clothing:** long sleeve, sweetheart neck, full skirted green velvet gown with silver, red & green sequin trim on bodice, matching evening bag, silver & red bead drop earrings, pendant, ring & wide red pumps **Extras:** 2-piece pearl stand, red oval brush & 8x10 picture of doll **Head:** superstar **Head Markings:** inside or outside rim © Mattel Inc 1976 +/- country **Arms:** bent **Body:** tan tnt **Body Markings:** © Mattel Inc 1966/ China **Black Version:** model **#:** 2696 **Hair Color:** brunette **Face:** green eyes, black brows, red lips & blush **Head:** Christie **Head Markings:** © Mattel Inc./ 1987 **Body:** dark brown tnt **Notes:** 4th in series

Model #: 1429 **Name:** Happy Holidays **Box Date:** 1992 **Hair Color:** blonde **Hairstyle:** front & sides pulled up with silver sequin hair ornament, rest curly waist length **Face:** blue eyes, brown brows, fuchsia lips & blush **Clothing:** long sleeve silver lamé gown with white tulle & silver glitter accents, beaded & sequined bodice & sleeves, silver & crystal drop earrings & ring, wide pearl pumps **Extras:** 2-piece pearl stand & pearl oval brush & 8x10 picture of doll **Head:** superstar **Head Markings:** inside or outside rim © Mattel Inc 1976 +/- country **Arms:** bent **Body:** tan tnt **Body Markings:** © Mattel Inc 1966/ China **Black Version:** model **#:** 2396 **Hair Color:** black **Face:** brown eyes, black brows, red lips & blush **Head:** Christie **Head Markings:** © Mattel Inc./ 1987 **Body:** dark brown tnt **Notes:** 5th in series

Model #: 10824 **Name:** Happy Holidays **Box Date:** 1993 **Hair Color:** blonde **Hairstyle:** 1 side & front pulled into red ribbon with poinsettia & gold trim **Face:** green eyes, brown brows, red lips & blush **Clothing:** gown with gold lamé bodice, red tulle with gold glitter & gold edge skirt with poinsettias on bodice & red satin bows at shoulders, sewn in panties, red gold drop earrings, ring & wide red bow pumps **Extras:** 2-piece gold stand, gold oval brush, 5x7 picture of doll **Head:** superstar **Head Markings:** inside or outside rim © Mattel Inc 1976 +/- country **Arms:** bent **Body:** ivory tnt **Body Markings:** © Mattel Inc 1966/ China **Black Version:** model #: 10911 **Box Date:** 1993 **Hair Color:** black **Face:** brown eyes, black brows, red lips & blush **Head:** Christie **Head Markings:** © Mattel Inc./ 1987 **Body:** dark brown tnt **Notes:** 6th in series

Model #: 12155 **Name:** Happy Holidays **Box Date:** 1994 **Hair Color:** blonde **Hairstyle:** curly waist length, pulled back with green gold & red beaded headband **Face:** green eyes, light brown brows, frosted wine lips **Clothing:** long sleeve sweetheart neck gold lamé gown with faux fur hem & white and gold lace insert in skirt, holly & faux fur trim at shoulders, gold & red bead drop earrings & ring, wide gold pumps **Extras:** 2-piece pearl stand, pearl oval brush & 5x7 picture of doll **Head:** superstar **Head Markings:** inside or outside rim © Mattel Inc 1976 +/- country **Arms:** bent **Body:** tan tnt **Body Markings:** © Mattel Inc 1966/ China **Notes:** brunette version Festival exclusive **Black Version:** model #: 12156 **Hair Color:** black **Face:** green eyes, black brows, frosted wine lips & blush **Head:** Christie **Head Markings:** © Mattel Inc./ 1987 **Body:** dark brown tnt **Notes:** 7th in series

Model #: 14123 **Name:** Happy Holidays **Box Date:** 1995 **Hair Color:** blonde **Hairstyle:** front section pulled back with small silver & sequin hair ornament, rest waist length, ends curled under **Face:** green eyes, light brown brows, red lips & blush **Clothing:** puffed sleeves green lamé gown with silver holly trim collar, white lace insert, red & silver poinsettia trim at waist, silver holly print on skirt, silver, red, green drop earrings, pendant & ring, wide red pumps **Extras:** 2-piece white stand, red oval brush & 8x10 picture of doll **Head:** superstar **Head Markings:** inside or outside rim © Mattel Inc 1976 +/- country **Arms:** Shani **Body:** tan tnt, B panties **Body Markings:** © Mattel Inc 1966/ China **Black Version:** model #: 14124 **Hair Color:** black **Face:** brown eyes, black brows, red lips & blush **Head:** Christie **Head Markings:** © Mattel Inc./ 1987 **Body:** dark brown tnt, B panties **Notes:** 8th in series

Model #: 12701 **Name:** Hollywood Legends Dorothy from Wizard of Oz **Box Date:** 1994 **Hair Color:** brunette **Hairstyle:** middle part, braided waist-length pigtails tied with blue ribbons **Face:** brown eyes, light brown brows, red lips & blush **Clothing:** blue & white gingham jumper with white puff sleeve sewn in blouse, white petticoat, white panties, blue anklets, wicker basket, brown plastic cairn terrier dog, red metallic plastic heels with molded bow **Extras:** 2-piece yellow stand, gold oval brush **Booklet:** COA **Head:** superstar **Head Markings:** inside or outside rim © Mattel Inc 1976 +/- country **Arms:** bent **Body:** tan tnt, B panties **Body Markings:** © Mattel Inc.1966/ Indonesia

Model #: 13676 **Name:** Hollywood Legends Maria from Sound of Music **Box Date:** 1995 **Hair Color:** blonde **Hairstyle:** earlobe length pageboy with bangs **Face:** blue eyes, light brown brows, pink lips **Clothing:** straw hat, dress with tan bodice, white satin sleeves & bodice insert trimmed in lace with pastel floral skirt, off-white petticoat, guitar, white tights and pale pink pearl flats **Extras:** 2-piece pearl stand **Booklet:** COA **Head:** superstar **Head Markings:** inside or outside rim © Mattel Inc 1976 +/- country **Arms:** Shani **Body:** tan tnt **Body Markings:** © Mattel Inc 1966/ China

Model #: 12741 **Name:** Hollywood Legends Rhett Butler **Box Date:** 1994 **Hair Color:** painted black & gray **Face:** brown eyes, brows & mustache, pale pink lips **Clothing:** black coat with sewn on cape, black suit, white ruffled shirt, white bow tie & vest, black lace-up oxford shoes, black top hat, silver watch chain **Extras:** 2-piece black stand **Booklet:** COA **Head:** modified Alan **Head Markings:** © 1991 Mattel Inc **Arms:** bent **Body:** tan tnt **Body Markings:** © Mattel Inc 1966/ China

Model #: 12997 **Name:** Hollywood Legends Scarlett **Box Date:** 1994 **Hair Color:** brunette **Hairstyle:** mid-back length with ends curled **Face:** green eyes, rooted lashes, brown brows, red lips & blush **Clothing:** sleeveless scoop neck green & white print long dress with green velvet wide waistband, lace & ribbon trim at neckline, green parasol, white petticoat & pantaloons, wide brim straw hat with green ribbon tie, pointed green flats **Extras:** 2-piece pearl stand **Booklet:** COA **Head:** superstar **Head Markings:** inside or outside rim © Mattel Inc 1976 +/- country **Arms:** Shani **Body:** pink tnt **Body Markings:** © Mattel Inc 1966/ China

Model #: 12045 Name: Hollywood Legends Scarlett Box Date: 1994 Hair Color: brunette Hairstyle: loose shoulder-length ringlets Face: green eyes, rooted lashes, brown brows, red lips & blush Clothing: green velvet & satin long sleeve full skirted gown trimmed in gold braid, green satin hat with gold tassel, gold ring, wide dark green pumps Extras: 2-piece pearl stand Booklet: COA Head: superstar Head Markings: inside or outside rim © Mattel Inc 1976 +/- country Arms: bent Body: pink tnt Body Markings: © Mattel Inc 1966/ China

Model #: 13254 Name: Hollywood Legends Scarlett Box Date: 1994 Hair Color: brunette Hairstyle: pulled back on sides with below shoulder-length ringlets Face: green eyes, rooted lashes, brown brows, red lips & blush Clothing: white gown, pearl buttons up center front with black leaf pattern sleeves, pantaloons, white lace trimmed petticoat, white hat w/black veil, white muff, coral & gold drop earrings & brooch, gold ring, wide black pumps Extras: 2-piece pearl stand Booklet: COA Head: superstar Head Markings: inside or outside rim © Mattel Inc 1976 +/- country Arms: Shani Body: pink tnt Body Markings: © Mattel Inc 1966/ China

Model #: 12815 Name: Hollywood Legends Scarlett Box Date: 1994 Hair Color: brunette Hairstyle: pulled back to nape of neck, ringlets dangling from top of head held with red sequin trim, curly bangs Face: green eyes, rooted lashes, pale brown brows, red lips & blush Clothing: deep red velvet slim gown with sweetheart neck trimmed in red rhinestones framed in gold, gold filigree earrings with red jewel & matching bracelet, long red gloves, matching tulle wrap trimmed with feathers, wide black pumps Extras: 2-piece pearl stand Booklet: COA Head: Mackie Head Markings: © 1991 Mattel Inc Arms: bent Body: pink tnt Body Markings: © Mattel Inc 1966/ China

International/Dolls of the World Series

Model #: 3626 Name: Dolls of the World Australian Box Date: 1992 Hair Color: blonde Hairstyle: waist length, ends curled, bangs Face: blue eyes, brown brows, red lips & blush Clothing: tan denim vest & long skirt with lace at hem, red, white and tan short sleeve blouse, red neckerchief, brown belt, hat with gold tie under chin, gold stud earrings & ring, brown cowboy boots Extras: 2-piece white pearl stand & red oval brush Head: superstar Head Markings: inside or outside rim © Mattel Inc 1976 +/- country Arms: bent Body: ruddy tan tnt Body Markings: © Mattel Inc 1966/ Malaysia

Model #: 9094 **Name:** Dolls of the World Brazilian **Box Date:** 1989 **Hair Color:** brunette **Hairstyle:** below shoulders curled under, pulled back from face & banded **Face:** brown eyes, brown brows, deep pink lips & blush **Clothing:** metallic mauve sleeveless crop top in shades of pink, nylon ruffle at neckline, matching skirt raised mid-thigh in front, almost to ankle in back, matching cuffs, ankle cuffs & headdress, hot pink mules **Extras:** 2-piece clear stand & hot pink oval brush **Head:** Hispanic **Head Markings:** inside rim © Mattel Inc, 1983 **Arms:** bent **Body:** dark tan tnt **Body Markings:** © Mattel Inc 1966/ China

Model #: 4928 **Name:** Dolls of the World Canadian **Box Date:** 1987 **Hair Color:** blonde **Hairstyle:** pulled back from face, mid-back-length ponytail at nape of neck **Face:** blue eyes, light brown brows, red lips & blush **Clothing:** red velvet military style jacket with gold buttons & brown vinyl belt with shoulder strap & pouch, black riding pants with yellow woven stripe up sides, black riding boots, brown Mounties hat, rhinestone ring **Extras:** 2-piece clear stand **Head:** superstar **Head Markings:** inside or outside rim © Mattel Inc 1976 +/- country **Arms:** bent **Body:** tan tnt **Body Markings:** © Mattel Inc 1966/ China

Model #: 11180 **Name:** Dolls of the World Chinese **Box Date:** 1993 **Hair Color:** black **Hairstyle:** thigh length, front section pulled into small ponytail, curly bangs **Face:** brown eyes, black brows, pink lips & blush **Clothing:** deep pink, black, red & yellow floral print robe over slim ankle-length skirt of same fabric with black & gold braided trim around neckline, hem & cuffs, gold stud earrings & ring, gold & pink floral hair ornament, black pointed flats **Extras:** 2-piece white pearl stand & red oval brush **Head:** Oriental **Head Markings:** © Mattel Inc 1980 **Arms:** bent **Body:** dark tan tnt **Body Markings:** © Mattel Inc 1966/ Malaysia **Notes:** available in 3 doll gift set: Dutch, Chinese, Kenya

Model #: 7330 **Name:** Dolls of the World Czechoslovakian **Box Date:** 1990 **Hair Color:** blonde **Hairstyle:** waist-length side ponytail twisted with red ribbon, bangs **Face:** blue eyes, light brown brows, deep pink lips **Clothing:** knee-length dress with black bodice, white elbow-length sleeves, white lace at scoop neckline, black, yellow, blue, white & red cotton print tiered full skirt with lace at hem & red grosgrain ribbon trim at waist, red tights, red stud earrings & ring, black lace-up knee-high boots **Extras:** 2-piece clear stand & red oval brush **Head:** superstar **Head Markings:** inside or outside rim © Mattel Inc 1976 +/- country **Arms:** bent **Body:** tan tnt **Body Markings:** © Mattel Inc 1966/ China

Model #: 11104 **Name:** Dolls of the World Dutch **Box Date:** 1993 **Hair Color:** blonde **Hairstyle:** waist-length braids **Face:** blue eyes, light brown brows, deep pink lips & blush **Clothing:** long turquoise & white vertically striped skirt, solid turquoise long sleeved square neck top with woven white, red, blue, green ribbon detailing at neckline & waist, white hat with lace trim, white "wooden" shoes, red stud earrings & ring **Extras:** 2-piece white pearl stand & royal blue oval brush **Head:** superstar **Head Markings:** inside or outside rim © Mattel Inc 1976 +/- country **Arms:** bent **Body:** tan tnt **Body Markings:** © Mattel Inc 1966/ China **Notes:** available in 3 doll gift set: Dutch, Chinese, Kenya

Model #: 4973 **Name:** Dolls of the World English **Box Date:** 1991 **Hair Color:** blonde **Hairstyle:** waist-length side ponytail **Face:** blue eyes, light brown brows, red lips & blush **Clothing:** red riding jacket, blue lapels, blue top hat with tulle, green, red & blue print blouse, ascot with gold jewel & matching blue ribbon, long blue split skirt, red riding boots & navy crop, silver stud earrings & ring **Extras:** 2-piece clear stand & hot pink oval brush **Head:** superstar **Head Markings:** inside or outside rim © Mattel Inc 1976 +/- country **Arms:** bent **Body:** ivory tnt **Body Markings:** © Mattel Inc 1966/ China

Model #: 3898 **Name:** International Eskimo **Box Date:** 1981 **Hair Color:** black **Hairstyle:** mid-back length, side part **Face:** brown eyes, black brows, deep peach lips & blush **Clothing:** white knee-length hooded parka dress with gray faux fur trim at hood, cuffs & hem with white & black braided trim & red woven trim for accents, matching over-the-knee white fabric boots, rhinestone ring **Extras:** 2-piece clear stand **Head:** Oriental **Head Markings:** © Mattel Inc 1980 **Arms:** bent **Body:** dark tan tnt **Body Markings:** © Mattel Inc 1966/ Taiwan

Model #: 9844 **Name:** Dolls of the World Eskimo reissue **Box Date:** 1990 **Hair Color:** black **Hairstyle:** mid-back length, middle part **Face:** brown eyes, black brows, orange red lips & blush **Clothing:** white knee-length hooded parka dress with gray faux fur trim at hood, cuffs and hem with silver & black braided trim & red woven trim for accents, matching over-the-knee white fabric boots, silver ring **Extras:** 2-piece clear stand, light blue oval brush **Head:** Oriental **Head Markings:** © Mattel Inc 1980 **Arms:** bent **Body:** dark tan tnt **Body Markings:** © Mattel Inc 1966/ China

Model #: 3188 **Name:** Dolls of the World German **Box Date:** 1986 **Hair Color:** blonde **Hairstyle:** mid-back-length ponytail at nape of neck, middle part **Face:** aqua blue eyes, brown brows, red lips & blush **Clothing:** red velvet jacket with 3 brass buttons & white ruffle trim at collar & cuffs, navy print skirt, white satin lace trimmed apron, blue flower on yellow ribbon tied at neck, gold, green, blue & red brocade hat with peach satin bow, pair of white stockings, black flats, rhinestone ring **Extras:** 2-piece clear stand **Head:** Steffie **Head Markings:** inside rim © 1971 Mattel Inc & country **Arms:** bent **Body:** tan tnt **Body Markings:** © Mattel, Inc. 1966/ Hong Kong

Model #: 12698 **Name:** Dolls of the World German reissue **Box Date:** 1994 **Hair Color:** blonde **Hairstyle:** braided pigtails with blue ribbon ties at ends & then pulled up **Face:** light blue eyes, light brown brows, red lips & blush **Clothing:** mid-calf-length dress with black bodice, blue long sleeves with white cuffs, white fringed shawl, red full skirt with black ribbon trim, white apron with blue ribbon trim, red flower at neck, gold ribbon accent on bodice, white pearl stud earrings & ring, white painted legs with black painted ballet slippers **Extras:** 2-piece white stand & red oval brush **Head:** superstar **Head Markings:** inside or outside rim © Mattel Inc 1976 +/- country **Arms:** Shani **Body:** tan tnt **Body Markings:** © Mattel Inc 1966/ China **Notes:** available in 3 doll gift set: Irish, German, Polynesian

Model #: 2997 **Name:** Dolls of the World Greek **Box Date:** 1985 **Hair Color:** brown **Hairstyle:** mid-back-length ponytail at nape of neck **Face:** brown eyes, brown brows, light red lips **Clothing:** long red taffeta print full skirt with double gold ribbon piping, black & white print jacket with red lapels & cuffs with white cloth accents at cuffs, white blouse, red stocking cap with yellow fringe, black modified ballet slippers, red ring **Extras:** 2-piece clear stand **Head:** superstar **Head Markings:** inside or outside rim © Mattel Inc 1976 +/- country **Arms:** bent **Body:** tan tnt **Body Markings:** © Mattel Inc.1966/ Philippines

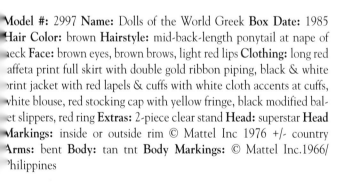

Model #: 3189 **Name:** Dolls of the World Icelandic **Box Date:** 1986 **Hair Color:** blonde **Hairstyle:** pigtails twisted to waist, hair wrapped around bands parted in middle **Face:** blue eyes, light brown brows, deep pink lips & blush **Clothing:** white long sleeve blouse with lace at collar, blue velveteen vest with gold stencil & gold braid trim, long blue velvet skirt with light blue satin apron trimmed in blue & gold, rhinestone ring, blue velvet hat with gold tassel, black pointed flats **Extras:** 2-piece clear stand **Head:** superstar **Head Markings:** inside or outside rim © Mattel Inc 1976 +/- country **Arms:** bent **Body:** tan tnt **Body Markings:** © Mattel, Inc. 1966/ Hong Kong

Model #: 7517 Name: International Irish Box Date: 1983 Hair Color: red-brown Hairstyle: below shoulder length, ends curled, middle part Face: green eyes, brown brows, orange lips & blush Clothing: green taffeta jumper with black velvet waistband & long skirt trimmed in lace at hem with woven ribbon accent, white blouse, white cap with lace trim, black modified ballet shoes, rhinestone ring Extras: 2-piece clear stand Booklet: BIC 1983 Head: Steffie Head Markings: inside rim © 1971 Mattel Inc & country Arms: bent Body: pink tnt Body Markings: © Mattel Inc 1966/ Taiwan

Model #: 12998 Name: Dolls of the World Irish reissue Box Date: 1994 Hair Color: red Hairstyle: waist length, ends curled Face: green eyes, brown-red brows, red lips & blush Clothing: kelly green long sleeved dress with dropped waist, white lace accents at collar, cuffs, bodice & sides of skirt, white lace cap, shamrock gold trimmed brooch, gold stud earrings & ring, wide green pumps Extras: 2-piece white stand & white oval brush Head: superstar Head Markings: inside or outside rim © Mattel Inc 1976 +/- country Arms: Shani Body: pink tnt Body Markings: © Mattel Inc.1966/ Indonesia Notes: available in 3 doll gift set: Irish, German, Polynesian

Model #: 1602 Name: International Italian Box Date: 1979 Hair Color: brunette Hairstyle: mid-back length, ends curled, side part cello on head Face: light brown eyes, brown brows, pale pink lips Clothing: white peasant blouse with lace at scoop neck & armholes, long red, white & green striped skirt, blue apron with white fringe, green rickrack & red woven trim, straw bag with yellow & green plastic flowers, straw hat with red ribbon, tan soled red plastic lace-up wedgies, rhinestone stud earrings & ring Extras: 2-piece clear stand Booklet: BWOF 1981 Head: Italian Head Markings: © 1978 Mattel Inc/ Taiwan Arms: bent Body: dark tan tnt Body Markings: © Mattel Inc 1966/ Taiwan Notes: head mold originally used in 1970 on unaffiliated Mattel doll

Model #: 2256 Name: Dolls of the World Italian reissue Box Date: 1992 Hair Color: brunette Hairstyle: waist length, pulled back from face, ends curled Face: blue-green eyes, brown brows, red lips & blush Clothing: red short jacket with multicolor fabric insert at waist & sleeves, white scoop neck blouse, purple taffeta skirt with yellow pattern fabric & blue taffeta ribbon trim apron, white knee-length stockings, gold hoop earrings, gold choker & ring, purple & yellow ribbon accent in hair, wide red pumps Extras: 2-piece white pearl stand & light blue oval brush Head: Teresa Head Markings: © 1990, Mattel/ Inc Arms: bent Body: tan tnt Body Markings: © Mattel Inc 1966/ China

Model #: 4647 Name: Dolls of the World Jamaican Box Date: 1991
Hair Color: black Hairstyle: shoulder length pulled back from face,
curly Face: brown eyes, black brows, orange-red lips & blush
Clothing: ankle-length long sleeved high neck blue print dress with
orange, yellow and white striped trim at hem & bodice, matching
vest, orange, blue & white print kerchief in the hair with matching
apron, silver hoop earrings & ring, blue pointed flats Extras: 2-piece
clear stand & orange hair pick Head: Christie Head Markings: ©
Mattel Inc./ 1987 Arms: bent Body: dark brown tnt Body Markings:
© Mattel Inc 1966/ China

Model #: 9481 Name: Dolls of the World Japanese Box Date: 1984
Hair Color: black Hairstyle: pulled up to top of head in bun Face:
brown eyes, black brows, red-orange lips & blush Clothing: red satin
kimono with black, white, blue, green & yellow floral print, gold
satin obi with black & gold braided accent, red & gold hair trim,
punch out cardboard fan, red ring, pair of red slip on sandals Extras:
2-piece clear stand Head: Oriental Head Markings: © Mattel Inc
1980 Arms: bent Body: light tan tnt Body Markings: © Mattel Inc
1966/ Taiwan

Model #: 11181 Name: Dolls of the World Kenyan Box Date: 1993
Hair Color: black Hairstyle: short cropped close to scalp Face:
brown eyes, black brows, light red lips & blush Clothing: red & white
checked sleeveless dress below knee, split on one side to hip with red
& white print shawl dress accent, multicolor banded collar, yellow-
green bracelets & ankle bracelets, yellow headband with gold beads,
red hoop earrings & ring Extras: 2-piece white pearl stand Head:
Nichelle Head Markings: © 1990/ Mattel Inc Arms: bent Body:
dark brown tnt Body Markings: © Mattel Inc 1966/ Malaysia Notes:
available in 3 doll gift set: Dutch, Chinese, Kenya

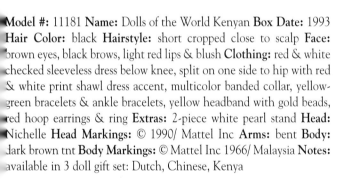

Model #: 4929 Name: Dolls of the World Korean Box Date: 1987
Hair Color: black Hairstyle: side ponytail twisted to waist, middle
part Face: brown eyes, black brows, deep pink lips & blush Clothing:
deep pink & light green satin traditional gown with gold braided trim
and gold glitter accents, pink hair ornament, pink ring, pink pointed
flats Extras: 2-piece clear stand Head: Oriental Head Markings: ©
Mattel Inc 1980 Arms: bent Body: tan tnt Body Markings: ©
Mattel Inc 1966/ China

Model #: 7329 Name: Dolls of the World Malaysian Box Date: 1990 Hair Color: black Hairstyle: pulled up to top of head, mid-back-length ponytail with gold & fuchsia metallic rose ornament on band Face: brown eyes, black brows, mauve lips & blush Clothing: metallic fuchsia long sleeve knee-length robe over ankle-length metallic gold, pink & black print slim skirt, same print sash trimmed with gold rose, gold braid around neck, gold stud earrings & ring, black mules Extras: 2-piece clear stand & fuchsia oval brush Head: Oriental Head Markings: © Mattel Inc 1980 Arms: bent Body: dark tan tnt Body Markings: © Mattel Inc 1966/ Malaysia

Model #: 1917 Name: Dolls of the World Mexican Box Date: 1988 Hair Color: brunette Hairstyle: waist length, pulled back from face into partial ponytail, ends curled under Face: brown eyes, dark brown brows, orange lips & blush Clothing: white short sleeved peasant blouse with orange, blue, white & green floral trim & lace, multicolor striped belt, orange satin tiered skirt with white lace petticoat, blue hair ornament, hoop earrings & ring, white lace mantilla, orange pointed flats Extras: 2-piece clear stand & blue oval brush Head: Hispanic Head Markings: inside rim © Mattel Inc, 1983 Arms: bent Body: dark tan tnt Body Markings: © Mattel Inc 1966/ China

Model #: 1753 Name: Dolls of the World Native American I Box Date: 1992 Hair Color: black Hairstyle: thigh length, middle part, side sectioned into pigtails with blue bands Face: brown eyes, black brows, red lips Clothing: off-white knee length, short sleeve shirt with Indian bead print, off-white fringe & silver fringe trim, matching pouch with ribbon strap, silver band bracelet & ring, silver & turquoise dangle earrings, matching off-white cloth boots Extras: 2-piece off-white display & royal blue oval brush Head: Diva Head Markings: © 1985 Mattel Inc. Arms: bent Body: dark tan tnt Body Markings: © Mattel Inc 1966/ Malaysia

Model #: 11609 Name: Dolls of the World Native American II Box Date: 1993 Hair Color: black Hairstyle: hip length, 2 pigtail braids on either side of face with silver cloth cylinder & blue & red feather trim Face: brown eyes, black brows, coral lips & blush Clothing: below-knee-length dress: turquoise top with elbow-length sleeves & long yellow fringe, off-white skirt, 3-row vertical multicolor seed bead front, silver belt with red & blue feather, cloth turquoise & off-white boots, turquoise dangle earrings & ring Extras: 2-piece white stand & turquoise oval brush Head: Teresa Head Markings: © 1990, Mattel/ Inc Arms: bent Body: dark tan tnt Body Markings: © Mattel Inc.1966/ Indonesia

Model #: 12699 **Name:** Dolls of the World Native American III **Box Date:** 1994 **Hair Color:** black **Hairstyle:** waist-length braids, middle part **Face:** brown eyes, black brows, mauve lips & blush **Clothing:** hip-length mauve satin tunic over matching long slim skirt, white, green, turquoise & olive woven trim at waist, hip & hem, white fringe at hip & hem, multicolor seed bead necklace, turquoise dangle earrings & ring, woven white feather headband, white purple & green pattern on bodice, white cloth knee-high boots **Extras:** 2-piece white stand & purple oval brush **Booklet:** 1995 PB **Head:** Teresa **Head Markings:** © 1990, Mattel/ Inc **Arms:** Shani **Body:** dark tan tnt **Body Markings:** © Mattel Inc.1966/ Indonesia

Model #: 7376 **Name:** Dolls of the World Nigerian **Box Date:** 1989 **Hair Color:** black **Hairstyle:** pulled back from face, curly shoulder length **Face:** brown eyes, black brows, red lips & blush **Clothing:** brown, white, dark brown pattern halter dress mid-thigh length over slim ankle-length skirt with gold accents at neckline, waist & hem, gold arm bands, matching fabric tie in hair, gold dangle earrings & ring, gold mules **Extras:** 2-piece clear stand & gold oval brush **Head:** Christie **Head Markings:** © Mattel Inc./ 1987 **Arms:** bent **Body:** dark brown tnt **Body Markings:** © Mattel Inc 1966/ China

Model #: 3262 **Name:** International Oriental **Box Date:** 1980 **Hair Color:** black **Hairstyle:** mid-back length, middle part with bangs, cello on head **Face:** brown eyes, dark brown brows, mauve lips & blush **Clothing:** red & gold brocade long sleeved jacket, gold slim dress split on both sides of skirt to knee with red braided trim at split & collar, rhinestone stud earrings & ring, cardboard fan, gold braid necklace with red disk trim, pair of red ankle straps **Extras:** 2-piece clear stand **Booklet:** BWOF 1980 **Head:** Oriental **Head Markings:** © Mattel Inc 1980 **Arms:** bent **Body:** pink tnt **Body Markings:** © Mattel Inc 1966/ Taiwan

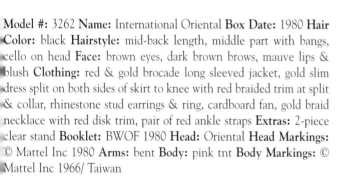

Model #: 1600 **Name:** International Parisian **Box Date:** 1979 **Hair Color:** light red **Hairstyle:** pulled to top of head hanging loosely with black & pink hair trim **Face:** green eyes, black brows, light pink lips & blush, black beauty mark on right cheek **Clothing:** pink satin knee-length halter dress with black lace insert on bodice, black lace-up trim at waist, white ruffles at hem, matching garter, black panty-hose, pink ankle straps, black ribbon with cameo accent at neck, rhinestone earrings & ring **Extras:** 2-piece clear stand **Booklet:** BWOF 1979 **Head:** Steffie **Head Markings:** inside rim © 1971 Mattel Inc & country **Arms:** bent **Body:** pink tnt **Body Markings:** © Mattel Inc 1966/ Taiwan

Model #: 9843 Name: Dolls of the World Parisian reissue Box Date: 1990 Hair Color: reddish blonde Hairstyle: pulled up to top of head with curls, black and pink feather shaped hair ornament Face: blue eyes, dark blonde brows, red lips & blush, black beauty mark Clothing: pink satin knee-length halter dress, black & silver lace trim at bodice & lower skirt, black braid trim around bodice & black lacing, white ruffle at lower hem, black knit stockings, black cameo at throat, gold stud earrings & ring, matching garter, black mules Extras: 2-piece clear stand & pink oval brush Head: Steffie Head Markings: inside rim © 1971 Mattel Inc & country Arms: bent Body: tan tnt Body Markings: © Mattel Inc 1966/ China

Model #: 2995 Name: Dolls of the World Peruvian Box Date: 1985 Hair Color: brunette Hairstyle: braids to mid-back, middle part Face: brown eyes, dark brown brows, deep pink lips Clothing: medium blue long sleeved top with woven red, green and white trim at cuffs neck & waist, dark blue below knee skirt with multicolor ribbon trim & green hem, turquoise cape with pink ribbon trim, blue hat with multicolor flower trim, pink ring, hot pink slip on sandals & pink ribbons for hair Extras: 2-piece display stand Head: Steffie Head Markings: inside rim © 1971 Mattel Inc & country Arms: bent Body: tan tnt Body Markings: © Mattel Inc.1966/ Philippines

Model #: 12700 Name: Dolls of the World Polynesian Box Date: 1994 Hair Color: black Hairstyle: thigh length Face: brown eyes, black brows, red lips & blush Clothing: red & white print 2-piece swimsuit with green grass skirt & multicolor wooden bead accent at hip, multicolor floral lei and matching band for hair, pearl stud earrings & ring Extras: 2-piece white stand & red oval brush Head: Oriental Head Markings: © Mattel Inc 1980 Arms: bent Body: dark tan tnt Body Markings: © Mattel Inc 1966/ Malaysia Notes: available in 3 doll gift set: Irish, German, Polynesian

Model #: 1601 Name: International Royal Box Date: 1979 Hair Color: blonde Hairstyle: mid-back-length ponytail with dangling curls, middle part Face: turquoise blue eyes, light brown brows, pale pink lips Clothing: white sleeveless gown with tiered ruffled skirt & red ribbon sash trimmed with gold medallions, gold necklace, rhinestone earrings & ring, gold crown, scepter, white ankle straps Extras: 2-piece clear stand Booklet: BWOF 1979 Head: superstar Head Markings: inside or outside rim © Mattel Inc 1976 +/- country Arms: bent Body: pink tnt Body Markings: © Mattel Inc 1966/ Taiwan

Model #: 1916 **Name:** Dolls of the World Russian **Box Date:** 1988 **Hair Color:** blonde **Hairstyle:** mid-back length, ends curled **Face:** blue eyes, light brown brows, deep pink lips **Clothing:** ankle-length long sleeve high collar deep pink velour tunic with dark brown faux fur trim at shoulders, gold collar, gold braid trim at cuffs, bodice & hem, black & gold cloth boots, rhinestone stud earrings & ring, black faux fur hat with rhinestone jewel & gold trim **Extras:** 2-piece clear stand & pink oval brush **Head:** superstar **Head Markings:** inside or outside rim © Mattel Inc 1976 +/- country **Arms:** bent **Body:** tan tnt **Body Markings:** © Mattel Inc 1966/ China

Model #: 3263 **Name:** International Scottish **Box Date:** 1980 **Hair Color:** red **Hairstyle:** waist length, middle part, cello on head **Face:** green eyes, brown brows, deep pink lips & blush **Clothing:** black velvet long sleeve top with lace at cuffs, collar & bodice front, long full tartan plaid skirt with tartan sash, black tam hat with tartan trim & red pom, rhinestone stud earrings & ring, black ankle straps **Extras:** 2-piece clear stand **Booklet:** BWOF 1980 **Head:** superstar **Head Markings:** inside or outside rim © Mattel Inc 1976 +/- country **Arms:** bent **Body:** pink tnt **Body Markings:** © Mattel Inc 1966/ Taiwan

Model #: 9845 **Name:** Dolls of the World Scottish reissue **Box Date:** 1990 **Hair Color:** red **Hairstyle:** waist length, ends curled **Face:** green eyes, red-brown brows, red lips & blush **Clothing:** black velvet long sleeve jacket with white & gold lace at cuffs, collar & jacket front, red, black, gold, and blue tartan plaid sash & long full skirt, black velvet tam with plaid accents & red pom, gold stud earrings & ring, wide black pumps **Extras:** 2-piece clear stand & red oval brush **Head:** superstar **Head Markings:** inside or outside rim © Mattel Inc 1976 +/- country **Arms:** bent **Body:** light tan tnt **Body Markings:** © Mattel Inc 1966/ China

Model #: 4031 **Name:** International Spanish **Box Date:** 1980 **Hair Color:** black **Hairstyle:** middle part, ponytail at top of head & nape of neck, ends curled, double row ribbon trim at topknot **Face:** brown eyes, brown brows, light red lips & blush **Clothing:** red nylon scoop neck dress knee-length in front/ankle in back with black lace trim at armholes & five tiered ruffled trim at hem, black lace fan, rhinestone ring, black ankle straps **Extras:** 2-piece clear stand **Head:** Hispanic **Head Markings:** inside rim © Mattel Inc, 1983 **Arms:** bent **Body:** dark tan tnt **Body Markings:** © Mattel Inc 1966/ Taiwan

Model #: 4963 **Name:** Dolls of the World Spanish reissue **Box Date:** 1991 **Hair Color:** black **Hairstyle:** mid-back length, ends curled, pulled back from face with black lace & gold hair accent **Face:** brown eyes, black brows, red lips & blush **Clothing:** black nylon long sleeved high neck blouse with yellow, orange, black & white print shawl with black fringe, green taffeta full skirt mid-calf length with orange, yellow, green & black print apron, white knee-high stockings, gold drop earrings, gold ring, wide black pumps & orange plastic hair ornament **Extras:** 2-piece clear stand & green oval brush **Head:** Steffie **Head Markings:** inside rim © 1971 Mattel Inc & country **Arms:** bent **Body:** dark tan tnt **Body Markings:** © Mattel Inc 1966/ China

Model #: 4032 **Name:** International Swedish **Box Date:** 1982 **Hair Color:** blonde **Hairstyle:** mid-back-length ponytail at nape of neck, side part **Face:** blue eyes, light brown brows, pale pink lips **Clothing:** white long sleeved blouse with lace at cuffs & neck, black lace-up vest, long royal blue skirt to ankle with white apron & woven ribbon trim, white cap trimmed in white lace, blue ring, royal blue ankle straps **Extras:** 2-piece clear stand **Booklet:** BIC 1983 **Head:** superstar **Head Markings:** inside or outside rim © Mattel Inc 1976 +/- country **Arms:** bent **Body:** pink tnt **Body Markings:** © Mattel Inc 1966/ Taiwan

Model #: 7541 **Name:** International Swiss **Box Date:** 1983 **Hair Color:** blonde **Hairstyle:** mid-back-length pigtails, side part **Face:** blue eyes, light brown brows, deep pink lips & blush **Clothing:** white short sleeved blouse, blue bodice & gold lace-up accent, blue ribbon at neck, red print velveteen skirt mid-calf length, white knee-high stockings, rhinestone ring, straw hat with blue ribbon & 2 red flowers, royal blue tennis shoes **Extras:** 2-piece clear stand **Booklet:** BIC 1983 **Head:** superstar **Head Markings:** inside or outside rim © Mattel Inc 1976 +/- country **Arms:** bent **Body:** tan tnt **Body Markings:** © Mattel Inc 1966/ Taiwan

Jubilee Series

Model #: 12009 **Name:** Jubilee Series Gold Jubilee Barbie **Box Date:** 1994 **Hair Color:** blonde **Hairstyle:** thigh-length ponytail on top of head with sideswept bangs **Face:** blue eyes, rooted lashes, blonde brows, rose lips & blush **Clothing:** gold slim gown encrusted with pearls & iridescent beads with open leg of mutton sleeves, gold & ivory brocade coat encrusted with pearls & iridescent beads, metallic pink lining with embroidered 'B', beaded tiara, pearl & jeweled dangle earrings, gold ring, gold heart shaped Barbie bracelet, gold Brazil shoes **Extras:** 2-piece white pearl & gold stand **Booklet:** story & COA **Head:** superstar **Head Markings:** inside or outside rim © Mattel Inc 1976 +/- country **Arms:** bent **Body:** ivory tnt **Body Markings:** © Mattel Inc 1966/ China

194

Bob Mackie Series

Model #: 5405 **Name:** Mackie Designer Gold **Box Date:** 1990 **Hair Color:** blonde **Hairstyle:** pulled to top of head, waist-length ponytail held with gold & crystal encrusted hair ornament **Face:** blue eyes, blonde brows, red lips & blush **Clothing:** white sleeveless crossover bodice gown with gold sequined skirt flared in back, bodice encrusted with gold beads, silver beads & bugle beads, rhinestone drop sphere earrings & gold ring, white feather boa, gold Brazil shoes **Extras:** 2-piece black stand **Booklet:** story **Head:** superstar **Head Markings:** inside or outside rim © Mattel Inc 1976 +/- country **Arms:** bent **Body:** tan tnt **Body Markings:** © Mattel Inc 1966/ China **Notes:** 1st in series & also available without acrylic case

Model #: 4247 **Name:** Mackie Empress Bride **Box Date:** 1992 **Hair Color:** blonde **Hairstyle:** pulled back into thigh-length braided ponytail **Face:** lavender-blue eyes, blonde brows, frosted hot pink lips & blush **Clothing:** white gown, large hoop skirt with pleated tulle, white brocade overskirt embroidered with gold, encrusted with pearls, sequins & seed beads, matching bodice & angel cap sleeves, veil with tiara, pearl drop earrings, elaborate pearl choker, gold ring, white pantyhose with gold lace panties, white, iridescent & gold rose bouquet, wide white pumps **Extras:** 2-piece pearl stand & design sketch **Booklet:** story **Head:** superstar **Head Markings:** inside or outside rim © Mattel Inc 1976 +/- country **Arms:** bent **Body:** tan tnt **Body Markings:** © Mattel Inc 1966/ China **Notes:** 5th in series

Model #: 14056 **Name:** Mackie Goddess of the Sun **Box Date:** 1995 **Hair Color:** yellow **Hairstyle:** pulled to top of head with 3 hard pin curls popping out of headdress **Face:** lilac-green eyes, brown brows, red lips & blush **Clothing:** slim gold off-the-shoulder gown flared at knee, heavily encrusted with seed beads, sequins & gold beads, matching beaded sun flare wings & headdress, gold sun dangle earrings, ring, yellow pantyhose & wide gold pumps **Extras:** 2-piece pearl stand & design sketch **Booklet:** story **Head:** Mackie **Head Markings:** © 1991 Mattel Inc **Arms:** Shani **Body:** tan tnt **Body Markings:** © Mattel Inc 1966/ China **Notes:** 8th in series

Model #: 10803 **Name:** Mackie Masquerade Ball **Box Date:** 1993 **Hair Color:** red **Hairstyle:** front & sides pulled to top of head, braided & wrapped under hat, rest of hair inside a black & gold beaded snood **Face:** aqua eyes, reddish-blonde brows, red lips & blush **Clothing:** off-the-shoulder multicolor beaded gown in a diamond pattern with gold bead accents, black velvet & gold beaded partial collar, matching cuffs, choker & hat with large orange jewel & black feathers, black mask, orange drop earrings, wide black pumps **Extras:** 2-piece black stand, black oval brush & design sketch **Booklet:** story **Head:** Mackie **Head Markings:** © 1991 Mattel Inc **Arms:** 1 ptr, 1 bent **Body:** tan tnt **Body Markings:** © Mattel Inc 1966/ China **Notes:** 6th in series, doll is scented

Model #: 4248 **Name:** Mackie Neptune Fantasy **Box Date:** 1992 **Hair Color:** white & green **Hairstyle:** pulled onto top of head forming giant pin curl with green sequin beaded hair ornament, crystal drop on forehead **Face:** green eyes, dark blonde brows, red lips & blush **Clothing:** green velvet sequined & heavily beaded gown, green velvet & bugle beaded coat with flared upsweep, green & crystal drop earrings, green beaded choker, wide green pumps **Extras:** 2-piece black stand & design sketch **Booklet:** story **Head:** Mackie **Head Markings:** © 1991 Mattel Inc **Arms:** 1 ptr, 1 bent **Body:** tan tnt **Body Markings:** © Mattel Inc 1966/ China **Notes:** 4th in series

Model #: 2703 **Name:** Mackie Platinum **Box Date:** 1991 **Hair Color:** blonde **Hairstyle:** pulled to top of head & upswept with silver & rhinestone bugle bead decorations **Face:** blue eyes, blonde brows, frosted red lips & blush **Clothing:** v-neck floor-length white sequined gown with silver sequins, seed beads, bugle beads encrusted on bodice, white ruffled cape heavily encrusted with iridescent sequins, silver seed beads & bugle beads, silver & crystal dangle earrings, silver ring, wide white pumps **Extras:** 2-piece pearl stand **Booklet:** story **Head:** superstar **Head Markings:** inside or outside rim © Mattel Inc 1976 +/- country **Arms:** bent **Body:** tan tnt **Body Markings:** © Mattel Inc 1966/ China **Notes:** 3rd in series, early gown sequins had blue cast

Model #: 12046 **Name:** Mackie Queen of Hearts **Box Date:** 199? **Hair Color:** black **Hairstyle:** pulled to top of head & tucked under forming a heart shape, red sequined & feather hat attached to head **Face:** lavender eyes, black brows, red lips & blush, black beauty mark on chin **Clothing:** red sequined and beaded full-length sleeveless gown with heart shaped red velvet cape encrusted with sequins, rhinestones & crystal bugle beads, heart shaped crystal drop earring & silver ring, wide red pumps **Extras:** 2-piece black stand & design sketch **Booklet:** story **Head:** Mackie **Head Markings:** © 1991 Mattel Inc **Arms:** Shani **Body:** tan tnt **Body Markings:** © Mattel Inc 1966/ China **Notes:** 7th in series

Model #: 2704 **Name:** Mackie Starlight Splendor **Box Date:** 1991 **Hair Color:** black **Hairstyle:** curly black topknot with heavily encrusted silver & white beaded skullcap **Face:** brown-green eyes, black brows, red lips & blush **Clothing:** halter-style sequined, beaded gown of silver, white & black, silver & white beaded cuffs, silver disk earrings & ring, back of gown has black & white feathers, wide black pumps **Extras:** 2-piece black stand **Booklet:** story **Head:** Christie **Head Markings:** © Mattel Inc./ 1987 **Arms:** bent **Body:** dark brown tnt **Body Markings:** © Mattel Inc 1966/ China **Notes:** 2nd in series

Musical Ballerina Series

Model #: 5472 **Name:** Musical Ballerina Series Nutcracker **Box Date:** 1991 **Hair Color:** blonde **Hairstyle:** pulled up to top of head in fan shape with curled tendrils at neck, silver & flower sequined tiara **Face:** blue eyes, light brown brows, hot pink lips & blush **Clothing:** pink, lavender & silver tutu with petal skirt, pink glitter tights, silver stud earrings, pink pearl toe shoes with pink satin ribbons **Extras:** stand/music box plays Dance of the Sugarplum Fairy, large pink base, clear background with white stencil & pink top **Booklet:** instructions **Head:** superstar **Head Markings:** inside or outside rim © Mattel Inc 1976 +/- country **Arms:** ballerina split fingers **Body:** tan tnt **Body Markings:** © Mattel Inc 1966/ China

Model #: 1648 **Name:** Musical Ballerina Series Swan Lake **Box Date:** 1991 **Hair Color:** blonde **Hairstyle:** 6 sections of hair twisted with gold glitter piled on top of head with topknot, feather & pearl hair ornament **Face:** light blue eyes, blonde brows, deep pink frosted lips & blush **Clothing:** white glitter tutu with iridescent bead & sequin accents, white glitter tights, silver stud earrings, white toe shoes with white ribbon ties **Extras:** light blue music box/stand plays Swan Lake, large blue base, clear background with white stencil sides & clear top **Booklet:** instructions **Head:** superstar **Head Markings:** inside or outside rim © Mattel Inc 1976 +/- country **Arms:** ballerina split fingers **Body:** tan tnt **Body Markings:** © Mattel Inc 1966/ China

My First/My Size

Model #: 1875 **Name:** My First Barbie **Box Date:** 1980 **Hair Color:** blonde **Hairstyle:** middle part, 2 ponytails 1 tied with pink ribbon **Face:** turquoise eyes, brown brows, peach lips & blush **Clothing:** yellow wrap bodysuit with turquoise trim, matching yellow pants, turquoise knee-length skirt, multicolor stripe sleeveless top, yellow mules **Extras:** pointed yellow brush & comb **Booklet:** MFB 1980 **Head:** superstar **Head Markings:** inside or outside rim © Mattel Inc 1976 +/- country **Arms:** ptr **Body:** tan tnt non b/l **Body Markings:** © Mattel Inc.1966/ Philippines

Model #: 1875 **Name:** My First Barbie **Box Date:** 1982 **Hair Color:** blonde **Hairstyle:** side part, pulled into 2 pigtails, tied with pink ribbon **Face:** blue eyes, blonde brows, pink lips & blush **Clothing:** pink sleeveless bodysuit with white lace trim at bodice and sleeve, pink & white gingham full knee-length skirt, hot pink mules **Booklet:** BWOF 1984 & MFB 1982 **Head:** superstar **Head Markings:** inside or outside rim © Mattel Inc 1976 +/- country **Arms:** ptr **Body:** tan tnt non b/l **Body Markings:** © Mattel Inc.1966/ Philippines

Model #: 1875 **Name:** My First Barbie **Box Date:** 1984 **Hair Color:** blonde **Hairstyle:** front & sides pulled back with pink ribbon rest mid-back length, bangs **Face:** blue eyes, blonde brows, pink lips & blush **Clothing:** white short sleeve knee-length dress with pink ribbon trim & lace edging at neck, arm & hem, narrow pink pumps **Extras:** pointed pink brush & comb **Booklet:** BWOF 1984 & MFB 1984 **Head:** superstar **Head Markings:** inside or outside rim © Mattel Inc 1976 +/- country **Arms:** ptr **Body:** tan tnt non b/l **Body Markings:** © Mattel Inc.1966/ Philippines **Black Version:** model #: 9858 **Hair Color:** black **Face:** brown eyes, brown brows, light red lips & blush **Head:** Hispanic **Head Markings:** inside rim © Mattel Inc, 1983 **Body:** dark brown tnt non b/l

Model #: 1788 **Name:** My First Barbie **Box Date:** 1986 **Hair Color:** blonde **Hairstyle:** sides & front pulled back, pink elastic & tulle headband, rest mid-back length, ends curled under, curly bangs **Face:** turquoise eyes, blonde brows, pink lips & blush **Clothing:** pink leotard, pink tulle skirt with petal hem falling below knee and matching arm bands, pink ballet slippers with ribbon ties **Extras:** pointed lilac brush & sheet of cardboard punch outs **Booklet:** BWOF 1987 & MFB 1986 **Head:** superstar **Head Markings:** inside or outside rim © Mattel Inc 1976 +/- country **Arms:** ptr **Body:** tan tnt non b/l **Body Markings:** © Mattel Inc.1966/ Philippines **Black Version:** model #: 1801 **Hair Color:** brunette **Face:** brown eyes, black brows, mauve lips & blush **Head:** Hispanic **Head Markings:** inside rim © Mattel Inc, 1983 **Body:** dark brown tnt non b/l

Model #: 1280 **Name:** My First Barbie **Box Date:** 1988 **Hair Color:** blonde **Hairstyle:** sides & front pulled back with iridescent fabric bow, rest waist length, ends curled under, bangs **Face:** blue eyes, blonde brows, hot pink lips & blush **Clothing:** white leotard with glitter dots & white iridescent tulle knee-length skirt, white ballet slippers with ribbon ties **Extras:** white oval brush & sheet of cardboard punch outs **Booklet:** BWOF 1988 **Head:** superstar **Head Markings:** inside or outside rim © Mattel Inc 1976 +/- country **Arms:** ptr **Body:** tan tnt non b/l **Body Markings:** © Mattel Inc 1966/ Malaysia **Black Version:** model #: 1281 **Hair Color:** black **Face:** brown eyes, brown brows, hot pink lips & blush **Head:** Christie **Head Markings:** © Mattel Inc./ 1987 **Body:** dark brown tnt non b/l **Hispanic Version:** model #: 1282 **Hair Color:** brunette **Face:** brown eyes, brown brows, mauve lips **Head:** Hispanic **Head Markings:** inside rim © Mattel Inc, 1983 **Body:** dark tan tnt non b/l

Model #: 9942 **Name:** My First Barbie **Box Date:** 1989 **Hair Color:** blonde **Hairstyle:** sides & front pulled back, rest waist length, ends curled under, bangs, iridescent tiara **Face:** blue eyes, blonde brows, pink lips **Clothing:** gown with purple drop waist bodice, iridescent white puffed sleeves & skirt, wide white pumps **Extras:** pearl oval brush & sheet of cardboard punch outs **Booklet:** BWOF 1988 **Head:** superstar **Head Markings:** inside or outside rim © Mattel Inc 1976 +/- country **Arms:** ptr **Body:** tan tnt non b/l **Body Markings:** © Mattel, Inc.1966/ Mexico **Notes:** lip paint may bleed into surrounding vinyl **Black Version:** model #: 9943 **Hair Color:** black **Face:** hazel eyes, black brows, hot pink lips & blush **Head:** Christie **Head Markings:** © Mattel Inc./ 1987 **Body:** dark brown tnt non b/l **Body Markings:** © Mattel Inc 1966/ Malaysia **Hispanic Version:** model #: 9944 **Hair Color:** brunette **Face:** brown eyes, brown brows, hot pink lips & blush **Head:** Hispanic **Head Markings:** inside rim © Mattel Inc, 1983 **Body:** dark tan tnt non b/l **Body Markings:** © Mattel Inc 1966/ Malaysia

Model #: 3839 **Name:** My First Barbie **Box Date:** 1991 **Hair Color:** blonde **Hairstyle:** pulled back with blue tulle band into side waist-length ponytail, ends curled under with bangs **Face:** lilac-blue eyes, light brown brows, deep pink lips & blush **Clothing:** blue & lilac metallic design leotard with blue iridescent tulle knee-length skirt & accents at shoulders, blue ballet slippers with ribbon ties **Extras:** blue oval brush **Head:** superstar **Head Markings:** inside or outside rim © Mattel Inc 1976 +/- country **Arms:** ptr **Body:** tan tnt non b/l **Body Markings:** © Mattel Inc 1966/ China **Black Version:** model #: 3861 **Hair Color:** brunette **Face:** light brown eyes, black brows, pink lips & blush **Head:** Christie **Head Markings:** © Mattel Inc./ 1987 **Body:** dark brown tnt non b/l **Body Markings:** © Mattel Inc 1966/ Malaysia **Hispanic Version:** model #: 3864 **Hair Color:** black **Face:** hazel eyes, black brows, pink lips & blush **Head:** Steffie **Head Markings:** inside rim © 1971 Mattel Inc & country **Arms:** ptr **Body:** dark tan tnt non b/l **Body Markings:** © Mattel Inc 1966/ Malaysia

Model #: 2516 **Name:** My First Barbie **Box Date:** 1992 **Hair Color:** blonde **Hairstyle:** mid-back length, sides & front pulled back with pink ribbon & iridescent tulle accent **Face:** teal eyes, blonde brows, pink lips & blush **Clothing:** white glitter leotard with pink tulle accents at shoulder, matching tutu skirt of white glitter fabric & pink iridescent tulle **Extras:** pink oval brush **Head:** superstar **Head Markings:** inside or outside rim © Mattel Inc 1976 +/- country **Arms:** ptr **Body:** tan tnt non b/l, white molded legs, pink molded ballet slippers **Body Markings:** © Mattel Inc.1966/ Indonesia **Black Version:** model #: 2767 **Hair Color:** black **Face:** hazel eyes, dark brown brows, hot pink lips & blush **Head:** Christie **Head Markings:** © Mattel Inc./ 1987 **Body:** dark brown tnt non b/l, white molded legs, molded pink ballet slippers **Body Markings:** © Mattel Inc 1966/ China **Hispanic Version:** model #: 2770 **Hair Color:** brunette **Face:** olive green eyes, brown brows, pink lips & blush **Head:** Teresa **Head Markings:** © 1990, Mattel/ Inc **Body:** dark tan tnt non b/l, white molded legs, pink molded ballet slippers **Body Markings:** © Mattel Inc 1966/ China

Model #: 11294 **Name:** My First Barbie **Box Date:** 1993 **Hair Color:** blonde **Hairstyle:** sides pulled back with lilac ribbon & white iridescent tulle accent, rest mid-back length, ends curled under with bangs **Face:** turquoise eyes, light brown brows, purple lips & blush **Clothing:** lilac glitter leotard with white tulle accents at shoulders, matching tutu of lilac glitter fabric & white iridescent tulle **Extras:** lilac oval brush **Head:** superstar **Head Markings:** inside or outside rim © Mattel Inc 1976 +/- country **Arms:** ptr **Body:** tan tnt non b/l, white molded legs, lilac molded ballet slippers **Body Markings:** © Mattel Inc.1966/ Indonesia **Black Version:** model #: 11340 **Hair Color:** brunette **Face:** brown eyes, black brows, hot pink lips & blush **Head:** Christie **Head Markings:** © Mattel Inc./ 1987 **Body:** dark brown tnt non b/l, white molded legs, lilac molded ballet slippers **Body Markings:** © Mattel Inc 1966/ China **Hispanic Version:** model #: 11341 **Hair Color:** brunette **Face:** olive green eyes, brown brows, pink lips & blush **Head:** Teresa **Head Markings:** © 1990, Mattel/ Inc **Body:** dark tan tnt non b/l, white molded legs, lilac molded ballet slippers **Body Markings:** © Mattel Inc 1966/ China **Asian Version:** model #: 11342 **Hair Color:** black **Face:** brown eyes, black brows, orange lips & blush **Head:** Oriental **Head Markings:** © Mattel Inc 1980 **Body:** tan tnt non b/l, white molded legs, lilac molded ballet slippers **Body Markings:** © Mattel Inc 1966/ China

Model #: 13064 **Name:** My First Barbie **Box Date:** 1994 **Hair Color:** blonde **Hairstyle:** sides & front pulled back, rest crinkled thigh length, bangs, gold tiara with gold & turquoise jewel **Face:** turquoise eyes, light blonde brows, deep pink lips **Clothing:** turquoise mini dress with sheer turquoise glitter fabric overskirt & neck detail, gold & turquoise jewel neck accent, decorated with multi color bows, turquoise stud earrings **Extras:** turquoise oval brush **Head:** superstar **Head Markings:** inside or outside rim © Mattel Inc 1976 +/- country **Arms:** ptr **Body:** tan tnt non b/l, light blue molded legs, turquoise molded ballet slippers & panties **Body Markings:** © Mattel Inc.1966/ Indonesia **Black Version:** model #: 13065 **Hair Color:** black **Face:** purple-green eyes, black brows, dark pink lips & blush **Head:** Christie **Head Markings:** © Mattel Inc./ 1987 **Body:** dark brown tnt non b/l, light blue molded legs, turquoise molded ballet slippers & panties **Hispanic Version:** model #: 13066 **Hair Color:** brunette **Face:** blue-brown eyes, brown brows, deep pink lips & blush **Head:** Teresa **Head Markings:** © 1990, Mattel/ Inc **Body:** dark tan tnt non b/l, light blue molded legs, turquoise molded ballet slippers & panties **Asian Version:** model #: 13067 **Hair Color:** black **Face:** brown eyes, black brows, rose lips & blush **Head:** Oriental **Head Markings:** © Mattel Inc 1980 **Body:** dark tan tnt non b/l, light blue molded legs, turquoise molded ballet slippers & panties

Model #: 1389 Name: My First Ken Box Date: 1988 Hair Color: painted blonde Face: blue eyes, dark blonde brows, mauve lips Clothing: 1-piece white ballet bodysuit with glitter dot accent & glitter leggings, blue short jacket with iridescent lapels & cummerbund, white dance oxfords Extras: sheet of cardboard punch outs Booklet: BWOF 1988 Head: 1983 Ken Head Markings: © 1983 Mattel Inc Arms: ptr Body: tan non b/l Body Markings: © Mattel Inc 1968/ Malaysia

Model #: 9940 Name: My First Ken Box Date: 1989 Hair Color: painted blonde Face: aqua teal eyes, dark blonde brows, mauve lips Clothing: 1-piece white halter-style dance bodysuit with iridescent bow tie & purple double breasted satin blazer with iridescent lapels, iridescent crown & white dance oxfords Extras: sheet of cardboard punch outs Head: 1983 Ken Head Markings: © 1983 Mattel Inc Arms: ptr Body: tan non b/l Body Markings: © Mattel Inc 1968/ Malaysia

Model #: 3841 Name: My First Ken Box Date: 1991 Hair Color: painted blonde Face: blue eyes, blonde brows, mauve lips Clothing: long sleeve light blue dance shirt with multicolor inserts, solid light blue pants, white dance oxfords Head: 1983 Ken Head Markings: © 1983 Mattel Inc Arms: ptr Body: dark tan non b/l Body Markings: © Mattel Inc 1968/ Malaysia Black Version: model #: 1807 Hair Color: painted black Face: brown eyes, dark brown brows, dark mauve lips Head: 1987 black Ken Head Markings: © Mattel Inc 1987 Body: dark brown non b/l

Model #: 1503 **Name:** My First Ken **Box Date:** 1992 **Hair Color:** painted blonde **Face:** turquoise eyes, light brown brows, mauve lips **Clothing:** white & silver strand long sleeve shirt & vest combination with iridescent vest panels & blue iridescent trim at cuffs and neckline, white pants with iridescent blue wide waistband, white dance oxfords **Head:** 1991 Secret Hearts Ken **Head Markings:** © 1991 Mattel Inc **Arms:** ptr **Body:** dark tan non b/l **Body Markings:** © Mattel Inc 1968/ Malaysia **Black Version:** model #: 3876 **Hair Color:** painted brunette **Face:** brown eyes, brown brows, dark mauve lips **Head:** 1987 black Ken **Head Markings:** © Mattel Inc 1987 **Body:** dark brown non b/l

Model #: 2517 **Name:** My Size **Box Date:** 1992 **Hair Color:** blonde **Hairstyle:** curly waist length with curly bangs **Face:** blue eyes, blonde brows, deep pink lips **Clothing:** pink stretch bodysuit with v-shaped iridescent sequin trim insert, tiered pink glitter tulle long skirt, pink stud earrings, tied on pink tiara, pink booties/ballet slippers with ribbon ties **Extras:** pink clip on earrings for child **Booklet:** instructions **Head:** superstar **Head Markings:** © Mattel Inc. 1976 **Arms:** my size pts **Body:** tan 3 ft s/l **Body Markings:** © 1992 Mattel, Inc./ Mexico **Notes:** #11212 black "dipped" version also available

Model #: 12053 **Name:** My Size Bride black version **Box Date:** 1994 **Hair Color:** brunette **Hairstyle:** sides & top pulled back, rest mid-back length with bangs **Face:** brown eyes, black brows, pink-peach lips **Clothing:** white stretch bodysuit with iridescent ruffle trim, white long skirt with white tulle overskirt & iridescent glitter dots, matching tulle puffed sleeves, white stud earrings, matching tulle veil, crystal heart necklace, white stretch booties with iridescent ribbons **Booklet:** instructions **Head:** superstar **Head Markings:** © Mattel Inc. 1976 **Arms:** my size pts **Body:** dark brown 3 ft s/l **Body Markings:** © 1992 Mattel, Inc./ Mexico **Notes:** "dipped" #12052 white version available & #14108 brunette Toys R Us exclusive

Model #: 13767 **Name:** My Size Princess **Box Date:** 1995 **Hair Color:** blonde **Hairstyle:** sides & top pulled back, rest mid-back length with bangs **Face:** blue eyes, blonde brows, pink lips & blush **Clothing:** white stretch sleeveless bodysuit, pink glitter flower accent, long pink & white alternating strips of tulle overskirt, pink petal accents at waistline with glitter, matching petal sleeves, pink headband with attached silver tiara & pink rose trim, pearl rose earrings, white booties/ballet slippers with ribbon ties **Extras:** pink rose clip on earrings for child **Booklet:** instructions **Head:** superstar **Head Markings:** © Mattel Inc. 1976 **Arms:** my size pts **Body:** tan 3 ft s/l **Body Markings:** © 1992 Mattel, Inc./ Mexico **Notes:** #13768 black "dipped" version also available

Model #: 11590 **Name:** 35th Anniversary Barbie **Box Date:** 1993 **Hair Color:** blonde **Hairstyle:** ponytail with ends curled below shoulders & curly bangs **Face:** no eye color, brown pointed or curved brows, red lips & blush **Clothing:** black & white striped 1-piece strapless swimsuit, wrist tag, white sunglasses with blue lenses, gold hoop earrings, black mules **Extras:** 3-piece clear stand, replica nostalgic doll box with white liner **Booklet:** 35th story **Head:** nostalgic **Head Markings:** © Mattel Inc/ 1958 **Arms:** straight - much shorter than original vintage regular arms **Body:** ivory, painted nails, nostalgic **Body Markings:** Barbie/ © 1958,1993/ Mattel, Inc./ Malaysia **Notes:** 1st version rounded brows, 2nd pointed **Brunette Version:** model #: 11782 **Hair Color:** brunette

Model #: 13675 **Name:** Busy Gal **Box Date:** 1995 **Hair Color:** brunette **Hairstyle:** below shoulder-length ponytail with ends curled & curly bangs **Face:** blue eyes, brown brows, red lips & blush **Clothing:** red & white striped sleeveless bodysuit with fabric bow at neck, red short jacket with elbow length sleeves lined with red & white striped fabric, slim red skirt, navy belt, navy hat, black glasses, designer portfolio with sketches, pearl stud earrings, navy mules **Extras:** 3-piece clear stand **Booklet:** instructions **Head:** nostalgic **Head Markings:** © Mattel Inc/ 1958 **Arms:** straight **Body:** tan, painted nails, nostalgic **Body Markings:** Barbie/ © 1958,1993/ Mattel, Inc./ Malaysia **Notes:** elastic holding glasses to wrist may cause wrist to shrink

Model #: 13534 **Name:** Solo in the Spotlight **Box Date:** 1994 **Hair Color:** blonde **Hairstyle:** below shoulder-length ponytail with ends curled & curly bangs **Face:** blue eyes, brown brows, red lips & blush **Clothing:** black sparkle strapless slim gown with flared tulle skirt at knee & red rose accent, long black gloves, pearl stud earrings, four strand clear bead choker, pink chiffon scarf, gray floor stand microphone, black mules **Extras:** 3-piece clear stand & black oval brush **Booklet:** instructions **Head:** nostalgic **Head Markings:** © Mattel Inc/ 1958 **Arms:** straight **Body:** tan, painted nails, nostalgic **Body Markings:** Barbie/ © 1958,1993/ Mattel, Inc./ Malaysia **Brunette Version:** model #: 13820 **Hair Color:** brunette

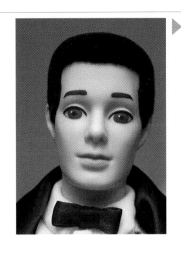

Model #: 1110 **Name:** 30th Anniversary Ken **Box Date:** 1991 **Hair Color:** brunette **Hairstyle:** flocked close cut **Face:** blue eyes, black brows, pink lips **Clothing:** replica Tuxedo outfit: long sleeve white shirt with pique yoke & pearl buttons, wine satin bow tie & cummerbund, black tuxedo jacket, satin lapels & white flower, matching pants, white undershirt & boxer shorts, black socks, black lace-up oxfords (new), silver replica wrist tag on chain **Extras:** 2-piece ivory stand **Booklet:** COA & story **Head:** porcelain flocked Ken **Arms:** pts **Body:** porcelain nostalgic Ken serial # painted on back **Body Markings:** © 1960 1990/ Mattel Inc/ Malaysia

Model #: 7957 **Name:** 30th Anniversary Midge **Box Date:** 1992 **Hair Color:** red **Hairstyle:** flipped up at nape of neck with curly bangs **Face:** blue eyes, reddish brows, peach lips, blush & light brown freckles **Clothing:** replica Senior Prom outfit: strapless green & light blue satin bodice, green & turquoise alternating tulle strips over a green satin skirt, pearl stud earrings, wrist corsage, green & pearl necklace, white faux fur stole, sheer stockings, white panties & merry widow, green mules with pearl **Extras:** 2-piece ivory stand **Booklet:** COA & story **Head:** porcelain Midge **Arms:** reg **Body:** porcelain nostalgic serial # painted on back **Body Markings:** © Mattel, Inc/ 1958,1962/ Malaysia

Model #: 11396 **Name:** 30th Anniversary Skipper **Box Date:** 1993 **Hair Color:** blonde **Hairstyle:** waist length, parted in middle with bangs **Face:** blue eyes, dark blonde brows, red lips & blush **Clothing:** replica Happy Birthday outfit: light blue & white sleeveless full skirt dress, white with blue trim petticoat, off-white straw hat & blue ribbon hatband, short white gloves, panties, silver headband, doily birthday cake & 6 candles, gold birthday present, 4 napkins, 2 pink poppers, 1 invitation, white anklets, white flats, foil wrist tag **Extras:** 2-piece white Skipper stand **Booklet:** COA & story **Head:** porcelain Skipper **Body:** porcelain nostalgic Skipper serial # painted on back **Body Markings:** © 1963/ Mattel Inc./ Malaysia

Model #: 5475 **Name:** Benefit Performance **Box Date:** 1987 **Hair Color:** brunette **Hairstyle:** sides pulled to top of head held with red ribbon, bangs, rest waist length **Face:** blue eyes, rooted lashes, brown brows, red lips & blush **Clothing:** replica Benefit Performance outfit: red velvet sleeveless crossover tunic with white tulle full underskirt decorated with red bows, rhinestones at waist, drop earrings, graduated necklace, long gloves, white teddy, full petticoat, white stockings & white mules **Extras:** 2-piece white stand **Booklet:** COA & story **Head:** porcelain nostalgic **Arms:** straight **Body:** porcelain nostalgic, serial # painted on back **Body Markings:** © 1966'76'91 Mattel, Inc./ Japan **Notes:** 3rd in porcelain series

Model #: 1708 **Name:** Blue Rhapsody **Box Date:** 1986 **Hair Color:** blonde **Hairstyle:** waist length, part on side **Face:** blue eyes, blonde brows, hot pink lips & blush **Clothing:** royal blue taffeta gown with long sleeves, square neck with pleated bodice, full skirt with black tulle silver & blue glitter design overlay, blue rhinestone double choker necklace, stud earrings, wearing blue lacy lingerie, full petticoat, shimmery blue stockings & clear blue glitter mules **Extras:** 2-piece black stand **Booklet:** COA & story **Head:** superstar porcelain **Arms:** straight **Body:** porcelain serial # painted on back **Body Markings:** © 1966'76'91 Mattel, Inc./ Japan **Notes:** 1st in porcelain series

Model #: 3415 **Name:** Enchanted Evening **Box Date:** 1986 **Hair Color:** blonde **Hairstyle:** ponytail with curly bangs **Face:** blue eyes, brown brows, deep pink lips & blush **Clothing:** pink satin gown with sequin trim at waist, fake fur stole, vinyl handless gloves, pale pink merry widow with white glitter stockings, gold glitter mules **Extras:** 2-piece black stand **Booklet:** COA & story **Head:** porcelain nostalgic **Arms:** reg **Body:** porcelain nostalgic serial # written on back **Body Markings:** © Mattel, Inc./ 1958/ Japan **Notes:** 2nd in porcelain series

Model #: 9973 **Name:** Gay Parisienne Porcelain Treasurers **Box Date:** 1991 **Hair Color:** brunette **Hairstyle:** mid-back-length ponytail, ends curled with curly bangs **Face:** no eye color, brown brows, red lips & blush **Clothing:** replica Gay Parisienne outfit: navy with white dot print strapless gown with knee-length bubble skirt, matching bows at hem and back, white faux fur stole, mustard color velvet clutch purse, pearl drop earrings & necklace, blue tulle headband hat, long white gloves, light blue stockings, blue panties with garters, strapless blue bra, navy mules **Extras:** 2-piece white stand **Booklet:** COA & story **Head:** porcelain nostalgic **Arms:** reg **Body:** porcelain nostalgic serial # painted on back **Body Markings:** © Mattel, Inc/ 1958/ Malaysia **Notes:** 1st in Treasures series, blonde & red hair versions available at Disney show & JCPenney

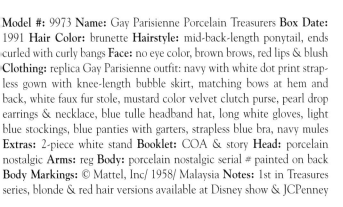

Model #: 7526 **Name:** Plantation Belle Porcelain Treasurers **Box Date:** 1991 **Hair Color:** red **Hairstyle:** mid-back-length ponytail, ends curled under, front section of hair swept across forehead into ponytail **Face:** blue eyes, brown brows, deep pink lips & blush **Clothing:** replica Plantation Belle outfit: sleeveless pale pink dotted swiss knee-length dress trimmed with white lace, pink pearl stud earrings, necklace, 3 strand bracelet, short white gloves, pink straw purse with beaded trim, big straw hat with pink trim, white stockings, white tulle petticoat, strapless chemise with attached garters & matching tap pants, pink mules **Extras:** 2-piece white stand **Booklet:** COA & story **Head:** porcelain nostalgic **Arms:** reg **Body:** porcelain nostalgic serial # painted on back **Body Markings:** © Mattel, Inc/ 1958/ Malaysia **Notes:** 2nd in Treasures series, blonde version Disney show exclusive

Model #: 1249 **Name:** Silken Flame Porcelain Treasurers **Box Date:** 1992 **Hair Color:** brunette **Hairstyle:** layered short cut **Face:** blue eyes, brown brows, coral lips & blush **Clothing:** replica Silken Flame & Red Flare outfits: strapless knee-length full skirt dress with red velvet top & white satin skirt, wide gold belt, red velvet coat with puff sleeves, matching hat, matching red clutch purse, gold clutch purse, long white gloves, pearl stud earrings, 3 strand pearl choker, white stockings, red merry widow, red mules **Extras:** white 2-piece stand **Booklet:** COA & story **Head:** porcelain nostalgic **Arms:** straight **Body:** porcelain nostalgic with serial # written on back **Body Markings:** © Mattel, Inc/ 1958/ Malaysia **Notes:** 3rd in Treasures series, blonde version Disney show exclusive

Model #: 7613 **Name:** Solo in the Spotlight **Box Date:** 1989 **Hair Color:** blonde **Hairstyle:** mid-back-length ponytail with curled end & bangs **Face:** blue eyes, light brown brows, red lips & blush **Clothing:** replica Solo in the Spotlight outfit: black sparkle slim strapless gown with tulle flare at knee accented with deep pink rose, pink chiffon scarf, black merry widow with beige stockings, long black gloves, 3 strand pearl choker & bracelet, pearl drop earrings, gray floor stand microphone, black mules **Extras:** 2-piece black stand **Booklet:** COA **Head:** porcelain nostalgic **Arms:** straight **Body:** porcelain nostalgic serial # written on back **Body Markings:** © Mattel, Inc./ 1958/ Japan **Notes:** 5th in porcelain series

Model #: 5313 **Name:** Sophisticated Lady **Box Date:** 1990 **Hair Color:** brunette **Hairstyle:** bobbed to nape of neck with bangs **Face:** blue eyes, brown brows, deep rose lips & blush **Clothing:** replica Sophisticated Lady outfit: pink taffeta sleeveless gown with silver lace insert at bodice & waist, full-length rose velvet sleeveless coat with large collar & silver buttons, pink pearl stud earrings, pearl & pink pearl necklace, silver tiara encrusted with pearls & pink stones, white long handless gloves, pink teddy, garter belt, stockings, deep pink mules **Extras:** 2-piece pearl stand **Booklet:** COA & story **Head:** porcelain nostalgic **Arms:** straight **Body:** porcelain nostalgic serial # painted on back **Body Markings:** © Mattel, Inc./ 1958/ Malaysia **Notes:** 6th in porcelain series

Model #: 2641 **Name:** Wedding Party Barbie **Box Date:** 1989 **Hair Color:** blonde **Hairstyle:** mid-back-length ponytail, ends curled & curly bangs **Face:** no eye color, brown brows, coral lips & blush **Clothing:** replica Wedding Day outfit: full-length gown with white iridescent lace overlay & tiered skirt, matching veil with pearl halo, pearl drop earrings, pearl necklace, pink & white bouquet with ribbon streamers, white merry widow & panties, stockings, blue garter, white mules **Extras:** 2-piece ivory stand **Booklet:** COA & story **Head:** #1 ponytail **Arms:** reg **Body:** porcelain nostalgic serial # painted on back **Body Markings:** © Mattel, Inc./ 1958/ Japan **Notes:** 4th in porcelain series

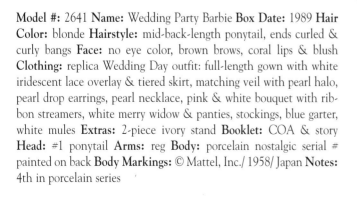  

Model #: 14479 Name: 50th Anniversary Mattel Barbie Box Date: 1995 Hair Color: blonde Hairstyle: pulled to top of head curled under, 3 fabric roses with gold bead centers in center of hair Face: light blue eyes, blonde brows, red lips & blush Clothing: long sleeve red velvet slim gown with gold pleated flared skirt at knee, heavy seed bead accent above gold pleating, 50 red ribbon roses, gold centers & red velvet & gold pleated stole, red & gold drop earrings, gold Mattel 50th bracelet, red mules & gold bead accent Extras: 2-piece white & gold stand Booklet: certificate & story Head: superstar porcelain Arms: bent Body: porcelain serial # painted on back & gold 50 years seal on shoulder Body Markings: © 1966'76'91 Mattel Inc./ Malaysia

Model #: 10246 Name: Gold & Silver Set Gold Sensation Box Date: 1993 Hair Color: blonde Hairstyle: upswept with long cascades Face: turquoise eyes, brown brows, red lips & blush Clothing: gold lamé full skirt gown with spaghetti straps, elaborate beaded & flowered trim across front of bodice & matching large hair ornament, gold drop earrings & "B" bracelet, pantyhose, wide gold pumps Extras: 2-piece ivory stand Booklet: COA & story Head: superstar porcelain Arms: bent Body: porcelain serial # on back Body Markings: © 1966'76'91 Mattel Inc./ Malaysia

Model #: 11305 Name: Gold & Silver Set Silver Starlight Box Date: 1993 Hair Color: black Hairstyle: hair pulled to top of head forming large loose bun held in place with silver ornament Face: lavender eyes, brown brows, deep pink lips & blush Clothing: scoop neck long sleeve silver lamé gown trimmed with silver flowers at neckline, long sterling silver drop earrings, "B" bracelet, pantyhose, wide silver pumps Extras: 2-piece black stand Booklet: COA & story Head: superstar porcelain Arms: bent Body: porcelain serial # on back Body Markings: © 1966'76'91 Mattel Inc./ Malaysia

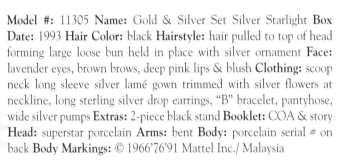

Model #: 1553 Name: Presidential Series Crystal Rhapsody Box Date: 1992 Hair Color: blonde Hairstyle: pulled top of head in large upsweep held with black headband Face: blue eyes, brown brows, red lips & blush Clothing: white satin rhinestone bodice gown with slim black velvet skirt & white satin shirred backdrop behind bodice & skirt, stud earrings, wide black flocked pumps with rhinestone on top center Extras: 2-piece black stand Booklet: COA & story Head: superstar porcelain Arms: straight Body: porcelain with serial # Body Markings: © 1966'76'91 Mattel Inc./ Malaysia Notes: brunette version Disney show exclusive

Model #: 10950 **Name:** Presidential Series Royal Splendor **Box Date:** 1993 **Hair Color:** blonde **Hairstyle:** waist length **Face:** lavender-blue eyes, brown brows, red lips & blush **Clothing:** purple silk peplum jacket heavily embroidered & matching slim skirt with partial overskirt of same fabric, matching hat, iridescent large bead earrings, wide purple pumps **Extras:** 2 black piece stand **Booklet:** COA & story **Head:** superstar porcelain **Arms:** straight **Body:** porcelain with serial # painted on back **Body Markings:** © 1966'76'91 Mattel Inc./ Malaysia

Model #: 12953 **Name:** Wedding Flower Collection Star Lily Bride **Box Date:** 1994 **Hair Color:** blonde **Hairstyle:** pulled back shoulder length, ends curled under **Face:** blue eyes, reddish-brown brows, coral lips & blush **Clothing:** white tulle veil with iridescent edging & flower trim, long ivory brocade gown with long sleeves, high neck, with iridescent rhinestone trim, white panties & pantyhose, large glittery lily bouquet, pearl stud earrings & wide white pumps **Extras:** 2-piece white stand **Booklet:** COA & story **Head:** superstar porcelain **Arms:** bent **Body:** porcelain with serial # painted on back **Body Markings:** © 1966'76'91 Mattel Inc./ Malaysia

Stars & Stripes/Military Series

Model #: 3966 **Name:** American Beauties Army Barbie **Box Date:** 1989 **Hair Color:** blonde **Hairstyle:** chin-length curly bob parted in middle **Face:** blue eyes, dark blonde brows, deep pink lips & blush **Clothing:** navy blue short jacket with matching long skirt & short skirt, white blouse, blue hat, pearl stud earrings & ring, wide black pumps **Extras:** white oval brush **Head:** superstar **Head Markings:** inside or outside rim © Mattel Inc 1976 +/- country **Arms:** bent **Body:** tan tnt **Body Markings:** © Mattel Inc 1966/ China **Notes:** 2nd & final doll in American Beauties series, customarily grouped with Stars & Stripes

Model #: 3360 **Name:** Stars & Stripes Air Force Barbie **Box Date:** 1990 **Hair Color:** blonde **Hairstyle:** chin-length bob **Face:** turquoise eyes, blonde brows, pink lips & blush **Clothing:** brown vinyl bomber jacket, blue scarf, olive green flight suit, pearl stud earrings & ring, navy hat, black hiking boots **Extras:** pearl oval brush **Booklet:** BWOF 1988 **Head:** superstar **Head Markings:** inside or outside rim © Mattel Inc 1976 +/- country **Arms:** bent **Body:** tan tnt **Body Markings:** © Mattel Inc 1966/ China

Model #: 11552 **Name:** Stars & Stripes AF Thunderbirds Barbie **Box Date:** 1993 **Hair Color:** blonde **Hairstyle:** chin-length bob **Face:** blue eyes, blonde brows, light red lips & blush **Clothing:** red long sleeve flight suit with appliqué insignias, white sewn in scarf, navy flight bag, black sunglasses, pearl ring, blue Air Force hat, black hiking boots **Extras:** red oval brush & blue plastic Thunderbirds insignia **Head:** superstar **Head Markings:** inside or outside rim © Mattel Inc 1976 +/- country **Arms:** bent **Body:** tan tnt **Body Markings:** © Mattel Inc 1966/ Malaysia **Black Version:** model #: 11553 **Hair Color:** black **Face:** brown eyes, black brows, red lips & blush **Head:** Christie **Head Markings:** © Mattel Inc./ 1987 **Body:** dark brown tnt **Notes:** also Barbie & Ken 2 doll gift set in white & black versions

Model #: 11554 **Name:** Stars & Stripes AF Thunderbirds Ken **Box Date:** 1993 **Hair Color:** painted blonde **Face:** blue eyes, blonde brows, peach lips **Clothing:** navy blue long sleeve flight suit with insignias & white scarf sewn in at throat, navy flight bag, navy Air Force hat, black sunglasses, black socks & loafers **Extras:** blue plastic Thunderbirds insignia **Head:** 1991 military Ken **Head Markings:** © 1991 Mattel Inc **Arms:** bent **Body:** dark tan tnt **Body Markings:** © Mattel Inc.1968/ Malaysia **Black Version:** model #: 11555 **Hair Color:** painted black **Face:** brown eyes, black brows, dark mauve lips **Head:** 1987 black Ken **Head Markings:** © Mattel Inc 1987 **Body:** dark brown tnt **Notes:** also Barbie & Ken 2 doll gift set in white & black versions

Model #: 7549 **Name:** Stars & Stripes Marine Barbie **Box Date:** 1991 **Hair Color:** blonde **Hairstyle:** chin-length bob **Face:** turquoise eyes, light brown brows, light red lips & blush **Clothing:** white sleeveless blouse with red collar accent, navy uniform jacket with gold buttons & matching knee-length skirt, gold stud earrings & ring, white hat with black brim, white gloves, wide black pumps **Extras:** 2-piece white stand & pearl oval brush & sheet of cardboard punch outs **Head:** superstar **Head Markings:** inside or outside rim © Mattel Inc 1976 +/- country **Arms:** bent **Body:** tan tnt **Body Markings:** © Mattel Inc 1966/ Malaysia **Black Version:** model #: 7594 **Hair Color:** black **Face:** brown eyes, black brows, red lips & blush **Head:** Christie **Head Markings:** © Mattel Inc./ 1987 **Body:** dark brown tnt **Notes:** also Barbie & Ken 2 doll gift set in white & black versions

Model #: 7574 **Name:** Stars & Stripes Marine Ken **Box Date:** 1991 **Hair Color:** painted blonde **Face:** turquoise eyes, blonde brows, mauve lips **Clothing:** navy military coat with white belt & matching blue pants with red piping up sides, white gloves, white military hat with black brim, black loafers **Extras:** sheet of cardboard punch outs **Head:** 1991 military Ken **Head Markings:** © 1991 Mattel Inc **Arms:** bent **Body:** dark tan tnt **Body Markings:** © Mattel Inc.1968/ Malaysia **Black Version:** model #: 5352 **Hair Color:** painted brunette **Face:** brown eyes, black brows, dark mauve lips **Head:** 1987 black Ken **Head Markings:** © Mattel Inc 1987 **Body:** dark brown tnt **Notes:** also Barbie & Ken 2 doll gift set in white & black versions

Model #: 9693 **Name:** Stars & Stripes Navy Barbie **Box Date:** 1990 **Hair Color:** blonde **Hairstyle:** chin-length curly bob **Face:** turquoise eyes, blonde brows, deep pink lips & blush **Clothing:** white middy long sleeve top with black tie, matching knee-length skirt & bell bottom pants, gold stud earrings & ring, black & white sailor hat, black pointed flats, wide black pumps **Extras:** white oval brush, map & sheet of cardboard punch outs **Head:** superstar **Head Markings:** inside or outside rim © Mattel Inc 1976 +/- country **Arms:** bent **Body:** tan tnt **Body Markings:** © Mattel Inc 1966/ China **Black Version:** model #: 9694 **Hair Color:** black **Face:** brown eyes, black brows, red lips & blush **Head:** Christie **Head Markings:** © Mattel Inc./ 1987 **Body:** dark brown tnt

Model #: 1234 **Name:** Stars & Stripes Rendezvous with Destiny Barbie **Box Date:** 1992 **Hair Color:** blonde **Hairstyle:** chin-length bob **Face:** blue eyes, blonde brows, red lips & blush **Clothing:** burgundy beret, tan camouflage quilted vest, long sleeve shirt & pants, pearl ring, green field medical cases, tan hiking boots **Extras:** white oval brush & sheet of cardboard punch outs **Head:** superstar **Head Markings:** inside or outside rim © Mattel Inc 1976 +/- country **Arms:** bent **Body:** tan tnt **Body Markings:** © Mattel Inc 1966/ Malaysia **Black Version:** model #: 5618 **Hair Color:** black **Face:** brown eyes, black brows, red lips & blush **Head:** Christie **Head Markings:** © Mattel Inc./ 1987 **Body:** dark brown tnt **Notes:** also Barbie & Ken 2 doll gift set in white & black versions

Model #: 1237 **Name:** Stars & Stripes Rendezvous with Destiny Ken **Box Date:** 1992 **Hair Color:** painted brown **Face:** turquoise eyes, light brown brows, mauve lips **Clothing:** tan camouflage quilted vest, long sleeve shirt & pants, wine colored beret, green field bag, black binoculars, quilted helmet, tan ankle high boots **Extras:** sheet of cardboard punch outs **Head:** 1991 military Ken **Head Markings:** © 1991 Mattel Inc **Arms:** bent **Body:** dark tan tnt **Body Markings:** © Mattel Inc.1968/ Malaysia **Black Version:** model #: 5619 **Hair Color:** painted black **Face:** brown eyes, black brows, dark mauve lips **Head:** 1987 black Ken **Head Markings:** © Mattel Inc 1987 **Body:** dark brown tnt **Notes:** also Barbie & Ken 2 doll gift set in black & white versions

Winter Princess Series

Model #: 12123 **Name:** Winter Princess Collection Evergreen Princess **Box Date:** 1994 **Hair Color:** blonde **Hairstyle:** waist length, ends curled, rest pulled back with braid headband of hair & gold ribbon **Face:** green eyes, brown brows, red lips & light blush **Clothing:** green gown, velvet long sleeve bodice, gathered fabric at shoulders, 3 filigree gold buttons down front, full skirt of green satin & gold ribbon, black tulle petticoat & black panties, matching gold choker, drop earrings & ring, wide dark green pumps & green velvet purse with gold handle **Extras:** 2-piece white pearl stand & dark green oval brush **Booklet:** COA **Head:** superstar **Head Markings:** inside or outside rim © Mattel Inc 1976 +/- country **Arms:** bent **Body:** tan tnt **Body Markings:** © Mattel Inc 1966/ China **Notes:** 2nd in series, red hair version Disney show exclusive

Model #: 13598 **Name:** Winter Princess Collection Peppermint Princess **Box Date:** 1994 **Hair Color:** blonde **Hairstyle:** mid-back length, ends curled under, pulled back with faux fur headband decorated with gold beads & red ribbon ornament **Face:** lavender eyes, blonde brows, red lips & blush **Clothing:** sleeveless scoop neck gown with red velvet bodice & matching drape with faux fur trim tassels on full overskirt of white & red satin stripes, white faux fur neckline, long white satin handless gloves, red velvet pouch purse, gold detail at waist, red panties, gold filigree & red jewel drop earrings, gold ring, wide red pumps **Extras:** 2-piece white stand & oval brush **Head:** superstar **Head Markings:** inside or outside rim © Mattel Inc 1976 +/- country **Arms:** bent **Body:** tan tnt **Body Markings:** © Mattel Inc.1966/ Indonesia **Notes:** 3rd in series

211

Model #: 10655 **Name:** Winter Princess Collection Winter Princess **Box Date:** 1993 **Hair Color:** blonde **Hairstyle:** faux white fur headband with 3 blue roses, rest waist length, ends curled **Face:** blue eyes, light brown brows, fuchsia lips & blush **Clothing:** blue velvet long sleeve gown with silver brocade insert in skirt, faux fur trim at neck, bodice & cuffs, muff with 3 blue roses, pearl & gold earrings, necklace, ring, net underskirt, wide blue pumps **Extras:** 2-piece white stand & white oval brush **Booklet:** COA **Head:** superstar **Head Markings:** inside or outside rim © Mattel Inc 1976 +/- country **Arms:** bent **Body:** tan tnt **Body Markings:** © Mattel Inc 1966/ China **Notes:** 1st in series

Model #: 5854 Name: Ames Country Looks Box Date: 1992 Hair Color: blonde Hairstyle: sides & front pulled back with bandanna, rest waist length, ends curled under Face: blue eyes, blonde brows, red lips & blush Clothing: white crop top with sleeveless red bandanna shirt tied at waist, black & white gingham shorts, matching ruffle skirt of shirt & shorts fabric, white hoop earrings & ring, red cowboy boots Extras: white oval brush Head: superstar Head Markings: inside or outside rim © Mattel Inc 1976 +/- country Arms: bent Body: tan tnt Body Markings: © Mattel Inc 1966/ China

Model #: 2452 Name: Ames Denim 'n Lace Box Date: 1992 Hair Color: blonde Hairstyle: sides partially braided rest waist length, ends curled under, partial bangs Face: blue eyes, light brown brows, hot pink lips & blush Clothing: short sleeve multicolor floral blouse & matching bag, denim jacket & mini skirt trimmed in white lace, white straw hat with light blue ribbon & floral trim, pearl stud earrings & ring, white footless tights & tennis shoes Extras: hot pink oval brush Head: superstar Head Markings: inside or outside rim © Mattel Inc 1976 +/- country Arms: bent Body: tan tnt Body Markings: © Mattel Inc 1966/ Malaysia

Model #: 5756 Name: Ames Hot Looks Box Date: 1991 Hair Color: blonde Hairstyle: sides & front pulled back, curly bangs, rest waist length Face: blue eyes, dark blonde brows, purple lips & blush Clothing: hot pink floral sleeveless mini dress, matching jacket with sheer blue sleeves, sheer blue overskirt, blue stretch pants trimmed in lace, blue belt & headband, pink hoop earrings & ring, wide blue pumps Extras: hot pink oval brush Head: superstar Head Markings: inside or outside rim © Mattel Inc 1976 +/- country Arms: bent Body: tan tnt Body Markings: © Mattel Inc 1966/ Malaysia

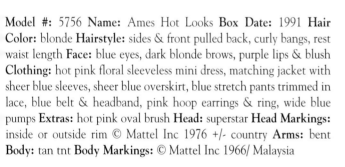

Model #: 2909 Name: Ames Party in Pink Box Date: 1991 Hair Color: blonde Hairstyle: front & sides pulled back with silver fabric hair ornament, bangs Face: green eyes, dark blonde brows, fuchsia lips & blush Clothing: pink mini dress with black boat neck, black tulle sheer long sleeves, black tulle & silver ruffle tiered mini skirt, black knee-high stretch pants trimmed in lace, black belt, pink hoop earrings & ring, wide black pumps Extras: hot pink oval brush Head: superstar Head Markings: inside or outside rim © Mattel Inc 1976 +/- country Arms: bent Body: tan tnt Body Markings: © Mattel Inc 1966/ Malaysia

Model #: 3406 **Name:** Applause Holiday **Box Date:** 1991 **Hair Color:** blonde **Hairstyle:** sides pulled up with white tulle & pink fabric tie, bangs, mid-back length, ends curled under **Face:** blue eyes, blonde brows, pink lips & blush **Clothing:** long sleeve scoop neck silver lamé gown trimmed with pink accents, white tulle overskirt, wide pink pearl wide pumps **Extras:** 2-piece pink pearl stand & oval brush **Head:** superstar **Head Markings:** inside or outside rim © Mattel Inc 1976 +/- country **Arms:** bent **Body:** tan tnt **Body Markings:** © Mattel Inc 1966/ China

Model #: 5313 **Name:** Applause Style **Box Date:** 1990 **Hair Color:** blonde **Hairstyle:** pulled up to top of head, very curly ponytail with hot pink bow **Face:** blue-green eyes, blonde brows, hot pink lips & blush **Clothing:** sleeveless gown with white satin top, full white satin multicolor "B" print fabric, sewn in white tulle slip, large hot pink sash & bow at waist, matching bolero jacket, pink bow earrings & ring, white panties, wide hot pink bow shoes **Extras:** 2-piece pearl stand & hot pink oval brush **Head:** superstar **Head Markings:** inside or outside rim © Mattel Inc 1976 +/- country **Arms:** bent **Body:** tan tnt **Body Markings:** © Mattel Inc 1966/ China

Model #: 14452 **Name:** Bloomingdale's Donna Karan **Box Date:** 1995 **Hair Color:** brunette **Hairstyle:** mid-back length **Face:** brown eyes, brown brows, red lips & blush **Clothing:** black turtleneck long sleeve leotard, matching tights, black wrap mini skirt, wide black belt with gold buckle, gold stud earrings, gold beaded necklace & ring, black beret with gold accent, gold vinyl bag, red fringed shawl, Bloomie's Big Brown Bag, wide black pumps **Extras:** 2-piece black stand & red oval brush **Head:** superstar **Head Markings:** inside or outside rim © Mattel Inc 1976 +/- country **Arms:** 1 bent & 1 Shani **Body:** tan tnt **Body Markings:** © Mattel Inc 1966/ China **Blonde Version:** model #: 14545 **Hair Color:** blonde **Face:** green eyes, light brown brows, red lips & blush **Notes:** beret may cause dent in head if left touching forehead

Model #: 12152 Name: Bloomingdale's Savvy Shopper Box Date: 1994 Hair Color: blonde Hairstyle: pulled back with black ribbon, mid-back length, ends curled under Face: blue eyes, blonde brows, red lips & blush Clothing: sleeveless black velvet mini dress, Nicole Miller Barbie print black silk swing coat, black velvet purse, gold sunglasses, white Bloomingdale's shopping bag, gold dangle earrings, black & gold bead choker, gold ring, wide black pumps Extras: 2-piece black stand & hot pink oval brush Head: superstar Head Markings: inside or outside rim © Mattel Inc 1976 +/- country Arms: bent Body: tan tnt Body Markings: © Mattel Inc 1966/ Malaysia

Model #: 10247 Name: Disney Fun Box Date: 1992 Hair Color: blonde Hairstyle: mid-back length, ends curled Face: turquoise eyes, blonde brows, hot pink lips & blush Clothing: multicolor crop top with ruffle neckline, matching knee-high stretch shorts with attached chartreuse ruffle skirt, black & white Mickey print, multi hot pink, black, orange, chartreuse splotch print, matching tote bag, hot pink hoop earrings & ring, black Mickey Mouse ears hat & matching hot pink balloon, hot pink tennis shoes Extras: hot pink oval brush Head: superstar Head Markings: inside or outside rim © Mattel Inc 1976 +/- country Arms: bent Body: tan tnt Body Markings: © Mattel Inc 1966/ China

Model #: 11650 Name: Disney Fun Box Date: 1994 Hair Color: blonde Hairstyle: mid-thigh length with curly bangs Face: blue eyes, blonde brows, hot pink lips & blush Clothing: white sleeveless scoop neck mini dress with black, orange & pink print, hot pink vinyl short jacket with gold lamé accents, hot pink hoop earrings & ring, black Mickey Mouse ears hat, matching purse & yellow balloon, hot pink tennis shoes Extras: orange oval brush Head: superstar Head Markings: inside or outside rim © Mattel Inc 1976 +/- country Arms: bent Body: tan tnt, white panties Body Markings: © Mattel Inc 1966/ Malaysia

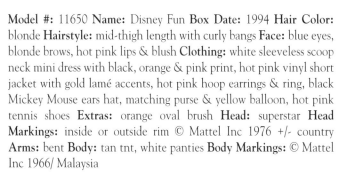

Model #: 11587 Name: Stacie Mickey's Toontown Box Date: 1993 Hair Color: blonde Hairstyle: thigh length with bangs Face: blue eyes, blonde brows, deep pink lips & blush Clothing: white T-shirt with Toontown appliqué, black, white, turquoise, yellow & red checked suspender shorts with yellow & red accents, matching baseball hat & jacket, red stud earrings, yellow Mickey balloon, white anklets, black flower flats with fabric bows Extras: red oval brush Head: 1991 Stacie Head Markings: © Mattel Inc./ 1991 Body: tan b/l Body Markings: Malaysia

Model #: 11481 Name: Club Doll Beach Fun Box Date: 1993 Hair Color: B=blonde K=painted blonde Hairstyle: B=sides & front pulled back, bangs, rest waist length, ends curled under Face: B=aqua eyes, blonde brows, hot pink lips & blush K=turquoise eyes, light brown brows, peach lips Clothing: B=green 1-piece swimsuit with multi-color ruffle on bottom & matching mini skirt, hot pink stud earrings, yellow-green sunglasses K=multicolor white, pink, yellow-green, purple & black tank top with purple trunks & visor Extras: hot pink oval brush Head: B=superstar K=modified Alan Head Markings: B=inside or outside rim © Mattel Inc 1976 +/- country K=© 1991 Mattel Inc Arms: both=ptr Body: B=dark tan tnt K=dark tan b/l Body Markings: B=© Mattel Inc 1966/ Malaysia K=© Mattel Inc 1968/ Malaysia

Model #: 12371 Name: Club Doll Denim'N Ruffles Gift Set Box Date: 1994 Hair Color: blonde Hairstyle: crinkled to top of thigh with bangs Face: blue-gray eyes, light brown brows, deep pink lips & blush Clothing: denim, hot pink, gold trim sleeveless crop top with gold cuffs, mini skirt of hot pink & denim with flower appliqué, gold star earrings & ring, hot pink cowboy hat & boots Extras: hot pink oval brush & High Stepper horse Head: superstar Head Markings: inside or outside rim © Mattel Inc 1976 +/- country Arms: bent Body: tan tnt, white panties Body Markings: © Mattel Inc 1966/ China Notes: includes regular issue High Stepper horse

Model #: 3196 Name: Club Doll Fantastica Box Date: 1992 Hair Color: black Hairstyle: thigh length, pulled back with headband of red fabric flowers Face: brown eyes, brown brows, red lips & blush Clothing: white peasant top & matching long full skirt trimmed in lace with green, red & white ribbon trim, white lace petticoat, white scarf with red edging, red choker, gold filigree earrings & ring, wide white pumps Extras: red oval brush Head: Teresa Head Markings: © 1990, Mattel/ Inc Arms: bent Body: dark tan tnt Body Markings: © Mattel Inc 1966/ Malaysia

Model #: 10339 Name: Club Doll Festiva Box Date: 1993 Hair Color: black Hairstyle: thigh length, ends curled under Face: brown eyes, black brows, red lips & blush Clothing: dress with white peasant top, full red skirt with black sewn in belt, red lace at hem, multi-color rick rack & ribbon decorations, turquoise hoop earrings & ring, choker, white straw hat with turquoise fabric flowers & red ribbon trim tied with green fabric scarf, wide white pumps Extras: turquoise oval brush Head: Teresa Head Markings: © 1990, Mattel/ Inc Arms: bent Body: dark tan tnt Body Markings: © Mattel Inc 1966/ Malaysia

216

Model #: 10379 **Name:** Club Doll Island Fun Gift Set **Box Date:** 1993 **Hair Color:** B=2 shades of blonde K=painted 2-tone blonde **Hairstyle:** B=thigh length, curly bangs, ends curled under **Face:** B=aqua eyes, blonde brows, hot pink lips & blush K=teal eyes, blonde brows, mauve lips **Clothing:** B=turquoise multicolor 1-piece swimsuit, hot pink wrap mini skirt & matching lei K=light green crop tank top, turquoise multicolor swim trunks, orange pendant **Extras:** hot pink oval brush **Head:** B=superstar K=modified Alan **Head Markings:** B=inside or outside rim ©Mattel Inc 1976 +/- country K=© 1991 Mattel Inc **Arms:** both=ptr **Body:** B=dark tan tnt K=dark tan b/l **Body Markings:** B=© Mattel Inc 1966/ Malaysia K=© Mattel Inc 1968/ Malaysia

Model #: 2366 **Name:** Club Doll Jewel Jubilee **Box Date:** 1991 **Hair Color:** blonde **Hairstyle:** 1 side & top pulled back with gold bow, bangs, waist length, ends curled under **Face:** turquoise eyes, light brown brows, light red lips & blush **Clothing:** white satin gown with white tulle & gold glitter dot overskirt, matching stole, large metallic gold bow at hip & matching fabric at neckline with red marquise jewel, gold stud earrings & ring, wide white pumps **Extras:** white oval brush **Booklet:** Hawaiian Fun 1991 **Head:** superstar **Head Markings:** inside or outside rim © Mattel Inc 1976 +/- country **Arms:** bent **Body:** tan tnt **Body Markings:** © Mattel Inc 1966/ Malaysia

Model #: 13744 **Name:** Club Doll Me and My Mustang **Box Date:** 1994 **Hair Color:** blonde **Hairstyle:** thigh length **Face:** turquoise eyes, blonde brows, red lips & blush **Clothing:** red & white striped cropped T-shirt with sewn on red vest, blue mini skirt, red & white hat, blue sunglasses, hoop earrings, watch, ring, red hat box style purse, red cowboy boots **Extras:** red oval brush & sheet of cardboard punch outs **Head:** superstar **Head Markings:** inside or outside rim © Mattel Inc 1976 +/- country **Arms:** bent **Body:** tan tnt, B panties **Body Markings:** © Mattel Inc 1966/ China **Notes:** also packaged with regular issue Mustang car

Model #: 9025 **Name:** Club Doll Party Sensation **Box Date:** 1990 **Hair Color:** blonde **Hairstyle:** thigh length, sides & front pulled back, tied with hot pink ribbon & fabric flower, ends curled under **Face:** blue eyes, blonde brows, pink lips & blush **Clothing:** hot pink & red gown with multi-tiered pink & red skirt, separate long sleeves, hot pink metallic stud earrings, pendant & ring, wide red pumps **Extras:** red oval brush **Head:** superstar **Head Markings:** inside or outside rim © Mattel Inc 1976 +/- country **Arms:** bent **Body:** tan tnt **Body Markings:** © Mattel Inc 1966/ Malaysia

Model #: 7009 **Name:** Club Doll Peach Blossom **Box Date:** 1992 **Hair Color:** blonde **Hairstyle:** sides & front pulled back, tied with peach & gold glitter tulle & matching flower **Face:** turquoise eyes, blonde brows, peach lips & blush **Clothing:** short sleeve scoop neck peach gown with peach & gold tulle overlay, pearl stud earrings, choker & ring, wide peach pumps **Extras:** white pearl oval brush **Head:** superstar **Head Markings:** inside or outside rim © Mattel Inc 1976 +/- country **Arms:** bent **Body:** tan tnt **Body Markings:** © Mattel Inc 1966/ China

Model #: 1858 **Name:** Club Doll Royal Romance **Box Date:** 1992 **Hair Color:** blonde **Hairstyle:** waist length, 1 side & front pulled back with blue & silver lace fabric & ribbon hair ornament **Face:** blue eyes, light brown brows, pink lips & blush **Clothing:** metallic royal blue slim gown with silver lace & blue fabric overskirt, split in center accented with silver fabric roses & metallic sashes, long metallic blue handless gloves, silver stud earrings, choker & ring, wide royal blue pumps **Extras:** royal blue oval brush **Head:** superstar **Head Markings:** inside or outside rim © Mattel Inc 1976 +/- country **Arms:** bent **Body:** tan tnt **Body Markings:** © Mattel Inc 1966/ Malaysia

Model #: 12384 **Name:** Club Doll Season's Greetings **Box Date:** 1994 **Hair Color:** blonde **Hairstyle:** waist length, ends curled under **Face:** green eyes, taupe brows, red lips & blush **Clothing:** red velvet jacket with green & red cuffs & collar, gold jewel closure, long full red & green velvet brocade skirt & matching hat with green holly & gold jewel trim, gold stud earrings & ring, wide red pumps **Extras:** green oval brush **Head:** superstar **Head Markings:** inside or outside rim © Mattel Inc 1976 +/- country **Arms:** bent **Body:** tan tnt **Body Markings:** © Mattel Inc 1966/ China

Model #: 10929 **Name:** Club Doll Secret Hearts Barbie Gift Set **Box Date:** 1993 **Hair Color:** B=blonde K=blonde painted **Hairstyle:** waist length, 1 side & front pulled back, ends curled under **Face:** B=blue eyes, brown brows, frosted deep pink lips & blush K=blue eyes, blonde brows, mauve lips **Clothing:** B=sleeveless iridescent white mini dress with light pink heart trim, white glitter tulle long skirt, pink heart drop earrings & pendant, silver ring, white wide pumps K=white nylon bodysuit with iridescent collar & tie, matching suit coat, pink flower, white socks & oxfords **Extras:** pearl oval brush, iridescent heart shaped bag & pink tray for ice cube & water **Booklet:** instructions **Head:** superstar & modified Alan **Head Markings:** B=inside or outside rim © Mattel Inc 1976 +/- country K=© 1991 Mattel Inc **Arms:** both bent **Body:** both tan tnt **Body Markings:** B=© Mattel Inc/1966 China K=© Mattel Inc/ 1968 China **Notes:** different Ken from regular issue Secret Hearts doll. Modified Alan head mold, blonde painted hair, & different outfit

Model #: 1859 Name: Club Doll Very Violet Box Date: 1992 Hair Color: blonde Hairstyle: waist length, pulled back with purple & silver fabric ornament, ends curled under Face: blue eyes, light brown brows, deep pink lips & blush Clothing: purple gown with lilac glitter tulle overskirt, purple purse, lilac metallic earrings, ring & pendant, wide purple pumps Extras: purple oval brush Head: superstar Head Markings: inside or outside rim © Mattel Inc 1976 +/- country Arms: bent Body: tan tnt Body Markings: © Mattel Inc 1966/ Malaysia

Model #: 10924 Name: Club Doll Wedding Fantasy Gift Set Box Date: 1993 Hair Color: B=blonde K=painted light brown Hairstyle: B=thigh length crinkled, sides pulled back Face: B=blue eyes, dark blonde brows, deep pink lips & blush K=brown eyes, brown brows, deep mauve lips Clothing: B=tulle veil, white gown with pink fabric roses on bodice & bouquet with pink ribbon streamers, white panties, pearl stud earrings, necklace, silver ring, wide white pumps K=1-piece bodysuit with pink shirt, white collar, silver ascot, gray pinstripe pants, light gray vest, gray tuxedo tails, pink flower in lapel, black socks, black loafers Extras: white oval brush Head: B=superstar K=Secret Hearts Head Markings: B= inside or outside rim © Mattel Inc 1976 +/-country K=© 1991 Mattel Inc. Arms: both=bent Body: B=tan tnt K=tan tnt Body Markings: B=© Mattel Inc 1966/ China K=Mattel Inc 1968/ China

Model #: 10658 Name: Club Doll Winter Royale Box Date: 1993 Hair Color: blonde Hairstyle: waist length, ends curled under Face: lavender eyes, light brown brows, red lips & blush Clothing: long sleeve scoop neck purple & lilac flocked gown with white faux fur trim at cuffs & neckline, gold braid belt with faux fur poms & matching hat, wide purple pumps Extras: white oval brush Head: superstar Head Markings: inside or outside rim © Mattel Inc 1976 +/- country Arms: bent Body: tan tnt Body Markings: © Mattel Inc 1966/ Malaysia

Model #: 13613 Name: Club Doll Winters Eve Box Date: 1994 Hair Color: blonde Hairstyle: pulled to top of head, ends curled under to form bun with 2 loose tendrils over ears, plaid ribbon & silver ornament trim Face: green eyes, blonde brows, red lips & blush Clothing: green satin long sleeve bodice with faux fur collar & cuffs, silver lacing, red, green, gold & black plaid full long skirt, silver dangle earrings & ring, wide red pumps Extras: green oval brush Head: superstar Head Markings: inside or outside rim © Mattel Inc 1976 +/- country Arms: bent Body: tan tnt Body Markings: © Mattel Inc 1966/ China

Model #: 11182 **Name:** Grocery B Mine **Box Date:** 1993 **Hair Color:** blonde **Hairstyle:** sides & front pulled back with pink band, bangs, crinkle to top of thigh **Face:** blue eyes, dark blonde brows, red lips & blush **Clothing:** red satin mini dress with white & pink hearts, sheer pink sleeves & neckline, red heart drop earrings, ring, wide red pumps **Extras:** hot pink oval brush & 3 valentines **Head:** superstar **Head Markings:** inside or outside rim © Mattel Inc 1976 +/- country **Arms:** bent **Body:** tan tnt, white panties **Body Markings:** © Mattel Inc 1966/ Malaysia

Model #: 10217 **Name:** Grocery Back to School **Box Date:** 1994 **Hair Color:** blonde **Hairstyle:** sides & front pulled back with red satin ribbon, rest mid-back length, ends curled under **Face:** turquoise eyes, dark blonde brows, orange-red lips & blush **Clothing:** red, white & blue v-neck pullover "B" top, red plaid mini skirt with sewn in panties, red stud earrings & ring, white tennis shoes **Extras:** red oval brush **Head:** superstar **Head Markings:** inside or outside rim © Mattel Inc 1976 +/- country **Arms:** bent **Body:** tan tnt **Body Markings:** © Mattel Inc 1966/ Malaysia

Model #: 13966 **Name:** Grocery Caroling Fun **Box Date:** 1995 **Hair Color:** blonde **Hairstyle:** thigh length with bangs **Face:** green eyes, brown brows, red lips & blush **Clothing:** white, green & red print long sleeve sweatshirt, green knit pants, white mittens on ribbons, white ear muffs on ribbon, pearl stud earrings & ring, red hiking boots **Extras:** red oval brush & cardboard punch outs **Head:** superstar **Head Markings:** inside or outside rim © Mattel Inc 1976 +/- country **Arms:** bent **Body:** tan tnt **Body Markings:** © Mattel Inc.1966/ Indonesia

Model #: 11276 **Name:** Grocery Easter Fun **Box Date:** 1993 **Hair Color:** blonde **Hairstyle:** sides & front pulled back with hot pink ribbon, bangs, rest waist length, ends turned under **Face:** turquoise eyes, dark blonde brows, hot pink lips & blush **Clothing:** mutli color Easter egg print mini dress with full skirt & sewn in panties, scoop neck, short sleeves, pink disk earrings, ring, wide hot pink pumps **Extras:** hot pink oval brush, egg decorating stickers & sheet of cardboard punch outs **Head:** superstar **Head Markings:** inside or outside rim © Mattel Inc 1976 +/- country **Arms:** bent **Body:** tan tnt **Body Markings:** © Mattel Inc 1966/ Malaysia

Model #: 12793 Name: Grocery Easter Party Box Date: 1994 Hair Color: blonde Hairstyle: pulled back with pink band, partial bangs, rest mid-back length, ends curled under Face: blue eyes, blonde brows, pink lips & blush Clothing: pink Easter print mini dress with yellow collar & pink satin bow at neck, pink disk earrings & ring, wide hot pink pumps Extras: hot pink oval brush, Easter egg stickers, dye & sheet of cardboard punch outs Head: superstar Head Markings: inside or outside rim © Mattel Inc 1976 +/- country Arms: bent Body: tan tnt, pink panties Body Markings: © Mattel Inc 1966/ Malaysia

Model #: 12192 Name: Grocery Holiday Dreams Box Date: 1994 Hair Color: blonde Hairstyle: waist length with ends curled under Face: green eyes, light brown brows, red lips & blush Clothing: long sleeve short nightshirt of red Christmas print fabric with white collar and green satin ribbon, red & white Santa hat, white stud earrings & ring, blue gift, red felt scuffs Extras: green oval brush Head: superstar Head Markings: inside or outside rim © Mattel Inc 1976 +/- country Arms: bent Body: tan tnt Body Markings: © Mattel Inc.1966/ Indonesia

Model #: 10280 Name: Grocery Holiday Hostess Box Date: 1992 Hair Color: blonde Hairstyle: mid-back length, bangs, green ribbon headband Face: green eyes, brown brows, red lips & blush Clothing: red and white velour scoop neck long sleeve dress, wide black belt with brass buckle, green ribbon trim, gold stud earrings & ring, wide black pumps Extras: white oval brush Head: superstar Head Markings: inside or outside rim © Mattel Inc 1976 +/- country Arms: bent Body: tan tnt Body Markings: © Mattel Inc 1966/ Malaysia

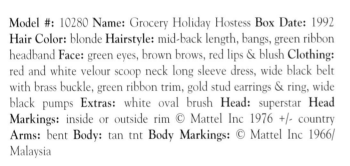

Model #: 2001 Name: Grocery Party Premiere Box Date: 1992 Hair Color: blonde Hairstyle: mid-back length, ends curled under with bangs Face: blue eyes, blonde brows, wine colored lips & blush Clothing: gold lamé, wine & gold glitter scoop neck, short sleeve mini dress with sewn in panties, bow at neckline, wine stud earrings, wide wine pumps Extras: wine oval brush Head: superstar Head Markings: inside or outside rim © Mattel Inc 1976 +/- country Arms: ptr Body: tan tnt Body Markings: © Mattel Inc 1966/ Malaysia

Model #: 2901 Name: Grocery Pretty Hearts Box Date: 1991 Hair Color: blonde Hairstyle: pulled back with red ribbon, bangs, rest waist length Face: blue eyes, light brown brows, red lips & blush Clothing: 2-piece knee-length dress, red heart shaped bodice with white puffed sleeves & red flocked hearts, matching white skirt with red hearts & sewn in panties, wide red pumps Extras: white oval brush Head: superstar Head Markings: inside or outside rim © Mattel Inc 1976 +/- country Arms: ptr Body: tan tnt Body Markings: © Mattel Inc 1966/ China

Model #: 3161 Name: Grocery Red Romance Box Date: 1992 Hair Color: blonde Hairstyle: sides & front pulled back in small ponytail, loose curls to mid-back Face: blue eyes, brown brows, red lips & blush Clothing: pink mini dress with white sheer sleeves & overskirt, red heart trim at waist, wide pink bow pumps Extras: pink oval brush Head: superstar Head Markings: inside or outside rim © Mattel Inc 1976 +/- country Arms: ptr Body: tan tnt Body Markings: © Mattel Inc 1966/ Malaysia

Model #: 13741 Name: Grocery Schooltime Fun Box Date: 1994 Hair Color: blonde Hairstyle: mid-back-length ponytail tied with red ribbon, ends curled under, bangs Face: blue eyes, blonde brows, red lips & blush Clothing: white long sleeve scoop neck T-shirt with multicolor alpha print mini jumper with red satin bow, red & yellow backpack, red star earrings & ring, red tennis shoes Extras: yellow oval brush & sheet of cardboard punch outs Head: superstar Head Markings: inside or outside rim © Mattel Inc 1976 +/- country Arms: bent Body: tan tnt Body Markings: © Mattel Inc 1966/ Malaysia

Model #: 3477 Name: Grocery Spring Bouquet Box Date: 1992 Hair Color: blonde Hairstyle: sides & front pulled back with pink fabric tie, rest curly waist length, bangs Face: blue eyes, blonde brows, dark pink lips & blush Clothing: long sleeve scoop neck multicolor pastel dress with sheer pink sleeves, bodice & waist insert, sewn in panties, pink stud earrings, pink pearl wide pumps Extras: pink pearl oval brush Head: superstar Head Markings: inside or outside rim © Mattel Inc 1976 +/- country Arms: ptr Body: tan tnt Body Markings: © Mattel Inc 1966/ Malaysia

Model #: 3208 Name: Grocery Sweet Spring Box Date: 1991 Hair Color: blonde Hairstyle: sides & front pulled back with band, rest curly mid-back length, bangs Face: blue eyes, brown brows, pink lips & blush Clothing: multicolor slim mini dress of pink, yellow, white, blue & wine with hot pink net ruffles on skirt & matching fabric bow at neck, yellow straw hat with fabric flowers, matching bag with flowers, hot pink stud earrings, wide fuchsia pumps Extras: fuchsia oval brush Head: superstar Head Markings: inside or outside rim © Mattel Inc 1976 +/- country Arms: ptr Body: tan tnt Body Markings: © Mattel Inc 1966/ Malaysia

Model #: 2783 Name: Grocery Trail Blazin' Box Date: 1991 Hair Color: blonde Hairstyle: sides & front pulled back with red bandanna, rest mid-back length, ends curled under Face: blue eyes, dark blonde brows, orange lips & blush Clothing: white long sleeve top with bandanna cuffs, red denim fringe vest, red bandanna & denim tiered mini skirt with sewn in panties, red cowboy boots Extras: white oval brush Head: superstar Head Markings: inside or outside rim © Mattel Inc 1976 +/- country Arms: ptr Body: tan tnt Body Markings: © Mattel Inc 1966/ Malaysia

Model #: 12675 Name: Grocery Valentine Box Date: 1994 Hair Color: blonde Hairstyle: sides & front pulled back with red ribbon, bangs, rest thigh length Face: lavender-blue eyes, blonde brows, red lips & blush Clothing: white scoop neck short sleeve full skirt mini dress with valentine print fabric & red satin trim, pearl stud earrings, red ring, white choker with red heart, wide red pumps Extras: red oval brush & cardboard punch outs Head: superstar Head Markings: inside or outside rim © Mattel Inc 1976 +/- country Arms: bent Body: tan tnt, white panties Body Markings: © Mattel Inc 1966/ Malaysia

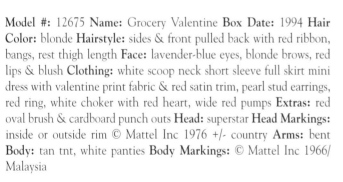

Model #: 14106 Name: Hallmark Holiday Memories Box Date: 1995 Hair Color: blonde Hairstyle: mid-back length, sides pulled to back of head, ends curled under Face: green eyes, blonde brows, red lips & blush Clothing: white long sleeve flocked white satin coat with red buttons, brown faux fur collar & cuffs, red satin slim long underskirt, white & red satin hat with holly trim, red stud earrings & ring, brown knee-high lace-up boots Extras: 2-piece gold stand & 2 Barbie size Christmas cards Head: superstar Head Markings: inside or outside rim © Mattel Inc 1976 +/- country Arms: Shani Body: pink tnt, B panties Body Markings: © Mattel Inc.1966/ Indonesia

Model #: 12579 **Name:** Hallmark Victorian Elegance **Box Date:** 1994 **Hair Color:** brunette **Hairstyle:** pulled to center back of head, ends turned under into large bun, burgundy & faux fur ruffled headband **Face:** lavender eyes, light brown brows, red lips & blush **Clothing:** Victorian style long sleeve burgundy skating costume with light brown faux fur collar, cuffs, muff, gold stud earrings & ring, black ice skates **Extras:** 2-piece pearl stand & 2 Barbie size Christmas cards **Head:** superstar **Head Markings:** inside or outside rim © Mattel Inc 1976 +/- country **Arms:** bent **Body:** tan tnt **Body Markings:** © Mattel Inc 1966/ China

Model #: 1879 **Name:** Hills Blue Elegance **Box Date:** 1992 **Hair Color:** blonde **Hairstyle:** sides pulled up into small ponytail, rest waist length with ends curled **Face:** blue eyes, light brown brows, deep pink lips & blush **Clothing:** metallic blue gown with full tulle skirt & matching stole, long blue handless gloves, silver stud earrings, choker, ring, wide blue pumps **Extras:** blue oval brush **Head:** superstar **Head Markings:** inside or outside rim © Mattel Inc 1976 +/- country **Arms:** bent **Body:** tan tnt **Body Markings:** © Mattel Inc 1966/ Malaysia

Model #: 3274 **Name:** Hills Evening Sparkle **Box Date:** 1990 **Hair Color:** blonde **Hairstyle:** sides & front pulled up to small ponytail, rest mid-back length with ends curled **Face:** blue eyes, blonde brows, pink lips & blush **Clothing:** iridescent strapless mini dress with turquoise & iridescent multi level overskirt, turquoise ruffled stole, silver stud earrings & ring, wide light blue pumps **Extras:** lavender oval brush **Head:** superstar **Head Markings:** inside or outside rim © Mattel Inc 1976 +/- country **Arms:** bent **Body:** tan tnt **Body Markings:** © Mattel Inc 1966/ Malaysia

Model #: 3549 **Name:** Hills Moonlight Rose **Box Date:** 1991 **Hair Color:** blonde **Hairstyle:** waist-length ponytail, ends curled with bangs **Face:** blue eyes, brown brows, deep pink lips & blush **Clothing:** silver lamé mini dress with full pink long skirt & matching stole, silver stud earrings & ring, wide fuchsia pumps **Extras:** white oval brush **Head:** superstar **Head Markings:** inside or outside rim © Mattel Inc 1976 +/- country **Arms:** bent **Body:** tan tnt **Body Markings:** © Mattel Inc 1966/ Malaysia

Model #: 4843 Name: Hills Party Lace Box Date: 1989 Hair Color: blonde Hairstyle: mid-back length, ends curled Face: blue eyes, light brown brows, pink lips & blush Clothing: lilac off-the-shoulder mini dress with lavender & silver lace trim, matching small purse, silver stud earrings & ring, wide lilac pumps Extras: lilac oval brush Head: superstar Head Markings: inside or outside rim © Mattel Inc 1976 +/- country Arms: bent Body: tan tnt Body Markings: © Mattel Inc 1966/ China

Model #: 12412 Name: Hills Polly Pocket Box Date: 1994 Hair Color: blonde Hairstyle: sides pulled up in small ponytail tied with pink ribbon, rest crinkled thigh length, bangs Face: blue eyes, light brown brows, pink lips Clothing: multicolor mini jumper dress of pink, yellow, green & purple with white long sleeves sewn in top, hot pink dangle earrings & ring, 2 Polly pocket dolls, wide hot pink pumps Extras: hot pink oval brush Head: superstar Head Markings: inside or outside rim © Mattel Inc 1976 +/- country Arms: bent Body: tan tnt, white panties Body Markings: © Mattel Inc.1966/ Indonesia

Model #: 13940 Name: Hills Sea Pearl Mermaid Box Date: 1995 Hair Color: blonde Hairstyle: sides pulled up into ponytail tied with sheer pink fabric, rest crinkled thigh length Face: blue eyes, brown brows, deep pink lips & blush Clothing: blue iridescent bra with pearl accents, matching fishtail with sheer pink fabric accents, pearl drop earrings & ring Extras: pink pearl oval brush Head: superstar Head Markings: inside or outside rim © Mattel Inc 1976 +/- country Arms: Shani Body: tan tnt Body Markings: © Mattel Inc.1966/ Indonesia

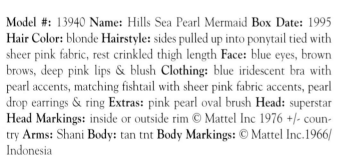

Model #: 1865 Name: Home Shopping Club Evening Flame Box Date: 1991 Hair Color: blonde Hairstyle: sides pulled up, ponytail tied with gold ribbon, waist length wavy Face: blue eyes, light brown brows, wine color lips & blush Clothing: long red nylon gown with gold dots on skirt, panties, sheer bodice & long sleeves, red tulle with gold dots shawl, gold stud earrings, ring, gold bead choker, wide red pumps, gold foil wrist tag Extras: 2-piece black stand & red oval brush Booklet: COA Head: superstar Head Markings: inside or outside rim © Mattel Inc 1976 +/- country Arms: bent Body: tan tnt Body Markings: © Mattel Inc 1966/ China

Model #: 13912 **Name:** International Travel Barbie **Box Date:** 1994 **Hair Color:** blonde **Hairstyle:** below shoulder length **Face:** lavender eyes, light brown brows, deep pink lips & blush **Clothing:** hot pink satin mini dress with white travel print short coat, ticket, passport, "B" blue garment bag, 2 pink suitcases, silver hoop earrings & ring, black sunglasses, wide deep pink pumps **Extras:** pink oval brush **Head:** superstar **Head Markings:** inside or outside rim © Mattel Inc 1976 +/- country **Arms:** bent **Body:** tan tnt **Body Markings:** © Mattel Inc 1966/ China **Notes:** sold in duty free shops, also available in small narrow box sold on board several airlines

Model #: 2702 **Name:** JC Penney Enchanted Evening **Box Date:** 1991 **Hair Color:** blonde **Hairstyle:** mid-back length, curled under **Face:** blue eyes, blonde brows, hot pink lips & blush **Clothing:** sleeveless v-neck metallic lilac slim gown with pleated accents, black, gold, green & lilac metallic full-length coat with white faux fur trim, matching hat with marquise jewel, lilac metallic stud earrings, choker, ring, purple metallic Brazil pumps **Extras:** lilac oval brush **Head:** superstar **Head Markings:** inside or outside rim © Mattel Inc 1976 +/- country **Arms:** bent **Body:** tan tnt **Body Markings:** © Mattel Inc 1966/ Malaysia

Model #: 7057 **Name:** JC Penney Evening Elegance **Box Date:** 1990 **Hair Color:** blonde **Hairstyle:** pulled back to waist-length ponytail **Face:** light blue eyes, blonde brows, pink lips & blush **Clothing:** gown with pink bodice, silver lamé insert to hip, white tulle with silver glitter dot tiered skirt, pink underskirt, pink & white tulle long sleeve short jacket with silver bow accents, silver stud earrings & ring, wide pink pumps **Extras:** pink oval brush **Booklet:** BWOF 1988 **Head:** superstar **Head Markings:** inside or outside rim © Mattel Inc 1976 +/- country **Arms:** bent **Body:** tan tnt **Body Markings:** © Mattel Inc 1966/ China

Model #: 1278 **Name:** JC Penney Evening Sensation **Box Date:** 1992 **Hair Color:** blonde **Hairstyle:** mid-back-length ponytail held with blue iridescent ornament & pear shape diamond jewel, ends curled under **Face:** aqua eyes, blonde brows, red lips & blush **Clothing:** spaghetti strap royal blue crushed velvet slim gown with iridescent blue bow at neckline, metallic blue, purple, green & gold striped cape, blue & gold drop earrings, pendant, ring, metallic blue Brazil pumps **Extras:** purple oval brush **Head:** superstar **Head Markings:** inside or outside rim © Mattel Inc 1976 +/- country **Arms:** bent **Body:** tan tnt **Body Markings:** © Mattel Inc 1966/ China

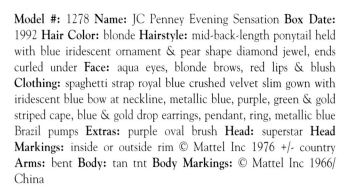

Model #: 10684 **Name:** JC Penney Golden Winter **Box Date:** 1993 **Hair Color:** blonde **Hairstyle:** sides & front pulled back with black faux fur & gold bow ornament, rest waist length, ends turned under **Face:** blue eyes, blonde brows, red lips & blush **Clothing:** black satin spaghetti strap full skirt gown with red, blue & gold paisley print, gold lamé jacket with long sleeves, black faux fur collar & cuffs, gold drop earrings, choker, ring, gold Brazil or wide black pumps **Extras:** red oval brush **Head:** superstar **Head Markings:** inside or outside rim © Mattel Inc 1976 +/- country **Arms:** bent **Body:** tan tnt **Body Markings:** © Mattel Inc 1966/ China

Model #: 12191 **Name:** JC Penney Night Dazzle **Box Date:** 1994 **Hair Color:** blonde **Hairstyle:** sides & top pulled back with large red taffeta bow, rest waist length, ends curled under **Face:** blue eyes, blonde brows, red lips & blush **Clothing:** long sleeve gown with red bodice, black & white flocked overskirt with red taffeta underskirt and matching large bow at hip, black & silver drop earrings, choker & ring, wide black pumps **Extras:** black oval brush **Head:** superstar **Head Markings:** inside or outside rim © Mattel Inc 1976 +/- country **Arms:** bent **Body:** tan tnt **Body Markings:** © Mattel Inc 1966/ China **Notes:** brunette version Festival exclusive

Model #: 14010 **Name:** JC Penney Royal Enchantment **Box Date:** 1995 **Hair Color:** blonde **Hairstyle:** sides & front pulled back with green ribbon, gold & green rose trim, rest waist length, ends turned under **Face:** green eyes, brown brows, red lips & blush **Clothing:** metallic green long sleeve gown with ivory satin & gold glitter underskirt, 3 gold bows on bodice, green & gold drop earrings, gold choker & ring, wide gold pumps **Extras:** gold oval brush **Head:** superstar **Head Markings:** inside or outside rim © Mattel Inc 1976 +/- country **Arms:** bent **Body:** tan tnt **Body Markings:** © Mattel Inc 1966/ Malaysia

Model #: 4870 **Name:** K-Mart Peach Pretty Barbie **Box Date:** 1989 **Hair Color:** blonde **Hairstyle:** front & 1 side pulled up with silver band & peach fabric, bangs, rest thigh length wavy **Face:** light blue eyes, brown brows, deep peach lips & blush **Clothing:** peach gown with iridescent bodice & silver bolero jacket, silver glitter dots on skirt, silver stud earrings & ring, wide aqua pumps **Extras:** 2-piece clear stand & aqua oval brush **Head:** superstar **Head Markings:** inside or outside rim © Mattel Inc 1976 +/- country **Arms:** bent **Body:** tan tnt **Body Markings:** © Mattel Inc 1966/ China

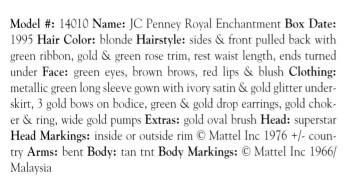

Model #: 3117 **Name:** K-Mart Pretty in Purple **Box Date:** 1992 **Hair Color:** blonde **Hairstyle:** front & 1 side pulled up with purple & white fabric hair ornament, rest waist length curly **Face:** lavender eyes, light brown brows, red frosted lips & blush **Clothing:** purple lamé mini dress with white tulle & glitter dot overskirt, neckline & shoulder detail, lavender stud earrings & ring, wide purple pumps **Extras:** purple oval brush **Head:** superstar **Head Markings:** inside or outside rim © Mattel Inc 1976 +/- country **Arms:** bent **Body:** tan tnt **Body Markings:** © Mattel Inc 1966/ Malaysia **Black Version:** model #: 3121 **Hair Color:** black **Face:** brown eyes, black brows, red frosted lips **Head:** Christie **Head Markings:** © Mattel Inc./ 1987 **Body:** dark tan tnt

Model #: 1511 **Name:** McGlynn's Bakery **Box Date:** 1991 **Hair Color:** blonde **Hairstyle:** waist-length ponytail tied with iridescent tulle bow, ends curled under with bangs **Face:** blue eyes, light brown brows, pink lips & blush **Clothing:** pink with pink lace iridescent tutu, pink ballet slippers **Head:** superstar **Head Markings:** inside or outside rim © Mattel Inc 1976 +/- country **Arms:** ptr **Body:** tan tnt **Body Markings:** © Mattel Inc 1966/ China **Notes:** usually attributed to McGlynn's but sold by many bakeries as cake decoration - not intended for sale to the public without a cake, black version model # 1534 with Christie head mold

Model #: 10051 **Name:** Meijers Shopping Fun **Box Date:** 1992 **Hair Color:** blonde **Hairstyle:** front & sides pulled back with hot pink band, rest waist length **Face:** blue eyes, blonde brows, hot pink lips & blush **Clothing:** white cotton mini dress with pink, purple, yellow, green & orange check design, pink polka dot bolero jacket, shopping bag, hot pink hoop earrings, ring, wide hot pink pumps **Extras:** hot pink oval brush **Booklet:** coupon book **Head:** superstar **Head Markings:** inside or outside rim © Mattel Inc 1976 +/- country **Arms:** bent **Body:** tan tnt **Body Markings:** © Mattel Inc 1966/ China

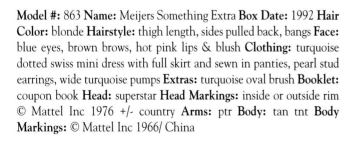

Model #: 863 **Name:** Meijers Something Extra **Box Date:** 1992 **Hair Color:** blonde **Hairstyle:** thigh length, sides pulled back, bangs **Face:** blue eyes, brown brows, hot pink lips & blush **Clothing:** turquoise dotted swiss mini dress with full skirt and sewn in panties, pearl stud earrings, wide turquoise pumps **Extras:** turquoise oval brush **Booklet:** coupon book **Head:** superstar **Head Markings:** inside or outside rim © Mattel Inc 1976 +/- country **Arms:** ptr **Body:** tan tnt **Body Markings:** © Mattel Inc 1966/ China

Model #: 4983 Name: Mervyn's Ballerina Barbie Box Date: 1983 Hair Color: blonde Hairstyle: middle part, sides pulled back to nape of neck, rest in ponytail curled under in bun with silver crown on top of head Face: turquoise eyes, blonde brows, peach lips & blush Clothing: white spaghetti strap tutu, red plastic rose with green leaves, white ballet slippers Extras: 2-piece white stand Head: superstar Head Markings: inside or outside rim © Mattel Inc 1976 +/- country Arms: ballerina Body: tan tnt Body Markings: © Mattel Inc 1966/ Taiwan Notes: many foreign versions of this doll exist

Model #: 7093 Name: Mervyn's Fabulous Fur Box Date: 1983 Hair Color: blonde Hairstyle: side part, mid-back-length ponytail at nape of neck, ends curled under Face: blue eyes, brown brows, pink lips & blush Clothing: metallic blue short sleeve 1-piece pantsuit, iridescent wide belt, white faux fur full-length coat, rhinestone stud earrings & ring, narrow blue pumps Extras: pointed white comb & brush Booklet: instructions Head: superstar Head Markings: inside or outside rim © Mattel Inc 1976 +/- country Arms: bent Body: tan tnt Body Markings: © Mattel Inc 1966/ Taiwan Notes: many foreign versions of this doll exist

Model #: 10997 Name: Naf Naf Barbie Box Date: 1993 Hair Color: blonde Hairstyle: waist length with bangs Face: blue eyes, blonde brows, red lips & blush Clothing: hot pink pattern long sleeve jacket with Naf insignia, orange nylon T-shirt, denim mini skirt, yellow nylon stretch pants, Naf Naf yellow & red baseball hat, extra lavender Naf Naf tank top, large multicolor nylon suitcase, blue disk earrings & ring, lavender tennis shoes, hot pink tennis shoes Extras: hot pink oval brush & sheet of stickers Booklet: passport to the WOF 1993 Head: superstar Head Markings: inside or outside rim © Mattel Inc 1976 +/- country Arms: bent Body: tan tnt Body Markings: © Mattel Inc 1966/ China Notes: foreign issue available in some specialty stores

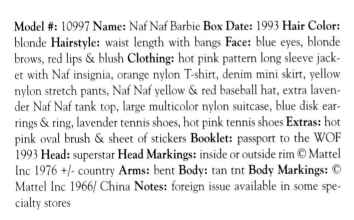

Model #: 3808 Name: Osco Picnic Pretty Box Date: 1992 Hair Color: blonde Hairstyle: mid-back length, ends curled Face: blue eyes, light brown brows, pink lips & blush Clothing: pink halter bodysuit with yellow ribbon at center neck, yellow & pink gingham full mini skirt with matching bag, white straw hat with pink flowers, pearl stud earrings & ring, wide pink pumps Extras: white oval brush Head: superstar Head Markings: inside or outside rim © Mattel Inc 1976 +/- country Arms: bent Body: tan tnt Body Markings: © Mattel Inc 1966/ Malaysia

Model #: 2998 Name: Sears 100th Celebration Box Date: 1986 Hair Color: blonde Hairstyle: side part, waist-length ponytail banded at nape of neck, ends curled Face: blue eyes, light brown brows, hot pink lips Clothing: silver lamé spaghetti strap bodysuit with pink tulle & silver glitter ruffled stole & matching long skirt, pink mules Extras: 2-piece hot pink stand & pointed brush Booklet: BWOF 1986 Head: superstar Head Markings: inside or outside rim © Mattel Inc 1976 +/- country Arms: bent Body: tan tnt Body Markings: © Mattel Inc 1966/ Malaysia

Model #: 3817 Name: Sears Blossom Beautiful Box Date: 1992 Hair Color: blonde Hairstyle: mid-back length, ends curled under with 1 small section caught in band with white flower & green ribbon trim Face: green eyes, light brown brows, light orange lips & blush Clothing: sleeveless long mint green gown with overlay of white tulle & gold glitter dots, white satin leaf-shaped accents, gold ring, pearl & gold drop earrings, gold bead necklace, mint green pearl shoes Extras: 2-piece white pearl stand & pink oval brush Head: superstar Head Markings: inside or outside rim © Mattel Inc 1976 +/- country Arms: bent Body: tan tnt Body Markings: © Mattel Inc 1966/ China

Model #: 2306 Name: Sears Dream Princess Box Date: 1992 Hair Color: blonde Hairstyle: curly bangs, rest waist length with ends curled under, iridescent fabric tiara Face: aqua eyes, light brown brows, pink lips & blush Clothing: aqua lace puff sleeve scoop neck short dress, matching long skirt with self fabric ruffle, fabric bow at waist, pearl stud earrings, ring & necklace, wide aqua pearl pumps Extras: aqua pearl oval brush & sheet of cardboard punch outs Head: superstar Head Markings: inside or outside rim © Mattel Inc 1976 +/- country Arms: bent Body: tan tnt Body Markings: © Mattel Inc 1966/ China

Model #: 3596 Name: Sears Evening Enchantment Box Date: 1989 Hair Color: blonde Hairstyle: pulled back into very curly ponytail, tied with blue satin ribbon & iridescent flower & pearl trim Face: blue eyes, brown brows, hot pink lips & blush Clothing: white long sleeve scoop neck iridescent blouse with blue ruffled neckline, long light blue skirt with white iridescent ruffle accent & underskirt, pearl stud earrings & ring, wide white pumps Extras: white oval brush Head: superstar Head Markings: inside or outside rim © Mattel Inc 1976 +/- country Arms: bent Body: tan tnt Body Markings: © Mattel Inc 1966/ China

Model #: 9049 **Name:** Sears Lavender Surprise **Box Date:** 1989 **Hair Color:** blonde **Hairstyle:** tied back with lilac fabric flower into waist-length ponytail at nape of neck, ends curled **Face:** aqua-blue eyes, light brown brows, hot pink lips & blush **Clothing:** lavender spaghetti strap mini sheath dress with ruffle at neckline & fabric flower, matching puff skirt with elastic ruffle hem, silver stud earrings & ring, wide lilac pumps **Extras:** lilac oval brush **Booklet:** BWOF 1988 **Head:** superstar **Head Markings:** inside or outside rim © Mattel Inc 1976 +/- country **Arms:** bent **Body:** tan tnt **Body Markings:** © Mattel Inc 1966/ China **Black Version:** model #: 5588 **Hair Color:** brunette **Face:** light brown eyes, black brows, hot pink lips & blush **Head:** Christie **Head Markings:** © Mattel Inc./ 1987 **Body:** dark brown tnt

Model #: 7669 **Name:** Sears Lilac and Lovely **Box Date:** 1987 **Hair Color:** blonde **Hairstyle:** sides & front pulled back into mid-back-length ponytail, curly bangs, ends curled under **Face:** lavender eyes, light brown brows, pale pink lips & blush **Clothing:** lilac satin spaghetti strap drop waist gown with full lace skirt, tulle boa, matching long handless gloves, rhinestone stud earrings & ring, wide lilac pumps **Extras:** lilac oval brush **Booklet:** BWOF 1988 **Head:** superstar **Head Markings:** inside or outside rim © Mattel Inc 1976 +/- country **Arms:** bent **Body:** tan tnt **Body Markings:** © Mattel Inc 1966/ China

Model #: 13911 **Name:** Sears Ribbons & Roses **Box Date:** 1994 **Hair Color:** blonde **Hairstyle:** sides & front pulled back with gold ribbon, rest waist length, ends curled under **Face:** lavender-green eyes, brown brows, red lips & blush **Clothing:** square neck white gown with gold striped bodice & metallic skirt with outline of red & purple flowers & green leaves, large gold ribbon bow at waist, gold drop earrings, choker & ring, wide pearl pumps **Extras:** pearl oval brush **Head:** superstar **Head Markings:** inside or outside rim © Mattel Inc 1976 +/- country **Arms:** bent **Body:** tan tnt **Body Markings:** © Mattel Inc 1966/ Malaysia

Model #: 12410 **Name:** Sears Silver Sweetheart **Box Date:** 1994 **Hair Color:** blonde **Hairstyle:** front & 1 side pulled into ponytail with silver lamé bow, rest waist length, ends curled under, curly bangs **Face:** blue eyes, blonde brows, deep pink lips & blush **Clothing:** light blue spaghetti strap drop waist gown, white tulle & silver glitter dot overskirt, silver lamé accent at neckline with large blue marquise jewel, matching large bow at hip, silver stud earrings & ring, wide blue pumps **Extras:** blue oval brush **Head:** superstar **Head Markings:** inside or outside rim © Mattel Inc 1976 +/- country **Arms:** bent **Body:** tan tnt **Body Markings:** © Mattel Inc 1966/ Malaysia

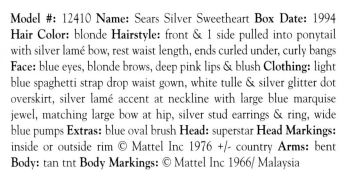

Model #: 2586 **Name:** Sears Southern Belle **Box Date:** 1991 **Hair Color:** blonde **Hairstyle:** 1 side pulled into ponytail, rest waist length, ends curled under **Face:** blue-lavender eyes, light brown brows, hot pink lips & blush **Clothing:** peach color tiered gown with purple set in waist & parasol, converts to short dress, white straw hat with peach ribbon ties, lilac stud earrings & ring, wide lilac bow pumps **Extras:** lilac oval brush **Head:** superstar **Head Markings:** inside or outside rim © Mattel Inc 1976 +/- country **Arms:** bent **Body:** tan tnt **Body Markings:** © Mattel Inc 1966/ China

Model #: 4550 **Name:** Sears Star Dream **Box Date:** 1987 **Hair Color:** blonde **Hairstyle:** side part, rest pulled into below shoulder-length ponytail, ends curled, iridescent fabric tiara with turquoise marquise stone **Face:** blue eyes, light brown brows, deep pink frosted lips & blush **Clothing:** white long sleeve skating outfit with matching long skirt, blue underskirt, rhinestone stud earrings & ring, 3 hot pink plastic roses & green leaves, shimmering pantyhose, wide white pumps **Extras:** pink oval brush & sheet of cardboard punch outs **Booklet:** BWOF 1987 **Head:** superstar **Head Markings:** inside or outside rim © Mattel Inc 1976 +/- country **Arms:** bent **Body:** tan tnt **Body Markings:** © Mattel Inc 1966/ China

Model #: 1132 **Name:** Sears Walking Jamie **Box Date:** 1969 **Hair Color:** blonde brunette titian **Hairstyle:** side part, shoulder-length flip tied with pink scarf, cello on head **Face:** brown eyes, rooted lashes, brown brows, deep pink lips & blush **Clothing:** yellow/green tunic mini dress with small orange elastic belt, yellow nylon shorts, orange mid-calf boots **Extras:** clear X stand **Booklet:** LB 1969 **Head:** tnt **Head Markings:** inside rim © 1966 Mattel Inc & country **Arms:** walking **Body:** tan b/l, walking mechanism **Body Markings:** © 1967 Mattel, Inc./ U.S. Patented/ Patd. Canada 1967/ other Pats. Pend./ Japan **Notes:** press panel on back & head turns, limbs swing, doll also available in 2 Sears gift sets: Strollin in Style & Furry Friends

Model #: 1364 **Name:** Service Merchandise Blue Rhapsody **Box Date:** 1991 **Hair Color:** blonde **Hairstyle:** waist length, ends curled under, bangs **Face:** blue eyes, light brown brows, fuchsia lips & blush **Clothing:** long gown with gold bodice & tiered royal blue nylon with gold glitter skirt, matching blue and gold hat, gold stud earrings, pendant & ring, wide royal blue pumps **Extras:** hot pink oval brush **Head:** superstar **Head Markings:** inside or outside rim © Mattel Inc 1976 +/- country **Arms:** bent **Body:** tan tnt **Body Markings:** © Mattel Inc 1966/ China

Model #: 12005 Name: Service Merchandise City Sophisticate Box Date: 1994 Hair Color: blonde Hairstyle: waist length, ends curled under Face: blue-green eyes, blonde brows, light red lips & blush Clothing: floor-length gold lamé & black satin long sleeve coat dress with matching belt, pirate style black satin hat with gold sequin trim, gold stud earrings, choker & ring, wide black pumps Extras: black oval brush Head: superstar Head Markings: inside or outside rim © Mattel Inc 1976 +/- country Arms: bent Body: tan tnt Body Markings: © Mattel Inc 1966/ China

Model #: 13612 Name: Service Merchandise Ruby Romance Box Date: 1995 Hair Color: blonde Hairstyle: sides pulled up to top of head, waist length, ends curled under, black satin & red tulle hair bow Face: blue eyes, light brown brows, red lips & blush Clothing: red satin & nylon gown with black glitter dots & edging at overskirt, black satin bow at waist, long black satin handless gloves, silver drop earrings, choker & ring, wide black pumps Extras: black oval brush Head: superstar Head Markings: inside or outside rim © Mattel Inc 1976 +/- country Arms: bent Body: tan tnt Body Markings: © Mattel Inc 1966/ China

Model #: 1886 Name: Service Merchandise Satin Nights Box Date: 1992 Hair Color: blonde Hairstyle: sides & front pulled back into waist-length ponytail, ends curled under Face: blue eyes, light brown brows, red lips & blush Clothing: long gown with white satin drop waist top, black satin skirt, large white bow accent at side, long tulle handless gloves, matching black hat with tulle trim, white pearl drop earrings & ring, wide black pumps Extras: white oval brush Head: superstar Head Markings: inside or outside rim © Mattel Inc 1976 +/- country Arms: bent Body: tan tnt Body Markings: © Mattel Inc 1966/ China

Model #: 10994 Name: Service Merchandise Sparkling Splendor Box Date: 1993 Hair Color: blonde Hairstyle: thigh length Face: blue eyes, light brown brows, frosted red lips & blush Clothing: long red satin gown with white piping trim, sheer sleeves and neckline with white cuffs, large silver glitter red tulle overskirt, red satin and silver glitter hat, silver stud earrings & ring, wide red pumps Extras: white oval brush Head: superstar Head Markings: inside or outside rim © Mattel Inc 1976 +/- country Arms: bent Body: tan tnt Body Markings: © Mattel Inc 1966/ Malaysia

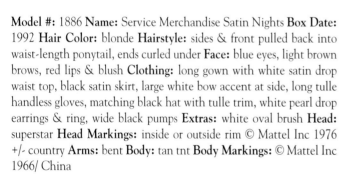

Model #: 3142 Name: Shopko/Venture Blossom Beauty Box Date: 1991 Hair Color: blonde Hairstyle: sides pulled up away from face tied with purple floral fabric trim, waist length, ends curled Face: blue eyes, light brown brows, pink lips & blush Clothing: gown with fuchsia below elbow puffed sleeves, rose dropped waist bodice, full multicolor floral skirt of white, pink, rose, purple, green, black & yellow, self fabric flower trim at hip, metallic rose stud earrings, ring & necklace, wide purple pumps Extras: purple oval brush Head: superstar Head Markings: inside or outside rim © Mattel Inc 1976 +/- country Arms: bent Body: tan tnt Body Markings: © Mattel Inc 1966/ Malaysia

Model #: 1876 Name: Shopko/Venture Party Perfect Box Date: 1992 Hair Color: blonde Hairstyle: sides pulled up, held with pink ribbon with white & silver tulle trim, waist length, ends curled Face: blue eyes, brown brows, pink lips & blush Clothing: fitted pink metallic long gown with multicolor print of pink, blue, green with white & silver tulle, pink fabric accents at shoulder & hip, pink fabric train to ankle, wide pink pearl shoes Extras: pink pearl oval brush Head: superstar Head Markings: inside or outside rim © Mattel Inc 1976 +/- country Arms: bent Body: tan tnt Body Markings: © Mattel Inc 1966/ Malaysia

Model #: 0 Name: Singapore Girl I Box Date: 1991 Hair Color: brunette Hairstyle: layered short cut Face: brown eyes, black brows, mauve lips Clothing: brown, navy, white & rust color cotton print blouse & sarong, white panties, navy double strap wedgies Extras: 2-piece clear stand & white oval brush Head: Oriental Head Markings: © Mattel Inc 1980 Arms: ptr Body: dark tan tnt Body Markings: © Mattel Inc 1966/ Malaysia Note: for sale by Singapore Airlines

Model #: 0 Name: Singapore Girl II Box Date: 1991 Hair Color: brunette Hairstyle: layered short cut Face: brown eyes, black brows, red lips Clothing: brown, navy, rust & white print blouse & sarong, white panties, navy double strapped wedgies Extras: 2-piece clear stand & white oval brush Head: Oriental Head Markings: © Mattel Inc 1980 Arms: ptr Body: dark tan tnt Body Markings: © Mattel Inc 1966/ Malaysia Note: for sale by Singapore Airlines

Model #: 4116 **Name:** Spiegel Regal Reflections **Box Date:** 1992 **Hair Color:** blonde **Hairstyle:** black fan shaped blue jeweled hair accessory clasped in partial ponytail at center back of head with rest of hair below shoulder length, ends curled **Face:** blue eyes, light brown brows, red lips & light blush **Clothing:** gold, blue & black full skirted gown trimmed in lace with black bodice & long sleeves, black tulle petticoat, black nylon panties, royal blue wide pumps, gold stud earrings & ring **Extras:** black 2-piece stand & pink oval brush **Head:** superstar **Head Markings:** inside or outside rim © Mattel Inc 1976 +/- country **Arms:** bent **Body:** tan tnt **Body Markings:** © Mattel Inc 1966/ Malaysia

Model #: 10969 **Name:** Spiegel Royal Invitation **Box Date:** 1993 **Hair Color:** blonde **Hairstyle:** waist length, ends curled **Face:** blue eyes, brown brows, fuchsia lips & blush **Clothing:** black & fuchsia dotted tulle in diamond pattern with gold ruffle trim full skirt, fuchsia bodice with black tulle long sleeves & overlay, fuchsia hat, earrings, ring & wide pumps **Extras:** 2-piece black stand & fuchsia oval brush **Head:** superstar **Head Markings:** inside or outside rim © Mattel Inc 1976 +/- country **Arms:** bent **Body:** tan tnt **Body Markings:** © Mattel Inc 1966/ Malaysia

Model #: 14009 **Name:** Spiegel Shopping Chic **Box Date:** 1995 **Hair Color:** blonde **Hairstyle:** waist length **Face:** brown eyes, light brown brows, frosted coral lips & blush **Clothing:** gold lamé mini dress, black satin short coat trimmed in faux leopard skin with gold jeweled belt, matching purse & hat, gold drop earrings & ring, black stockings, wide black pumps, black poodle dog with gold chain leash **Extras:** 2-piece black stand, black oval brush, sheet of cardboard punch outs **Head:** superstar **Head Markings:** inside or outside rim © Mattel Inc 1976 +/- country **Arms:** Shani **Body:** tan tnt **Body Markings:** © Mattel Inc 1966/ Malaysia

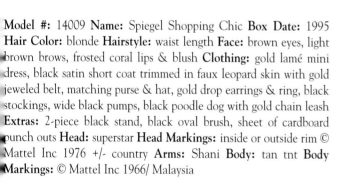

Model #: 3347 **Name:** Spiegel Sterling Wishes **Box Date:** 1991 **Hair Color:** blonde **Hairstyle:** mid-back length, ends curled, small section of front pulled into ponytail with tulle trim **Face:** blue eyes, light brown brows, red lips & blush **Clothing:** metallic silver & black off-the-shoulder gown with white & silver glitter tulle trim & slip, silver stud earrings, choker & ring, wide black pumps **Extras:** 2-piece black stand & black oval brush **Head:** superstar **Head Markings:** inside or outside rim © Mattel Inc 1976 +/- country **Arms:** bent **Body:** tan tnt **Body Markings:** © Mattel Inc 1966/ China

Model #: 12077 **Name:** Spiegel Theater Elegance **Box Date:** 1994 **Hair Color:** blonde **Hairstyle:** upsweep with dangling curls & bangs **Face:** blue eyes, light brown brows, deep pink lips & blush **Clothing:** black velvet fitted gown with flared skirt at knee, crystal beaded appliqué & hot pink satin flower, hot pink satin wrap, crystal drop bead earrings, choker, silver ring, wide black pumps, black mask with handle **Extras:** 2-piece white stand & white oval brush **Head:** superstar **Head Markings:** inside or outside rim © Mattel Inc 1976 +/- country **Arms:** bent **Body:** tan tnt **Body Markings:** © Mattel Inc 1966/ China

Model #: 4583 **Name:** Target Baseball Date **Box Date:** 1992 **Hair Color:** blonde **Hairstyle:** shoulder length, ends curled up **Face:** blue eyes, brown brows, red lips & blush **Clothing:** blue & yellow T-shirt with striped vest, red & white striped shorts, blue nylon shorts, red tote bag, red & blue baseball cap, yellow anklets, red stud earrings & ring, white tennis shoes **Extras:** red oval brush **Head:** superstar **Head Markings:** inside or outside rim © Mattel Inc 1976 +/- country **Arms:** bent **Body:** tan tnt **Body Markings:** © Mattel Inc 1966/ China

Model #: 7970 **Name:** Target Bathtime Fun Skipper **Box Date:** 1992 **Hair Color:** blonde **Hairstyle:** sides & front pulled back with hot pink band, rest curly thigh length, curly bangs **Face:** blue eyes, blonde brows, deep pink lips & blush **Clothing:** multicolor swimsuit of yellow, light blue, pink & lilac, blue foam rubber flowers at wrist & matching skirt **Extras:** white oval brush & can of foam soap **Head:** 1987 Skipper **Head Markings:** © Mattel Inc./ 1987 **Arms:** slight bend **Body:** tan tnt **Body Markings:** © Mattel, Inc.1987/ Malaysia

Model #: 2954 **Name:** Target Cute'n Cool **Box Date:** 1991 **Hair Color:** blonde **Hairstyle:** mid-thigh length with multicolored fabric headband **Face:** blue eyes, blonde brows, pink lips & blush **Clothing:** long sleeve turtleneck multicolor tunic top with capri pants & scarf of pink, orange, white, green, yellow & purple, purple crop tank top & short slim skirt, yellow hat box purse, notebook, alarm clock, soda can, portable phone & pencil, purple pointed flats, wide orange pumps **Extras:** hot pink oval brush **Head:** superstar **Head Markings:** inside or outside rim © Mattel Inc 1976 +/- country **Arms:** ptr **Body:** tan tnt **Body Markings:** © Mattel Inc 1966/ Malaysia

Model #: 3203 **Name:** Target Dazzlin' Date **Box Date:** 1992 **Hair Color:** blonde **Hairstyle:** sides & front pulled into ponytail tied with aqua ribbon & black tulle rose, rest thigh length, ends curled under **Face:** aqua eyes, dark blonde brows, hot pink lips & blush **Clothing:** teal satin bodysuit with black tulle & silver glitter neckline, black tulle rose on bodice, short bolero jacket, full mini skirt & black tulle with silver glitter dots petticoat, silver stud earrings & ring, wide black pumps **Extras:** dark turquoise oval brush **Head:** superstar **Head Markings:** inside or outside rim © Mattel Inc 1976 +/- country **Arms:** bent **Body:** tan tnt **Body Markings:** © Mattel Inc 1966/ Malaysia

Model #: 7476 **Name:** Target Gold and Lace **Box Date:** 1989 **Hair Color:** blonde **Hairstyle:** below shoulder-length ponytail, ends curled, curly bangs **Face:** blue eyes, blonde brows, pink lips **Clothing:** gold halter-style bodysuit, white bolero jacket with multicolor glitter & gold trim, gold & white lace mini skirt, silver stud earrings & ring, wide white pumps **Extras:** white oval brush **Head:** superstar **Head Markings:** inside or outside rim © Mattel Inc 1976 +/- country **Arms:** bent **Body:** tan tnt **Body Markings:** © Mattel Inc 1966/ Malaysia

Model #: 2587 **Name:** Target Golden Evening **Box Date:** 1991 **Hair Color:** blonde **Hairstyle:** sides & front pulled up into ponytail, rest mid-back length with ends curled under **Face:** blue eyes, dark blonde brows, red lips & blush **Clothing:** strapless black velvet with gold accents, gold & white lace peplum, black velvet short slim skirt, gold short bolero jacket, gold stud earrings & ring, black velvet & gold purse, wide black pumps **Extras:** gold oval brush **Head:** superstar **Head Markings:** inside or outside rim © Mattel Inc 1976 +/- country **Arms:** bent **Body:** tan tnt **Body Markings:** © Mattel Inc 1966/ Malaysia

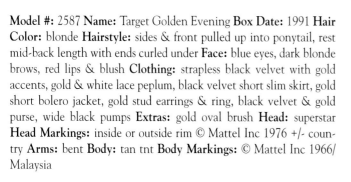

Model #: 10202 **Name:** Target Golf Date **Box Date:** 1992 **Hair Color:** blonde **Hairstyle:** front pulled into small ponytail, curly bangs, rest waist length, ends curled under **Face:** blue-green eyes, brown brows, hot pink lips **Clothing:** white T-shirt with blue, green and black argyle vest, blue shorts, blue stud earring & ring, green visor, yellow golf club, 3 balls, putting cup, white tennis shoes **Extras:** royal blue oval brush **Booklet:** contest **Head:** superstar **Head Markings:** inside or outside rim © Mattel Inc 1976 +/- country **Arms:** bent **Body:** tan tnt **Body Markings:** © Mattel Inc 1966/ Malaysia

Model #: 5955 **Name:** Target Party Pretty **Box Date:** 1990 **Hair Color:** blonde **Hairstyle:** mid-back length, ends curled **Face:** blue eyes, blonde brows, red lips & blush **Clothing:** black sparkle mini dress with black and white trim at hem, cross over straps on bodice, white lace bolero jacket, silver stud earrings & ring, small black shoulder bag, pearl triangle hand bag, wide black pumps **Extras:** pearl oval brush **Head:** superstar **Head Markings:** inside or outside rim © Mattel Inc 1976 +/- country **Arms:** bent **Body:** tan tnt **Body Markings:** © Mattel Inc 1966/ Malaysia

Model #: 5413 **Name:** Target Pretty in Plaid **Box Date:** 1992 **Hair Color:** blonde **Hairstyle:** sides pulled up to small ponytail, curly bangs, rest wavy waist length **Face:** green eyes, light brown brows, wine colored lips **Clothing:** plaid 3/4 sleeve jacket of white, dark green, peach & dark peach with elastic waist, light peach scarf & thigh high stockings, green floral skirt with sewn in peach panties, pearl stud earrings & ring, white straw hat with green, peach & orange trim, wide wine pumps **Extras:** peach oval brush **Head:** superstar **Head Markings:** inside or outside rim © Mattel Inc 1976 +/- country **Arms:** bent **Body:** tan tnt **Body Markings:** © Mattel Inc 1966/ Malaysia

Model #: 14110 **Name:** Target Steppin' Out **Box Date:** 1995 **Hair Color:** blonde **Hairstyle:** front & 1 side pulled into small ponytail, rest waist length, ends curled under **Face:** lavender eyes, blonde brows, deep pink lips & blush **Clothing:** hot pink satin full skirt long sleeve mini dress with black velvet scoop neck collar & sewn in panties, cuffs, belt with silver jewel trim, matching purse, black beret hat, silver & black dangle earrings & ring, wide black pumps **Extras:** hot pink oval brush **Head:** superstar **Head Markings:** inside or outside rim © Mattel Inc 1976 +/- country **Arms:** bent **Body:** tan tnt **Body Markings:** © Mattel Inc 1966/ Malaysia

Model #: 411 **Name:** Target Wild Style **Box Date:** 1992 **Hair Color:** blonde **Hairstyle:** mid-back length **Face:** blue-green eyes, blonde brows, hot pink lips & blush **Clothing:** multicolor pants of black, yellow, hot pink & white, short blue denim skirt, black vinyl jacket with gold buckle, yellow short sleeve T-shirt, gold trim chain around neck, hot pink hoop earrings, hot pink satin jockey cap, black vinyl spats, wide black pumps **Extras:** hot pink oval brush **Head:** superstar **Head Markings:** inside or outside rim © Mattel Inc 1976 +/- country **Arms:** ptr **Body:** tan tnt **Body Markings:** © Mattel Inc 1966/ China

Model #: 4589 Name: Wal-Mart 25th Year Pink Jubilee Box Date: 1987 Hair Color: blonde Hairstyle: side part, mid-back-length ponytail, ends curled Face: blue eyes, brown brows, pink lips & blush Clothing: pink & silver dot mini dress, pink & silver glitter pantyhose, long slim pink skirt split up front side, pink overskirt multi length, faux fur stole, wide silver belt, rhinestone stud earrings & ring, wide pink pumps Extras: pink oval brush & sheet of cardboard punch outs Booklet: BWOF 1987 & instructions Head: superstar Head Markings: inside or outside rim © Mattel Inc 1976 +/- country Arms: bent Body: tan tnt Body Markings: © Mattel Inc 1966/ China

Model #: 2282 Name: Wal-Mart Anniversary Star Box Date: 1992 Hair Color: blonde Hairstyle: sides & front pulled up, secured with pink fabric ornament, rest waist length, ends curled Face: blue eyes, light brown brows, deep pink lips & blush Clothing: pink gown with pink tulle & silver glitter dot overskirt & cap sleeves, elbow length handless silver gloves, silver stud earrings & ring, wide pink pumps Extras: pink oval brush Head: superstar Head Markings: inside or outside rim © Mattel Inc 1976 +/- country Arms: bent Body: tan tnt Body Markings: © Mattel Inc 1966/ Malaysia

Model #: 3678 Name: Wal-Mart Ballroom Beauty Box Date: 1991 Hair Color: blonde Hairstyle: sides & front pulled up into small iridescent lilac hair ornament, rest wavy waist length, ends curled Face: blue eyes, light brown brows, pink lips & blush Clothing: iridescent bodice & long slim skirt with lilac tulle layered overskirt & stole, metallic lilac stud earrings, choker & ring, wide lilac pumps Extras: lilac oval brush Head: superstar Head Markings: inside or outside rim © Mattel Inc 1976 +/- country Arms: bent Body: tan tnt Body Markings: © Mattel Inc 1966/ Malaysia

Model #: 13614 Name: Wal-Mart Country Bride Box Date: 1994 Hair Color: blonde Hairstyle: pulled back with pink gingham & white tulle veil, waist length, ends curled under Face: blue-lavender eyes, light brown brows, pink lips & blush Clothing: white dotted swiss wedding gown with short puffed sleeves & pink trim, small daisy bouquet, white pearl stud earrings & ring, wide white pumps Extras: pink oval brush Head: superstar Head Markings: inside or outside rim © Mattel Inc 1976 +/- country Arms: bent Body: tan tnt Body Markings: © Mattel Inc 1966/ Malaysia Black Version: model #: 13615 Hair Color: black Face: lavender-brown eyes, black brows, light red lips & blush Head: Christie Head Markings: © Mattel Inc./ 1987 Body: dark brown tnt Hispanic Version: model #: 13616 Hair Color: brunette Face: brown eyes, brown brows, light red lips & blush Head: Teresa Head Markings: © 1990, Mattel/ Inc Body: dark tan tnt

Model #: 11646 **Name:** Wal-Mart Country Star **Box Date:** 1994 **Hair Color:** blonde **Hairstyle:** sides pulled back & braided, rest waist length with ends curled **Face:** blue eyes, light brown brows, red lips & blush **Clothing:** long sleeve white blouse with multicolor yoke & gold fringe, multicolor skirt short in front long in back with purple petticoat, silver stud earrings & ring, hot pink cowboy hat & cowboy boots **Extras:** hot pink oval brush, black hand held microphone, cardboard punch out guitar **Head:** superstar **Head Markings:** inside or outside rim © Mattel Inc 1976 +/- country **Arms:** bent **Body:** tan tnt, white panties **Body Markings:** © Mattel Inc 1966/ Malaysia

Black Version: model **#:** 12096 **Hair Color:** black **Face:** brown eyes, black brows, hot pink lips & blush **Head:** Christie **Head Markings:** © Mattel Inc./ 1987 **Body:** dark brown tnt, white panties **Hispanic Version:** model **#:** 12097 **Hair Color:** brunette **Face:** green eyes, brown brows, red lips & blush **Head:** Teresa **Head Markings:** © 1990, Mattel/ Inc **Body:** dark tan tnt, white panties

Model #: 7335 **Name:** Wal-Mart Dream Fantasy **Box Date:** 1990 **Hair Color:** blonde **Hairstyle:** front & sides pulled up into twisted ponytail, rest waist length with ends curled **Face:** blue eyes, light brown brows, coral lips & blush **Clothing:** silver bodysuit with full long aqua overskirt & matching tulle trim at sleeves & waist, silver stud earrings, pendant & ring, wide aqua pumps **Extras:** lavender oval brush **Booklet:** IIB 1990 **Head:** superstar **Head Markings:** inside or outside rim © Mattel Inc 1976 +/- country **Arms:** bent **Body:** tan tnt **Body Markings:** © Mattel Inc 1966/ Malaysia

Model #: 1374 **Name:** Wal-Mart Frills and Fantasy **Box Date:** 1988 **Hair Color:** blonde **Hairstyle:** sides & top pulled up into ponytail, rest mid-back length, ends curled **Face:** blue eyes, light brown brows, deep pink lips & blush **Clothing:** light blue & white mini dress with multi layered blue & white tulle mid-calf-length skirt with tulle accents at shoulders, blue stud earrings, pendant, ring, barrette, wide light blue pumps **Extras:** blue pearl oval brush **Booklet:** BWOF 1988 **Head:** superstar **Head Markings:** inside or outside rim © Mattel Inc 1976 +/- country **Arms:** bent **Body:** tan tnt **Body Markings:** © Mattel Inc 1966/ China

Model #: 3963 Name: Wal-Mart Lavender Look Box Date: 1989 Hair Color: blonde Hairstyle: front & sides pulled up in small pony-tail, rest mid-back length, ends curled Face: lavender eyes, light brown brows, deep pink lips & blush Clothing: lavender mini dress with lavender & white tulle, pink dot overskirt with varying hem length, matching cuff accents, silver stud earrings & ring, wide laven-der pumps Extras: lavender oval brush Head: superstar Head Markings: inside or outside rim © Mattel Inc 1976 +/- country Arms: bent Body: tan tnt Body Markings: © Mattel Inc 1966/ China

Model #: 10592 Name: Wal-Mart Superstar Box Date: 1993 Hair Color: blonde Hairstyle: sides pulled up with small pink fabric hair ornament, rest waist length, ends curled under, curly bangs Face: blue eyes, blonde brows, deep pink lips & blush Clothing: full skirted sleeveless gown with iridescent bodice inset, rest pink with deep pink glitter dots, pink stud earrings & ring, white Barbie trophy, wide hot pink pumps Extras: hot pink oval brush, cardboard superstar poster Head: superstar Head Markings: inside or outside rim © Mattel Inc 1976 +/- country Arms: bent Body: tan tnt Body Markings: © Mattel Inc 1966/ China Black Version: model #: 10711 Hair Color: black Face: lavender eyes, black brows, deep pink lips & blush Head: Christie Head Markings: © Mattel Inc./ 1987 Body: light brown tnt

Model #: 11645 Name: Wal-Mart Toothfairy blue Box Date: 1994 Hair Color: blonde Hairstyle: sides pulled up into small ponytail tied with pink ribbon, bangs, rest waist length, ends curled under Face: blue eyes, light brown brows, pink lips & blush Clothing: turquoise, pink & white tutu style dress with sewn in panties, white stud earrings & matching blue pouch Extras: pink oval brush & sheet of cardboard punch outs Head: superstar Head Markings: inside or outside rim © Mattel Inc 1976 +/- country Arms: bent Body: tan tnt, white legs & molded pink ballet slippers Body Markings: © Mattel Inc.1966/ Indonesia

Model #: 11645 Name: Wal-Mart Toothfairy purple Box Date: 1994 Hair Color: blonde Hairstyle: sides pulled up into small ponytail tied with pink ribbon, bangs, rest waist length, ends curled under Face: lavender eyes, light brown brows, pink lips & blush Clothing: purple, pink, white tutu style dress with sewn in panties, white stud earrings & matching purple pouch Extras: pink oval brush & sheet of cardboard punch outs Head: superstar Head Markings: inside or outside rim © Mattel Inc 1976 +/- country Arms: ptr Body: tan tnt, white legs & molded pink ballet slippers Body Markings: © Mattel Inc.1966/ Indonesia

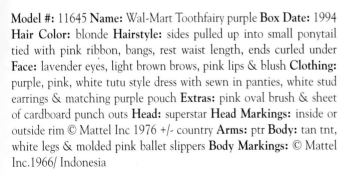

Model #: 3210 Name: Montgomery Wards Barbie Box Date: 1972 Hair Color: brunette Hairstyle: shoulder-length ponytail with curly bangs & curled ends Face: blue eyes, brown brows, red lips Clothing: black & white striped strapless swimsuit, wrist tag, white mules Head: Barbie Head Markings: inside rim Copr.© 1958 Mattel, Inc. Arms: reg Body: dark tan s/l Body Markings: MidgeT.M./ © 1962/Barbie®/ 1958/ by/ Mattel, Inc./ Patented Notes: pink box sold in store, sent through catalog in brown shipping box, some dolls have nails painted red

Model #: 7637 Name: Winn Dixie Party Pink Box Date: 1989 Hair Color: blonde Hairstyle: middle part, mid-back length, ends curled Face: blue eyes, light brown brows, hot pink lips & blush Clothing: off the shoulder pink nylon mini dress, silver & pale pink sheer sleeve & skirt detail, wide pink bow pumps Extras: pink oval brush Head: superstar Head Markings: inside or outside rim © Mattel Inc 1976 +/- country Arms: ptr Body: tan tnt Body Markings: © Mattel Inc 1966/ China

Model #: 5410 Name: Winn Dixie Pink Sensation Box Date: 1990 Hair Color: blonde Hairstyle: mid-back length with ends curled, sides pulled up into ponytail with hair wrap & bangs Face: blue eyes, light brown brows, pink lips & blush Clothing: solid pink & pink & white print mini dress with sewn in pink panties, wide deep pink pumps Extras: deep pink oval brush Head: superstar Head Markings: inside or outside rim © Mattel Inc 1976 +/- country Arms: ptr Body: tan tnt Body Markings: © Mattel Inc 1966/ Malaysia

Model #: 3284 Name: Winn Dixie Southern Beauty Box Date: 1991 Hair Color: blonde Hairstyle: waist-length side ponytail tied with thin white satin ribbon, ends curled Face: green eyes, light brown brows, dark orange lips & blush Clothing: light orange sleeveless full skirted mini dress with sewn in panties & double white petticoat, wide white satin ribbon at waist, white lace trim at neckline with white satin bow, pearl stud earrings & ring, wide white pumps Extras: white oval brush Head: superstar Head Markings: inside or outside rim © Mattel Inc 1976 +/- country Arms: bent Body: tan tnt Body Markings: © Mattel Inc 1966/ Malaysia

Model #: 4842 **Name:** Woolworth's Special Expressions **Box Date:** 1989 **Hair Color:** blonde **Hairstyle:** sides & front pulled back, curly bangs, rest curly to waist **Face:** blue eyes, light brown brows, pink lips & blush **Clothing:** white halter mini dress with white & silver tulle accents on skirt, wide white bow pumps **Extras:** white oval brush **Head:** superstar **Head Markings:** inside or outside rim © Mattel Inc 1976 +/- country **Arms:** ptr **Body:** tan tnt **Body Markings:** © Mattel Inc 1966/ China **Black Version:** model # 7346 **Hair Color:** black **Face:** brown eyes, black brows, hot pink lips & blush **Head:** Christie **Head Markings:** © Mattel Inc./ 1987 **Body:** dark brown tnt

Model #: 5504 **Name:** Woolworth's Special Expressions **Box Date:** 1990 **Hair Color:** blonde **Hairstyle:** waist length, ends curled under **Face:** lavender eyes, blonde brows, deep pink lips & blush **Clothing:** pink, peach & hot pink mini dress with matching panties, wide hot pink pumps **Extras:** hot pink oval brush **Head:** superstar **Head Markings:** inside or outside rim © Mattel Inc 1976 +/- country **Arms:** ptr **Body:** tan tnt **Body Markings:** © Mattel Inc 1966/ Malaysia **Black Version:** model #: 5505 **Hair Color:** brunette **Face:** brown eyes, black brows, hot pink lips & blush **Head:** Christie **Head Markings:** © Mattel Inc./ 1987 **Body:** dark brown tnt

Model #: 2582 **Name:** Woolworth's Special Expressions **Box Date:** 1991 **Hair Color:** blonde **Hairstyle:** front & sides pulled up with aqua fabric tie, rest waist length, ends curled under **Face:** aqua eyes, light brown brows, mauve lips & blush **Clothing:** aqua mini dress with silver lace accents, matching panties, wide aqua pumps **Extras:** aqua oval brush **Head:** superstar **Head Markings:** inside or outside rim © Mattel Inc 1976 +/- country **Arms:** ptr **Body:** tan tnt **Body Markings:** © Mattel Inc 1966/ Malaysia **Black Version:** model #: 2583 **Hair Color:** black **Face:** hazel eyes, black brows, coral lips & blush **Head:** Christie **Head Markings:** © Mattel Inc./ 1987 **Body:** dark brown tnt

Model #: 3197 **Name:** Woolworth's Special Expressions **Box Date:** 1992 **Hair Color:** blonde **Hairstyle:** front & sides pulled back, rest mid-back length, ends curled under **Face:** blue eyes, light brown brows, lavender lips & blush **Clothing:** peach satin off-the-shoulder mini dress with iridescent tulle trim at skirt & neckline with sewn in panties, peach stud earrings, wide peach pumps **Extras:** peach pearl oval brush **Head:** superstar **Head Markings:** inside or outside rim © Mattel Inc 1976 +/- country **Arms:** ptr **Body:** tan tnt **Body Markings:** © Mattel Inc 1966/ Malaysia **Black Version:** model #: 3198 **Hair Color:** black **Face:** brown eyes, black brows, deep pink lips & blush **Head:** Christie **Head Markings:** © Mattel Inc./ 1987 **Body:** dark brown tnt **Hispanic Version:** model #: 3200 **Hair Color:** brunette **Face:** lavender eyes, light brown brows, orange lips & blush **Head:** Steffie **Head Markings:** inside rim © 1971 Mattel Inc & country **Body:** dark tan tnt

Model #: 10048 **Name:** Woolworth's Special Expressions **Box Date:** 1992 **Hair Color:** blonde **Hairstyle:** side section pulled back with light blue fabric tie, rest mid-back length, ends curled under **Face:** blue eyes, blonde brows, hot pink lips & blush **Clothing:** confetti color long sleeve boat neck mini dress with light blue sheer shoulder straps, light blue panties, turquoise stud earrings, wide turquoise pumps **Extras:** turquoise oval brush **Head:** superstar **Head Markings:** inside or outside rim © Mattel Inc 1976 +/- country **Arms:** ptr **Body:** tan tnt **Body Markings:** © Mattel Inc 1966/ China **Black Version:** model #: 10049 **Hair:** black **Face:** brown eyes, black brows, deep pink lips & blush **Head:** Christie **Head Markings:** © Mattel, Inc/ 1987 **Body:** dark brown tnt **Hispanic Version:** model #: 10050 **Hair Color:** brunette **Face:** brown eyes, light brown brows, pink lips & blush **Head:** Teresa **Head Markings:** © 1990, Mattel/ Inc **Body:** dark tan tnt

Model #: 2522 **Name:** Woolworth's Sweet Lavender **Box Date:** 1992 **Hair Color:** blonde **Hairstyle:** sides & front pulled back, rest waist length, ends turned under **Face:** blue eyes, blonde brows, hot pink lips & blush **Clothing:** off-the-shoulder gown with white & metallic splatter print, full skirt of pink, purple & gold tulle overlay with purple fabric roses at hips and shoulders, metallic splatter long handless gloves, silver stud earrings & ring, wide purple pumps **Extras:** pink oval brush **Head:** superstar **Head Markings:** inside or outside rim © Mattel Inc 1976 +/- country **Arms:** bent **Body:** tan tnt **Body Markings:** © Mattel Inc 1966/ Malaysia **Black Version:** model #: 2523 **Hair Color:** brunette **Face:** brown eyes, black brows, hot pink lips & blush **Head:** Christie **Head Markings:** © Mattel Inc./ 1987 **Body:** dark brown tnt

Model #: 5979 **Name:** Zayre's My First Barbie Pink tutu Hispanic **Box Date:** 1987 **Hair Color:** brunette **Hairstyle:** sides & front pulled back, rest mid-back length, bangs, pink headband with pink tulle accent **Face:** brown eyes, brown brows, deep pink lips & blush **Clothing:** pink leotard, pink tulle knee-length skirt with petal hem & matching arm bands, pink ballet slippers with ribbon ties **Extras:** pointed pink brush & sheet of cardboard punch outs **Booklet:** BWOF 1987 & MFB 1986 **Head:** Hispanic **Head Markings:** inside rim © Mattel Inc, 1983 **Arms:** ptr **Body:** dark tan tnt non b/l **Body Markings:** © Mattel Inc 1966/ Malaysia

Toy Store Exclusives

Model #: 4385 **Name:** Child's World Disney Barbie **Box Date:** 1990 **Hair Color:** blonde **Hairstyle:** sides pulled to back of head, curly bangs, rest waist length with ends curled under **Face:** blue eyes, blonde brows, deep pink lips & blush **Clothing:** Minnie Mouse white T-shirt, blue denim short jacket, pink mini skirt over pink & white checked knee-high knit shorts, silver stud earrings & ring, matching pink pants, black Mickey Mouse ears hat, pink socks, white tennis shoes **Extras:** pink oval brush **Head:** superstar **Head Markings:** inside or outside rim © Mattel Inc 1976 +/- country **Arms:** bent **Body:** tan tnt **Body Markings:** © Mattel Inc 1966/ China **Black Version:** model #: 9385 **Hair Color:** black **Face:** brown eyes, black brows, hot pink lips & blush **Head:** Christie **Head Markings:** © Mattel Inc./ 1987 **Body:** dark brown tnt

Model #: 13257 **Name:** FAO Schwarz Circus Star **Box Date:** 1994 **Hair Color:** blonde **Hairstyle:** below shoulder length, ends curled **Face:** blue eyes, light brown brows, pink lips & blush **Clothing:** black, blue, pink & gold pattern costume with black & gold cuffs, black pantyhose, black & gold hat with multicolor feather trim, black boots with gold cuffs, black velvet cape with gold & hot pink satin lining, multicolor gold trimmed umbrella, gold stud earrings & gold ring **Extras:** 2-piece black stand & hot pink oval brush **Head:** superstar **Head Markings:** inside or outside rim © Mattel Inc 1976 +/- country **Arms:** Shani **Body:** tan tnt **Body Markings:** © Mattel Inc 1966/ Malaysia

Model #: 7734 **Name:** FAO Schwarz Golden Greetings **Box Date:** 1989 **Hair Color:** blonde **Hairstyle:** waist length, ends curled & front portion in ponytail **Face:** blue eyes, light brown brows, pink lips & blush **Clothing:** gold lamé fitted gown with gold & white lace & tulle formed into gathered skirt short in front long in back, gold stud earrings & ring, wide pearl pumps **Extras:** white pearl oval brush **Head:** superstar **Head Markings:** inside or outside rim © Mattel Inc 1976 +/- country **Arms:** bent **Body:** tan tnt **Body Markings:** © Mattel Inc 1966/ Malaysia

Model #: 14001 **Name:** FAO Schwarz Jeweled Splendor Signature Collection **Box Date:** 1995 **Hair Color:** blonde **Hairstyle:** sides pulled back to top of head held in place with gold & multicolor jeweled tiara, rest waist length, ends curled under **Face:** green eyes, rooted lashes, light brown brows, red lips & blush **Clothing:** black velvet gown, sequined & seed bead encrusted multicolor bodice, spaghetti straps, large leg of mutton black velvet & gold lamé sleeves, cuffs trimmed in black lace, full black velvet skirt with gold & black lace, multicolor sequin trim at hem, gold & red drop earrings, gold choker & ring, black sheer pantyhose, black sewn in tulle slip, wide black pumps **Extras:** 2-piece stand **Booklet:** COA **Head:** superstar **Head Markings:** inside or outside rim © Mattel Inc 1976 +/- country **Arms:** bent **Body:** ivory tnt **Body Markings:** © Mattel Inc 1966/ China **Notes:** unusual display box has black flocked decoration, 1st in series doll commemorates 125th anniversary of FAO

Model #: 1539 **Name:** FAO Schwarz Madison Ave **Box Date:** 1991 **Hair Color:** blonde **Hairstyle:** upsweep with curl at ears **Face:** blue eyes, light brown brows, deep pink lips & blush **Clothing:** hot pink suit with bright green satin blouse & coat, hot pink pantyhose, hot pink lace teddy, pink & green vinyl handbag, gold & pearl drop earrings, pearl choker, black glasses, FAO paper shopping bag, wide hot pink pumps **Extras:** 2-piece black stand **Head:** superstar **Head Markings:** inside or outside rim © Mattel Inc 1976 +/- country **Arms:** bent **Body:** tan tnt **Body Markings:** © Mattel Inc 1966/ China

Model #: 2921 **Name:** FAO Schwarz Night Sensation **Box Date:** 1991 **Hair Color:** blonde **Hairstyle:** sides & front pulled into ponytail, rest waist length, ends curled under **Face:** blue-green eyes, blonde brows, pink lips & blush **Clothing:** black sleeveless bodice with multi-layer fuchsia satin ruffles, black edging & silver braid trim at neckline with large pearl shaped rhinestone, black full satin skirt, black pants, silver stud earrings & ring, wide black pumps & silver wrist tag **Extras:** 2-piece black stand & hot pink oval brush **Head:** superstar **Head Markings:** inside or outside rim © Mattel Inc 1976 +/- country **Arms:** bent **Body:** tan tnt **Body Markings:** © Mattel Inc 1966/ Malaysia

Model #: 2017 **Name:** FAO Schwarz Rockettes **Box Date:** 1992 **Hair Color:** blonde **Hairstyle:** waist length, ends curled, front pulled into small ponytail **Face:** blue eyes, light brown brows, red lips & blush **Clothing:** multicolor white leotard, purple stockings, white satin tuxedo jacket with tails & purple lapels, gold bow tie, white glitter top hat, gold cane, gold stud earrings & ring, extra multicolor headpiece, armlets, tiered overskirt, gold Brazil pumps & Radio City lobby poster & ticket **Extras:** 2-piece white stand & purple oval brush **Head:** superstar **Head Markings:** inside or outside rim © Mattel Inc 1976 +/- country **Arms:** bent **Body:** tan tnt **Body Markings:** © Mattel Inc 1966/ Malaysia

Model #: 12749 **Name:** FAO Schwarz Shopping Spree **Box Date:** 1994 **Hair Color:** blonde **Hairstyle:** waist length with bangs **Face:** blue eyes, light brown brows, pink lips **Clothing:** white sweatshirt with FAO logo, purple leggings, white tennis shoes, multicolor FAO baseball cap, purple stud earrings & ring with FAO paper shopping bag **Extras:** purple oval brush & sheet of cardboard punch outs **Head:** superstar **Head Markings:** inside or outside rim © Mattel Inc 1976 +/- country **Arms:** bent **Body:** tan tnt **Body Markings:** © Mattel Inc 1966/ Malaysia

Model #: 11652 **Name:** FAO Schwarz Silver Screen **Box Date:** 1993 **Hair Color:** blonde **Hairstyle:** nape of neck length, ends curled, parted on side **Face:** blue eyes, rooted lashes, light brown brows, red lips, black beauty mark **Clothing:** silver lamé fitted gown flared at knee with feather stole & silver jeweled trim, silver stud earrings, ring, rhinestone choker, pearlized white mules, white satin teddy & white monogrammed robe **Extras:** 2-piece white stand **Head:** superstar **Head Markings:** inside or outside rim © Mattel Inc 1976 +/- country **Arms:** bent **Body:** tan tnt **Body Markings:** © Mattel Inc 1966/ Malaysia

Model #: 5946 **Name:** FAO Schwarz Winter Fantasy **Box Date:** 1990 **Hair Color:** blonde **Hairstyle:** waist length, ends curled, faux fur snowflake & ribbon hair ornament **Face:** blue eyes, light brown brows, deep pink lips & blush **Clothing:** medium blue velour gown with faux fur trim at hem & collar, silver ribbon belt, matching muff with snowflake & ribbon accent, white tulle slip, blue stud earrings, ring & matching necklace, wide blue pumps **Extras:** white pearl oval brush **Head:** superstar **Head Markings:** inside or outside rim © Mattel Inc 1976 +/- country **Arms:** bent **Body:** tan tnt **Body Markings:** © Mattel Inc 1966/ China **Notes:** blue stud earrings later replaced with rhinestone because of color bleeding

Model #: 12149 **Name:** Toys R Us Astronaut **Box Date:** 1994 **Hair Color:** blonde **Hairstyle:** middle part, mid-back length, ends curled under **Face:** dark blue eyes, blonde brows, red lips & blush **Clothing:** white vinyl, silver & red trimmed 1-piece flight suit, helmet, neck ring, Barbie flag, backpack, moon rock bag, 3 moon rocks, earphones, red stud earrings & ring, silver boots **Extras:** red oval brush, Apollo XXV badge for child, sheet of stickers & sheet of cardboard punch outs **Booklet:** instructions **Head:** superstar **Head Markings:** inside or outside rim © Mattel Inc 1976 +/- country **Arms:** bent **Body:** tan tnt **Body Markings:** © Mattel Inc 1966/ China **Black Version:** model **#:** 12150 **Hair Color:** brunette **Face:** lilac-green eyes, black brows, red lips & blush **Head:** Christie **Head Markings:** © Mattel Inc./ 1987 **Body:** dark brown tnt

Model #: 3177 **Name:** Toys R Us Barbie & Friends **Box Date:** 1991 **Hair Color:** B & SK=blonde K=painted two tone blonde **Hairstyle:** B=sides & front pulled back with red band, rest waist length, ends curled under & bangs, SK=sides pulled back, rest waist length, ends curled under, bangs **Face:** B=blue eyes, blonde brows, light red lips & blush, SK=lavender eyes, blonde brows, light orange lips & blush, K=blue eyes, brown brows, mauve lips **Clothing:** B=red Minnie Mouse T-shirt, white & turquoise multicolor print mini skirt, sewn in panties, black Mickey Mouse ears, red stud earrings & ring, wide purple pumps SK=white Donald Duck T-shirt, red knit shorts, black Mickey Mouse ears, red flats K=white Mickey Mouse T-shirt, white multicolor print pants, large turquoise pockets, black Mickey Mouse ears, red Mickey Mouse balloon, white tennis shoes **Extras:** yellow oval brush **Head:** B=superstar SK=1987 Skipper K=1988 Ken **Head Markings:** B=inside or outside rim © Mattel Inc 1976 +/- country SK=© Mattel Inc/ 1987 K=© M.I. 1988 **Arms:** B & K=bent SK=slight bend **Body:** B=tan tnt SK=tan 1987 Skipper K=dark tan tnt **Body Markings:** B=© Mattel Inc 1966/ Malaysia SK=© Mattel, Inc 1987/ Malaysia K=© Mattel Inc 1968/ Malaysia

Model #: 3722 **Name:** Toys R Us Barbie for President **Box Date:** 1991 **Hair Color:** blonde **Hairstyle:** front & sides pulled back, rest waist length, ends curled under **Face:** turquoise eyes, brown brows, red lips & blush **Clothing:** gown with silver lamé bodice trimmed in red satin with blue full skirt with 1 tier having silver stars, pearl stud earrings & ring, red bolero jacket & matching knee-length skirt, white blouse with gold & white stripe tie, white briefcase, wide red pumps **Extras:** red oval brush, sheet of cardboard punch outs & Barbie for President badge for child **Head:** superstar **Head Markings:** inside or outside rim © Mattel Inc 1976 +/- country **Arms:** bent **Body:** tan tnt **Body Markings:** © Mattel Inc 1966/ China **Black Version:** model #: 3940 **Hair Color:** black **Face:** purple eyes, black brows, red lips & blush **Head:** Christie **Head Markings:** © Mattel Inc./ 1987 **Body:** dark brown tnt **Notes:** first boxes used unauthorized presidential seal

Model #: 9324 Name: Toys R Us Beauty Pageant Skipper Box Date: 1991 Hair Color: blonde Hairstyle: front & sides pulled back with pink ribbon, rest thigh length, ends curled under Face: turquoise eyes, blonde brows, pink lips & blush Clothing: pink bodysuit with silver stripe insert, long pink skirt with sheer pink & silver glitter dot accents, matching shoulder detail, Skipper pink ribbon sash, pink pearl bowler hat, cane, pink pearl bow shoes Extras: pink pearl oval brush & sheet of cardboard punch outs Head: 1987 Skipper Head Markings: © Mattel Inc./ 1987 Arms: slight bend Body: tan tnt Body Markings: © Mattel, Inc.1987/ Malaysia

Model #: 1490 Name: Toys R Us Cool 'N Sassy Box Date: 1992 Hair Color: blonde Hairstyle: front pulled back, rest waist length, ends curled under Face: turquoise eyes, blonde brows, rose lips & blush Clothing: yellow tank top, yellow knee-high stretch shorts with lace trim, multicolor long sleeve short blue jacket with fuchsia lace, blue multicolor mini skirt, fuchsia tulle full mini skirt, yellow star earrings & ring, hot pink cordless phone, bottle, fork, piece of cake on plate, soda, cassette player, wide yellow pumps Extras: yellow oval brush Head: superstar Head Markings: inside or outside rim © Mattel Inc 1976 +/- country Arms: bent Body: tan tnt Body Markings: © Mattel Inc 1966/ China Body: dark brown tnt Black Version: model #: 4110 Hair Color: black Face: brown eyes, black brows, red lips & blush Head: Christie Head Markings: © Mattel Inc./ 1987 Arms: bent

Model #: 4893 Name: Toys R Us Cool City Blues Box Date: 1989 Hair Color: B & SK=blonde K=painted blonde Hairstyle: B=sides & front pulled back, rest curly mid-back length, bangs pulled into small band SK=front & sides pulled back, rest curly mid-back length, curly bangs Face: B=turquoise eyes, blonde brows, hot pink lips & blush K=turquoise eyes, brown brows, peach lips SK=turquoise eyes, blonde brows, pink lips & blush Clothing: B=pink, white & silver stripe short sleeve blouse, denim yoke & high collar with pink & silver accents, jeweled belt, mid-calf flared denim skirt, silver earrings, pink fabric boots K=white, light blue & pink glitter T-shirt, denim long sleeve jacket, jeans, tan print vinyl boots SK=pink long sleeve T-shirt, cat appliqué, denim mini skirt, pink belt, pink bow flats Extras: pink oval brush Head: B=superstar K=1983 Ken SK=1987 Skipper Head Markings: B=inside or outside rim © Mattel Inc 1976 +/- country SK=© Mattel Inc/ 1987 K=©1983 Mattel Inc Arms: B & K=ptr SK=slight bend Body: B=tan tnt K=dark tan b/l SK=tan tnt Body Markings: B=© Mattel Inc 1966/ Malaysia SK=© Mattel, Inc 1987/ China K=© Mattel Inc 1968/ Malaysia

Model #: 5947 **Name:** Toys R Us Cool Looks **Box Date:** 1990 **Hair Color:** blonde **Hairstyle:** pulled up in side ponytail, waist length, several strands on side pulled to back of head with curly ends, bangs **Face:** turquoise eyes, dark blonde brows, fuchsia lips & blush **Clothing:** light green top, orange appliqué T-shirt with hot pink trim, matching mini skirt with yellow charm, hot pink knee-high stretch shorts, black record print vest, pink hoop earrings & ring, cordless phone, soda can, notebook, pencil, yellow hat box tote, hot pink tennis shoes **Extras:** hot pink hair pick & sheet of stickers **Head:** superstar **Head Markings:** inside or outside rim © Mattel Inc 1976 +/- country **Arms:** bent **Body:** tan tnt **Body Markings:** © Mattel Inc 1966/ Malaysia

Model #: 9058 **Name:** Toys R Us Dance Sensation **Box Date:** 1984 **Hair Color:** blonde **Hairstyle:** side part, banded at nape of neck split into 2 twisted ponytails with hot pink fabric hair ties, mid-back length **Face:** blue eyes, blonde brows, red lips & blush **Clothing:** fuchsia satin bodysuit with matching long slim skirt, tiered knee-length skirt of satin & multicolor chiffon tiers, matching harem pants, pink tutu, white & purple glitter dickey with purple tie, pink tights, striped leggings, purple & pink full-length leotard, 2 hangers, hot pink ankle strap ballet shoes & mules **Booklet:** BWOF 1984 **Head:** superstar **Head Markings:** inside or outside rim © Mattel Inc 1976 +/- country **Arms:** bent **Body:** tan tnt **Body Markings:** © Mattel Inc.1966/ Philippines

Model #: 1075 **Name:** Toys R Us Dream Date Skipper **Box Date:** 1990 **Hair Color:** 2-tone blonde **Hairstyle:** curly mid-back length with curly bangs & light blonde long wavy fall **Face:** blue eyes, blonde brows, pink lips & blush **Clothing:** light blue v-neck sleeveless mid-thigh bodysuit with flocked blue bow tulle mini skirt & matching ankle-length skirt, gold choker & bracelet, light blue heart shape purse, disk, light blue flats **Extras:** 2-piece blue stand, light blue oval brush, sheet of stickers & sheet of cardboard punch outs **Booklet:** IIB 1990 & instructions **Head:** 1987 Skipper **Head Markings:** © Mattel Inc./ 1987 **Arms:** slight bend **Body:** tan tnt **Body Markings:** © Mattel, Inc.1987/ China

Model #: 9180 **Name:** Toys R Us Dream Time **Box Date:** 1988 **Hair Color:** blonde **Hairstyle:** shoulder length, side ponytail, curly ends **Face:** purple eyes, blonde brows, fuchsia lips & blush **Clothing:** long pink nightgown with white lace trim & matching peignoir of pink, white rose print with tie front, pink teddy bear with silver bow, rhinestone ring, pink mules **Extras:** pointed pink comb & brush **Head:** superstar **Head Markings:** inside or outside rim © Mattel Inc 1976 +/- country **Arms:** bent **Body:** tan tnt **Body Markings:** © Mattel Inc 1966/ China **Notes:** original issue in 1985 in lavender gown

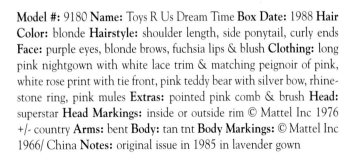  

Model #: 10712 **Name:** Toys R Us Dream Wedding Gift Set **Box Date:** 1993 **Hair Color:** B=blonde ST=blonde T=brunette **Hairstyle:** B=sides & front pulled back, rest waist length, ends curled under ST=thigh length, ends curled under T=fuzzy short **Face:** B=blue eyes, blonde brows, pink lips & blush ST=blue eyes, blonde brows, pink lips & blush T=turquoise eyes, brown brows, peach lips & blush **Clothing:** B=white scoop neck long sleeve gown, tulle glitter overskirt & matching bouquet with multicolor ribbons, veil, pearl stud earrings, necklace & ring, wide white pumps ST=pink satin short sleeve knee-length dress with tulle overskirt, lace at neckline, wide pink ribbon waistband, bouquet & white hat with multicolor ribbons, pearl stud earrings, pink pearl flower flats T=white bodysuit with white shirt, pink collar, lilac tie, pink cummerbund, white satin pants, white satin tuxedo coat with pink flower in lapel, white ring pillow trimmed in lace with ring & white flower flats **Extras:** pink pearl oval brush **Head:** B=superstar ST=1991 Stacie T=1990 Todd **Head Markings:** B=inside or outside rim © Mattel Inc 1976 +/- country ST=© Mattel Inc/ 1991 T=©1990/ Mattel Inc **Arms:** B=bent ST & T=ptr **Body:** B=tan tnt ST & T=tan Todd **Body Markings:** B=© Mattel Inc 1966/ Malaysia ST & T=© Malaysia **Black Version:** model #: 10713 **Hair Color:** B=black ST=black T=brunette **Face:** B=brown eyes, black brows, hot pink lips & blush ST=brown eyes, black brows, pink lips & blush T=brown eyes, brown brows, dark mauve lips & blush **Head:** B=Christie **Head Markings:** © Mattel Inc/ 1987 **Body:** B=dark brown tnt ST & T=dark brown Todd

Model #: 12322 **Name:** Toys R Us Emerald Elegance **Box Date:** 1994 **Hair Color:** red **Hairstyle:** sides & front pulled back with teal satin ribbon & fabric flower, rest thigh length, ends curled under **Face:** aqua eyes, reddish brows, fuchsia lips & blush **Clothing:** dark aqua & teal satin gown with dropped waist & iridescent lace overskirt, matching bolero jacket, fabric flower & ribbon trim at hip, aqua drop earrings, pendant, ring, wide aqua pumps **Extras:** aqua oval brush **Head:** superstar **Head Markings:** inside or outside rim © Mattel Inc 1976 +/- country **Arms:** bent **Body:** tan tnt **Body Markings:** © Mattel Inc.1966/ Indonesia **Black Version:** model #: 12323 **Hair Color:** black **Face:** brown eyes, black brows, deep pink lips & blush **Head:** Christie **Head Markings:** © Mattel Inc./ 1987 **Body:** light brown tnt

Model #: 1882 **Name:** Toys R Us Fashion Brights **Box Date:** 1992 **Hair Color:** blonde **Hairstyle:** waist length, ends curled under with bangs **Face:** lavender-aqua eyes, blonde brows, deep pink lips & blush **Clothing:** hot pink teddy with lace insert, pink & white bikini, multicolor tank top & matching yellow-green knee-high stretch shorts, white mini dress with purple tulle overdress & hot pink ribbon waistband, rose & purple bolero jacket, pearl stud earrings, hot pink visor & Frisbee, 2 hangers, hot pink tennis shoes, wide purple pumps **Extras:** purple oval brush **Head:** superstar **Head Markings:** inside or outside rim © Mattel Inc 1976 +/- country **Arms:** ptr **Body:** tan tnt **Body Markings:** © Mattel Inc 1966/ China **Black Version:** model #: 4112 **Hair Color:** brunette **Face:** lavender eyes, black brows, hot pink lips & blush **Head:** Christie **Head Markings:** © Mattel Inc./ 1987 **Body:** dark brown tnt

Model #: 13553 **Name:** Toys R Us Firefighter **Box Date:** 1994 **Hair Color:** blonde **Hairstyle:** mid-back-length ponytail tied with red ribbon, bangs **Face:** blue eyes, blonde brows, red lips & blush **Clothing:** white long sleeve shirt with decal, yellow vinyl pants, red suspenders & matching jacket, yellow fire hat, Dalmatian dog, white pearl earrings & ring, emergency bag, clipboard, belt, beeper, blood pressure gauge, adhesive bandage box, pill bottle, cough syrup, 2 bottles, knee-high yellow boots **Extras:** yellow oval brush, sheet of stickers, Barbie Fire Rescue child's badge **Booklet:** instructions **Head:** superstar **Head Markings:** inside or outside rim © Mattel Inc 1976 +/- country **Arms:** Shani **Body:** tan tnt **Body Markings:** © Mattel Inc 1966/ China **Black Version:** model #: 13472 **Hair Color:** black **Face:** lavender eyes, black brows, red lips & blush **Booklet:** instructions **Head:** Christie **Head Markings:** © Mattel Inc./ 1987 **Body:** dark brown tnt

Model #: 10507 **Name:** Toys R Us Love to Read **Box Date:** 1992 **Hair Color:** B=blonde Baby 1=blonde Baby 2=brunette **Hairstyle:** B=front & sides pulled back with pink ribbon rest thigh length, ends curled under Baby1=front & sides pulled back divided in 2 & tied with lilac ribbon rest waist length Baby 2=hair pulled to top of head with pink ribbon curl hair & bangs **Face:** B=aqua eyes, blonde brows, dark pink lips & blush Baby 1=blue eyes, blonde brows, rose lips & blush Baby 2=brown eyes, black brows, pink lips & blush **Clothing:** B=lilac & white short sleeve scoop neck full skirt mini dress, stripe & floral print with white satin belt & purple rose accent, white panties, pearl stud earrings, necklace, ring, wide fuchsia bow pumps Baby 1=white T-shirt, lilac & white striped shorts, white bow flats Baby 2=sun dress with light green ribbon straps & bows, white, multicolor skirt, lilac bow flats **Extras:** fuchsia oval brush & little golden book "Mother Goose Rhymes" **Booklet:** Storytime Fun **Head:** B=superstar Babies=1976 **Head Markings:** B=inside or outside rim © Mattel Inc 1976 +/- country babies=© Mattel Inc. 1976 **Arms:** B=bent **Body:** B=tan tnt Baby 1=tan 1976 Baby 2=dark brown 1976 **Body Markings:** B=© Mattel Inc 1966/ China kids= 1976 Mattel Inc/ China **Note:** babies may vary

Model #: 4581 Name: Toys R Us Malt Shop Box Date: 1992 Hair Color: blonde Hairstyle: mid-back-length ponytail, ends curled with extra pink band mid way through ponytail, curly bangs Face: blue eyes, blonde brows, pale pink lips & blush Clothing: pink flannel scoop neck 3/4 sleeve bodysuit, light blue satin poodle skirt with sheer pink petticoat & white belt, pink scarf, pearl stud earrings & ring, pink tray, 2 pink sodas, 2 glasses, white tennis shoes Extras: pink oval brush & Dairy Queen coupon Head: superstar Head Markings: inside or outside rim © Mattel Inc 1976 +/- country Arms: bent Body: tan tnt Body Markings: © Mattel Inc 1966/ Malaysia

Model #: 10608 Name: Toys R Us Moonlight Magic Box Date: 1993 Hair Color: black Hairstyle: top & front pulled back with gold fabric flower, rest thigh length, ends curled under Face: brown eyes, brown brows, red lips & blush Clothing: black & gold glitter gown with metallic gold partial overskirt, black & gold ribbon bows at hips, long gold handless gloves, gold drop earrings, pendant, ring, wide black pumps Extras: gold oval brush Head: superstar Head Markings: inside or outside rim © Mattel Inc 1976 +/- country Arms: bent Body: light tan tnt Body Markings: © Mattel Inc 1966/ Malaysia Black Version: model #: 10609 Hair Color: black Face: brown eyes, black brows, red lips & blush Head: Christie Head Markings: © Mattel Inc./ 1987 Body: light brown tnt

Model #: 13239 Name: Toys R Us POGS Box Date: 1994 Hair Color: blonde Hairstyle: thigh length crinkled, pulled back with turquoise & white dot headband, bangs Face: blue eyes, dark blonde brows, deep pink lips & blush Clothing: cropped long sleeve multi-color stripe Barbie T-shirt with matching mid-thigh shorts, turquoise & white dot mini skirt with hot pink waistband, hot pink disk earrings & ring, clear vinyl pog bag, hot pink tennis shoes Extras: hot pink oval brush, 6 pogs Booklet: 1994 PB Head: superstar Head Markings: inside or outside rim © Mattel Inc 1976 +/- country Arms: bent Body: tan tnt Body Markings: © Mattel Inc.1966/ Indonesia

Model #: 12243 **Name:** Toys R Us Party Time **Box Date:** 1994 **Hair Color:** blonde **Hairstyle:** thigh length crinkled, pulled back with peach ribbon **Face:** blue eyes, dark blonde brows, peach lips & blush **Clothing:** blue scoop neck short sleeve full skirted mini dress with white lace trim, peach satin bow at waist, peach bow earrings, ring, watch, wide peach pumps **Extras:** peach oval brush & child's peach watch **Booklet:** instructions **Head:** superstar **Head Markings:** inside or outside rim © Mattel Inc 1976 +/- country **Arms:** bent **Body:** tan tnt **Body Markings:** © Mattel Inc.1966/ Indonesia **Black Version:** model #: 14274 **Hair Color:** black **Face:** brown eyes, black brows, red lips & blush **Head:** Christie **Head Markings:** © Mattel Inc./ 1987 **Body:** dark brown tnt **Hispanic Version:** model #: 12244 **Hair Color:** brunette **Hairstyle:** pulled back with pink ribbon **Face:** lavender-green eyes, brown brows, pink lips & blush **Clothing:** green scoop neck short sleeve full skirted mini dress with white lace trim, pink satin bow at waist, pink bow earrings, ring, watch, wide hot pink pumps **Extras:** hot pink oval brush & pink child's size watch **Head:** Teresa **Head Markings:** © 1990, Mattel/ Inc **Body:** dark tan tnt

Model #: 4885 **Name:** Toys R Us Party Treats **Box Date:** 1989 **Hair Color:** blonde **Hairstyle:** sides & front pulled back, rest mid-back length, ends curled under **Face:** turquoise eyes, light brown brows, hot pink lips & blush **Clothing:** pink spaghetti strap bodysuit with appliqué, pink iridescent tulle knee-length skirt & puffed sleeves, wide pink pumps **Extras:** aqua oval brush **Head:** superstar **Head Markings:** inside or outside rim © Mattel Inc 1976 +/- country **Arms:** ptr **Body:** tan tnt **Body Markings:** © Mattel Inc 1966/ Malaysia

Model #: 4869 **Name:** Toys R Us Pepsi Spirit Barbie **Box Date:** 1989 **Hair Color:** blonde **Hairstyle:** thigh length crinkled, sides & front pulled back **Face:** blue eyes, blonde brows, red lips & blush **Clothing:** long sleeve red, white & blue Pepsi shirt, denim mini skirt, white belt, Pepsi duffel bag, 1-piece blue, white & red swimsuit, denim vest, white vinyl baseball hat, blue stretch pants, white socks, red headband, Pepsi towel, red tennis shoes **Extras:** red oval brush **Head:** superstar **Head Markings:** inside or outside rim © Mattel Inc 1976 +/- country **Arms:** bent **Body:** tan tnt **Body Markings:** © Mattel Inc 1966/ China

Model #: 4867 **Name:** Toys R Us Pepsi Spirit Skipper **Box Date:** 1989 **Hair Color:** blonde **Hairstyle:** waist length, sides & front pulled back, ends turned under **Face:** blue eyes, blonde brows, peach lips & blush **Clothing:** white long sleeve Pepsi shirt with red cuffs & collarband, Pepsi fanny pack, blue denim mini skirt with red waistband, blue knee-high shorts, 2-piece red, white & blue bathing suit, white tote bag, red socks, white tennis shoes **Extras:** red oval brush **Head:** 1987 Skipper **Head Markings:** © Mattel Inc./ 1987 **Arms:** slight bend **Body:** tan tnt **Body Markings:** © Mattel, Inc.1987/ China

Model #: 10689 **Name:** Toys R Us Police Officer **Box Date:** 1993 **Hair Color:** brunette **Hairstyle:** waist length, ends curled under **Face:** brown eyes, black brows, red lips & blush **Clothing:** navy police uniform shirt with tie & matching pants with black belt & gold buckle, matching hat, gold stud earrings & ring, mini dress of gold lamé with spaghetti strap bodice, white satin & gold glitter tulle overskirt, gold fabric rose at waist, black tennis shoes & wide white pumps **Extras:** white oval brush & Barbie Police Dept. badge for child & sheet of cardboard punch outs **Head:** Christie **Head Markings:** © Mattel Inc./ 1987 **Body:** light brown tnt **Body Markings:** © Mattel Inc 1966/ Malaysia +/- country **Arms:** bent **Caucasian version:** model # 10688 **Hair Color:** blonde **Face:** blue eyes, blonde brows, peach lips & blush **Head:** superstar **Head Markings:** inside or outside rim © Mattel Inc 1976 **Body:** tan tnt

Model #: 13555 **Name:** Toys R Us Purple Passion **Box Date:** 1995 **Hair Color:** red **Hairstyle:** waist length, sides & top pulled back with purple ribbon & fabric flower trim **Face:** purple-turquoise eyes, reddish brows, pink lips & blush **Clothing:** purple gown with satin pleated crossover bodice, glitter tulle skirt, sheer long sleeves and neckline insert, iridescent bead earrings, choker, gold ring, wide purple pumps **Extras:** purple oval brush **Head:** superstar **Head Markings:** inside or outside rim © Mattel Inc 1976 +/- country **Arms:** bent **Body:** light tan tnt, B panties **Body Markings:** © Mattel Inc 1966/ China **Black Version:** model #: 13554 **Hair Color:** brunette **Face:** lavender eyes, black brows, hot pink lips & blush **Head:** Christie **Head Markings:** © Mattel Inc./ 1987 **Body:** light brown tnt, B panties

Model #: 11928 **Name:** Toys R Us Quinceanera Teresa **Box Date:** 1994 **Hair Color:** brunette **Hairstyle:** curly waist length, pulled back with iridescent headband, curly bangs **Face:** brown eyes, brown brows, hot pink lips & blush **Clothing:** long pink gown with fabric rose at bodice, pearl stud earrings, necklace & ring, pink 3 flower bouquet with iridescent ribbon, wide pearl pumps **Extras:** pearl oval brush & sheet of cardboard punch outs **Head:** Teresa **Head Markings:** © 1990, Mattel/ Inc **Arms:** bent **Body:** dark tan tnt **Body Markings:** © Mattel Inc 1966/ China **Notes:** celebrating a Hispanic girl's 15th birthday

Model #: 1276 **Name:** Toys R Us Radiant in Red **Box Date:** 1992 **Hair Color:** red **Hairstyle:** front & sides pulled back with red bow, rest wavy thigh length, ends curled under **Face:** green eyes, brown brows, red lips & blush **Clothing:** red taffeta gown with gold lace overlay on bodice & sleeves, red bows at cuffs & red marquise jewel at neckline, large red bow at hip, red tulle with gold glitter overlay on skirt, gold stud earrings, ring, wide red pumps **Extras:** red oval brush **Head:** superstar **Head Markings:** inside or outside rim © Mattel Inc 1976 +/- country **Arms:** bent **Body:** light tan tnt **Body Markings:** © Mattel Inc 1966/ Malaysia **Black Version:** model #: 4113 **Hair Color:** brunette **Face:** green eyes, brown brows, red lips & blush **Head:** Christie **Head Markings:** © Mattel Inc./ 1987 **Body:** light brown tnt

Model #: 13255 **Name:** Toys R Us Sapphire Dream **Box Date:** 1995 **Hair Color:** blonde **Hairstyle:** sides & front pulled back with navy & gold trimmed ribbon, rest thigh length, ends curled under **Face:** blue eyes, rooted lashes, dark blonde brows, red lips & blush **Clothing:** sleeveless navy velvet gown with flared skirt at mid-thigh, gold & rhinestone jewels at shoulders & waist, sheer navy & gold cape, gold & rhinestone drop earrings & ring, blue panties, wide navy pumps **Extras:** 2-piece black stand & blue oval brush **Head:** superstar **Head Markings:** inside or outside rim © Mattel Inc 1976 +/- country **Arms:** Shani **Body:** tan tnt **Body Markings:** © Mattel Inc 1966/ China

Model #: 2721 **Name:** Toys R Us School Fun **Box Date:** 1991 **Hair Color:** blonde **Hairstyle:** waist-length pigtails, ends curled under with bangs **Face:** blue eyes, light brown brows, deep pink lips & blush **Clothing:** white multicolor print top, matching mini skirt with purple insert and sewn in panties, hot pink letter jacket with initial "B" & white vinyl long sleeves with purple cuffs & waistband, matching backpack, white hoop earrings & ring, 2 small pencils, hot pink tennis shoes **Extras:** hot pink oval brush **Head:** superstar **Head Markings:** inside or outside rim © Mattel Inc 1976 +/- country **Arms:** bent **Body:** tan tnt **Body Markings:** © Mattel Inc 1966/ China **Black Version:** model #: 4111 **Hair Color:** black **Face:** purple eyes, black brows, hot pink lips & blush **Head:** Christie **Head Markings:** © Mattel Inc./ 1987 **Body:** dark brown tnt

Model #: 10682 **Name:** Toys R Us School Spirit **Box Date:** 1993 **Hair Color:** blonde **Hairstyle:** 1/2 of front & 1 side pulled back with pink band & braided, rest thigh length with bangs **Face:** turquoise eyes, light brown brows, hot pink lips & blush **Clothing:** multicolor scoop neck short sleeve mini dress with sewn in panties, matching backpack, pink satin "B" jacket with white satin sleeves & turquoise cuffs, collar & waistband, hot pink hoop earrings & ring, 2 small pencils, white tennis shoes **Extras:** hot pink oval brush **Head:** superstar **Head Markings:** inside or outside rim © Mattel Inc 1976 +/- country **Arms:** bent **Body:** tan tnt **Body Markings:** © Mattel Inc 1966/ Malaysia **Black Version:** model #: 10683 **Hair Color:** black **Face:** hazel eyes, black brows, fuchsia lips & blush **Head:** Christie **Head Markings:** © Mattel Inc./ 1987 **Body:** light brown tnt

Model #: 7799 **Name:** Toys R Us Show n' Ride **Box Date:** 1988 **Hair Color:** blonde **Hairstyle:** middle part, mid-back length, ends curled under **Face:** blue eyes, blonde brows, red lips & blush **Clothing:** white blouse with lace trim, short red riding jacket, tan riding pants, navy ankle-length flared skirt, light brown riding cap, blue ribbon, riding crop, horse blanket, 4 horse leg warmers & horseshoes, light brown riding boots **Extras:** red oval curved handle brush **Booklet:** BWOF 1988 **Head:** superstar **Head Markings:** inside or outside rim © Mattel Inc 1976 +/- country **Arms:** bent **Body:** tan tnt **Body Markings:** © Mattel Inc 1966/ China

257

Model #: 7513 Name: Toys R Us Ski Fun Midge Box Date: 1990 Hair Color: red Hairstyle: waist-length side ponytail, ends curled under with bangs Face: aqua-green eyes, brown brows, deep pink lips & blush, brown freckles Clothing: white long sleeve turtleneck multicolor mini dress with turquoise faux fur hem, silver & turquoise vest with turquoise faux fur collar, ski ticket, turquoise faux fur hat, turquoise skis & poles, hot pink goggles, silver stud earrings & ring, silver mittens, turquoise ski boots, wide turquoise pumps Extras: turquoise oval brush & sheet of cardboard punch outs Booklet: instructions Head: Diva Head Markings: © 1985 Mattel Inc. Arms: bent Body: tan tnt Body Markings: © Mattel Inc 1966/ China

Model #: 10491 Name: Toys R Us Spots 'N Dots Barbie Box Date: 1993 Hair Color: blonde Hairstyle: waist length, ends curled under with red ribbon headband & bow Face: blue eyes, brown brows, red lips & blush Clothing: short sleeve scoop neck mini dress with black & white print top & red full skirt, red hoop & triangle earrings & ring, Dalmatian plastic dog with red ribbon leash, wide red pumps Extras: red oval brush Head: superstar Head Markings: inside or outside rim © Mattel Inc 1976 +/- country Arms: bent Body: tan tnt Body Markings: © Mattel Inc 1966/ China Teresa Version: model #: 10885 Hair Color: brunette Face: brown eyes, brown brows, red lips & blush Head: Teresa Head Markings: © 1990, Mattel/ Inc Body: dark tan tnt

Model #: 7008 Name: Toys R Us Spring Parade Box Date: 1991 Hair Color: blonde Hairstyle: middle part with bangs, waist length, ends curled under Face: aqua eyes, blonde brows, lilac lips & blush Clothing: white gown with lilac metallic thread, lilac tulle overskirt & ruffle trim, white fabric flowers at shoulders, pearl stud earrings, necklace & ring, white straw hat with yellow fabric ties, white basket with flowers, wide lilac pumps Extras: pink oval brush Head: superstar Head Markings: inside or outside rim © Mattel Inc 1976 +/- country Arms: bent Body: tan tnt Body Markings: © Mattel Inc 1966/ China Black Version: model #: 2257 Hair Color: black Face: hazel eyes, black brows, coral lips & blush Head: Christie Head Markings: © Mattel Inc./ 1987 Body: dark brown tnt

Model #: 13488 **Name:** Toys R Us Sunflower Barbie **Box Date:** 1994 **Hair Color:** blonde **Hairstyle:** mid-thigh length **Face:** aqua eyes, blonde brows, deep pink lips & blush **Clothing:** scoop neck short sleeve mini dress with black & white gingham top, rest hot pink sunflower print, matching hat, sunflower on bodice & hat, hot pink disk earrings & ring, yellow heart purse decorated with sunflower, wide hot pink pumps **Extras:** hot pink oval brush **Head:** superstar **Head Markings:** inside or outside rim © Mattel Inc 1976 +/- country **Arms:** bent **Body:** tan tnt, B panties **Body Markings:** © Mattel Inc.1966/ Indonesia **Teresa Version:** model #: 13489 **Hair Color:** brunette **Face:** lilac-green eyes, brown brows, deep pink lips & blush **Clothing:** same outfit but colors are hot pink & white gingham on top & purple on bottom, hot pink heart shaped sunflower decorated purse, wide purple pumps **Extras:** purple oval brush **Head:** Teresa **Head Markings:** © 1990, Mattel/ Inc **Body:** dark tan tnt, B panties

Model #: 2917 **Name:** Toys R Us Sweet Romance **Box Date:** 1991 **Hair Color:** blonde **Hairstyle:** thigh length, ends curled under **Face:** blue eyes, dark blonde brows, fuchsia lips & blush **Clothing:** long blue gown with halter-style metallic blue drop waist bodice, full blue shimmering skirt, matching long handless gloves, silver stud earrings & ring **Extras:** blue perfume pendant for child **Head:** superstar **Head Markings:** inside or outside rim © Mattel Inc 1976 +/- country **Arms:** bent **Body:** tan tnt **Body Markings:** © Mattel Inc 1966/ China

Model #: 7635 **Name:** Toys R Us Sweet Roses **Box Date:** 1989 **Hair Color:** blonde **Hairstyle:** sides & front pulled back, rest waist length, ends curled under **Face:** lavender-blue eyes, dark blonde brows, pink lips & blush **Clothing:** pink crossover long slim gown with white flower accents at shoulders, pink ruffle accessories, white apron with lace trim, silver stud earrings, ring, wide pink pumps **Extras:** lilac oval brush **Booklet:** BWOF 1988 **Head:** superstar **Head Markings:** inside or outside rim © Mattel Inc 1976 +/- country **Arms:** bent **Body:** tan tnt **Body Markings:** © Mattel Inc 1966/ Malaysia

Model #: 7801 **Name:** Toys R Us Tennis Stars **Box Date:** 1988 **Hair Color:** B=blonde K=painted brunette **Hairstyle:** B=side part, side sections pulled to back, rest mid-back length, ends curled under **Face:** B=turquoise eyes, blonde brows, deep pink lips & blush K=turquoise eyes, blonde brows, peach lips **Clothing:** B=white halter-style bodysuit with gold stripes & pink collar, pink tennis skirt, gold waistband, white socks & tennis racket, pink tennis shoes K=white short sleeve tennis shirt with gold stripes & navy collar, blue shorts, white socks, tennis racket, blue tennis shoes **Extras:** pointed pink brush, tennis net, tennis net brace & sheet of cardboard punch outs **Booklet:** BWOF 1988 & instructions **Head:** B=superstar K=1983 Ken **Head Markings:** B=inside or outside rim© Mattel Inc 1976 +/- country K=© 1983 Mattel Inc **Arms:** both=ptr **Body:** B=tan tnt K=tan b/l **Body Markings:** B=© Mattel Inc 1966/ Malaysia K=©Mattel Inc 1968/ Malaysia

Model #: 1433 **Name:** Toys R Us Totally Hair Courtney **Box Date:** 1991 **Hair Color:** brunette **Hairstyle:** sides & front pulled back with green tulle band, rest crinkled past floor length, curly bangs **Face:** brown eyes, brown brows, deep pink lips & blush **Clothing:** long sleeve scoop neck mini dress of turquoise, green, hot pink, purple & white, white panties, turquoise flats **Extras:** turquoise hair pick & tube of Dep gel **Head:** 1987 Skipper **Head Markings:** © Mattel Inc./ 1987 **Arms:** slight bend **Body:** tan tnt **Body Markings:** © Mattel, Inc.1987/ Malaysia

Model #: 1430 **Name:** Toys R Us Totally Hair Skipper **Box Date:** 1991 **Hair Color:** blonde **Hairstyle:** sides & front pulled back with hot pink tulle band, rest crinkled past floor length with curly bangs **Face:** blue eyes, blonde brows, deep pink lips & blush **Clothing:** long sleeve scoop neck mini dress of hot pink, turquoise, pink, purple, yellow-green & white with matching shorts, hot pink flats **Extras:** hot pink hair pick & tube of Dep gel **Head:** 1987 Skipper **Head Markings:** © Mattel Inc./ 1987 **Arms:** slight bend **Body:** tan tnt **Body Markings:** © Mattel, Inc.1987/ Malaysia

Model #: 1675 **Name:** Toys R Us Vacation Sensation blue **Box Date:** 1986 **Hair Color:** blonde **Hairstyle:** side part, sides pulled to back of head, rest mid-back length, ends curled under **Face:** dark blue eyes, blonde brows, red lips & blush **Clothing:** 1-piece long sleeve turquoise blue jumpsuit, rhinestone earrings & ring, hot pink initial "B" garment bag, matching duffel bag, suitcase, luggage carrier, white top, yellow shorts, pink bodysuit, matching skirt, multicolor scarf, white lace knee socks, camera, umbrella, white tennis shoes, turquoise mules **Extras:** sheet of cardboard punch outs **Head:** superstar **Head Markings:** inside or outside rim © Mattel Inc 1976 +/- country **Arms:** bent **Body:** tan tnt **Body Markings:** © Mattel Inc.1966/ Philippines

Model #: 1675 **Name:** Toys R Us Vacation Sensation pink **Box Date:** 1988 **Hair Color:** blonde **Hairstyle:** front & sides pulled back, rest waist length, ends curled under **Face:** lilac eyes, blonde brows, pink lips & blush **Clothing:** pink & white stripe long sleeve jumpsuit, rhinestone earrings & ring, large white vinyl garment bag, duffel bag, pink suitcase, luggage carrier, purple bodysuit & matching skirt, multicolor scarf, white knee socks, white top with pink hearts, pink shorts, camera, umbrella, white tennis shoes, purple mules **Extras:** sheet of cardboard punch outs **Booklet:** BWOF 1988 **Head:** superstar **Head Markings:** inside or outside rim © Mattel Inc 1976 +/- country **Arms:** bent **Body:** tan tnt **Body Markings:** © Mattel Inc 1966/ China

Model #: 13557 **Name:** Toys R Us Wedding Party Gift Set **Box Date:** 1994 **Hair Color:** B=blonde ST=blonde T=brunette **Hairstyle:** B=thigh length, ends curled under ST=pulled back with yellow band, waist length with bangs T=fuzzy short **Face:** B=blue eyes, blonde brows, light red lips & blush ST=blue eyes, blonde brows, deep pink lips & blush T=blue eyes, light brown brows, mauve lips **Clothing:** B=white long sleeve drop waist gown, lace top, tulle overskirt, veil with 3 rose trim, matching bouquet, pearl stud earrings, necklace & ring, wide white pumps ST=yellow long sleeve knee-length taffeta dress with pink rose & green ribbon trim at neck, small pink flower bouquet, pearl stud earrings, yellow flower flats T=1-piece bodysuit with white shirt, white collar, yellow tie & cummerbund, white satin pants, white satin tuxedo coat with pink flower in lapel, white flower flats **Extras:** yellow oval brush **Head:** B=superstar ST=1991 Stacie T=1990 Todd **Head Markings:** B=inside or outside rim ©Mattel Inc 1976 +/- country ST=© Mattel Inc/ 1991 T=© 1990/ Mattel Inc **Arms:** B=bent **Body:** B=tan tnt ST & T=Todd **Body Markings:** B=©Mattel Inc 1966/ Malaysia ST & T= Malaysia **Black Version:** model #: 13556 **Hair Color:** B=black ST=black T=brunette **Face:** B=brown eyes, black brows, fuchsia lips & blush ST=brown eyes, black brows, fuchsia lips & blush T=brown eyes, black brows, wine lips & blush **Head:** B=Christie **Head Markings:** © Mattel Inc/ 1987 **Body:** B=dark brown tnt ST & T=dark brown Todd

Model #: 13478 Name: Toys R Us Western Stampin' Gift Set black version Box Date: 1995 Hair Color: black Hairstyle: sides & front pulled back with black band, rest crinkled waist length Face: brown eyes, black brows, wine lips & blush Clothing: black & gold top with red short sleeve fringed jacket with gold & black trim, red & gold flared mini skirt with sewn in panties, gold cowboy hat dangle earrings & ring, red pants, gold scarf, red cowboy hat & boots with gold stamper spurs Extras: palomino horse, blonde & glitter strand tail & mane, red oval brush, red saddle, saddle blanket, bridle, 6 horseshoes, brush, horse socks, 4 barrettes, 3 shoe covers, glitter, stamp pad Booklet: instructions Head: Christie Head Markings: © Mattel Inc./ 1987 Arms: bent Body: light brown tnt Body Markings: © Mattel Inc 1966/ China Notes: regular black issue had darker skin tone & blue outfit, white doll same as regular issue Western Stampin', horse & saddle made in Mexico

Model #: 5949 Name: Toys R Us Winter Fun Box Date: 1990 Hair Color: blonde Hairstyle: waist length, ends turned under Face: lilac eyes, blonde brows, deep pink lips & blush Clothing: white glitter turtleneck top, white stretch pants, white satin jacket with white faux fur cuffs & shoulder insert, iridescent fanny pack, white glitter leggings with faux fur cuffs, silver stud earrings & ring, hot pink skis & poles, white ski boots Extras: hot pink oval brush & sheet of stickers Booklet: IIB 1989 & instructions Head: superstar Head Markings: inside or outside rim © Mattel Inc 1976 +/- country Arms: bent Body: tan tnt Body Markings: © Mattel Inc 1966/ Malaysia

Gift Sets

Model #: 13181 Name: Barbie and Champion Box Date: 1994 Hair Color: white Hairstyle: front & sides pulled back with pink band rest thigh length Face: blue-lilac eyes, blonde brows, hot pink lips & blush Clothing: blue, green, fuchsia plaid long sleeve jacket with silver cuffs, lapels & 3 pearl buttons, black jockey hat, silver lamé pants, pearl stud earrings, hot pink scarf, black riding crop, silver loving cup, black riding boots Extras: dark brown horse with black tail & mane, blue plaid saddle blanket, silver ribbon, Velcro ribbon, winner's ribbon, breast collar, beads, turquoise saddle, reins, bit, bridle, stirrups, horseshoes, brush & turquoise oval doll brush Booklet: Barbie 1995 & instructions Head: superstar Head Markings: inside or outside rim © Mattel Inc 1976 +/- country Arms: gymnast Body: tan gymnast Body Markings: © 1993 Mattel, Inc./ Malaysia

Model #: 4431 **Name:** Barbie and Friends: Ken Barbie P.J. **Box Date:** 1982 **Hair Color:** B=blonde PJ=light brown K=brunette painted **Hairstyle:** B=side part, mid-back length PJ=center part, band at nape of neck, mid-back length **Face:** B & PJ= blue eyes, brown brows, peach lips K=blue eyes, brown brows, peach lips **Clothing:** Ken=red pants, light red top, white tennis shoes PJ= rhinestone stud earrings & ring, blue & white mini dress, fuchsia belt, navy mules B=rhinestone stud earrings & ring, multicolor stripe top & pink mini skirt, striped knee socks, light blue tennis shoes **Head:** PJ = Steffie B=superstar K=superstar **Head Markings:** B=inside or outside rim ©Mattel Inc 1976 +/- country PJ=inside rim © 1971 Mattel Inc & country K=inside rim © Mattel Inc 1977 **Arms:** all=bent **Body:** tan tnt **Body Markings:** B & PJ=© Mattel Inc 1966/ Taiwan K=© Mattel Inc 1968/ Taiwan

Model #: 4984 **Name:** Barbie and Ken Camping Out **Box Date:** 1983 **Hair Color:** B=blonde K=painted blonde **Hairstyle:** B=parted in middle, waist length **Face:** B=blue eyes, brown brows, peach lips & blush K=blue eyes, brown brows, peach lips **Clothing:** B=white short sleeve mid-thigh bodysuit, red sewn on vest & brown belt, white tennis shoes K=red short sleeve shirt, white shorts, brown belt, white tennis shoes, red backpack, tent frame, poles, backpack frame, camp stove shields, strap, camping stove, field glasses, connector, cup, lantern, dishes, fry pan, 2 pots, coffee pot, orange tent, blue sleeping bag **Extras:** sheet of stickers **Booklet:** instructions **Head:** B=superstar K=superstar **Head Markings:** B=inside or outside rim © Mattel Inc 1976 +/- country K=inside rim © Mattel Inc 1977 **Arms:** both=ptr **Body:** B=tan tnt K=tan b/l **Body Markings:** B=© Mattel Inc 1966/ Hong Kong K=© Mattel Inc 1968/ Hong Kong

Model #: 11589 **Name:** Birthday Fun at McDonald's Gift Set **Box Date:** 1993 **Hair Color:** B & ST=blonde T=brunette **Hairstyle:** B=thigh length, curly bangs, ends curled under, pulled back with blue denim headband ST=thigh length, curly bangs, ends curled under T=short fuzzy hair **Face:** B=turquoise eyes, dark blonde brows, hot pink lips & blush ST=blue eyes, blonde brows, deep pink lips & blush T=blue eyes, light brown brows, orange lips & brown freckles **Clothing:** B=floral bodysuit & mid-thigh shorts, turquoise denim blouse tied in front, cone hat, hot pink stud earrings & ring, wide white pumps ST=green swimsuit, multicolor stripe skirt, lace trim, long sleeve jacket, hot pink stud earrings, cone hat, happy meal box, white lace anklets, blue flower flats T=striped T-shirt with green collar & cuffs, turquoise denim short overalls, cone hat, happy meal box, white socks, black high-top athletic shoes **Extras:** white oval brush, birthday cake, sheet of cardboard punch outs **Head:** B=superstar, Stacie & Todd **Head Markings:** B=inside or outside rim © Mattel Inc 1976 +/- country ST=© Mattel Inc/ 1991 T=©1990/ Mattel Inc **Arms:** B=bent **Body:** B=tan tnt ST & T=tan **Body Markings:** B=©Mattel Inc 1966/ Malaysia ST & T=Malaysia

Model #: 2483 **Name:** My First Barbie Gift Set **Box Date:** 1991 **Hair Color:** blonde **Hairstyle:** front & sides pulled back with pink lace tie, rest waist length with curly bangs **Face:** blue eyes, blonde brows, pink lips & blush **Clothing:** pink with silver glitter dot sleeveless bodysuit with pink tulle & silver overskirt with hot pink flower trim at waist, white satin bolero jacket with faux fur long sleeves & white dotted swiss 3 tier ruffle mini skirt, purple tank style drop waist mini dress with iridescent ruffle skirt & bow at hip, green satin strapless mini dress, white lace at neck & hem, purple bow at waist, pink & silver T-shirt with silver star & purple ribbon trim, white lace footless tights, hot pink spaghetti strap bodysuit, lilac hanger, hot pink tennis shoes, pink ballet slippers with ribbon ties, wide white pumps **Extras:** lilac oval brush **Head:** superstar **Head Markings:** inside or outside rim © Mattel Inc 1976 +/- country **Arms:** ptr **Body:** tan tnt, no b/l **Body Markings:** © Mattel Inc 1966/ China

Model #: 5716 **Name:** Sharin Sisters Gift Set **Box Date:** 1991 **Hair Color:** blonde **Hairstyle:** B=crinkled thigh length, bangs, pulled back with splatter color headband SK=front and sides pulled back with pink band, ponytail braided thigh length, partial bangs ST=front & sides pulled back with pink band, twisted, rest crinkled thigh length, partial bangs **Face:** all=blue eyes, blonde brows, deep pink lips & blush **Clothing:** B=turtleneck sleeveless mini dress, splatter top & purple denim skirt, matching short sleeve jacket & pants, hot pink stud earrings & ring, hot pink tennis shoes SK=pink short sleeve T-shirt, splatter mini skirt & knee-length shorts, sleeveless jacket, turquoise fanny pack & stud earrings, hot pink flats ST=yellow dress with silver rhinestones, turquoise tulle overskirt & hat, splatter print panties & socks, pink long sleeve jacket & lilac flower flats **Extras:** hot pink oval brush **Head:** B=superstar SK=1987 Skipper ST=1991 Stacie **Head Markings:** B=inside or outside rim © Mattel Inc 1976 +/- country SK=© Mattel Inc/ 1987 ST=© Mattel Inc/ 1991 **Arms:** B=bent SK=slight bend **Body:** B=tan tnt SK=tan tnt T=tan b/l Todd **Body Markings:** B=© Mattel Inc 1966/ Malaysia SK=© Mattel Inc 1987/ Malaysia ST=Malaysia

Model #: 10143 **Name:** Sharin Sisters Gift Set **Box Date:** 1992 **Hair Color:** blonde **Hairstyle:** B=thigh length pulled back with fabric headband, bangs SK=sides and front pulled back with blue band, partial bangs, rest waist length & curly ST=waist length with ends curly **Face:** B=green eyes, blonde brows, hot pink lips & blush SK=turquoise eyes, blonde brows, hot pink lips & blush ST=turquoise eyes, blonde brows, hot pink lips & blush **Clothing:** B=royal blue print halter-style mini dress, white lace trim & sheer short sleeve jacket, white lace knee-high shorts, white ring, wide pink pumps SK=blue print T-shirt style top with white lace vest & mini skirt, pink stretch shorts, iridescent heart shaped belt with pink fabric flower, pink flats ST=pink lace trimmed mini dress with blue print shorts, lace hat with pink flower, royal blue flower flats **Extras:** pink oval brush **Head:** B=superstar SK=1987 Skipper ST=1991 Stacie **Head Markings:** B=inside or outside rim © Mattel Inc 1976 +/- country SK=© Mattel Inc/ 1987 ST=© Mattel Inc/ 1991 **Arms:** B=bent SK=slight bend **Arms:** B=bent SK=slight bend **Body:** B=tan tnt SK=tan tnt ST=tan tnt b/l **Body Markings:** B=© Mattel Inc 1966/ Malaysia SK=© Mattel Inc 1987/ Malaysia ST=Malaysia

Model #: 1992 Name: Snap 'N Play Gift Set Box Date: 1992 Hair Color: blonde Hairstyle: 1 side & front pulled back, rest mid-back length, ends curled under Face: blue eyes, blonde brows, frosted fuchsia lips & blush Clothing: plastic crop tops: lilac, turquoise, lime green plastic tank tops: hot pink & yellow, long skirt: lilac with sheer overskirt with white glitter dots, pink belt, short skirt: pink & white checked with yellow ruffle & pink waistband, white splatter print with turquoise waistband, turquoise & white stripe with pink & white dots, yellow waistband, yellow knee-length skirt with yellow iridescent lace ruffle at waist & hem, turquoise waistband, 2 barrettes, wide pumps: lime green, hot pink, turquoise Extras: hot pink oval brush Head: Teen Talk Head Markings: © 1991 Mattel Inc Arms: ptr Body: tan tnt Body Markings: © Mattel Inc 1966/ China Notes: regular Snap 'N Play doll has pink painted bra and panties

Model #: 10227 Name: Stacie & Butterfly Pony Gift Set Box Date: 1993 Hair Color: blonde Hairstyle: front & sides pulled back, rest waist length, ends curled under Face: blue eyes, light brown brows, hot pink lips & blush Clothing: hot pink silver splatter top with silver angel cap sleeves & belt, matching knee-high shorts, sheer hot pink & white dot mini skirt & matching hat, silver stud earrings, pink pony with purple mane & tail, hot pink & silver cloth saddle, 3 butterfly barrettes, hot pink bridle, lead, hot pink flower flats Extras: hot pink oval brush Booklet: instructions Head: 1991 Stacie Head Markings: © Mattel Inc./ 1991 Body: tan b/l Body Markings: Malaysia

Model #: 13742 Name: Strollin' Fun Barbie & Kelly Playset Box Date: 1995 Hair Color: blonde Hairstyle: B=waist length with bangs & floral visor K=ponytail tied with pink ribbon & bangs Face: B=blue eyes, brown brows, hot pink lips & blush K=blue eyes, light brown brows, pink lips & blush Clothing: B=blue denim vest & shorts, pink & white stripe cropped T-shirt, pink belt, pink sunglasses, pearl stud earrings, white anklets, pink hiking boots K=denim overall dress, pink jellies, pink bottle, 3 rattles, diaper, pacifier Extras: small round pink brush & comb, white & pink stroller with accessory bag & sheet of cardboard punch outs Booklet: instructions Head: B=superstar & Kelly Head Markings: B=inside or outside rim © Mattel Inc 1976 +/- country K=© 1994 Mattel Inc Arms: bent Body: B=tan tnt K=light tan Body Markings: B=© Mattel Inc 1966/ China K=© 1994/ Mattel, Inc/ China Black Version: model #: 13743 Hair Color: brunette Face: B=brown eyes, black brows, light red lips & blush K=brown eyes, black brows, deep pink lips Head: B=Christie Head Markings: ©Mattel Inc/ 1987 Body: B=dark brown tnt K=dark brown

Model #: 14073 **Name:** Travelin' Sisters Playset **Box Date:** 1995 **Hair Color:** blonde for all **Hairstyle:** B=bangs, rest thigh length SK=bangs, rest pulled back with red headband, thigh length K=1 & 1/2 of front pulled back with red ribbon & white bow rest mid-back length ST=thigh length **Face:** all: blue eyes & blonde brows, B & SK=red lips & blush K & ST=light red lips & blush **Clothing:** B=red plaid beret, pleated mini skirt, white turtleneck long sleeve blouse with lace, blue denim vest, white pearl studs & ring, red handled blue & white gingham purse, wide red pumps SK=white & black dot long sleeve bodysuit, denim blue & red plaid mini skirt jumper, red plastic heart shaped purse, white post earrings, white anklets, red ankle boots ST=white sleeveless shirt, blue jeans, red plaid long sleeve blouse tied at waist, white hat with black dots, pearl stud earrings, white high-top athletic shoes K=blue & white gingham 1-piece short sleeve playsuit with dog appliqué & white lace collar, black flats with strap over foot **Extras:** red oval brush, 3 pieces of luggage, 2 blue, 1 red all with initial "B", hair dryer, bottles, small red brush, soap, jar, perfume & sheet of cardboard punch outs **Head:** B=superstar SK=1993 Skipper K=1994 Kelly ST=1991 Stacie **Head Markings:** B=inside or outside rim ©Mattel Inc 1976 +/- country SK=© Mattel Inc 1993 ST=© Mattel Inc/ 1991 K=© 1994 Mattel Inc **Arms:** B=bent SK=slight bend **Body:** B=tan tnt, white panties SK= 1987 ST=tan b/t Todd **Body Markings:** B=© Mattel Inc 1966/ Malaysia SK=© Mattel Inc. 1987/ Malaysia ST: Malaysia K=© 1994/ Mattel, Inc/ Malaysia **Japanese Version:** - Barbie has Bob Mackie head. Japanese writing on box. **Head Markings:** B= 1991 Mattel Inc rest same **Notes:** both sets available in U.S.

Model #: 9852 **Name:** Wedding Day Kelly & Todd **Box Date:** 1990 **Hair Color:** K=blonde T=brunette **Hairstyle:** K=sides & top pulled back with pink ribbon, rest thigh length with curly bangs T=fuzzy cropped **Face:** K=blue eyes, blonde brows, pink lips, light brown freckles T=blue eyes, brown brows, peach lips, light brown freckles **Clothing:** K=long pink dotted swiss puffed sleeve dress trimmed in lace, white basket with pink tulle & 3 pink flowers, pink pearl flower flats T=1-piece jumpsuit with pink shirt, white high collar, gray pinstripe pants, light gray vest, silver ascot tie, gray tails tuxedo with pink flower, white satin pillow with ring, black socks, black flower flats **Head:** both=1990 Todd **Head Markings** K & T= ©1990 Mattel Inc **Body:** both=tan b/l Todd **Body Markings:** K & T=Malaysia **Notes:** sold by Toys R Us and JCPenney, also available as part of 6 doll gift set

Mail-In Specials

Model #: 10309 **Name:** Kool-Aid Wacky Warehouse **Box Date:** 1992 **Hair Color:** blonde **Hairstyle:** waist-length side ponytail, braided, tied with 2 hot pink bands **Face:** blue eyes, blonde brows, deep pink lips & blush **Clothing:** multicolor short sleeve crop top tied in center, matching mid-thigh-length light purple shorts with multicolor ruffle at hip, purple stud earrings & ring, purple tote bag, green visor, light purple socks, hot pink tennis shoes **Extras:** hot pink oval brush **Head:** superstar **Head Markings:** inside or outside rim © Mattel Inc 1976 +/- country **Arms:** bent **Body:** tan tnt **Body Markings:** © Mattel Inc 1966/ China

Model #: 11763 **Name:** Kool-Aid Wacky Warehouse **Box Date:** 1994 **Hair Color:** blonde **Hairstyle:** mid-thigh length with bangs **Face:** turquoise eyes, brown brows, hot pink lips & blush **Clothing:** yellow 1-piece swimsuit with multicolor front tie bolero top & short skirt, pink stud & blue dangle earrings & ring, pink Kool Aid carryall, hot pink floppy hat, hot pink mules **Extras:** yellow oval brush **Head:** superstar **Head Markings:** inside or outside rim © Mattel Inc 1976 +/- country **Arms:** bent **Body:** tan tnt **Body Markings:** © Mattel Inc 1966/ Malaysia

Model #: 0 **Name:** Kraft Treasurers Barbie **Box Date:** 1992 **Hair Color:** blonde **Hairstyle:** waist length **Face:** turquoise eyes, blonde brows, red lips & blush **Clothing:** long sleeve mini dress with white bodice, multicolor sleeves & skirt, blue collar, Cheesasaurus Rex appliqué, red vest, blue stretch pants, blue floppy hat, matching tote bag, red hoop earrings & ring, red tennis shoes **Extras:** red oval brush **Head:** superstar **Head Markings:** inside or outside rim © Mattel Inc 1976 +/- country **Arms:** bent **Body:** tan tnt **Body Markings:** © Mattel Inc 1966/ China

Model #: 0 **Name:** Lady Lovely Locks Starlight Blue Barbie **Box Date:** 1988 **Hair Color:** blonde **Hairstyle:** sides & front pulled back, rest curly waist length with curly bangs **Face:** blue eyes, blonde brows, pink lips & blush **Clothing:** light blue knee-length dress with iridescent blue ruffle on skirt, light blue wide pumps **Head:** superstar **Head Markings:** inside or outside rim © Mattel Inc 1976 +/- country **Arms:** ptr **Body:** tan tnt **Body Markings:** © Mattel Inc 1966/ China **Notes:** available by mail with proof of purchase, doll is same as Fashion Play Barbie released in Canada, some are developing pale splotches on legs

Model #: 10123 **Name:** Little Debbie **Box Date:** 1992 **Hair Color:** brown **Hairstyle:** mid-back length, ends curled under, curly bangs **Face:** turquoise eyes, light brown brows, deep pink lips & blush **Clothing:** blue & white short sleeve knee-length full skirt gingham dress with sewn in panties, white lace trimmed collar & cuffs, white lace apron, tan straw hat, black pointed flats **Extras:** 2-piece white stand & light blue oval brush **Booklet:** coupon **Head:** superstar **Head Markings:** inside or outside rim © Mattel Inc 1976 +/- country **Arms:** ptr **Body:** tan tnt **Body Markings:** © Mattel Inc 1966/ China

Name: Barbie pink silhouette box 1959-60 **Box Date:** 1959 **Clothing:** regular issue dolls, usually #1, #2 or #3 ponytail Barbie dressed in outfits for display in stores - not normally available for sale in the pink box, but as displays changed dolls were sold — model #s used were 100 less than outfit model # - known outfits: Barbie-Q, Busy Gal, Commuter Set, Enchanted Evening, Evening Splendour, Friday Night Date, Gay Parisienne, Let's Dance, Nighty Negligee, Plantation Belle (illus.), Resort Set, Roman Holiday, Silken Flame, Solo in the Spotlight, Suburban Shopper, Sweater Girl, Sweet Dreams, Wedding Day Set, Winter Holiday

Name: Barbie dressed box 1963-65 **Box Date:** 1962 **Clothing:** dressed straight leg Barbie dolls in special striped box with end panel stating dressed doll & clear inside cover with gold sticker, known outfits: After Five, American Airlines Stewardess, Black Magic, Bride's Dream, Career Girl, Country Fair, Dinner at Eight, Evening Splendor, Garden Party, Garden Tea Party, Ice Breaker, Knitting Pretty (illus.) pink or blue version, Masquerade, Mood for Music, Nighty Negligee, Orange Blossom, Peachy Fleecy, Registered Nurse, Senior Prom, Sheath Sensation, Solo in the Spotlight, Swinging Easy, Tennis Anyone?, Theatre Date, Barbie in Holland, Mexico, Switzerland, Arabian Nights, Cinderella, Guinevere

Name: Ken dressed box doll 1963-65 **Box Date:** 1962 **Clothing:** dressed straight leg Ken dolls in special box with stripes, end panel states dressed doll with outfit sticker & clear inside cover with gold seal, known outfits: Campus Hero, Casuals, Dr. Ken, Fraternity Meeting, Holiday, Sailor, Ski Champion (illus.), Time for Tennis, Touchdown, Ken in Holland, Mexico, Switzerland, Arabian Nights, King Arthur, the Prince

Name: Midge dressed box **Box Date:** 1963 **Clothing:** dressed straight leg doll, regular box but end panel says dressed doll & side panel has stripes, includes clear inside cover with gold label, known outfits: Crisp'N Cool (illus.), Fancy Free, Orange Blossom

Name: Skipper dressed box **Box Date:** 1964 **Clothing:** dressed regular straight leg doll, regular box but end panel says dressed doll & side panel has stripes, includes clear inside cover gold label, known outfits: Flower Girl (illus.), Happy Birthday, Masquerade Party, Red Sensation, School Days, Silk'N Fancy, Skating Fun

Baggie dolls are dolls from the 1970s repackaged in a plastic bag instead of box. They are considered leftovers and were usually sold for a discount. Talkers did not have a talking mechanism and all the dolls, with the exception of Francie and Casey, were previously issued dolls. The Francie Baggie is pictured here and the Casey Baggie is pictured with the regular Casey.

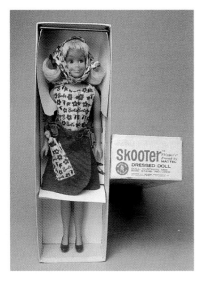

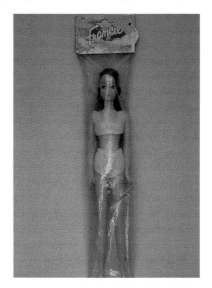

Name: Skooter dressed box **Issue Date:** 1965 **Box Date:** 1963 **Clothing:** found in retail display, dressed straight leg doll in Skipper dressed box with dressed Skooter end panel & outfit sticker (in photo sticker has fallen off) known outfit: Day at the Fair, **Notes:** usually not considered an official dressed box doll. This also applies to Allan dressed doll, which is found in retail display, dressed in Rovin' Reporter

Model #: 7699 **Name:** Francie Baggie **Tag Date:** 1974 **Hair Color:** brunette **Hairstyle:** waist length, parted on side **Face:** brown eyes, brown brows, light pink lips **Clothing:** yellow 2-piece swimsuit **Head:** Francie **Arms:** Mexico **Body:** pale pink s/l thin hollow **Body Markings:** © 1966/ Mattel, Inc./ Taiwan **Notes:** same face used on Quick Curl Francie

Model #: 1115 **Name:** Barbie Baggie **Tag Date:** 1972 **Hair Color:** red blonde brunette **Hairstyle:** parted on side & pulled back into loosely curled ponytail at nape of neck **Face:** blue center glance eyes, rooted lashes, light brown brows, pink lips **Clothing:** white vinyl bikini with gold net sleeveless cover-up **Extras:** clear X stand **Head:** tnt Barbie **Head Markings:** inside rim © 1966 Mattel Inc & country **Arms:** Mexico **Body:** pink talker **Body Markings:** © 1967/ Mattel, Inc./ U.S. & Foreign/ Pats.Pend./ Hong Kong **Notes:** this is one example of a baggie doll. Live Action Barbie is another known example

Model #: 1156 **Name:** P.J. Baggie **Tag Date:** 1973 **Hair Color:** blonde **Hair Style:** side part, flipped up below shoulders, 2 small sections on either side of part braided & tied off with seed beads **Face:** brown eyes, rooted lashes, light brown brows, orange lips & blush **Clothing:** orange long sleeve mini dress with sewn in orange pantyhose & knee high gold metallic boots, purple vest with fringe below knee, wrist tag **Head:** Midge **Head Markings:** inside rim © Mattel Inc. 1958 & country, date may be gone **Arms:** living **Body:** tan live action **Body Markings:** © 1968 Mattel Inc./ U.S. & Foreign Patented/ Patented in Canada 1967/ Other Patents pending/ Taiwan

Model #: 1159 **Name:** Ken Baggie **Tag Date:** 1973 **Hair Color:** brunette **Face:** blue eyes, brown brows, pink lips **Clothing:** gold satin pants, multicolor green, blue, yellow, white, hot pink long sleeve shirt with faux brown suede vest with fringe, brown loafers & wrist tag **Head:** 68 Ken **Head Markings:** © 1968 Mattel Inc **Body:** pink live action **Body Markings:** © 1968/ Mattel, Inc./ Taiwan/ U.S. & For.Patd./ Patented in/ Canada 1967/ Other Pats/ Pending **Notes:** This is just one example of a baggie Ken. Another known example is a nonfunctioning Talking Ken in turquoise & coral outfit

Bibliography

Augustyniak, J. Michael. *The Barbie® Doll Boom*. Collector Books, 1996.

Barbie® Bazaar, "Mattel & Christmas Catalog Reprints of Barbie Doll 1959-1965." Special edition 1994.

Barbie® Bazaar, "Mattel and Christmas Catalog Reprints 1969-1972." Special edition 1992.

Blitman, Joe. *Francie™ & Her Mod, Mod, Mod, Mod World of Fashion*. Hobby House Press, 1996.

Christensen, Alva and Laurel. "Dressed Box Dolls Part I." *Miller's Barbie® Collector*. Summer 1996.

DeWein, Sibyl. *Collectible Barbie Dolls 1977-1979*. Jostens, 1980.

DeWein, Sibyl and Evelyn Ashabraner. *Barbie Dolls and Collectibles*. Collector Books, 1977, updated 1990.

Rana, Margo. *Barbie® Exclusives*. Collector Books, 1995.

Rana, Margo. *Barbie™ Exclusives Book II*. Collector Books, 1996.

Theirault, Florence. *Theirault's Presents Barbie®*. Gold Horse Publishing, 1985.

Theirault, Florence. *Barbie® Rarities*. Gold Horse Publishing, 1992.

How to Use the Price Guide

First, please remember that this is presented as simply a guide. Pricing can fall within a huge range based on dealer and other indefinable variables. A doll may be purchased for $40 and found the very same day with another dealer for $15. Patience and comparison shopping alleviate some of the problem.

The "NRFB" (not removed from box) column contains what could best be called "factory fresh" condition for each doll. Some dolls are in a box encased in cellophane; others are in two-piece boxes that may be opened and the doll carefully removed. Rather than use two different terms, NRFB is used to describe mint, undisturbed perfection for each particular doll.

"Mint no box" is for a doll missing only its box. All original clothing and accessories are included. There has always been a "50% rule" in Barbie collecting: A mint doll missing only its box is worth 50% of a NRFB example. That is a very general rule, and in this price guide I have attempted to accurately reflect the real effect of the missing box. Some dolls are worth considerably less than 50% without their boxes and some are worth considerably more than 50% of the boxed doll price. These decisions are based on the individual availability and desirability of each doll.

Name	Average Retail	NRFB	Mint no Box	Page Number	Name	Average Retail	NRFB	Mint no Box	Page Number
100th Celebration Sears	15	90	45	230	Barbie and Friends: Ken Barbie P.J.	30	75	25	263
25th Year Pink Jubilee Wal-Mart	12	60	30	239	Barbie and Ken Camping Out	25	95	35	263
30th Anniversary Ken	200	200	100	204	Barbie and the All Stars Barbie	15	20	7	90
30th Anniversary Midge	200	200	100	204	Barbie and the All Stars Christie	15	20	7	99
30th Anniversary Skipper	200	200	100	204	Barbie and the All Stars Ken	15	20	7	156
35th Anniversary Barbie	35	35	15	203	Barbie and the All Stars Midge	15	40	15	81
35th Anniversary Barbie brunette hair	35	80	40	203	Barbie and the All Stars Teresa	15	35	10	103
50th Anniversary Mattel Barbie	600	600	300	207	Barbie Baggie	3	150	75	269
Air Force Barbie Stars & Stripes	20	45	22	208	Barbie bubblecut 1961 & 62 white, ginger & sable	3	650	325	12
Air Force Thunderbirds Barbie Stars & Stripes	20	25	10	209	Barbie bubblecut 1961 brunette & titian	3	350	175	12
Air Force Thunderbirds Barbie black version Stars & Stripes	20	25	10	209	Barbie bubblecut 1961 blondes	3	300	150	12
Air Force Thunderbirds Ken Stars & Stripes	20	25	10	209	Barbie bubblecut 1962-67 blondes	3	300	150	12
Air Force Thunderbirds Ken black Stars & Stripes	20	25	10	209	Barbie bubblecut 1962-67 brunette & titian	3	350	175	12
All American Barbie	15	20	5	42	Barbie bubblecut Sidepart	3	800	400	13
All American Christie	15	20	5	100	Barbie dressed box an average	8	700	200	268
All American Ken	15	20	5	157	Barbie for President Toys R Us	20	35	17	248
All American Kira	15	20	5	109	Barbie for President Toys R Us black version	20	35	17	248
All American Teresa	15	30	10	104	Barbie Hair Happenin's	8	1,800	600	20
All Star Ken	10	25	10	150	Barbie pink silhouette box an average #3 Ponytail	8	1,500	700	268
All Stars Barbie	15	20	7	39	Barbie Ponytail #1 blonde	3	6,000	4,000	11
All Stars Christie	15	20	7	99	Barbie Ponytail #1 brunette	3	9,000	7,000	11
All Stars Ken	15	20	7	156	Barbie Ponytail #2 blonde	3	4,000	3,500	11
All Stars Midge	15	40	15	81	Barbie Ponytail #2 brunette	3	5,000	4,500	11
All Stars Teresa	15	35	10	103	Barbie Ponytail #3 blonde	3	700	500	11
Allan bendable leg	5	650	175	167	Barbie Ponytail #3 brunette	3	1,000	800	11
Allan	3	135	55	167	Barbie Ponytail #4 blonde	3	450	300	11
American Beauties Army	20	40	20	208	Barbie Ponytail #4 brunette	3	600	400	11
American Beauty Mardi Gras	35	100	50	172	Barbie Ponytail #5 blondes	3	300	200	12
American Beauty Queen	12	25	12	45	Barbie Ponytail #5 brunette & titian	3	400	300	12
American Beauty Queen black version	12	35	15	67	Barbie Ponytail #6 & 7 blondes	3	300	200	12
American Girl 1965	5	975	450	14	Barbie Ponytail #6 & 7 brunette & titian	3	400	300	12
American Girl 1966	5	1,100	600	14	Barbie Swirl Ponytail ash & lemon blonde	3	400	300	13
American Girl 1966 high color	5	1,800	1,200	14	Barbie Swirl Ponytail brunette, titian & platinum	3	550	450	13
American Girl Side-Part	5	3,500	3,000	14	Barbie Talking orange bikini, bun in back	8	375	150	17
American Stories Series Colonial	25	25	8	172	Barbie Talking orange bikini, Stacey head mold	8	450	225	19
American Stories Series Pilgrim	25	25	8	172	Barbie Talking side ponytail	8	300	125	17
American Stories Series Pioneer	25	25	8	172	Barbie Talking Spanish	8	550	450	16
Ames Country Looks	10	25	12	213	Barbie Talking white bikini, gold coverup	8	500	175	19
Ames Denim 'n Lace	10	20	10	213	Barbie trade-in twist & turn	2	300	150	15
Ames Hot Looks	10	20	10	213	Barbie twist & turn flip hair, multicolor splotches	5	500	175	17
Ames Party in Pink	10	25	12	213	Barbie twist & turn flip hair, pink & white	5	500	175	18
Angel Face	12	30	10	30	Barbie twist & turn flip hair, psychedelic	5	550	175	18
Angel Lights	100	100	60	51	Barbie twist & turn orange net	5	450	175	15
Animal Lovin' Barbie	15	35	7	37	Barbie twist & turn pink check	5	550	175	16
Animal Lovin' Barbie black version	15	35	7	64	Barbie with Growin' Pretty Hair blue print dress	8	275	150	21
Animal Lovin' Ken	15	25	7	155	Barbie with Growin' Pretty Hair pink satin dress	8	275	150	19
Animal Lovin' Nikki	15	25	7	108	Baseball Date Target	10	20	10	236
Anniversary Star Wal-Mart	12	35	17	239	Basketball Kevin	10	15	5	130
Applause Holiday	45	55	20	214	Bath Blast	10	15	5	48
Applause Style	45	30	10	214	Bath Blast black version	10	15	5	69
Army American Beauties	20	40	20	208	Bath Magic	10	15	5	45
Astronaut	15	65	20	33	Bath Magic black version	10	15	5	67
Astronaut black version	15	80	25	62	Bathtime Fun	10	15	5	42
Astronaut Toys R Us	10	25	12	248	Bathtime Fun black version	10	15	5	66
Astronaut Toys R Us black version	20	20	10	248	Bathtime Fun Skipper Target	10	20	10	236
Australian Dolls of the World	20	40	20	184	Baton Twirler Skipper	10	15	5	121
B Mine	10	20	10	220	Baton Twirler Skipper black version	10	15	5	124
Babysitter Courtney	10	20	5	127	Baywatch Barbie	15	15	5	56
Babysitter Skipper	10	20	5	120	Baywatch Barbie black version	15	15	5	73
Babysitter Skipper black version	10	20	5	124	Baywatch Ken	15	15	5	162
Babysitter Skipper 3 babies	10	15	5	123	Baywatch Ken black version	15	15	5	166
Babysitter Skipper black version 3 babies	10	15	5	125	Baywatch Teresa	15	30	15	106
Back to School	10	20	10	220	Beach Blast Barbie	7	25	5	40
Baggie Barbie	3	150	75	269	Beach Blast Christie	7	25	5	99
Baggie Casey	3	150	75	134	Beach Blast Ken	7	25	5	155
Baggie Francie	3	150	75	269	Beach Blast Miko	7	25	5	109
Baggie Ken	3	100	45	269	Beach Blast Skipper	7	25	5	119
Baggie P.J.	3	150	75	269	Beach Blast Steven	7	25	5	169
Baggie/Pose 'N Play Skipper	3	75	40	114	Beach Blast Teresa	7	35	10	103
Bakery McGlynn's	15	150	75	228	Beach Fun Club Doll	20	45	22	216
Ballerina Barbie	10	60	30	24	Beautiful Bride 1976	10	250	125	25
Ballerina Barbie Mervyn's	15	65	30	229	Beautiful Bride 1978	10	175	90	26
Ballerina Cara	10	75	35	94	Beauty Pageant Skipper Toys R Us	15	30	17	249
Ballroom Beauties Collection-Starlight Waltz	75	75	35	173	Beauty Secrets Barbie	12	45	15	28
Ballroom Beauty Wal-Mart	12	20	10	239	Beauty Secrets Christie	12	45	15	96
Barbie & Friends Disney Toys R Us	30	65	25	248	Bedtime	15	15	3	51
Barbie & the Beat	15	25	7	39	Bedtime black version	15	15	3	70
Barbie & the Beat Christie	15	25	7	99	Benefit Ball Classique	50	200	100	173
Barbie & the Beat Midge	15	40	9	82	Benefit Performance porcelain	200	400	200	204
Barbie and Champion	45	60	20	262	Benetton Barbie	15	25	10	42
					Benetton Christie	15	25	10	100
					Benetton Kira	15	25	10	110

Name	Average Retail	NRFB	Mint no Box	Page Number	Name	Average Retail	NRFB	Mint no Box	Page Number
Bicyclin'	25	25	7	51	Christian Dior	100	150	75	173
Bicyclin' black version	25	25	7	70	Christie Talking	8	175	65	92
Billy Boy Feelin' Groovy	20	200	100	35	Christie Talking multicolor suit	8	250	125	93
Birthday Barbie black version, blue dress	15	20	7	70	Christie twist & turn	5	250	125	92
Birthday Barbie black version, white dress with blue sash	15	15	7	73	Circus Star FAO Schwarz	70	75	35	245
Birthday Barbie blue dress	15	20	7	52	City Sophisticate Service Merchandise	20	70	35	233
Birthday Barbie Hispanic version white dress with blue sash	15	15	7	79	City Style Classique	50	85	40	174
Birthday Barbie white dress with blue sash	15	15	7	56	Classique Benefit Ball	50	200	100	173
Birthday Fun at McDonald's Gift Set	25	30	10	263	Classique City Style	50	85	40	174
Birthday Party Barbie	15	30	7	48	Classique Evening Extravaganza	60	65	30	174
Birthday Party Barbie black version	15	30	7	69	Classique Evening Extravaganza black version	60	85	40	174
Birthday Surprise Barbie	15	30	7	45	Classique Midnight Gala	60	60	30	174
Birthday Surprise Barbie black version	15	30	7	67	Classique Opening Night	60	125	60	175
Black Barbie	15	50	25	60	Classique Uptown Chic	60	70	35	175
Black Francie 1st "colored" light version	5	1,600	900	131	Club Doll Beach Fun	20	45	22	216
Black Francie 2nd "colored" dark version	5	1,600	900	131	Club Doll Denim'N Ruffles Gift Set	35	45	22	216
Bloomingdale's Donna Karan	65	100	50	214	Club Doll Fantastica	20	45	22	216
Bloomingdale's Donna Karan brunette hair	65	125	60	214	Club Doll Festiva	20	45	22	216
Bloomingdale's Savvy Shopper	65	95	50	215	Club Doll Island Fun Gift Set	20	55	27	217
Blossom Beautiful Sears	45	400	200	230	Club Doll Jewel Jubilee	20	85	42	217
Blossom Beauty Shopko/Venture	15	45	22	234	Club Doll Me and My Mustang (doll only)	15	30	15	217
Blue Elegance Hills	12	70	35	224	Club Doll Party Sensation	20	50	25	217
Blue Rhapsody porcelain	200	700	350	205	Club Doll Peach Blossom	20	65	32	218
Blue Rhapsody Service Merchandise	20	300	150	232	Club Doll Royal Romance	20	70	35	218
Bob Mackie Designer Gold	150	850	425	195	Club Doll Season's Greetings	20	100	50	218
Bob Mackie Empress Bride	300	850	425	195	Club Doll Secret Hearts Barbie Gift Set	25	40	20	218
Bob Mackie Goddess of the Sun	200	200	100	195	Club Doll Very Violet	20	70	35	219
Bob Mackie Masquerade Ball	200	500	250	195	Club Doll Wedding Fantasy Gift Set	25	125	60	219
Bob Mackie Neptune Fantasy	200	900	450	196	Club Doll Winter Royale	20	100	50	219
Bob Mackie Platinum	200	600	300	196	Club Doll Winters Eve	20	25	13	219
Bob Mackie Queen of Hearts	200	250	125	196	Colonial Barbie American Stories Series	25	25	8	172
Bob Mackie Starlight Splendor	200	600	300	196	Color Magic cardboard box blonde hair	8	2,500	900	16
Boy, Billy Feelin' Groovy	20	200	100	35	Color Magic cardboard box midnight hair	8	3,500	1,500	16
Brad	5	125	150	168	Color Magic plastic box blonde hair	8	2,000	900	15
Brad Talking	8	450	175	168	Color Magic plastic box midnight hair	8	3,000	1,500	15
Brazilian Dolls of the World	20	70	35	185	Cookin' Goodies Tutti	8	450	175	138
Bubble Angel	10	10	5	56	Cool & Crimp Courtney	10	10	3	128
Bubble Angel black version	10	10	5	74	Cool & Crimp Kevin	10	10	3	130
Bubblecut Barbie 1961 & 62 white, ginger & sable	3	650	325	12	Cool & Crimp Skipper	10	10	3	122
Bubblecut Barbie 1961 brunette & titian	3	350	175	12	Cool & Crimp Skipper black version	10	10	3	125
Bubblecut Barbie 1961 blondes	3	300	150	12	Cool 'N Sassy Toys R Us	15	20	10	249
Bubblecut Barbie 1962-67 blondes	3	300	150	12	Cool 'N Sassy Toys R Us black version	15	20	10	249
Bubblecut Barbie 1962-67 brunette & titian	3	350	175	12	Cool City Blues Toys R Us	30	45	22	249
Bubblecut Barbie Sidepart	3	800	400	13	Cool Looks Toys R Us	15	20	10	250
Busy Barbie	6	200	100	21	Cool Times Barbie	15	30	7	38
Busy Francie	6	250	125	133	Cool Times Christie	15	30	7	98
Busy Gal	50	50	25	203	Cool Times Ken	15	30	7	155
Busy Ken	6	100	50	146	Cool Times Midge	15	50	25	81
Busy Steffie	8	200	100	86	Cool Times Teresa	15	35	10	103
Busy Talking Barbie	8	250	125	21	Cool Tops Courtney	10	20	5	127
Busy Talking Ken	8	175	100	146	Cool Tops Kevin	10	20	5	129
Busy Talking Steffie	8	250	125	86	Cool Tops Skipper	10	20	5	119
Butterfly Princess Barbie	15	15	6	56	Cool Tops Skipper black version	10	20	5	124
Butterfly Princess Barbie black version	15	15	6	74	Costume Ball Barbie	15	25	7	43
Butterfly Princess Teresa	15	15	6	106	Costume Ball Barbie black version	15	25	7	66
Caboodles	10	15	5	49	Costume Ball Ken	15	25	7	158
California Barbie	8	20	7	36	Costume Ball Ken black version	15	25	7	166
California Christie	8	20	7	97	Country Bride Wal-Mart	12	20	10	239
California Dream Barbie	8	20	7	36	Country Bride Wal-Mart black version	12	20	10	239
California Dream Christie	8	20	7	97	Country Bride Wal-Mart Hispanic version	12	25	12	239
California Dream Ken	8	20	7	154	Country Looks Ames	10	25	12	213
California Dream Midge	8	40	15	81	Country Star Wal-Mart	15	20	10	240
California Dream Teresa	8	35	10	102	Country Star Wal-Mart black version	15	20	10	240
California Ken	8	20	7	153	Country Star Wal-Mart Hispanic version	15	25	12	240
California Midge	8	40	15	81	Crystal Barbie	15	35	10	31
Camp Fun Barbie	10	10	5	52	Crystal Barbie black version	15	35	10	61
Camp Fun Barbie black version	10	15	5	71	Crystal Ken	15	25	7	151
Camp Fun Ken	10	20	7	161	Crystal Ken black version	15	50	10	164
Camp Fun Midge	10	10	5	83	Cut and Style all hair colors	13	13	5	57
Camp Fun Skipper	10	10	5	122	Cut and Style black version	13	13	5	74
Camp Fun Teresa	10	15	7	105	Cute'n Cool Target	10	20	10	236
Canadian Dolls of the World	20	80	40	185	Czechoslovakian Dolls of the World	20	125	60	185
Caroling Fun	10	25	12	220	Dance 'N Twirl	50	50	15	57
Casey	5	450	150	134	Dance 'N Twirl black version	50	50	15	74
Casey Baggie	3	150	75	134	Dance Club Barbie	15	50	15	40
Cheerleading Courtney	10	20	5	128	Dance Club Devon	15	40	10	99
Chelsie High School	15	30	8	134	Dance Club Kayla	15	65	20	91
Child's World Disney Barbie	15	35	15	245	Dance Club Ken	15	65	20	156
Child's World Disney Barbie black version	15	35	15	245	Dance Magic Barbie	15	25	7	40
Children's Collector Series Rapunzel	40	40	20	173	Dance Magic Barbie black version	15	25	7	64
Chinese Dolls of the World	20	20	10	185	Dance Magic Ken	15	20	5	156
Chris	5	250	100	140	Dance Magic Ken black version	15	25	7	166
					Dance Moves Barbie	15	15	5	58
					Dance Moves Barbie black version	15	15	5	75
					Dance Moves Teresa	15	15	5	106

Name	Average Retail	NRFB	Mint no Box	Page Number
Dance Sensation Toys R Us	15	25	12	250
Day-to-Night Barbie	15	30	10	32
Day-to-Night Barbie black version	15	30	10	61
Day-to-Night Barbie Hispanic version	15	60	20	77
Day-to-Night Ken	15	25	12	152
Day-to-Night Ken black version	15	25	12	164
Dazzlin' Date Target	10	25	10	237
Deluxe Quick Curl Barbie	5	75	35	24
Deluxe Quick Curl Cara	5	75	35	94
Deluxe Quick Curl P.J.	5	75	35	88
Denim 'n Lace Ames	10	20	10	213
Denim'N Ruffles Gift Set Club Doll	35	45	22	216
Desert Storm/Rendezvous with Destiny Barbie	20	25	10	210
Desert Storm/Rendezvous with Destiny Barbie black version	20	25	10	210
Desert Storm/Rendezvous with Destiny Ken	20	25	10	211
Desert Storm/Rendezvous with Destiny Ken black version	20	25	10	211
Designer Gold Bob Mackie	150	850	425	195
Disney Barbie black version Child's World/Children's Palace	15	35	15	245
Disney Barbie Child's World/Children's Palace	15	35	15	245
Disney Fun 1st release	25	35	10	215
Disney Fun 2nd release	25	35	10	215
Doctor Barbie	15	30	15	36
Doctor Ken	15	30	15	154
Dolls of the World Australian	20	40	20	184
Dolls of the World Brazilian	20	70	35	185
Dolls of the World Canadian	20	80	40	185
Dolls of the World Chinese	20	20	10	185
Dolls of the World Czechoslovakian	20	125	60	185
Dolls of the World Dutch	20	20	10	186
Dolls of the World English	20	50	25	186
Dolls of the World/International Eskimo	20	100	50	186
Dolls of the World Eskimo reissue	20	30	15	186
Dolls of the World German	20	100	45	187
Dolls of the World German reissue	20	20	10	187
Dolls of the World Greek	20	100	45	187
Dolls of the World Icelandic	20	100	50	187
Dolls of the World/International Irish	20	150	75	188
Dolls of the World Irish reissue	20	20	15	188
Dolls of the World/International Italian	20	185	90	188
Dolls of the World Italian reissue	20	20	10	188
Dolls of the World Jamaican	20	25	12	189
Dolls of the World Japanese	20	150	75	189
Dolls of the World Kenyan	20	20	10	189
Dolls of the World Korean	20	60	30	189
Dolls of the World Malaysian	20	35	17	190
Dolls of the World Mexican	20	40	20	190
Dolls of the World Native American I	20	25	12	190
Dolls of the World Native American II	20	30	15	190
Dolls of the World Native American III	20	20	10	191
Dolls of the World Nigerian	20	60	30	191
Dolls of the World/International Oriental	20	150	75	191
Dolls of the World/International Parisian	20	185	90	191
Dolls of the World Parisian reissue	20	20	10	192
Dolls of the World Peruvian	20	100	50	192
Dolls of the World Polynesian	20	20	10	192
Dolls of the World/International Royal	20	185	90	192
Dolls of the World Russian	20	50	25	193
Dolls of the World/International Scottish	20	150	75	193
Dolls of the World Scottish reissue	20	40	20	193
Dolls of the World/International Spanish	20	120	60	193
Dolls of the World Spanish reissue	20	40	20	194
Dolls of the World/International Swedish	20	120	60	194
Dolls of the World/International Swiss	20	110	55	194
Donna Karan Bloomingdale's	65	100	50	214
Donna Karan brunette hair Bloomingdale's	65	125	60	214
Dorothy from Wizard of Oz Hollywood Legends	45	45	25	183
Dr. Barbie	15	20	7	52
Dr. Barbie black version	15	20	7	71
Dr. Barbie with black baby	15	50	7	71
Dramatic New Living Barbie	5	250	125	18
Dramatic New Living Skipper	5	125	50	112
Dream Bride	30	45	10	45
Dream Date Barbie	15	40	20	30
Dream Date Ken	15	20	10	151
Dream Date P.J.	15	45	22	89
Dream Date Skipper Toys R Us	15	40	20	250
Dream Fantasy Wal-Mart	10	30	15	240
Dream Glow Barbie	15	40	7	33
Dream Glow Barbie black version	15	40	7	62
Dream Glow Barbie Hispanic version	15	75	20	77
Dream Glow Ken	15	20	5	152
Dream Glow Ken black version	15	20	5	164
Dream Princess Sears	25	70	35	230
Dream Time	10	25	7	33
Dream Time Toys R Us	15	45	10	250
Dream Wedding Gift Set Toys R Us	25	35	15	251
Dream Wedding Gift Set Toys R Us black version	25	35	15	251
Dress 'n Fun	7	20	3	176
Dress 'n Fun black version	7	20	3	176
Dress 'n Fun Hispanic version	7	25	3	176
Dressed box Barbie an average	8	700	200	268
Dressed box Ken an average	8	350	100	268
Dressed box Midge an average	8	750	150	268
Dressed box Skipper an average	8	350	75	268
Dressed box Skooter an average	8	350	75	269
Dude High School	15	60	15	134
Dutch Dolls of the World	20	20	10	186
Earring Magic Barbie all hair colors	15	20	7	49
Earring Magic Barbie black version	15	20	7	69
Earring Magic Ken	15	40	20	160
Earring Magic Midge	15	40	18	82
Easter Fun	10	30	15	220
Easter Party	10	25	12	221
Egyptian Queen Great Eras	60	70	35	178
Elizabethan Queen Great Eras	60	60	30	179
Emerald Elegance Toys R Us	20	40	20	251
Emerald Elegance Toys R Us black version	20	40	20	251
Empress Bride Bob Mackie	300	850	425	195
Enchanted Evening JC Penney	30	150	75	226
Enchanted Evening porcelain	200	400	200	205
Enchanted Seasons Collection Snow Princess	80	150	75	175
Enchanted Seasons Collection Spring Bouquet	80	100	50	175
English Dolls of the World	20	50	25	186
Eskimo International	20	100	50	186
Eskimo reissue Dolls of the World	20	30	15	186
Evening Elegance JC Penney	25	150	75	226
Evening Enchantment Sears	15	50	25	230
Evening Extravaganza black version Classique	60	85	40	174
Evening Extravaganza Classique	60	65	30	174
Evening Flame Home Shopping Club	50	150	75	225
Evening Sensation JC Penney	30	75	35	226
Evening Sparkle Hills	12	45	22	224
Evergreen Princess Winter Princess Series	80	150	75	211
Fabulous Fur Mervyn's	15	50	25	229
Fantastica Club Doll	20	45	22	216
FAO Schwarz Circus Star	70	75	35	245
FAO Schwarz Golden Greetings	50	250	100	246
FAO Schwarz Jeweled Splendor Signature Collection	250	350	175	246
FAO Schwarz Madison Ave	70	200	100	246
FAO Schwarz Night Sensation	50	175	65	246
FAO Schwarz Rockettes	70	175	65	247
FAO Schwarz Shopping Spree	30	30	15	247
FAO Schwarz Silver Screen	70	150	75	247
FAO Schwarz Winter Fantasy	50	200	100	247
Fashion Brights Toys R Us	15	25	12	252
Fashion Brights Toys R Us black version	15	25	12	252
Fashion Jeans Barbie	10	45	15	29
Fashion Jeans Ken	10	45	15	150
Fashion Photo Barbie	10	80	25	25
Fashion Photo Christie	10	80	25	95
Fashion Photo P.J.	10	85	30	88
Fashion Play white & lilac teddy	7	12	3	176
Fashion Play white & lilac teddy black doll	7	12	3	176
Fashion Play white & lilac teddy Hispanic doll	7	12	3	176
Fashion Play blue & pink playsuit	7	12	3	176
Fashion Play blue & pink playsuit black doll	7	12	3	176
Fashion Play blue & pink playsuit Hispanic doll	7	12	3	176
Fashion Queen	8	500	145	13
Fashion Queen Wig Wardrobe	5	250	50	13
Feelin' Groovy	20	200	100	35
Feeling Fun	10	20	7	38
Festiva Club Doll	20	45	22	216
Firefighter Toys R Us	20	30	15	252
Firefighter Toys R Us black version	20	30	15	252
Flapper Great Eras	60	175	85	179
Flight Time Barbie	15	30	10	40
Flight Time Barbie black version	15	25	7	65
Flight Time Barbie Hispanic version	15	45	15	78
Flight Time Ken	15	20	7	156
Fluff	5	125	50	126
Fountain Mermaid	10	15	5	52
Fountain Mermaid black version	10	15	5	71
Francie 1st "colored" black version light	5	1,600	900	131
Francie 2nd "colored" black version dark	5	1,600	900	131
Francie Baggie	3	150	75	269

Name	Average Retail	NRFB	Mint no Box	Page Number
Francie bendable leg	5	450	150	130
Francie Hair Happenin's	8	450	225	132
Francie no bangs	5	1,500	750	132
Francie straight leg	5	350	150	131
Francie twist & turn	5	450	150	131
Francie twist & turn short flip, multicolor	5	600	150	132
Francie twist & turn short flip, yellow & pink 1965	5	700	150	132
Francie with Growin' Pretty Hair	8	275	125	133
Free Moving Barbie	8	65	30	23
Free Moving Cara	8	65	30	93
Free Moving Curtis	8	35	15	169
Free Moving Ken	8	35	15	147
Free Moving P.J.	8	65	30	87
Frills and Fantasy Wal-Mart	10	30	15	240
Fun to Dress pink & white bra & panties	7	12	3	177
Fun to Dress pink & white bra & panties black doll	7	12	3	177
Fun to Dress pink teddy	7	12	3	177
Fun to Dress pink teddy black doll	7	12	3	177
Fun to Dress pink camisole & panties	7	12	3	177
Fun to Dress pink camisole & panties black doll	7	12	3	177
Fun to Dress pink camisole & panties Hispanic doll	7	12	3	177
Fun to Dress aqua towel	7	12	3	178
Fun to Dress aqua towel black doll	7	12	3	178
Fun to Dress aqua towel Hispanic doll	7	12	3	178
Funtime	10	20	7	35
Funtime black version	10	20	7	63
Garden Party	10	25	8	38
Gay Parisienne Porcelain Treasurers	200	300	150	205
German Dolls of the World	20	100	45	187
German reissue Dolls of the World	20	20	10	187
Gibson Girl Great Eras	60	100	45	179
Gift Giving Lace dress	10	25	8	38
Gift Giving Lavender dress	10	25	8	34
Glitter Beach Barbie	7	12	3	49
Glitter Beach Christie	7	12	3	102
Glitter Beach Jazzie	7	25	5	137
Glitter Beach Ken	7	12	3	160
Glitter Beach Kira	7	12	3	111
Glitter Beach Skipper	7	12	3	121
Glitter Beach Steven	7	12	3	170
Glitter Beach Teresa	7	25	5	105
Glitter Hair Barbie all hair colors	10	10	3	53
Glitter Hair Barbie black version	10	10	3	71
Goddess of the Sun Bob Mackie	200	200	100	195
Gold & Silver Set Gold Sensation	200	300	150	207
Gold & Silver Set Silver Starlight	200	400	200	207
Gold and Lace Target	10	25	10	237
Gold Jubilee Barbie Jubilee Series	300	1,000	500	194
Gold Medal Olympic Barbie	5	65	30	23
Gold Medal Olympic Barbie Skater	10	125	40	23
Gold Medal Olympic Barbie Skier	10	125	40	23
Gold Medal Olympic P.J. Gymnast	10	150	50	87
Gold Medal Olympic Skier Ken	10	125	35	148
Gold Sensation Gold & Silver Set	200	300	150	207
Golden Dreams Barbie	12	50	20	28
Golden Dreams Christie	12	50	20	96
Golden Evening Target	10	25	10	237
Golden Greetings FAO Schwarz	50	250	100	246
Golden Winter JC Penney	30	100	50	227
Golf Date Target	10	20	10	237
Gone with the Wind Hollywood Legends Rhett Butler	75	75	35	183
Gone with the Wind Hollywood Legends Scarlett Barbeque Dress	75	75	35	183
Gone with the Wind Hollywood Legends Scarlett Green Curtain	75	75	35	184
Gone with the Wind Hollywood Legends Scarlett New Orleans Dress	75	75	35	184
Gone with the Wind Hollywood Legends Scarlett Red Dress	75	75	35	184
Great Eras Egyptian Queen	60	70	35	178
Great Eras Elizabethan Queen	60	60	30	179
Great Eras Flapper	60	175	85	179
Great Eras Gibson Girl	60	100	45	179
Great Eras Medieval Lady	60	60	30	179
Great Eras Southern Belle	50	60	30	180
Great Shapes Barbie	10	15	5	31
Great Shapes Barbie black version	10	15	5	61
Great Shapes Ken	10	15	5	151
Great Shapes Skipper	10	15	5	116
Greek Dolls of the World	20	100	45	187
Growin' Pretty Hair Barbie blue print dress	8	275	150	21
Growin' Pretty Hair Barbie pink satin dress	8	275	150	19
Growin' Pretty Hair Francie	8	275	125	133
Growing Up Ginger	8	85	45	126

Name	Average Retail	NRFB	Mint no Box	Page Number
Growing Up Skipper	8	65	40	115
Gymnast	15	15	5	53
Gymnast black version	15	15	5	72
Hair Fair Barbie 1st card	5	150	45	15
Hair Fair Barbie 2nd card	5	150	45	17
Hair Fair Barbie white box	5	100	40	19
Hair Happenin's Barbie	8	1,800	600	20
Hair Happenin's Francie	8	450	225	132
Hallmark Holiday Memories	45	45	25	223
Hallmark Victorian Elegance	45	150	75	224
Happy Birthday Barbie 1st in multicolor dress	15	35	10	28
Happy Birthday Barbie 2nd in pink w/white dot dress	15	35	10	32
Happy Birthday Barbie pink multicolor dress	20	30	7	43
Happy Birthday Barbie pink multicolor dress black doll	20	30	7	66
Happy Holidays 1st in red dress	35	600	200	180
Happy Holidays 2nd in white dress	35	250	100	180
Happy Holidays 3rd in pink dress	35	100	40	181
Happy Holidays 3rd in pink dress black doll	35	100	40	181
Happy Holidays 4th in green velvet dress	35	170	85	181
Happy Holidays 4th in green velvet dress black doll	35	150	75	181
Happy Holidays 5th in silver dress	35	125	65	181
Happy Holidays 5th in silver dress black doll	35	125	65	181
Happy Holidays 6th in red & gold dress	35	90	45	182
Happy Holidays 6th in red & gold dress black doll	35	90	45	182
Happy Holidays 7th in gold dress	35	150	75	182
Happy Holidays 7th in gold dress black doll	35	150	75	182
Happy Holidays 8th in green satin dress	35	60	30	182
Happy Holidays 8th in green satin dress black doll	35	50	25	182
Happy Meal Janet	10	12	5	141
Happy Meal Stacie	10	12	5	141
Happy Meal Todd	10	12	5	143
Happy Meal Whitney	10	12	5	141
Hawaiian Barbie	8	100	35	24
Hawaiian Fun Barbie	7	15	3	43
Hawaiian Fun Christie	7	15	3	100
Hawaiian Fun Jazzie	7	15	3	136
Hawaiian Fun Ken	7	15	3	158
Hawaiian Fun Kira	7	15	3	110
Hawaiian Fun Skipper	7	15	3	120
Hawaiian Fun Steven	7	15	3	170
Hawaiian Ken with 1968 Ken face	8	50	25	149
Hawaiian Ken with Hispanic face	8	50	40	152
High School Chelsie	15	30	8	134
High School Dude	15	60	15	134
High School Jazzie	15	25	7	135
High School Stacie	15	65	30	136
Hills Blue Elegance	12	70	35	224
Hills Evening Sparkle	12	45	22	224
Hills Moonlight Rose	12	45	22	224
Hills Party Lace	10	45	22	225
Hills Polly Pocket	10	20	10	225
Hills Sea Pearl Mermaid	10	20	10	225
Hispanic Barbie	15	50	25	76
Holiday Barbie 1st in red dress	35	600	200	180
Holiday Barbie 2nd in white dress	35	250	100	180
Holiday Barbie 3rd in pink dress	35	100	40	181
Holiday Barbie 3rd in pink dress black doll	35	100	40	181
Holiday Barbie 4th in green velvet dress	35	170	85	181
Holiday Barbie 4th in green velvet dress black doll	35	150	75	181
Holiday Barbie 5th in silver dress	35	125	65	181
Holiday Barbie 5th in silver dress black doll	35	125	65	181
Holiday Barbie 6th in red & gold dress	35	90	45	182
Holiday Barbie 6th in red & gold dress black doll	35	90	45	182
Holiday Barbie 7th in gold dress	35	150	75	182
Holiday Barbie 7th in gold dress black doll	35	150	75	182
Holiday Barbie 8th in green satin dress	35	60	30	182
Holiday Barbie 8th in green satin dress black doll	35	50	25	182
Holiday Dreams	10	20	10	221
Holiday Hostess	10	40	20	221
Holiday Memories Hallmark	45	45	25	223
Hollywood Hair Barbie	15	20	5	50
Hollywood Hair Ken	15	20	5	160
Hollywood Hair Skipper	15	20	5	121
Hollywood Hair Teresa	15	30	15	105
Hollywood Legends Dorothy from Wizard of Oz	45	45	25	183
Hollywood Legends Maria from Sound of Music	50	50	25	183
Hollywood Legends Rhett Butler	75	75	35	183
Hollywood Legends Scarlett Barbeque Dress	75	75	35	183
Hollywood Legends Scarlett Green Curtain	75	75	35	184
Hollywood Legends Scarlett New Orleans Dress	75	75	35	184
Hollywood Legends Scarlett Red Dress	75	75	35	184
Home Pretty	15	20	7	43

Name	Average Retail	NRFB	Mint no Box	Page Number	Name	Average Retail	NRFB	Mint no Box	Page Number
Home Shopping Club Evening Flame	50	150	75	225	JC Penney Royal Enchantment	30	35	17	227
Homecoming Queen Skipper	10	20	5	119	Jewel Jubilee Club Doll	20	85	42	217
Homecoming Queen Skipper black version	10	20	5	123	Jewel Secrets Barbie	15	25	7	35
Horse Lovin' Barbie	10	45	20	31	Jewel Secrets Barbie black version	15	25	7	63
Horse Lovin' Ken	10	30	15	151	Jewel Secrets Ken	15	30	10	153
Horse Lovin' Skipper	10	30	15	116	Jewel Secrets Ken black version	15	25	7	165
Hot Looks Ames	10	20	10	213	Jewel Secrets Skipper	15	25	7	117
Hot Skatin' Barbie	15	15	5	58	Jewel Secrets Whitney	15	65	20	90
Hot Skatin' Barbie black	15	15	5	75	Jeweled Splendor FAO Schwarz				
Hot Skatin' Ken	15	15	5	162	Signature Collection	250	350	175	246
Hot Skatin' Midge	15	15	5	83	Jubilee Series Gold Jubilee Barbie	300	1,000	500	194
Hot Stuff Skipper	8	30	15	117	K-Mart Peach Pretty Barbie	25	35	17	227
Ice Capades Barbie	10	25	7	41	K-Mart Pretty in Purple	15	35	17	228
Ice Capades Barbie	10	25	7	44	K-Mart Pretty in Purple black version	15	35	17	228
Ice Capades Barbie black version	10	30	8	65	Karan, Donna Bloomingdale's	65	100	50	214
Ice Capades Ken	10	25	7	157	Karan, Donna Bloomingdale's brunette hair	65	125	60	214
Icelandic Dolls of the World	20	100	50	187	Kelly	12	12	4	143
International/Dolls of the World Australian	20	40	20	184	Kelly black version	12	12	4	143
International/Dolls of the World Brazilian	20	70	35	185	Ken Baggie	3	100	45	269
International/Dolls of the World Canadian	20	80	40	185	Ken bendable leg	5	450	150	144
International/Dolls of the World Chinese	20	20	10	185	Ken dressed box doll	8	350	100	268
International/Dolls of the World Czechoslovakian	20	125	60	185	Ken flocked hair	3	150	60	144
International/Dolls of the World Dutch	20	20	10	186	Ken painted hair	3	125	40	144
International/Dolls of the World English	20	50	25	186	Ken painted hair shortie	3	125	40	144
International Eskimo	20	100	50	186	Ken Talking blue outfit	8	225	100	145
International/Dolls of the World Eskimo reissue	20	30	15	186	Ken Talking red outfit	8	175	80	145
International/Dolls of the World German	20	100	45	187	Ken Talking Spanish blue & orange	8	250	125	145
International/Dolls of the World German reissue	20	20	10	187	Kenyan Dolls of the World	20	20	10	189
International/Dolls of the World Greek	20	100	45	187	Kevin	10	10	3	129
International/Dolls of the World Icelandic	20	100	50	187	Kissing Barbie	15	50	25	26
International Irish	20	150	75	188	Kissing Christie	15	65	32	95
International/Dolls of the World Irish reissue	20	20	15	188	Kool-Aid Wacky Warehouse I	0	65	30	266
International Italian	20	185	90	188	Kool-Aid Wacky Warehouse II	0	65	30	266
International/Dolls of the World Italian reissue	20	20	10	188	Korean Dolls of the World	20	60	30	189
International/Dolls of the World Jamaican	20	25	12	189	Kraft Treasurers Barbie	0	65	30	267
International/Dolls of the World Japanese	20	150	75	189	Lady Lovely Locks Starlight Blue Barbie	0	35	17	267
International/Dolls of the World Kenyan	20	20	10	189	Lavender Look Wal-Mart	10	25	12	241
International/Dolls of the World Korean	20	60	30	189	Lavender Surprise Sears	15	35	17	231
International/Dolls of the World Malaysian	20	35	17	190	Lavender Surprise Sears black version	15	35	17	231
International/Dolls of the World Mexican	20	40	20	190	Lights & Lace Barbie	15	35	7	44
International/Dolls of the World Native American I	20	25	12	190	Lights & Lace Christie	15	35	7	101
International/Dolls of the World Native American II	20	30	15	190	Lights & Lace Teresa	15	35	7	104
International/Dolls of the World Native American III	20	20	10	191	Lilac and Lovely Sears	15	60	30	231
International/Dolls of the World Nigerian	20	60	30	191	Little Debbie	15	65	32	267
International Oriental	20	150	75	191	Live Action Barbie	8	150	75	20
International Parisian	20	185	90	191	Live Action Christie	8	150	75	93
International/Dolls of the World Parisian reissue	20	20	10	192	Live Action Ken	8	120	50	146
International/Dolls of the World Peruvian	20	100	50	192	Live Action P.J.	8	150	75	85
International/Dolls of the World Polynesian	20	20	10	192	Living Barbie	5	250	125	20
International Royal	20	185	90	192	Living Skipper	5	150	60	113
International/Dolls of the World Russian	20	50	25	193	Locket Surprise Barbie	15	15	5	54
International Scottish	20	150	75	193	Locket Surprise Barbie black version	15	15	5	72
International/Dolls of the World Scottish reissue	20	40	20	193	Locket Surprise Kayla	15	20	7	92
International Spanish	20	120	60	193	Locket Surprise Ken	15	20	7	161
International/Dolls of the World Spanish reissue	20	40	20	194	Love to Read Toys R Us	20	30	15	252
International Swedish	20	120	60	194	Lovin' You	15	55	27	32
International Swiss	20	110	55	194	Mackie Designer Gold	150	850	425	195
International Travel Barbie	45	65	30	226	Mackie Empress Bride	300	850	425	195
Irish International	20	150	75	188	Mackie Goddess of the Sun	200	200	100	195
Irish reissue Dolls of the World	20	20	15	188	Mackie Masquerade Ball	200	500	250	195
Island Fun Barbie	7	15	3	37	Mackie Neptune Fantasy	200	900	450	196
Island Fun Christie	7	15	3	98	Mackie Platinum	200	600	300	196
Island Fun Club Doll Gift Set	20	55	27	217	Mackie Queen of Hearts	200	250	125	196
Island Fun Ken	7	15	3	154	Mackie Starlight Splendor	200	600	300	196
Island Fun Miko	7	15	3	108	Madison Avenue FAO Schwarz	70	200	100	246
Island Fun Skipper	7	15	3	117	Magic Curl	15	35	10	29
Island Fun Steven	7	15	3	169	Magic Curl black version	15	35	10	60
Island Fun Teresa	7	15	3	103	Magic Moves	20	25	7	34
Italian International	20	185	90	188	Magic Moves black version	20	25	7	62
Italian reissue Dolls of the World	20	20	10	188	Malaysian Dolls of the World	20	35	17	190
Jamaican Dolls of the World	20	25	12	189	Malibu Barbie	3	70	35	24
Japanese Dolls of the World	20	150	75	189	Malibu Barbie Beach Party	10	55	20	28
Jazzie High School	15	25	7	135	Malt Shop Toys R Us	25	35	17	253
Jazzie Sun Lovin'	15	40	15	136	Mardi Gras American Beauty	35	100	50	172
Jazzie Teen Dance	15	25	7	135	Maria from Sound of Music				
Jazzie Teen Looks Cheerleader	15	25	7	135	Hollywood Legends	50	50	25	183
Jazzie Teen Looks Swimsuit	15	25	7	135	Marine Barbie Stars & Stripes	20	25	10	209
Jazzie Teen Looks Workout	15	25	7	136	Marine Barbie Stars & Stripes black version	20	25	10	209
Jazzie Teen Scene	15	25	7	137	Marine Ken Stars & Stripes	20	25	10	210
JC Penney Enchanted Evening	30	150	75	226	Marine Ken Stars & Stripes black version	20	25	10	210
JC Penney Evening Elegance	25	150	75	226	Masquerade Ball Bob Mackie	200	500	250	195
JC Penney Evening Sensation	30	75	35	226	McDonald's Happy Meal Janet	10	12	5	141
JC Penney Golden Winter	30	100	50	227	McDonald's Happy Meal Todd	10	12	5	143
JC Penney Night Dazzle	30	60	30	227	McDonald's Happy Meal Whitney	10	12	5	141
					McDonald's Happy Meal Stacie	10	12	5	141

Name	Average Retail	NRFB	Mint no Box	Page Number
McGlynn's Bakery	15	150	75	228
Me and My Mustang (doll only) Club Doll	15	30	15	217
Me n' My Dog Tutti	8	500	200	138
Medieval Lady Great Eras	60	60	30	179
Meijers Shopping Fun	10	25	12	228
Meijers Something Extra	10	25	12	228
Melody in Pink Tutti	8	450	175	139
Mermaid	15	30	7	46
Mermaid - Fountain Mermaid	10	15	5	52
Mermaid - Fountain Mermaid black version	10	15	5	71
Mermaid - Sea Pearl Mermaid Hills	10	20	10	225
Mermaid Skipper & Sea Twins	10	20	5	122
Mervyn's Ballerina Barbie	15	65	30	229
Mervyn's Fabulous Fur	15	50	25	229
Mexican Dolls of the World	20	40	20	190
Mickey's Toontown Stacie	25	30	15	215
Midge bendable leg	5	650	325	80
Midge dressed box	8	750	150	268
Midge freckleless	3	500	250	80
Midge straight leg	3	175	65	80
Midge Wig Wardrobe	3	450	225	80
Midge with teeth	3	500	250	80
Midnight Gala Classique	60	60	30	174
Miss Barbie	8	750	350	14
Mod Hair Ken	5	80	40	147
Montgomery Ward Barbie	3	700	350	242
Moonlight Magic Toys R Us	20	20	10	253
Moonlight Magic Toys R Us black version	20	30	15	253
Moonlight Rose Hills	12	45	22	224
Musical Ballerina Series Nutcracker	100	200	100	197
Musical Ballerina Series Swan Lake	100	150	75	197
My First Barbie 1st in yellow outfit	10	30	15	197
My First Barbie 2nd in pink & white check dress	10	35	5	197
My First Barbie 3rd in white dress	10	25	3	198
My First Barbie 3rd in white dress black doll	10	25	3	198
My First Barbie 4th in pink tutu	10	25	3	198
My First Barbie 4th in pink tutu black doll	10	20	3	198
My First Barbie 5th in white tutu	10	20	3	198
My First Barbie 5th in white tutu black doll	10	20	3	198
My First Barbie 5th in white tutu Hispanic doll	10	20	3	198
My First Barbie 6th in purple & white	10	20	3	199
My First Barbie 6th in purple & white black doll	10	20	3	199
My First Barbie 6th in purple & white Hispanic doll	10	20	3	199
My First Barbie 7th in blue tutu	10	20	3	199
My First Barbie 7th in blue tutu black doll	10	20	3	199
My First Barbie 7th in blue tutu Hispanic doll	10	20	3	199
My First Barbie 8th in pink & white tutu	10	15	3	199
My First Barbie 8th in pink & white tutu black doll	10	15	3	199
My First Barbie 8th in pink & white tutu Hispanic doll	10	15	3	199
My First Barbie 9th in lilac & white tutu	10	15	3	200
My First Barbie 9th in lilac & white tutu black doll	10	15	3	200
My First Barbie 9th in lilac & white tutu Hispanic doll	10	15	3	200
My First Barbie 9th in lilac & white tutu Asian doll	10	20	3	200
My First Barbie 10th in blue dress	10	15	3	200
My First Barbie 10th in blue dress black doll	10	15	3	200
My First Barbie 10th in blue dress Hispanic doll	10	15	3	200
My First Barbie 10th in blue dress Asian doll	10	20	3	200
My First Barbie Gift Set (pink tutu)	20	20	3	264
My First Ken 1st in white & blue	10	20	3	201
My First Ken 2nd in purple & white	10	20	3	201
My First Ken 3rd in light blue	10	20	3	201
My First Ken 3rd in light blue black doll	10	20	3	201
My First Ken 4th in white & blue iridescent	10	15	3	202
My First Ken 4th in white & blue iridescent black doll	10	25	3	202
My Size all	135	150	75	202
My Size Bride all	135	135	70	202
My Size Princess all	135	135	70	202
Naf Naf Barbie	25	25	5	229
Native American I Dolls of the World	20	25	12	190
Native American II Dolls of the World	20	30	15	190
Native American III Dolls of the World	20	20	10	191
Navy Barbie Stars & Stripes	20	25	10	210
Navy Barbie Stars & Stripes black version	20	25	10	210
Neptune Fantasy Bob Mackie	200	900	450	196
New Good Lookin' Ken	5	175	60	145
Newport	8	175	65	22
Nigerian Dolls of the World	20	60	30	191
Night Dazzle JC Penney	30	60	30	227
Night Sensation FAO Schwarz	50	175	65	246
Night-Night Sleep Tight! Tutti	8	500	200	139
No Bangs Francie	5	1,500	750	132
Nostalgic 35th Anniversary Barbie	35	35	15	203
Nostalgic 35th Anniversary Barbie brunette hair	35	80	40	203
Nostalgic Busy Gal	50	50	25	203
Nostalgic Solo in the Spotlight blonde or brunette	30	30	15	203
Now Look Ken	5	80	40	148
Nurse Whitney	15	50	20	90
Nutcracker Ballerina Musical Series	100	200	100	197
Olympic Gold Medal Barbie	5	65	30	23
Olympic Gold Medal Barbie Skater	10	125	40	23
Olympic Gold Medal Barbie Skier	10	125	40	23
Olympic Gold Medal Ken Skier	10	125	35	148
Olympic Gold Medal P.J. Gymnast	10	150	50	87
Opening Night Classique	60	125	60	175
Oriental International	20	150	75	191
Osco Picnic Pretty	10	30	15	229
Oshogatsu	80	80	40	59
P.J. Baggie	3	150	75	269
P.J. Talking	8	200	90	85
P.J. twist & turn	5	275	100	84
Paint' n Dazzle all hair colors	15	15	5	54
Paint' n Dazzle black version	15	15	5	72
Parisian International	20	185	90	191
Parisian reissue Dolls of the World	20	20	10	192
Party in Pink Ames	10	25	12	213
Party Lace Hills	10	45	22	225
Party Perfect Shopko/Venture	15	45	22	234
Party Pink Winn Dixie	10	25	12	242
Party Premiere	10	25	12	221
Party Pretty Target	10	25	10	238
Party Sensation Club Doll	20	50	25	217
Party Time Toys R Us	15	15	7	254
Party Time Toys R Us black version	15	15	7	254
Party Time Toys R Us Hispanic version	15	15	7	254
Party Treats Toys R Us	15	15	7	254
Party' N Play Stacie	10	15	5	140
Party' N Play Stacie black version	10	15	5	141
Party' N Play Todd	10	15	5	143
Peach Blossom Club Doll	20	65	32	218
Peach Pretty K-Mart	25	35	17	227
Peaches n' Cream	15	45	15	33
Peaches n' Cream black version	15	40	12	62
Peppermint Princess Winter Princess Collection	80	80	40	211
Pepsi Spirit Barbie Toys R Us	20	35	17	254
Pepsi Spirit Skipper Toys R Us	20	35	17	255
Perfume Giving Ken	15	20	5	154
Perfume Giving Ken black version	15	20	5	165
Perfume Pretty Barbie	15	25	7	37
Perfume Pretty Barbie black version	15	25	7	64
Perfume Pretty Whitney	15	45	20	91
Peruvian Dolls of the World	20	100	50	192
Pet Pals Courtney	10	15	5	127
Pet Pals Kevin	10	15	5	129
Pet Pals Skipper	10	15	5	120
Pet Pals Skipper black version	10	15	5	124
Picnic Pretty Osco	10	30	15	229
Pilgrim Barbie American Stories Series	25	25	8	172
Pink Jubilee 25th Year Wal-Mart	12	60	30	239
Pink n' Pretty Barbie	10	50	20	30
Pink n' Pretty Christie	10	45	20	96
Pink Sensation Winn Dixie	10	25	12	242
Pink Silhouette Box Barbie an average #3 Ponytail	8	1,500	700	268
Pioneer Barbie American Stories Series	25	25	8	172
Pizza Party Courtney	10	10	3	128
Pizza Party Kevin	10	10	3	130
Pizza Party Skipper	10	10	3	123
Pizza Party Skipper black version	10	10	3	125
Plantation Belle Porcelain Treasurers	200	250	125	205
Platinum Bob Mackie	200	600	300	196
POGS Toys R Us	20	30	15	253
Police Officer Toys R Us	20	35	17	255
Police Officer Toys R Us black version	20	35	17	255
Polly Pocket Barbie Hills	10	20	10	225
Polly Pocket Janet	10	10	3	142
Polly Pocket Stacie	10	10	3	142
Polly Pocket Whitney	10	10	3	142
Polynesian Dolls of the World	20	20	10	192
Ponytail #1 Barbie blonde	3	6,000	4,000	11
Ponytail #1 Barbie brunette	3	9,000	7,000	11
Ponytail #2 Barbie blonde	3	4,000	3,500	11
Ponytail #2 Barbie brunette	3	5,000	4,500	11
Ponytail #3 Barbie blonde	3	700	500	11
Ponytail #3 Barbie brunette	3	1,000	800	11
Ponytail #4 Barbie blonde	3	450	300	11
Ponytail #4 Barbie brunette	3	600	400	11
Ponytail #5 Barbie blondes	3	300	200	12

Name	Average Retail	NRFB	Mint no Box	Page Number
Ponytail #5 Barbie brunette & titian	3	400	300	12
Ponytail #6 & 7 Barbie blondes	3	300	200	12
Ponytail #6 & 7 Barbie brunette & titian	3	400	300	12
Ponytail Swirl Barbie ash & lemon blonde	3	400	300	13
Ponytail Swirl Barbie brunette, titian & platinum	3	550	450	13
Porcelain Midge 30th Anniversary	200	200	100	204
Porcelain 50th Anniversary Mattel Barbie	600	600	300	207
Porcelain Benefit Performance	200	400	200	204
Porcelain Blue Rhapsody	200	700	350	205
Porcelain Crystal Rhapsody	200	350	175	207
Porcelain Enchanted Evening	200	400	200	205
Porcelain Gay Parisienne	200	300	150	205
Porcelain Gold Sensation	200	300	150	207
Porcelain Ken 30th Anniversary	200	200	100	204
Porcelain Plantation Belle	200	250	125	205
Porcelain Royal Splendor	200	300	150	208
Porcelain Silken Flame	200	250	150	206
Porcelain Silver Starlight Gold & Silver Set	200	400	200	207
Porcelain Skipper 30th Anniversary	200	200	100	204
Porcelain Solo in the Spotlight	200	200	100	206
Porcelain Sophisticated Lady	200	250	125	206
Porcelain Star Lily Bride Wedding Flower Collection	180	180	100	208
Porcelain Wedding Party Barbie	200	600	350	206
Pose 'N Play/baggie Skipper	3	75	40	114
Presidential Series Crystal Rhapsody	200	350	175	207
Presidential Series Royal Splendor	200	300	150	208
Pretty Changes	10	40	20	26
Pretty Dreams	20	20	7	59
Pretty Dreams black version	20	20	7	76
Pretty Hearts	10	30	15	222
Pretty in Plaid Target	10	25	10	238
Pretty in Purple black version K-Mart	15	35	17	228
Pretty in Purple K-Mart	15	35	17	228
Purple Passion Toys R Us	20	35	17	255
Purple Passion Toys R Us black version	20	35	17	255
Queen of Hearts Bob Mackie	200	250	125	196
Quick Curl Barbie	5	125	55	22
Quick Curl Cara	5	125	55	94
Quick Curl Francie	5	175	85	133
Quick Curl Kelley	5	175	85	87
Quick Curl Skipper	5	125	55	114
Quinceanera Teresa Toys R Us	20	30	15	256
Radiant in Red Toys R Us	20	20	10	256
Radiant in Red Toys R Us black version	20	35	17	256
Rappin' Rockin' Barbie	15	25	7	46
Rappin' Rockin' Christie	15	45	15	101
Rappin' Rockin' Ken	15	25	7	158
Rappin' Rockin' Teresa	15	65	20	104
Rapunzel Children's Collector Series	40	40	20	173
Red Romance	10	20	10	222
Regal Reflections Spiegel	50	400	200	235
Rendezvous with Destiny Barbie Stars & Stripes	20	25	10	210
Rendezvous with Destiny Barbie Stars & Stripes black version	20	25	10	210
Rendezvous with Destiny Ken Stars & Stripes	20	25	10	211
Rendezvous with Destiny Ken Stars & Stripes black version	20	25	10	211
Rhett Butler Hollywood Legends	75	75	35	183
Ribbons & Roses Sears	25	30	15	231
Ricky	3	135	55	128
Rocker Barbie	10	35	10	34
Rocker Barbie 2nd issue	10	20	7	35
Rocker Dana	10	35	10	107
Rocker Dana 2nd issue	10	20	7	108
Rocker Dee-Dee	10	20	7	97
Rocker Dee-Dee 2nd issue	10	20	7	97
Rocker Derek	10	35	10	167
Rocker Derek 2nd issue	10	35	10	168
Rocker Diva	10	35	10	90
Rocker Diva 2nd issue	10	35	10	90
Rocker Ken	10	35	10	153
Rockettes FAO Schwarz	70	175	65	247
Roller Skating Barbie	10	45	20	29
Roller Skating Ken	10	45	20	149
Rollerblades Barbie	15	35	10	46
Rollerblades Christie	15	40	12	101
Rollerblades Ken	15	25	7	159
Rollerblades Kira	15	40	12	110
Rollerblades Teresa	15	65	20	105
Romantic Bride	20	45	15	50
Romantic Bride black version	20	45	15	69
Royal Enchantment JC Penney	30	35	17	227
Royal International	20	185	90	192
Royal Invitation Spiegel	50	150	75	235
Royal Romance Club Doll	20	70	35	218
Ruby Romance Service Merchandise	20	50	25	233
Ruffle Fun	7	7	3	178
Ruffle Fun black version	7	7	3	178
Ruffle Fun Hispanic version	7	12	3	178
Russian Dolls of the World	20	50	25	193
Sapphire Dream Toys R Us 1st in series	80	80	40	256
Satin Nights Service Merchandise	20	70	35	233
Savvy Shopper Bloomingdale's	65	95	50	215
Scarlett Barbeque Dress Hollywood Legends	75	75	35	183
Scarlett Green Curtain Dress Hollywood Legends	75	75	35	184
Scarlett New Orleans Dress Hollywood Legends	75	75	35	184
Scarlett Red Dress Hollywood Legends	75	75	35	184
School Fun Toys R Us	15	20	10	257
School Fun Toys R Us black version	15	20	10	257
School Spirit Toys R Us	15	20	10	257
School Spirit Toys R Us black version	15	20	10	257
Schooltime Fun	10	20	10	222
Scott	5	65	35	129
Scottish International	20	150	75	193
Scottish reissue Dolls of the World	20	40	20	193
Sea Holiday Barbie	20	20	7	50
Sea Holiday Ken	20	20	7	160
Sea Holiday Midge	20	25	8	82
Sea Pearl Mermaid Hills	10	20	10	225
Sears 100th Celebration	15	90	45	230
Sears Blossom Beautiful	45	400	200	230
Sears Dream Princess	25	70	35	230
Sears Evening Enchantment	15	50	25	230
Sears Lavender Surprise	15	35	17	231
Sears Lavender Surprise black version	15	35	17	231
Sears Lilac and Lovely	15	60	30	231
Sears Ribbons & Roses	25	30	15	231
Sears Silver Sweetheart	25	35	17	231
Sears Southern Belle	15	60	30	232
Sears Star Dream	15	60	30	232
Sears Walking Jamie	5	275	150	232
Season's Greetings Club Doll	20	100	50	218
Secret Hearts Barbie	15	20	7	50
Secret Hearts Barbie black version	15	20	7	70
Secret Hearts Barbie Gift Set Club Doll	25	40	20	218
Secret Hearts Ken	15	30	15	161
Sensations Barbie	15	40	20	37
Sensations Becky	15	25	12	108
Sensations Belinda	15	25	12	98
Sensations Bopsy	15	25	12	91
Service Merchandise Blue Rhapsody	20	300	150	232
Service Merchandise City Sophisticate	20	70	35	233
Service Merchandise Ruby Romance	20	50	25	233
Service Merchandise Satin Nights	20	70	35	233
Service Merchandise Sparkling Splendor	20	50	25	233
Sharin Sisters Gift Set 1st set	30	50	20	264
Sharin Sisters Gift Set 2nd set	30	45	18	264
Shaving Fun Ken	15	15	5	163
Shopko/Venture Blossom Beauty	15	45	22	234
Shopko/Venture Party Perfect	15	45	22	234
Shopping Chic Spiegel	60	90	45	235
Shopping Fun Meijers	10	25	12	228
Shopping Spree FAO Schwarz	30	30	15	247
Show n' Ride Toys R Us	20	37	18	257
Silken Flame Porcelain Treasurers	200	250	150	206
Silver Screen FAO Schwarz	70	150	75	247
Silver Starlight Gold & Silver Set	200	400	200	207
Silver Sweetheart Sears	25	35	17	231
Singapore Girl I	20	175	85	234
Singapore Girl II	20	80	40	234
Ski Fun Barbie	15	25	7	46
Ski Fun Ken	15	25	7	159
Ski Fun Midge Toys R Us	15	35	18	258
Skipper bendable leg	5	350	125	112
Skipper dressed box	8	350	75	268
Skipper Pose 'N Play/baggie	3	75	40	114
Skipper reissue	5	300	150	114
Skipper straight leg	3	125	45	112
Skipper Trade-in	5	200	50	113
Skipper twist & turn orange & pink check	5	250	75	113
Skipper twist & turn pink & blue stripe	5	350	100	112
Skipper twist & turn yellow & orange	5	275	75	113
Skooter bendable leg	5	350	125	126
Skooter dressed box	8	350	75	269
Skooter straight leg	3	125	45	125
Slumber Party Barbie	15	15	3	58
Slumber Party Barbie black version	15	15	3	75
Slumber Party Midge	15	15	3	83
Slumber Party Teresa	15	15	3	107

Name	Average Retail	NRFB	Mint no Box	Page Number
Swirl Ponytail Barbie ash & lemon blonde	3	400	300	13
Swirl Ponytail Barbie brunette, titian & platinum	3	550	450	13
Swiss International	20	110	55	194
Talking Barbie orange bikini, bun in back	8	375	150	17
Talking Barbie orange bikini, Stacey head mold	8	450	225	19
Talking Barbie side ponytail	8	300	125	17
Talking Barbie Spanish	8	550	450	16
Talking Barbie white bikini, gold coverup	8	500	175	19
Talking Brad	8	450	175	168
Talking Christie	8	175	65	92
Talking Christie multicolor suit	8	250	125	93
Talking Ken blue outfit	8	225	100	145
Talking Ken red outfit	8	175	80	145
Talking Ken Spanish blue & orange	8	250	125	145
Talking P.J.	8	200	90	85
Talking Stacey blue & silver swimsuit	8	500	200	85
Talking Stacey striped bikini	8	400	175	84
Target Baseball Date	10	20	10	236
Target Bathtime Fun Skipper	10	20	10	236
Target Cute'n Cool	10	20	10	236
Target Dazzlin' Date	10	25	10	237
Target Gold and Lace	10	25	10	237
Target Golden Evening	10	25	10	237
Target Golf Date	10	20	10	237
Target Party Pretty	10	25	10	238
Target Pretty in Plaid	10	25	10	238
Target Steppin' Out	10	30	10	238
Target Wild Style	10	35	10	238
Teacher	25	25	10	60
Teacher black version	25	25	10	76
Teen Dance Jazzie	15	25	7	135
Teen Fun Skipper Cheerleader	10	15	5	118
Teen Fun Skipper Party Teen	10	15	5	118
Teen Fun Skipper Workout	10	15	5	118
Teen Looks Cheerleader Jazzie	15	25	7	135
Teen Looks Swimsuit Jazzie	15	25	7	135
Teen Looks Workout Jazzie	15	25	7	136
Teen Scene Jazzie	15	25	7	137
Teen Sweetheart Skipper	10	15	5	118
Teen Talk	30	35	15	47
Teen Talk black version	30	35	15	68
Teen Talk Math Is Tough	30	250	250	47
Teen Time Courtney	10	20	5	127
Teen Time Skipper	10	20	5	119
Tennis Stars Toys R Us	15	25	12	260
Theater Elegance Spiegel	50	200	100	236
Tiff Pose 'N Play	8	175	75	126
Todd	5	175	65	140
Todd Groom	10	35	17	167
Toothfairy Wal-Mart blue	10	10	5	241
Toothfairy Wal-Mart purple	10	10	5	241
Totally Hair Barbie	10	35	17	48
Totally Hair Barbie black version	10	25	12	68
Totally Hair Barbie brunette	10	25	12	48
Totally Hair Courtney Toys R Us	15	40	15	260
Totally Hair Ken	10	35	17	159
Totally Hair Skipper Toys R Us	15	40	15	260
Toys R Us Astronaut	10	25	12	248
Toys R Us Astronaut black version	20	20	10	248
Toys R Us Barbie & Friends Disney	30	65	25	248
Toys R Us Barbie for President	20	35	17	248
Toys R Us Barbie for President black version	20	35	17	248
Toys R Us Beauty Pageant Skipper	15	30	17	249
Toys R Us Cool 'N Sassy	15	20	10	249
Toys R Us Cool 'N Sassy black version	15	20	10	249
Toys R Us Cool City Blues	30	45	22	249
Toys R Us Cool Looks	15	20	10	250
Toys R Us Dance Sensation	15	25	12	250
Toys R Us Dream Date Skipper	15	40	20	250
Toys R Us Dream Time	15	45	10	250
Toys R Us Dream Wedding Gift Set	25	35	15	251
Toys R Us Dream Wedding Gift Set black version	25	35	15	251
Toys R Us Emerald Elegance	20	40	20	251
Toys R Us Emerald Elegance black version	20	40	20	251
Toys R Us Fashion Brights	15	25	12	252
Toys R Us Fashion Brights black version	15	25	12	252
Toys R Us Firefighter	20	30	15	252
Toys R Us Firefighter black version	20	30	15	252
Toys R Us Love to Read	20	30	15	252
Toys R Us Malt Shop	25	35	17	253
Toys R Us Moonlight Magic	20	20	10	253
Toys R Us Moonlight Magic black version	20	30	15	253
Toys R Us Party Time	15	15	7	254
Toys R Us Party Time black version	15	15	7	254
Toys R Us Party Time Hispanic version	15	15	7	254

Name	Average Retail	NRFB	Mint no Box	Page Number
Toys R Us Party Treats	15	15	7	254
Toys R Us Pepsi Spirit Barbie	20	35	17	254
Toys R Us Pepsi Spirit Skipper	20	35	17	255
Toys R Us POGS	20	30	15	253
Toys R Us Police Officer	20	35	17	255
Toys R Us Police Officer black version	20	35	17	255
Toys R Us Purple Passion	20	35	17	255
Toys R Us Purple Passion black version	20	35	17	255
Toys R Us Quinceanera Teresa	20	30	15	256
Toys R Us Radiant in Red	20	20	10	256
Toys R Us Radiant in Red black version	20	35	17	256
Toys R Us Sapphire Dream 1st in series	80	80	40	256
Toys R Us School Fun	15	20	10	257
Toys R Us School Fun black version	15	20	10	257
Toys R Us School Spirit	15	20	10	257
Toys R Us School Spirit black version	15	20	10	257
Toys R Us Show n' Ride	20	37	18	257
Toys R Us Ski Fun Midge	15	35	18	258
Toys R Us Spots 'N Dots Barbie	15	25	12	258
Toys R Us Spots 'N Dots Teresa	15	25	12	258
Toys R Us Spring Parade	20	25	12	258
Toys R Us Spring Parade black version	20	25	12	258
Toys R Us Sunflower Barbie	15	15	5	259
Toys R Us Sunflower Teresa	15	20	7	259
Toys R Us Sweet Romance	15	25	12	259
Toys R Us Sweet Roses	15	25	12	259
Toys R Us Tennis Stars	15	25	12	260
Toys R Us Totally Hair Courtney	15	40	15	260
Toys R Us Totally Hair Skipper	15	40	15	260
Toys R Us Vacation Sensation blue	15	40	15	261
Toys R Us Vacation Sensation pink	15	45	20	261
Toys R Us Wedding Party Gift Set	25	25	12	261
Toys R Us Wedding Party Gift Set black version	25	25	12	261
Toys R Us Western Stampin' Gift Set black version	25	25	12	262
Toys R Us Winter Fun	15	30	15	262
Tracy Bride	10	40	15	89
Trade-in Barbie twist & turn	2	300	150	15
Trail Blazin'	10	15	7	223
Travelin' Sisters Playset	40	50	25	266
Troll	10	15	5	51
Tropical Barbie	7	15	5	34
Tropical Barbie black version	7	15	5	63
Tropical Barbie Hispanic version	7	25	8	78
Tropical Ken	7	10	3	153
Tropical Ken black version	7	18	5	165
Tropical Miko	7	15	5	107
Tropical Skipper	7	15	5	117
Tropical Splash Barbie	7	7	3	59
Tropical Splash Christie	7	7	3	102
Tropical Splash Ken	7	7	3	163
Tropical Splash Kira	7	7	3	111
Tropical Splash Skipper	7	7	3	123
Tropical Splash Steven	7	7	3	171
Tropical Splash Teresa	7	7	3	107
Tutti and Todd Sundae Treat Set	10	550	200	140
Tutti Cookin' Goodies	8	450	175	138
Tutti Me n' My Dog	8	500	200	138
Tutti Melody in Pink	8	450	175	139
Tutti Night-Night Sleep Tight!	8	500	200	139
Tutti pink checked outfit	5	150	75	138
Tutti solid pink bodice & floral skirt or vice versa	5	125	50	138
Tutti Swing-A-Ling	8	650	225	139
Tutti Walkin' My Dolly	8	500	200	139
Twinkle Lights	20	20	7	55
Twinkle Lights black version	20	20	7	73
Twirley Curls	12	25	5	31
Twirley Curls black version	12	25	5	60
Twirley Curls Hispanic version	12	30	8	76
Twist & turn Barbie flip hair, multicolor splotches swimsuit	5	500	175	17
Twist & turn Barbie flip hair, pink & white swimsuit	5	500	175	18
Twist & turn Barbie flip hair, psychedelic swimsuit	5	550	175	18
Twist & turn Barbie orange net swimsuit	5	450	175	15
Twist & turn Barbie pink check swimsuit	5	550	175	16
Twist & turn Christie	5	250	125	92
Twist & turn Francie	5	450	150	131
Twist & turn Francie short flip, multicolor	5	600	150	132
Twist & turn Francie short flip, yellow & pink 1965	5	700	150	132
Twist & turn P.J.	5	275	100	84
Twist & turn Skipper orange & pink check	5	250	75	113
Twist & turn Skipper pink & blue stripe	5	350	100	112

Name	Average Retail	NRFB	Mint no Box	Page Number
Twist & turn Skipper yellow & orange	5	275	75	113
Twist & turn Stacey blue & pink floral suit	5	750	175	84
Twist & turn Stacey long ponytail	5	400	150	84
Twist & turn Stacey short flip, multicolor suit	5	500	175	85
UNICEF	20	20	5	41
UNICEF Asian version	20	40	15	79
UNICEF black version	20	20	5	65
UNICEF Hispanic version	20	30	8	78
Uptown Chic Classique	60	70	35	175
Vacation Sensation blue Toys R Us	15	40	15	261
Vacation Sensation pink Toys R Us	15	45	20	261
Valentine	10	20	10	223
Very Violet Club Doll	20	70	35	219
Victorian Elegance Hallmark	45	150	75	224
Wal-Mart 25th Year Pink Jubilee	12	60	30	239
Wal-Mart Anniversary Star	12	35	17	239
Wal-Mart Ballroom Beauty	12	20	10	239
Wal-Mart Country Bride	12	20	10	239
Wal-Mart Country Bride black version	12	20	10	239
Wal-Mart Country Bride Hispanic version	12	25	12	239
Wal-Mart Country Star	15	20	10	240
Wal-Mart Country Star black version	15	20	10	240
Wal-Mart Country Star Hispanic version	15	25	12	240
Wal-Mart Dream Fantasy	10	30	15	240
Wal-Mart Frills and Fantasy	10	30	15	240
Wal-Mart Lavender Look	10	25	12	241
Wal-Mart Pink Jubilee 25th Year	12	60	30	239
Wal-Mart Superstar	12	40	20	241
Wal-Mart Superstar black version	12	100	50	241
Wal-Mart Toothfairy blue	10	10	5	241
Wal-Mart Toothfairy purple	10	10	5	241
Walk Lively Barbie	8	145	60	21
Walk Lively Ken	8	80	35	147
Walk Lively Steffie	8	165	85	86
Walkin' My Dolly Tutti	8	500	200	139
Walking Jamie Sears	5	275	150	232
Wedding Day Alan	13	30	10	168
Wedding Day Barbie	13	25	8	44
Wedding Day Kelly & Todd	20	45	22	266
Wedding Day Ken	13	25	8	158
Wedding Day Midge	13	35	15	82
Wedding Fantasy	25	35	10	41
Wedding Fantasy black version	25	35	10	65
Wedding Fantasy Gift Set Club Doll	25	125	60	219
Wedding Flower Collection Star Lily Bride Porcelain	180	180	100	208
Wedding Party Barbie Porcelain	200	600	350	206
Wedding Party Gift Set Toys R Us	25	25	12	261
Wedding Party Gift Set Toys R Us black version	25	25	12	261
Western Barbie	10	50	25	29
Western Fun Barbie	10	20	7	41
Western Fun Barbie black version	10	20	7	66
Western Fun Ken	10	20	7	157
Western Fun Nia	10	20	7	109
Western Ken	10	40	15	150
Western Skipper	10	40	15	116
Western Stampin' Barbie	15	25	8	55
Western Stampin' Barbie black version	15	25	8	63
Western Stampin' Gift Set Toys R Us black version	25	25	12	262
Western Stampin' Ken	15	25	8	162
Western Stampin' Tara Lynn	15	75	35	92
Wet n' Wild Barbie	7	10	3	42
Wet n' Wild Christie	7	10	3	100
Wet n' Wild Ken	7	10	3	157
Wet n' Wild Kira	7	10	3	109
Wet n' Wild Skipper	7	10	3	120
Wet n' Wild Steven	7	10	3	169
Wet n' Wild Teresa	7	20	8	104
Wig Wardrobe Midge	3	450	225	80
Wild Style Target	12	20	10	238
Winn Dixie Party Pink	10	25	12	242
Winn Dixie Pink Sensation	10	25	12	242
Winn Dixie Southern Beauty	10	25	12	242
Winter Fantasy FAO Schwarz	50	200	100	247
Winter Fun Toys R Us	15	30	15	262
Winter Princess Collection Evergreen Princess	80	150	75	211
Winter Princess Collection Peppermint Princess	80	80	40	211
Winter Princess Collection Winter Princess	80	650	300	212
Winter Royale Club Doll	20	100	50	219
Winter Sport Barbie	15	15	5	59
Winter Sport Ken	15	15	5	163
Winter Sport Midge	15	15	5	83
Winters Eve Club Doll	20	25	13	219
Woolworth's Spec Expressions aqua dress	10	20	10	243
Woolworth's Spec Expressions aqua dress black doll	10	20	10	243
Woolworth's Spec Expressions multicolor dress	10	20	10	244
Woolworth's Spec Expressions multicolor dress black doll	10	25	13	244
Woolworth's Spec Expressions multicolor dress Hispanic doll	10	35	17	244
Woolworth's Spec Expressions peach satin dress	10	25	12	244
Woolworth's Spec Expressions peach satin dress black doll	10	25	12	244
Woolworth's Spec Expressions peach satin dress Hispanic doll	10	25	12	244
Woolworth's Spec Expressions pink chiffon	10	25	12	243
Woolworth's Spec Expressions pink chiffon black doll	10	25	12	243
Woolworth's Spec Expressions white dress	10	25	12	243
Woolworth's Spec Expressions white dress black doll	10	20	10	243
Woolworth's Sweet Lavender	20	25	12	244
Woolworth's Sweet Lavender black version	20	40	20	244
Yellowstone Kelley	10	400	175	87
Zayre's My First Barbie Pink tutu Hispanic	10	45	20	245